ARE MINORITY RIGHTS (STILL) HUMAN RIGHTS?

Marking the 75th anniversary of the Universal Declaration of Human Rights and the 25th anniversary of the Framework Convention for the Protection of National Minorities and European Charter for Regional or Minority Languages, this book investigates to what extent minority rights can, or should, be treated as part of the human rights regime.

Internationally renowned experts, both scholars and practitioners, critically assess the current state of protection from different disciplinary perspectives. Key themes include the historical trajectory from the League of Nations to ICCPR Article 27, the 'persons-belonging-to' formula, tensions between individual and collective protection, differences in normativity, and the absence of a universally binding definition of 'minority', with implications for non-derogability, enforcement, and sovereignty.

Designed for students, researchers, and practitioners of international human rights law, European human rights, and minority protection, the volume provides a multi-disciplinary map of doctrine and practice and a focused resource for courses in public international law, particularly human rights law, European law, and minority rights.

Are Minority Rights (Still) Human Rights?

Edited by
Miodrag Jovanović
and
Ana Zdravković

• HART •
OXFORD • LONDON • NEW YORK • NEW DELHI • SYDNEY

HART PUBLISHING

Bloomsbury Publishing Plc

Kemp House, Chawley Park, Cumnor Hill, Oxford, OX2 9PH, UK

1385 Broadway, New York, NY 10018, USA

Bloomsbury Publishing Ireland Limited, 29 Earlsfort Terrace, Dublin 2, D02 AY28, Ireland

HART PUBLISHING, the Hart/Stag logo, BLOOMSBURY and the Diana logo are trademarks of Bloomsbury Publishing Plc

First published in Great Britain 2026

A catalogue record for this book is available from the British Library.

A catalogue record for this book is available from the Library of Congress.

Library of Congress Control Number: 2025949156

ISBN: HB: 978-1-50998-454-1
ePDF: 978-1-50998-456-5
ePub: 978-1-50998-455-8

Typeset by Compuscript Ltd, Shannon

For product safety related questions contact productsafety@bloomsbury.com

To find out more about our authors and books visit www.hartpublishing.co.uk. Here you will find extracts, author information, details of forthcoming events and the option to sign up for our newsletters.

FOREWORD

PATRICK THORNBERRY

I am delighted to offer this brief Foreword to the present volume – a follow up to an international conference on the same question in Belgrade, November 2023. Editors and writers are to be congratulated in raising a difficult and ostensibly surprising question regarding minority rights, and all writers for registering intelligent, considered responses. The cast of authors represents an interdisciplinary vanguard of contemporary thinking about minority rights. The collection of responses addresses conceptual and institutional issues regarding human rights, minorities and minority rights, and provides a spectrum of applications of rights as well as reflections on societies and cultures, 'old' and 'new' minorities, and indigenous peoples.

It is perhaps not necessary to identify every author by name in the Foreword, except to recall the high standard of the contributors and their luminous catechisation of the characteristics and boundaries of minority and human rights. Equally, in light of the information provided elsewhere in the present collection, it is not necessary to recall in detail the history of minority rights via the political pragmatics of earlier centuries, through the League of Nations' system of minority rights, to the maturation of the current rights framework that contextualises our understanding of modern arrangements. We should, however, recall the humanitarian aspect of earlier emanations of minority rights even as rights focused on particular groups rather than evincing a universal customary standard.

Joseph L Kunz wrote in 1954, that '[t]oday the well-dressed international lawyer wears "human rights"',[1] perhaps distinct from distinct from the shabbier sartorial style of minority rights. In which respect the Universal Declaration of Human Rights of 1948 did not refer specifically to minorities, although the ground-breaking Article 27 of the International Covenant on Civil and Political Rights (ICCPR) did so, while intimations of 'groupness' were never completely absent from early UN-era instruments, including the 1948 Convention on the Prevention and Punishment of the Crime of Genocide. In many States, however, rights of minorities were not at the forefront of political consciousness in an age of ideological rivalry, burgeoning anti-colonialism, the perceived 'Europeanness' of

[1] Josef Kunz, 'The Present Status of the International Law for the Protection of Minorities' [1954] 48 AJIL, 282.

language and practice with regard to minorities, nation-building, and the promise and presumed social healing powers of universal individual rights. From the early heady days of the United Nations and regional organisations, instruments and the practice of human rights have expanded to form industrial-scale, intersecting networks of concepts, norms and institutions (international and domestic) that engage parliaments, courts, lawyers and civil society. It is also true that practice does not always accord with theory, that the texts are subject to constant reinterpretation and are always restlessly unfulfilled.

Dedicated and distinct minority rights instruments were inserted into the modern human rights *ordo rerum* relatively late on in its development. Key texts include the UN Declaration on the Rights of Persons Belonging to National or Ethnic, Religious and Linguistic Minorities (adopted by the UN General Assembly in 1992) and the Framework Convention for the Protection of National Minorities (adopted by the Committee of Ministers of the Council of Europe in 1994). These instruments emerged following the upheavals in Eastern Europe and in the face of opposition from States that had formidable philosophical, political or cultural objections to recognising minorities. The Declaration and the Framework Convention are weakly-worded instruments, reflecting degrees of caution in uploading them into legal spaces, soft or hard, occupied by texts of individual human rights. The nature and extent of the integration of streams of discourse is the profound subject matter of the present collection.

The dominant human rights framework has meant that, in many cases, minority rights are distinguished as incidental matters that arise from the interpretation of primary human rights instruments. Even Article 27 of the ICCPR is interpreted though its relationship with the International Covenant as a whole; in other words, as a piece of the larger jigsaw of a complex network of individual rights. This situation is replicated in a range of other 'universal' human rights texts. The edgy relationship between minority rights and the principle of non-discrimination means that the establishment of a minority rights regime for one group in a State is liable to be 'measured' against the non-discrimination standard proclaimed as fundamental and indefatigable. In a UN setting, the present writer's interest in minority rights was treated as verging on the risible in that that it was claimed that the non-discrimination principle would resolve dilemmas of rights and politics without reference to minority rights. Further, 'minority' has been extended in current discourse to accommodate myriad social phenomena including migration, voyaging across its paradigmatic application to self-defining historical communities. Minority rights also co-exist with formidable mainstays of the international system, such as indigenous rights, even where 'no sullen line of demarcation separates and cuts off the several orders from each other'.[2]

[2] Citation from Richard Brinsley Sheridan, in Declan Kiberd, *Irish Classics* (London, Granta Books, 2000).

Nonetheless, minorities and minority rights have had their effects on the wider matrix of human rights, working, as it were, from within. There is sensitivity to the existence and claims of ethnic, religious and linguistic minorities in human rights practice, international and domestic. This may be so even in instances where there is localised (governmental or popular) lack of acceptance of concepts of minorities and/or indigenous peoples. Academic authority has also observed a deep-seated 'culturalisation' of expressions of human rights,[3] within an otherwise unadorned latticework of principles and rules. Such is not a complete response to caveats against celebratory affirmations of collective minority rights but supplements our understanding of the nature of human rights.

There are other 'challenges' to accommodating minority rights in the family of human rights. Equality among groups is not of the same stripe as equality between individuals. Appreciations of 'ethnic' and 'ethnicity' are seemingly losing ground to vocabularies of 'race' and 'racism', notably but not exclusively in post-colonial contexts. Political developments have generated fresh impetus to nation-state ideologies redolent of minority-threatening eras of international law – loyalty and State security are accordingly demanded by dominant elites. Religious minorities may be undervalued in States dominated by alternative creeds or based, constitutionally and otherwise, on rigorously secular principles. Linguistic diversity is nominally and formally, but not always, substantively valued. Narratives of progress may depict concern for minorities and indigenous peoples as patronising, archaic, and as possibly concealing ambitions of State fragmentation. Polarisation of discourse regarding sub-State collectives may outweigh positive assessments of cultural diversity/difference as facets of national excellence.

These and related issues point to difficulties in mastering interactions between communities and States in contemporary settings – though this is not new. There is, however, a certain inevitability, rational and political, in addressing the concerns and rights of minorities and comparable groups. Minority and indigenous rights institutions and bodies memorialise an ethic of empathy and respect for the concerns of collectives. The properties of group rights also recall the consequential nature and ineffability of difference as well as commonality among human beings. In this garden of forking paths,[4] human rights present an important humanitarian language and minorities may prosper within their protective shade, even if the articulation of their rights to survive and flourish does not perfectly fit the available template.

[3] Federico Lenzerini, The Culturalization of Human Rights Law (Oxford University Press, 2014).
[4] A 'fiction' in Jorge Luis Borges, *Labyrinths* (Penguin Books, 1970).

PREFACE – ON PRINCIPLES AND REALITIES

TIBOR VÁRADY*

This volume was prompted by two anniversaries. Two truly important anniversaries. The Universal Declaration of Human Rights (UDHR) was accepted 75 years ago, the European Framework Convention for the Protection of National Minorities (FCNM) came into force 25 years ago. At the present moment, it can be said that the observance of human rights – and of minority rights within human rights – has become a generally accepted principle. This is, indeed, a ground for celebration.

The UDHR and the FCNM (followed by other declarations and treaties) set (or confirmed) a number a critically important principles. One must bear in mind, however, that although principles may provide a foothold for reality they cannot be equated with actuality. In the words of Samuel Johnson, the 18th Century English author and scholar 'A man may be very sincere in good principles, without having good practice.' Moving from principle to reality and practice remains a task. History has produced many examples where principles became divorced from content. Hence, the content of principles must remain in focus.

In Article 2 of the UDHR it is stated:

> Everyone is entitled to all the rights and freedoms set forth in this Declaration, without distinction of any kind, such as race, colour, sex, language, religion, political or other opinion, national or social origin, property, birth or other status. Furthermore, no distinction shall be made on the basis of the political, jurisdictional or international status of the country or territory to which a person belongs, whether it be independent, trust, non-self-governing or under any other limitation of sovereignty.

This is unequivocal. But 'unequivocality' also needs to be tested time and again, because different surroundings may foster different logics. Let me raise a contemporary question as an example. It is stated in Article 2 that 'the country or territory to which a person belongs' must not be a basis for distinction. Does this mean that a person belonging to a country that has committed aggression must not be distinguished from persons from other countries, and should not be disallowed, for example, to participate in a tennis tournament? And if this is, indeed, the true

* Member of the Serbian Academy of Sciences and Arts.

understanding, has this understanding become reality? Are we truly prepared to tie rights or sanctions to persons, notwithstanding the countries or territories to which they belong? Let me also mention that one of the core principles of human rights is equality. This is a critically important foothold of minority rights as well. Minority rights are, indeed, human rights. This has been unambiguously confirmed in the FCNM.

> According to Article 1: 'The protection of national minorities and of the rights and freedoms of persons belonging to those minorities forms an integral part of the international protection of human rights, and as such falls within the scope of international co-operation'.

The principle of equality (which is given strong emphasis in Article 2 of the UDHR) should extend to minority rights as well. Yet, in addition to accepting it, one needs to repeatedly scrutinise the principle of equality from the angle of different facts, different environments, and alternating destinies. A clear definition of this issue (and of this task) may be found in the well-known sentences of Judge Tanaka. In the South-West Africa Cases decided by the International Court of Justice in 1996, Judge Tanaka formulated the following opinion:

> The idea of equality of men as persons [...] underlies all modern, democratic and humanitarian law systems [...] This idea, however, does not exclude the different treatment of persons from the consideration of the differences of factual circumstances such as sex, age, language, religion, economic condition, education, etc. To treat different matters equally in a mechanical way would be as unjust as to treat equal matters differently.[1]

One of the clear consequences of this view is that minorities can only be equal when they have the right to be different. Minorities – just as majorities – have a right to preserve their identity. This also means that they should possess the means for preserving their linguistic, cultural, religious, or other identity. Equality means more than the right to join. Different treatment may be a means for denying equality, but it may also be a tool of forging equality.

The relevance of difference has often been the battleground of harsh debates. One of the most recent examples is the decision of the Supreme Court of the United States in the *Students for Fair Admissions Inc. v President and Fellows of Harvard College* case decided on June 29, 2023.[2] The key question was whether the admission practices of Harvard College and of the University of North Carolina – which rely on affirmative action – represent a violation or a confirmation of the Equal Protection Clause of the Fourteenth Amendment of the US Constitution. Affirmative action (confirmed by earlier court decisions)[3] permits preferential treatment of minorities (primarily black minorities) in order to redress centuries of discrimination, and to shape true equality. In its June 2023 decision, the Supreme

[1] *South West Africa Cases* (Second Phase) (*Ethiopia v South Africa*; *Liberia v South Africa*) [1966] ICJ Rep 6 (dissenting opinion of Judge Tanaka), 250–324, 303.

[2] *Students for Fair Admissions Inc v President and Fellows of Harvard College* [2023] 600 US 181.

[3] The crucial decision of the US Supreme Court was *Brown v Board of Education* [1954] 347 US 483.

Court held that affirmative action violates the Equal Protection Clause. In her dissenting opinion (that received much public attention) Justice Sotomayor raised counterarguments. In her opinion, 'colorblindness' may confirm discrimination instead of confirming equality. According to her words: 'Superficial colorblindness in a society that systematically segregates opportunity will cause a sharp decline in the rates at which underrepresented minority students enroll in our Nation's colleges and universities …'[4] In her closing words Justice Sotomayor states: 'The majority's vision of race neutrality will entrench racial segregation in higher education because racial inequality will persist so long as it is ignored'.[5]

This debate will continue, and it shows that one should never forget that equality cannot be achieved simply by accepting it as a principle. Principles must be turned into achievements, and this requires there to be a scrutiny of the actual circumstances – and it requires good intentions that go beyond acceptable phrases. One also must bear in mind that true equality (including equal rights to be different) is an element of normalcy. This is often forgotten. Such disregard is sometimes a consequence of prejudices, and at others it just follows from inertia. Normalcy must not be perceived as one of the synonyms of majority behaviour.

I remember a reception at an international conference in Switzerland. There were participants from many countries, including participants from Israel. The host tried to make a gesture towards guests from Israel, and on one of the tables on which food was offered, a tag was placed with the words 'Kosher Food'. On the other tables the tag stated: 'Normal Food'. This brought forth smiles rather than indignation, but the smiles were tinged with a shade of bitterness. The authors of the tags simply followed a predisposition that equates 'normalcy' with majority. One of the key preconditions of equality – and of minority rights in particular – is to include difference into the perception of normalcy.

There are many examples around us. In Croatia, the use of the Latin alphabet is obviously a part of normalcy, but the use of the Cyrillic alphabet by the Serbian minority, and in environments where the Serbian minority is present, should also be perceived within the picture of normalcy. The presence of Hungarian, Slovak, Romanian, Croatian or Ruthenian languages in schools, in the press or on billboards, in environments that include minorities, is a part of normalcy in the Vojvodina – along with the normal presence of the Serbian language. Minority rights are part of normalcy. Our aim should be to keep minority rights within the realm of acknowledged human rights – in other words, to maintain a sustainable normalcy.

Let me say that it is, indeed, a part of normalcy to accept diversity as a value. Such an acceptance is definitely a commendable gesture and forges a good principle. But principles are time and again tested in surroundings of new realities. The maintenance of normalcy implies confrontations with new challenges. Challenges

[4] *Students for Fair Admissions Inc v President and Fellows of Harvard College* [2023] 600 US 181 (dissenting opinion of Justice Sotomayor), 377–78.

[5] ibid, 383-84.

often take the form of legal issues. At this point, a true vision of the UDHR and the FCNM should always be present in the process of perception and decision-making.

It also needs to be mentioned that threats to human rights are constantly changing or being modified. Pictures of juxtaposition need to be reinvestigated. Perils may arise in different settings. An important present-day scenery is that of human rights in corporations.[6] It is critically important to recognise (and to comprehend) various settings in which human rights (including minority rights) may be impaired. Minority rights might also be affected within corporations – or may come into confrontation with corporations. I would like to mention here an interesting study, published in 2023, which examined a still ongoing conflict between the U'wa indigenous people in Colombia and the companies Shell and Occidental Petroleum. The basis of the confrontation is oil exploration on U'wa land. The article focuses on potential dangers, but also on various actors who can contribute to the defence of human rights (including the rights of indigenous people).[7]

Or, to give a further example, the principle (and aim) of equality may be jeopardised when equal rules apply to financially unequal people. A rather stunning example was noted in connection with the US bail system. A non-observance (or limited observance) of the presumption of innocence may aggravate the evolving situation. In a September 2014 article, the *New Yorker*[8] reported the case of Kalief Browder who was (wrongfully) arrested in May 2010 on the charge of stealing a backpack. He could have been released on bail, but the bail was set at $3,000, and Browder and his family were not able to pay that much. Awaiting his trial, Browder was kept in jail for about 3 years. He was released in 2013, because no evidence was found to confirm that he had really stolen a backpack. (As a matter of fact, there was no evidence of theft at the time of the arrest either. The backpack was not found in Browder's possession.) The years of imprisonment brought a lot of suffering. Shortly after being released, Kalief Browder committed suicide. In the Case Western Reserve Journal of International Law an article inspired by the Browder case appeared in 2022, under the title '*Guilty? Or Just Poor? Potential International Human Rights Violations in the U.S. Bail System*'.[9] The author (Alireza Nouriani-Dargiri) comes to the conclusion that: 'The United States bail system is broken, and international law might be the means to fix it'.[10] It may be debated whether decision-makers in New York were in a position to replace applicable

[6] See on this issue, eg Tibor Várady and Miodrag Jovanović (eds) Ana Zdravković (ass ed), *Human Rights in the 21st Century* (Eleven International Publishing, 2020), 151–256 – pt IV of the book is devoted to human rights in corporations.

[7] Pablo Rueda-Saiz, 'Targets, Fields, and Tactics: Multi-Institutional Legal Mobilization in the Campaign of the U'wa People in Colombia' (2023) 2 *Michigan Journal of Law and Society*, 38–81.

[8] Jennifer Gonnerman, 'A Boy Was Accused of Taking a Backpack. The Courts Took the Next Three Years of His Life' *The New Yorker* (New York, 29 September 2014).

[9] Alireza Nourani-Dargin, 'Guilty? Or Just Poor? Potential International Human Rights Violations in the U.S. Bail System', (2022) 54 *Case Western Reserve Journal of International Law*, 509–43.

[10] ibid, 510.

local rules with principles of international law. It is, however, a clear task of lawyers (and not only of lawyers), to provide access to principles of international law – and to fit emerging issues (including incipient problems with equality) within the principles of international human rights.

It is also a fact that the ideas and principles of the human rights conventions are sometimes challenged outside the realm of legal steps. These challenges also deserve attention. Principles set by the UDHR and by the FCNM could (and should) motivate human actions outside legal proceedings as well. In 1997, two prominent linguists (Robert Phillipson and Tove Skutnabb-Kangas) published an interesting study under the title '*Linguistic human rights and English in Europe*'.[11] Focusing on 'glimpses in the European language scene', the article notes that 'the British Foreign Minister greeted the fall of the Iron Curtain by proclaiming that English should become the first foreign language throughout eastern and central Europe'.[12] British arguments also included the assumption that 'English language is associated with democracy, the free market, and human rights …'[13] The article draws attention to a specific project focusing on Latvia, which assumes that 'English provides a bridge between the local participants, who were composed of both Russian and Latvian speaking members'.[14] One might say that it is, indeed, an important task to create a just and balanced cohabitation of Latvian and Russian languages on a territory in which Latvian had earlier been often discriminated, and where Russian just became a minority language. The article raises the question whether in this situation (and other similar situations in Central-Eastern Europe), the English language may offer a solution. According to the authors: 'The idea that 'English' can solve such problems is pure fantasy. An ecology of language perspective embracing use of all the relevant languages is needed'.[15]

The Preamble of the FCNM cites the considerations and intentions that represent the basis of the agreement. One of the considerations that are identified is the following:

> Considering that a pluralist and genuinely democratic society should not only respect the ethnic, cultural, linguistic and religious identity of each person belonging to a national minority, but also create appropriate conditions enabling them to express, preserve and develop this identity;

It is clear that acquiring the command of English, in addition to knowledge of one or more local languages, is an advantage. But there is a critical difference between 'in addition to' and 'instead of'. There is no reason to perceive the English language as a substitute for the local diversity. This would contradict the task set in

[11] Robert Phillipson and Tove Skutnabb-Kangas, 'Linguistic Human Rights and English in Europe' (1997) 16(1) *World Englishes*, 27–43.

[12] ibid, 28.

[13] ibid.

[14] ibid, 37-8.

[15] ibid, 39.

the Preamble – the creation of appropriate conditions enabling people to express, preserve, and develop their identity.

* * *

In the words of the poet T.S. Eliot 'Human kind cannot bear very much reality'.[16] It is important to perceive this as a warning, and as a call to transcend obstructive limits while aiming to comprehend realities. Principles can only remain principles if they keep a distance from phrases, if they remain tied to realities – and if they follow ongoing changes in the actual world. Human rights and minority rights cannot be respected if they are viewed from the angle of a single unchanging pattern of reality. One needs different insights and different tools while endeavouring to define and protect rights of old and new ethnic minorities, indigenous people, religious minorities, rich and poor – or, say, while observing human rights in the environment of corporations.

It is important to keep in mind that protection of human rights (and of minority rights within human rights) does not only require pledges and declarations. It also requires serious study, and an open mind at each juncture. Our environment is changing, and we need to address changing realities with thorough research.

I trust that contributions to this book will contribute to perceiving the true goals of the UDHR, of the FCNM, and of other international agreements devoted to human rights. True perception is a precondition of attainment.

[16] *Burnt Norton* (No 1 of *Four Quartets*).

CONTENTS

Foreword v
Patrick Thornberry

Preface – On Principles and Realities ix
Tibor Várady

List of Contributors xvii

Are Minority Rights (Still) Human Rights? Introduction 1
Miodrag Jovanović and Ana Zdravković

PART I
MINORITY RIGHTS AS HUMAN RIGHTS – VIEWS FROM THEORY AND PRACTICE

1. *Special Rights and Obligations: Why Minority Rights Need Institutional Frameworks* 15
   Tove H. Malloy

2. *Minority Rights as Human Rights? Concepts, Doctrine, and Practice* 37
   Miodrag Jovanović and Ivana Krstić

PART II
INSTITUTIONAL SETTING OF MINORITY RIGHTS PROTECTION

3. *The Framework Convention for the Protection of National Minorities and the Northern Ireland Peace Process* 59
   Elizabeth Craig

4. *25 Years of Implementation of the European Charter for Regional or Minority Languages* 75
   Vesna Crnić-Grotić

5. *Human Rights, Including Rights of Persons Belonging to Minorities, in the External Action of the European Union* 85
   Julia Szelivanov

PART III
SPECTRUM OF MINORITY RIGHTS PROTECTION

6. *'Battling' Nations and Minorities' Fundamental Educational Rights before the ECtHR:* Valiullina's *Promises and Missed Opportunities* *101*
Kristin Henrard

7. *Minorities' Participation in Public Affairs: A Human Rights Norm or a Conflict Prevention Technique?* *125*
Milica V. Matijević and Ana Knežević Bojović

8. *Assessing Non-Territorial Autonomy to Protect Minorities in the Digital Age and Digital Minorities* *151*
Antoni Abat i Ninet

PART IV
SOCIETY, CULTURE, DIVERSITY: OLD AND NEW MINORITIES

9. *New Minorities as a New Frontier for Minority Rights Regimes: The Case of Non-EU Citizens in the Context of EU Member States* *169*
Roberta Medda-Windischer and Katharina Crepaz

10. *Indigenous Peoples' Rights and the European Courts: A Category under Construction* *185*
Jessika Eichler

11. *Anthropological Theory, Stakeholder Inclusion and Minority Rights: Reflections on the Research and Safeguarding of Serbian Intangible Cultural Heritage in the Western Balkans* *205*
Miloš Milenković

Index *221*

LIST OF CONTRIBUTORS

Antoni Abat i Ninet (Talent Distinguished Researcher, Autonomous University of Barcelona, Spain)

Elizabeth Craig (Senior Lecturer in Law, University of Sussex, UK)

Katharina Crepaz (Senior Researcher at the Center for Autonomy Experience, European Academy of Bolzano, Italy)

Vesna Crnić-Grotić (Full Professor, University of Rijeka, Faculty of Law, Croatia)

Jessika Eichler (Postdoctoral Scholar, recently gained her HDR (habilitation) from Sciences Po Paris, France)

Kristin Henrard (Full Professor, Brussels School of Governance, Belgium)

Miodrag A. Jovanović (Full Professor, University of Belgrade, Faculty of Law)

Ana Knežević Bojović (Senior Research Associate, Institute of Comparative Law, Serbia)

Ivana Krstić (Full Professor, University of Belgrade Faculty of Law, Serbia)

Tove H. Malloy (Full Professor, Europa-Universität Flensburg, Germany)

Milica V. Matijević (Senior Research Associate, Institute of Comparative Law, Serbia)

Roberta Medda-Windischer (Senior Researcher and Group Leader for Equality and Diversity in Integrated Societies, European Academy of Bolzano, Italy)

Miloš Milenković (Full Professor, University of Belgrade, Faculty of Philosophy, Serbia)

Julia Szelivanov (Policy Officer, European External Action Service, Belgium)

Patrick Thornberry (Emeritus Professor, Keele University, UK)

Tibor Várady (Full Member, Serbian Academy of Sciences and Arts, Serbia)

Ana M. Zdravković (PhD Candidate and Research Assistant, Institute of Comparative Law, Serbia)

Are Minority Rights (Still) Human Rights? Introduction

MIODRAG JOVANOVIĆ* AND ANA ZDRAVKOVIĆ**

The title of this volume may appear at first glance unnecessarily intriguing. Why question something that seems self-evident, at least as enshrined in some major global and regional international legal instruments. Take, for instance, the Preamble of the 1992 UN Declaration on the Rights of Persons Belonging to National or Ethnic, Religious and Linguistic Minorities. By '[r]eaffirming that one of the basic aims of the United Nations … is to promote and encourage respect for human rights and for fundamental freedoms for all [as well as] reaffirming faith in fundamental human rights …',[1] the UN Declaration clearly operates on the premise that the minority protection ought to be treated as an integral part of the international human rights law structure. This assumption is even more clearly emphasised in the opening article of the 1995 Council of Europe Framework Convention for the Protection of National Minorities.[2]

However, neither a theoretical nor a historical perspective offers solid ground for such a confident rhetoric of the harmonious marriage of human and minority rights. In the groundbreaking political-theoretical treatise on minority rights, published in the same year as the Council of Europe's Convention, Kymlicka noted that although ethnocultural conflicts have become the most common source of political conflicts and violence around the world, '[t]he Western political tradition has been surprisingly silent on these issues.' Simply put, 'most Western political theorists have operated with an idealised model of the polis in which fellow citizens share a common descent, language, and culture'.[3] Hence, up to the 1990s minority protection has remained an unknown variable in the complex formula of a well-ordered liberal-democratic State. For that very reason, Kymlicka felt that

* Full Professor, Faculty of Law, University of Belgrade.
** Research Assistant, Institute of Comparative Law.

[1] General Assembly resolution 47/135, 18 December 1992.

[2] 'The protection of national minorities and of the rights and freedoms of persons belonging to those minorities forms an integral part of the international protection of human rights, and as such falls within the scope of international co-operation'. Council of Europe, H (95) 10.

[3] Will Kymlicka, *Multicultural Citizenship: A Liberal Theory of Minority Rights* (Oxford: Oxford University Press, 1995), 2.

his theory needed to 'clarify the basic building blocks for a liberal approach to minority rights'.[4]

Similarly, historical trajectories of minority and human rights protection at the international level have hardly gone hand in hand. In the aftermath of the First World War, the minority rights problem, at least at the European level, was largely addressed on the basis of the national self-determination principle, which was promoted by both a communist revolutionary, Vladimir Lenin, and the then American President, Woodrow Wilson.[5] It was clear from the outset that the neat application of the principle, even in the privileged part of the world,[6] was not possible. Therefore,

> [b]y way of compensation for the incomplete fulfilment of the implications of national self-determination, and insurance against the disturbance of international relations resulting from oppression and efforts to compel the assimilation of minorities, the great powers decided that national groups in certain countries of that region should be granted a special set of minority rights.[7]

However, not only did this experiment fail miserably, but many blamed the League of Nations' model of minority rights protection for opening the door for its misuse by the Nazi regime in its justification of the 1938 annexation of the Sudetenland. No wonder, therefore, that with the establishment of the United Nations after the Second World War, 'the concept of positive minority rights has not been given international endorsement'.[8] Moreover, the immediate upshot of the emphasis on human rights protection, which was captured in the 1948 UN Declaration on Human Rights, was the abandonment of the minority rights vocabulary. Simply put, '[t]he doctrine of human rights has been put forward as a substitute for the concept of minority rights, with the strong implication that minorities whose members enjoy individual equality of treatment cannot legitimately demand facilities for the maintenance of their ethnic particularism'.[9]

One may argue that the incorporation of minority rights into the fabric of the international legal regime of human rights successfully started with the enshrinement of Article 27 of the International Covenant on Civil and Political Rights (ICCPR), and that it culminated with the adoption of the aforementioned UN

[4] ibid.

[5] For a comparison between the two, see, Burkhard Olschowsky, 'Vladimir Ilyich Lenin and Woodrow Wilson on the Self-Determination of Nations', in Burkhard Olschowsky, Piotr Juszkiewicz, Jan Rydel (eds), *Central and Eastern Europe after the First World War* (Oldenburg: De Gruyter, 2021), 149–170.

[6] Calculli notes that while Lenin conceived the principle of self-determination 'as a right that all peoples could claim', Wilson construed it as 'self-government for a few European nations, keeping the colonial architecture of the world intact'. She argues that the Leninist 'meaning of self-determination triumphed, ultimately becoming an international norm after World War II'. Marina Calculli, 'Self-Determination: the Story of the Liberal Appropriation of a Socialist Principle', in Enrico Fassi and Vittorio Emanuele Parsi (eds), *The Liberal World Order and Beyond* (Milan: Vita & Pensiero, 2021), 138.

[7] Inis Claude, *National Minorities: An International Problem* (Cambridge, Mass.: Harvard University Press, 1955), 207–208.

[8] ibid, 208.

[9] ibid, 211.

Declaration and the Council of Europe Framework Convention. This development, however, has not eliminated some obvious tensions between the concepts of human and minority rights. We will here briefly mention the most obvious ones:

First, the dominant terminology of human rights instruments is framed, understandably, in individualistic language. Nevertheless, by using the so-called 'persons-belonging-to' formula, these instruments extend the same terminology to those rights that are traditionally perceived as minority rights. Hence, Article 27 states that '[i]n those States in which ethnic, religious or linguistic minorities exist, persons belonging to such minorities shall not be denied the right'.[10] This, in turn, raises the question whether communal aspects of minority protection are to be safeguarded by special group/collective measures.[11]

Second, there is a glaring difference between normativity of international/regional human and minority rights instruments. Understood as the capacity to guide human behaviour, normativity of (international) law can be gradated,[12] and, thus, Besson rightly notes that 'in terms of degree of normativity', international law 'now ranges from low-intensity or soft law to imperative law'.[13] On this specific spectrum of normativity, human rights instruments are generally closer to the extreme of imperative law, such as, for instance, in the provision of Article 11 of ICCPR, which stipulates that '[n]o one shall be imprisoned merely on the ground of inability to fulfil a contractual obligation'. Minority rights instruments, in contrast, tend to lean towards the opposite extreme of soft law. In d'Aspremont's words, these are legal instruments with 'soft negotium', that is, with the content which 'does not lay down any specific obligation' but is designed 'in such a way that the addressee retains a right to opt out or to define its scope of application'.[14] Take, for instance, the wording of Article 5 of the Framework Convention, which states that '[t]he Parties undertake to promote the conditions necessary for persons belonging to national minorities to maintain and develop their culture, and to preserve the essential elements of their identity, namely their religion, language, traditions and cultural heritage'.

Finally, this all may affect the status of human/minority rights provisions in the overall architectonics of the international legal order. For instance, it is well known

[10] The mere fact that the provision adds in the continuation – 'in community with the other members of their group'– does not quite rebut the stated problem, insofar that a number of traditional rights can be exercised only in the group (eg right to association, to assembly).

[11] Dinstein raised this problem as early as 1976, by arguing that '[i]nternational human rights are not monolithic, and a cardinal distinction must be drawn between individual and collective rights granted directly to human beings'. While the former 'are bestowed upon every single human being personally', the latter 'are afforded to human beings communally, that is to say, in conjunction with one another or as a group'. Yoram Dinstein, 'Collective Human Rights of Peoples and Minorities' (1976) 25 *International and Comparative Law Quarterly* 1, 102–103.

[12] See more in, Miodrag Jovanović, *The Nature of International Law* (Cambridge: Cambridge University Press, 2019), 78–156.

[13] Samantha Besson, 'Theorizing the Sources of International Law', in Samantha Besson and John Tasioulas (eds), *The Philosophy of International Law* (Oxford: Oxford University Press, 2010), 165.

[14] Jean d'Aspremont, 'Softness in International Law: A Self-Serving Quest for New Legal Materials' (2008) 19 *European Journal of International Law* 5, 1084.

that some human rights enjoy the status of absolute, ie non-derogable rights that cannot be suspended or restricted under any circumstances, even during states of emergency.[15] Both Article 4 of the ICCPR and Article 15 of the European Convention on Human Rights (ECHR) provide a list of such non-derogable human rights. By contrast, no such status is reserved for any minority right. According to some authors, non-derogability of certain human rights implies that they are hierarchically superior to other rights of human rights law.[16] If minority rights are treated as an integral part of international human rights law, they are, then, destined to stay at the bottom part of that ladder, a position that is not merely of theoretical significance, but also carries substantial practical implications.[17]

To state some of the most noticeable tensions between the concepts of human and minority rights by no means implies disregarding the fact that, apart from their own supervisory mechanisms, minority rights are today primarily protected through the adjudicatory machinery of human rights law, particularly that of the European Court of Human Rights.[18] This is but an example, albeit the important one, that the international legal doctrine largely operates on the assumption that minority rights *are* human rights. This volume, thus, takes into account each of the aspects of an intricate relationship between the two concepts, approaching them from the point of view of both international legal theory and practice.

***

The volume is divided into four parts. The first part is dedicated to 'Minority Rights as Human Rights – Views from Theory and Practice' and it opens with the contribution by Tove H. Malloy, titled 'Special Rights and Obligations: Why Minority Rights Need Institutional Frameworks'. The paper departs from the complex question of whether minority rights are a form of human rights. The relevance of this question stems from the belief that human rights are universal, meaning they are meant for everyone, whereas minority rights, though accessible to all in theory, are designed for specific groups, making them both universal and

[15] Ana Zdravković, 'How It All Began – Exploring the Theoretical Conceptualisations of Absolute Rights' (2024) 8 *Revista de Estudios Judiciales*, 5–47; See also Miodrag Jovanović, Ivana Krstić, 'Human Rights and the Constitutionalization of International Law' in Tibor Várady and Miodrag Jovanović (eds), *Human Rights in the 21st Century* (Eleven International Publishing and the Serbian Academy of Science and Arts, 2020), 31–35.

[16] Teraya Koji, 'Emerging Hierarchy in International Human Rights and Beyond: From the Perspective of Non-derogable Rights' (2001) 12 *European Journal of International Law* 5, 917–941.

[17] For practical examples of such ramifications, see Milica Matijević, Ana Zdravković, 'Use of Minority Languages in Administrative Proceedings in Serbia' in *Law on General Administrative Procedure: Contemporary Tendencies and Challenges* (Eurosfera & Partners, Institute of Comparative Law, 2024) 335–348; These issues could also be examined from a broader, systemic perspective, see Milica Matijević, Ana Zdravković, 'Breaking the Invisible Cage: Limits of Law in Structural Discrimination' (2024) 3 *Diritto, Immigrazione e Cittadinanza* 1–18.

[18] For a critical assessment, see, eg, Olgun Akbulut, 'Commentary: Shifting Standards? The ECtHR's Evolving Approach to Minority Rights' (2025) 24 *Journal on Ethnopolitics and Minority Issues in Europe* 2, 1–12.

particular. Although it can seem confusing, Malloy argues that the key to understanding it lies in the definition and the scope of application, or in other words, in revealing who is entitled to the rights, and how those rights are applied. Put differently, the paper claims that it is not the nature of the rights themselves that defines their character, but the intentions behind their implementation, hence the commitment and actions of those responsible for upholding the rights ultimately shape whether minority rights function as true human rights. Drawing on legal and philosophical theories, particularly Philip Allott's account of social exchange and Onora O'Neill's typology of perfect and imperfect obligations, it explores how societies determine which rights ought to be guaranteed in specific contexts. After analysing the Council of Europe's Framework Convention for the Protection of National Minorities (FCNM) and the reports of Advisory Committee on the FCNM, it concludes that minority rights are human rights, as long as they are effectively implemented and enforced, since it is not their universality in theory but their ability to deliver concrete protections that affirms their place within the human rights framework. This assessment is based on the fact that the provisions of FCNM guarantee material outcomes as they all have counterpart rights, either liberty rights or special rights.

In the paper 'Minority Rights as Human Rights? Concepts, Doctrine, and Practice', Miodrag Jovanović and Ivana Krstić critically examine whether there is any justificatory route for treating minority rights as an integral part of human rights. While minority protections have evolved after the emergence of international human rights law and are acknowledged in instruments such as the ICCPR and Council of Europe's FCNM, the analysis demonstrates that minority rights differ from human rights in several respects. As their recognition depends on legal and political acknowledgment (not inherent status), they often require collective protection, and their scope is limited to certain groups rather than being truly universal. Underlining the issues behind the lack of a universally accepted and binding international legal definition of 'minority', the paper reminds the reader of uncertainties and indeterminacy pertaining to the concept of minority rights. Moreover, it illustrates the inaptness of foundationalist justification behind human rights for minority rights and considers alternative positions, such as the 'political conception' of human rights. It is revealed that attempts to secure minority rights through anti-discrimination frameworks or human rights courts, such as the European Court of Human Rights and the Court of Justice of the European Union, were mostly based on individual remedies, thereby failing to fully address collective harms or group identities. Additionally, the enforceability of minority rights is weak, since legal instruments not only rely on vague commitments but also grant States broad discretion, thereby prioritising sovereignty over substantive rights of minorities. As a result, it is argued that minority rights lack the 'trump-over-sovereignty', which is a typical character of human rights, at least from the perspective of the 'political conception'. To elevate minority rights to this status, binding treaties with clear collective rights and enforcement mechanisms are necessary, but until then, the paper warns that minority rights remain secondary, conditional, and less enforceable than universal human rights.

The second part of the book offers two analyses regarding 'Institutional Setting of Minority Rights Protection', starting with Elizabeth Craig's chapter on 'The Framework Convention for the Protection of National Minorities and the Northern Ireland Peace Process'. It explores how the FCNM has evolved over the last thirty years, focusing on Northern Ireland's peace process. When the UK signed the FCNM in 1998, the same year as the Good Friday Agreement, it was hoped these developments would support peace by protecting minority rights, especially around language, culture, and identity and the FCNM – though cautious in its rights language – was recognised as a human rights treaty with the potential to adapt to changing contexts and identities. The paper illustrates how debates over the FCNM have often centred on its application to new minorities and the complexities of self-identification, highlighting how these debates have played out in Northern Ireland, especially with the recent official recognition of Ulster Scots as a national minority. From this recognition and legislative changes made in 2022, Craig concludes not only that there are still tensions around language and cultural identity, but also that risks of disregarding distinct identities have not been eliminated. Although new institutions have been created to address these issues, the paper identifies ongoing political disagreement and uncertainty about the best ways to protect minority rights. Ultimately, the chapter suggests that when it comes to minority rights as human rights, current understandings and applications of human rights serve primarily as guiding principles for political action, but they cannot offer definitive solutions to the complex challenges and changing demographics that arise in unique historical and geopolitical settings. It is therefore up to local governments and communities to interpret and implement these rights in ways that address the complex realities of their own societies.

The implementation of the European Charter for Regional or Minority Languages is analysed in the paper '25 Years of Implementation of the European Charter for Regional or Minority Languages' by Vesna Crnić-Grotić. The author seeks to assess what Charter has accomplished and to identify areas that still need improvement. Her findings indicate that the Charter takes a unique approach by focusing on preserving linguistic diversity as part of Europe's 'cultural heritage', offering States Parties considerable flexibility in the manner they implement its provisions. This includes a *menu-system* that allows countries to select specific protective measures for the languages they recognise, a system that is adaptable but also contains certain drawbacks, since it can make comparison between countries difficult. It is highlighted that the Charter's scope covers many areas of public life, from education and media to administration and culture, including endangered languages. However, the paper warns that challenges persist, such as varying national thresholds for language recognition, reluctance by some States to fully commit to its obligations and the development of new, electronic forms of media that were non-existent at the time the Charter was drafted. It is also shown in the chapter that the progress stemming from reporting mechanisms and oversight can often be slow. However, the paper recognises that the Charter has been successful in bringing attention to regional and minority languages, as it encourages both

States and speakers to appreciate linguistic diversity. Looking forward, the paper concludes that the Charter's relevance will rely on its ability to adapt to social and technological changes, as that is necessary to ensure that Europe's rich linguistic heritage is safe for future generations.

In the chapter 'Human Rights, Including Rights of Persons Belonging to Minorities, in the External Action of the European Union', Julia Szelivanov examines how the EU supports and promotes minority rights in its policies and activities outside the EU. While the EU doesn't have a unified legal framework for minority rights, it is explained that it consistently calls on States around the world to respect and protect the rights of national, ethnic, religious, and linguistic minorities, following international standards. The EU's approach is rooted in anti-discrimination and individual rights, but it also acknowledges the collective aspect of minority rights in some contexts. Despite the lack of binding EU rules, most Member States have ratified major international treaties on minority protection, hence the EU weaves minority rights into both its policy documents and country-based activities, including in the context of enlargement, using a mix of legal tools, funding programs, diplomatic pressure, and targeted sanctions. Moreover, special attention is given to vulnerable groups, such as the Roma and religious minorities, and it is shown that the EU also supports dialogue, inclusion, and equal participation in this regard. Ultimately, while internal EU differences limit the development of a single, comprehensive policy on minority rights, the paper praises the EU for remaining active in promoting and defending these rights internationally on both multilateral and bilateral levels, through a variety of instruments and strategies.

The third part of the volume delves into the 'Spectrum of Minority Rights Protection' and begins with the contribution by Kristin Henrard, titled '"Battling" Nations and Minorities' Fundamental Educational Rights Before the ECtHR: *Valiullina*'s Promises and Missed Opportunities', which firstly reminds that the relationship between nation-states and minorities has long been tense, since States often view demands for minority recognition as a threat to national unity and sovereignty. While States typically expect minorities to assimilate, the paper emphasises that minorities seek equal participation in society without losing their identity, hoping for integration as a two-way process. However, it is also stressed that instruments like the Council of Europe's FCNM combine general and minority-specific rights but leave States broad discretion. What is more, given that education central role in nation-building, the paper finds it unsurprising that powerholders often use it as a tool to assimilate different groups by enforcing their own language as the language of instruction. The main part of the analysis therefore focuses on the ECtHR's approach to education and language rights. While it is admitted that some landmark judgments did expand protection for minorities, it is estimated that ECtHR is often cautious, especially in politically charged contexts, as it typically grants States significant leeway. The research shows that the recent *Valiullina v Latvia* case exemplified this trend, which is concluded from the fact that the Court ultimately prioritised Latvia's nation building aims and granted a broad margin of appreciation, even though it has, at least nominally, recognised the importance of mother-tongue education and the principle of substantive equality. It is therefore estimated that the opportunity to firmly anchor minority-specific rights in the Court's jurisprudence was missed, hence the article concludes by urging the ECtHR to more robustly integrate minority rights and values, such as equality, identity, and inclusion, into its interpretation of the ECHR.

The following chapter, co-authored by Milica V. Matijević and Ana Knežević Bojović, titled 'Minorities' Participation in Public Affairs: A Human Rights Norm or a Conflict Prevention Technique?' explores how the protection of minority rights in Europe has evolved since the end of the Second World War, especially through the work of the Advisory Committee on the FCNM. The analysis creatively compares the development of these rights with the stages of human life, and ultimately suggests that that if they were human, minority rights would have by now reached an 'early adulthood' phase. The paper attempts to uncover whether the Committee's monitoring practices are guided more by aims to prevent conflicts than by broader human rights principles. After comparing the Committee's approach to the right to effective participation in public affairs across twelve countries with different EU integration trajectories, contrary to the authors' initial hypothesis, the research found no strong link between the intensity of the Committee's scrutiny and whether countries were subject to minority rights requirements as part of joining the EU. Instead, a more systematic and rigorous approach was observed in countries with a recent history of ethnic conflict, such as those emerging from Yugoslavia and the UK (regarding Northern Ireland). In these settings, ensuring minorities' representation in public bodies became part of post-conflict peacebuilding, which in turn influenced legal frameworks and monitoring practices. The authors argue that this conflict prevention angle has shaped how minority rights are enforced, by often prioritising practical stability over consistent legal standards. In the conclusion, the authors argue that while minority rights protection is rooted in human rights ideals, in practice it remains heavily influenced by the legacy of conflict resolution and peacekeeping in Europe, and thus often serves as a tool to manage and prevent ethnic tensions.

The paper 'Assessing Non-Territorial Autonomy to Protect Minorities in the Digital Age and Digital Minorities' by Antoni Abat i Ninet analyses epistemological components of the term 'minority', as it is more complex than just being fewer in number within a given territory. As being a minority always means being defined in relation to a majority, and because legal frameworks are often focused on numbers and territory, the author indicates that these categories are quickly losing their prominence in reality. For example, someone can be part of a linguistic minority nationally but belong to a majority in their hometown. The chapter shows that the true marker of minority status is not just numbers, but often power, social position, and the experience of discrimination. Traditional laws have thus often ignored groups defined by gender, sexuality, disability or socioeconomic status, even though these groups face similar forms of exclusion. The central part of the paper reminds the reader that nowadays territory extends beyond physical land borders and includes digital territories, such as cyberspace, and cultural territories and claims that in the digital era, new 'virtual minorities' are emerging with marginalised communities forming online and becoming targets of hate or discrimination that transcend borders. It is suggested that protecting these groups may require moving beyond theories focusing on physical territories, while also adopting new forms of self-governance that are not linked to a specific place, such as non-territorial autonomy, since both traditional and digital minorities could benefit from this approach. In the end, the chapter advocates for a more flexible and inclusive understanding of minority status and urges recognition that the old frameworks are no longer enough in today's rapidly changing, digitalised world.

The final part of the volume illuminates broader topics captioned as 'Society, Culture, Diversity: Old and New Minorities' and it firstly presents the chapter on 'New Minorities As a New Frontier for Minority Rights Regimes: The Case of Non-EU Citizens in the Context of EU Member States', co-authored by Roberta Medda-Windischer and Katharina Crepaz, which tackles the issue of defining who counts as a minority, especially when it comes to new (non-EU citizens) minorities in the EU. Despite legal references to minority rights in EU treaties, the authors underline that there is no universally accepted or binding definition of a 'minority', which means protection often depends on each State's approach. However, they claim that this ambiguity is both a challenge and, potentially, an opportunity, as it might allow more flexible protection for non-EU minorities like migrants, but it inevitably leads to inconsistent rights across countries. The chapter argues that new (non-EU) minorities face significant gaps in rights and political participation compared against long-established European third-country nationals. Although EU laws focus on anti-discrimination and long-term residency, this research indicates that barriers remain. This is even more so, considering that many new minorities are more interested in practical issues, like language, work, and voting rights, than in the symbolic protections often associated with traditional minorities. To address this, the authors propose the 'Tree Model' for diversity governance, which balances unity and diversity and envisions a society rooted in both human and minority rights, where both majority and minority groups interact on equal terms, and where only claims consistent with human rights standards are recognised. Ultimately, it is concluded that achieving this vision and true inclusion requires flexibility, willingness to cooperate, and continuous adaptation from both majority and minority groups.

Jessika Eichler claims in her piece on 'Indigenous Peoples' Rights and the European Courts: A Category Under Construction' that recognising collective rights for indigenous peoples as a unique legal category is becoming more important in human rights and decolonial contexts. While international law and regional frameworks such as the Council of Europe acknowledge some minority rights, she argues that true collective rights for indigenous groups are either missing or are weakly protected, because most European legal systems, including the ECHR and EU, focus mainly on individual rights. Consequently, it is rather difficult for indigenous communities to claim and protect their land, cultural practices, and self-governance. Her research indicates that legal protections often take the form of anti-discrimination rules or general rights, which do not fully meet indigenous peoples' specific needs for land, culture, and participation. The paper also points out that efforts to advance indigenous rights in Europe face obstacles, such as State-centric views, the priority given to economic interests over cultural survival, and fragmented legal frameworks. Although it is determined that some international bodies (such as the UN Human Rights Committee) provide more robust recognition, European courts have mostly relied on adapting existing individual rights to cover collective claims, leading to patchy protection and limited impact. Finally, it is also shown that recent jurisprudence made slow progress, with inconsistent and cautious advances in the form of occasional broadening of property and cultural rights and in the recognition of procedural disadvantages faced by indigenous groups. Overall, Europe's legal landscape remains fragmented and insufficient for fully recognising indigenous collective rights, with meaningful protection often depending on context, creative legal interpretation, and international pressure rather than clear, binding regional law. However, the author points out the potential impact of Article 56 (3) of the ECHR, which leaves space open for bringing a kind of legal pluralism to the table, as it allows for the Convention to be applied in certain territories 'with due regard to local requirements'. Even though it is not spelled out directly, Eichler maintains that this exception could be understood to allow for indigenous legal or political systems to be recognised alongside, or even in place of, local government structures that may fall short in supporting collective autonomy.

In the closing chapter of the book, dedicated to the topic 'Anthropological Theory, Stakeholder Inclusion and Minority Rights – Reflections on the Research and Safeguarding of Serbian Intangible Cultural Heritage in the Western Balkans' and written by Miloš Milenković, the focus shifts to the anthropology as a discipline that continues to grapple with how to engage real-world issues around identity, culture, and heritage, especially in contexts where people view these elements as concrete, lived realities. While many in the field of anthropology have often advocated for marginalised groups, author argues that anthropology is ambivalent about collective identities and rights, wary of essentialising culture, since for instance, there is a clear tension in debates about safeguarding intangible cultural heritage, the field where international frameworks tend to align with nation-states rather than with minorities. The paper reflects on the ongoing changes in heritage preservation and identity in Serbia and the Western Balkans, where these questions are especially pressing because minority groups often keep their identities on the margins of UNESCO's heritage protection framework, and post-conflict societies often return to traditionalism, particularly among young people. The chapter underlines the need for a balanced, participatory approach that would, on the one hand, respect the importance of identity and heritage in these societies, while on the other, maintain academic integrity. This would necessitate communities to be involved in research and heritage preservation, to connect theoretical considerations with practical realities and experiences. However, Milenković also understands that any attempt to challenge or break down ideas regarding identity is often perceived as betrayal, and that factors such as populism and resistance to outside influence may make these efforts considerably complicated. Ultimately, the paper proposes that anthropology should aim to promote peaceful coexistence by encouraging respect for collective identities, while still keeping the critical and thoughtful analysis that is central to the discipline. On that path, it is indicated that the UNESCO Convention for the Safeguarding of Intangible Cultural Heritage could 'ground' the Universal Declaration of Human Rights and the FCNM, while also serving as a guide toward renewed respect for individual differences in cases where collectives are strongly essentialised and heritage is largely defined along ethnic lines. However, reaching this goal calls for comparative studies, stronger interdisciplinary cooperation, and the sharing of knowledge and expertise, yet it may be worth it, as it is said to currently be a key platform for collaboration between the humanities and social sciences for advancing human and minority rights.

PART I

Minority Rights as Human Rights – Views from Theory and Practice

1

Special Rights and Obligations: Why Minority Rights Need Institutional Frameworks

TOVE H. MALLOY

1. Introduction

Claiming that minority rights are human rights is a mode of speaking that requires clarification. Some minority rights are universal; others are particular. Theoretically, human rights are universal because they belong to all humankind. Minority rights are also universal because they can be claimed by all members of society, but they are particular because they are assigned to specific persons or entities. This means they are special rights. This seems confusing. How can minority rights span from the universal to the particular? The answer lies in the *definition* of scope and the scope of *application*. Thus, in terms of scope there is a differentiation in who can actually enjoy the application of minority rights. We might say that the intentions and aims of minority rights protection require differentiation. In terms of the technical application of minority rights there are legal tools available whose material outcomes point to universal rights although scope, aims and intentions indicate particular rights-holders. It would seem that material outcomes are realised not as a result of the nature of rights but as a result of the intentions of duty-bearers. Intentions, therefore, are the foundation of the institutional frameworks guaranteeing minority rights.

This chapter begins with a short introduction to the problem area, that is the system of rights that we call human rights. I explore the nature of human rights and rights in general to better understand the dichotomy of the universal and the particular. This leads to the common knowledge about the background of human rights as deriving from natural rights. But it also poses questions of what type of rights are human rights, or perhaps more correctly, what is the nature of rights? And are there different types? I explore the nature (definition) of human rights in terms of the difference between general rights and special rights. This leads to the notion of 'promise', and I question how humanity decides what kind of rights should be promised in what situations. In a short discussion of the metatheoretical foundation of societal organisation, I draw on Philip Allott's theory of social exchange, or as I would call it the 'politics of social exchange'. It can assist us in understanding that we live in a constructed reality invented, developed and negotiated by human beings, including the way we conceptualise human rights and the assigning of rights to each other. His theory is complex. He explores how we use our consciousness to structure our societies, and he develops the notion of the legal relation in which duty is a key to the rights of the individual. Based on a number of principles that he develops, he eventually makes us see that all legal power is shared power, and thus we should all have an opportunity for equal access to power.

The notion of having to share power, leads to the field of ethical behaviour and the debates among scholars of ethical theory. A major problem facing human society is that we will never be 100 per cent equal, but we are bound to strive for improving the status of individuals as much as possible in the direction of equality. Indeed, a major aim of minority rights is to achieve equality for groups of difference. The principle of equality and its many dimensions are in focus. Unfortunately, this does not give clear answers; there are internal tensions in the principle, and non-discrimination does not secure minorities their rights to equality and equity. It shows how difficult the sharing of legal power is when it comes to securing equity for all. Because legal power is not distributed equally, one might ask how rights aimed at protecting the existence of minorities ethically might be found? This is a question the British philosopher Onora O'Neill has written extensively about. She provides interesting insights into the ethical dimensions of rights and obligations. Her theory of perfect and imperfect obligations leads to the questions of how to secure that rights and obligations are matched.[1]

One way of investigating this is by empirically examining the approach taken by the contemporary minority rights protection scheme, the European minority rights regime, as set out in the only legally binding instrument in Europe, the Council of Europe's Framework Convention for the Protection of National Minorities (FCNM).[2] In focus is the theoretical approach taken by the Advisory Committee on the FCNM. A good source on this is the discussion provided in the Thematic Commentary No. 4 (TC4).[3] The three categories

[1] Onora O'Neill, Towards Justice and Virtue: A Constructive Account of Practical Reasoning (Cambridge: Cambridge University Press, 1996).

[2] Council of Europe, *Framework Convention for the Protection of National Minorities and Explanatory Report*, ETS No 157 www.coe.int/en/web/conventions/cets-number-/-abridged-title-known?module=treaty-detail&treatynum=157.

[3] Advisory Committee on the Framework Convention for the Protection of National Minorities, The Framework Convention: A Key Tool to Managing Diversity through Minority Rights – The Scope of Application of the Framework Convention for the Protection of National Minorities, Thematic Commentary No 4 (Council of Europe 2016) www.coe.int/en/web/minorities/thematic-commentaries-of-the-advisory-committee.

of scope of application that the TC4 introduces are, therefore, linked to the debate on perfect and imperfect ethical obligations. Institutions are a key to this debate. In a short discussion, the question of how we institutionalise obligations and how we might identify obligation-bearers is addressed, and it is asked what institutions will take on the obligations? In concluding, it is argued that minority rights are still human rights because the analysis of the FCNM provisions shows that they are all guaranteed material outcomes in so far that they all have counterpart rights. Thus, it is not the scope that determines whether minority rights are human rights, but rather the intentions that guarantee material outcomes through institutional frameworks.

2. The Nature of Rights

It is common knowledge that human rights derive from natural rights, or the idea that there is a higher law and set of standards that are universal.[4] Such standards are not framed according to specific societies. They pertain to all individuals and belong to all human beings. This is a world that is organised on the basis of ideas of morality. Natural rights are therefore not positive law, or what we might call man-made law, nor are they made by States and governing bodies. They are inherent, fundamental, inalienable and universal rights that we all enjoy and may claim from day one of our lives.

The idea of natural rights has influenced our thinking about rights since the times of the philosophers of Ancient Greece. Later, in modern times, with the Reformation and philosophers like John Locke, natural rights became a key notion of the development of humane societies. The influence of natural rights became clear in eminent documents, such as, the U.S. Declaration of Independence (1776) and the French Declaration of the Rights of Man and the Citizen (1789) through to the United Nations Charter (1945) and the United Nations Universal Declaration on Human Rights (1948).

Today, human rights have, by and large, been transformed into man-made law, or positive law. Still, they are inherent, fundamental, inalienable and universal rights. Of course, the jurisprudence of human rights law has shown that they are also gradable and seldom absolute, but are nevertheless inherent and universal. However, to transform human rights into positive law, it is necessary to take into account that which is particular and identifiable in terms of time and space. The particular is that which we all generate as individuals: personality, culture, communities, histories, and all the things that are particular to some of us, but never to all of us.

[4] John Finnis, *Natural Law and Natural Rights* (Oxford: Clarendon Press, 1980).

2.1. General vs. Special Rights

The difference between the universal and the particular in terms of rights is legally epitomised in the difference between general and special rights. Drawing on H. L. A. Hart, Jeremy Waldron has explained it as a question of contingent events. 'A special right', Waldron argues, 'is a right which a person is conceived to have by virtue of the occurrence of some contingent event or transaction'.[5] Waldron clarifies this by noting that a special right 'arises out of some special transaction or relationship, that is, a transaction or relationship which is, in some sense, peculiar to those who happen to have entered into it'.[6] This type of right is also called a right *in personam* as opposed to the notion of a right *in rem* (which is a legal term describing the power a court may exercise over a person over whom the court does not have *in personam* jurisdiction). The term *in rem* is Latin and refers to things which are tangible, such as property, whereas *in personam* in Latin refers to the individual human being. Granted, Waldron's concern is the particular situation of property law. However, in philosophy, the right to property has been defined to include an individual's personal being to which no one has a right but him or herself. John Locke, the English philosopher, developed this theory at a time when property ownership was for the few.[7] In the view of Locke, a person's labour and the work that the body provides, is also a property and thus a right, which should be protected. This is why Alf Ross has argued that 'a right of disposal is (normally) equipped with protection *in rem* and a right of claim with protection *in personam*'.[8]

Waldron further argues that general rights also impose obligations but do not arise from a special relationship; they are rights that every person can claim on an equal basis. Nevertheless, it is also possible to redescribe a special right as a general right. The caveat is that a special right redescribed as a general right is 'a general right which is conditional in its content'.[9] Such a general right is in fact a conditional right but a right that a rights-holder can have in common with everyone else *ab initio* as a direct consequence of the moral rule about promises. And promises have been in focus from the ancients to the medieval, to the moderns and beyond, according to Allen Habib, who notes that theorists have sought to explain the normative force of promises.[10] Theorists have a standard taxonomy of the main types of promissory theory, which includes normative power views,

[5] Jeremy Waldron, *The Right to Private Property* (Oxford: Oxford University Press, 1990), 112.

[6] ibid, 107.

[7] John Locke, *Two Treatises of Government* [1689] in Thomas Hollis (ed), (A Millar et al 1764) https://www.yorku.ca/comninel/courses/3025pdf/Locke.pdf.

[8] Alf Ross, 'The Theory of Rights In Rem and Rights In Personam' in Jakob v H Holtermann (ed), *On Law and Justice* (Uta Bindreiter tr., Oxford University Press, 2019), 227–241.

[9] Waldron, The Right to Private Property (n 5), 106.

[10] Allen Habib, 'Promises' in Edward N Zalta and Uri Nodelman (eds), *The Stanford Encyclopedia of Philosophy* www.plato.stanford.edu/archives/win2022/entries/promises/.

conventionalist views, expectation views, and joint commitment views. But for our purposes it suffices to know that a general rule means that 'promises produce moral obligations; they are of a peculiar sort. Unlike paradigmatic moral duties, the duty not to harm for example, promissory obligations are not owed equally to everyone, but rather only those we have promised'.[11] On this view, one could argue that a special right *in personam* may also be of a general nature as long as there is a special promise in the definition.

Promises must of course be made by human beings to other human beings. This seems to indicate that there is a relationship of obligation, or as it is often described in law, a relationship of duties. There are numerous opinions among ethical philosophers as to what a promissory obligation entails, depending on the view of philosophy. For instance, rule utilitarians, also called conventionalists, defend promissory obligations on the grounds that the rule of promise-keeping is productive of the best consequences. There is not space here to discuss all the views. Suffice to say that understanding promises, and the act of promising, points us to the issue of how members of society organise and negotiate promises. How do societies organise such complex matters? Who gets to decide?

3. The 'Politics of Social Exchange'

Philip Allott has developed a very interesting and complex theory of societal self-organisation through the actions of social exchange, including promise-keeping.

Society, as a structure and a system within consciousness, creates itself by conceiving of itself within consciousness in the perspective of its constitution, by willing and acting with a view to the constant re-conceiving of that constitution, and by willing and acting with a view to actualising the constitution. The structure-system of society contains an exchange of energy. The social exchange transforms natural power into social power, exchanges power for purpose. Social power created under the legal constitution takes the form of legal relations.[12]

Social power is here the key to how we organise our societies. Allott summarises for us that:

> … the constitution is the structure-system of a society which enables social power to be applied to make the transformations which enable a society to create itself from its possibilities, to actualise its possibilities through willing and acting in fulfilment of its purposes, to make the social exchange.[13]

[11] ibid.
[12] Philip Allott, *Eunomia: New Order for a New World* (Oxford: Oxford University Press, 1990), 145.
[13] ibid, 152.

The Social Exchange is visualised by Allott in a diagram:

Figure 1 The Social Exchange

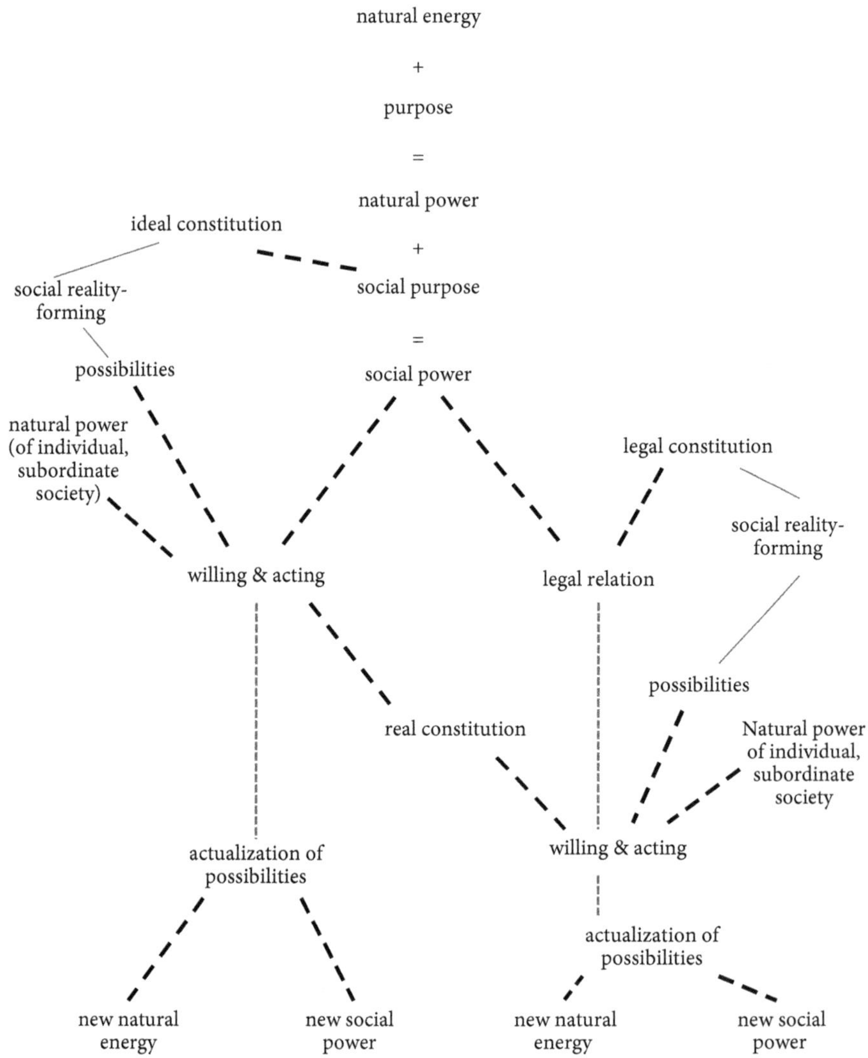

Source: Author's adaptation of graphic from Allott, Eunomia. Fig. 7 at 153.

Allott specifically explains the legal aspect of social exchange with the concept of legal relation, which is the mechanism that establishes relationships between members of society, or legal relators. The legal relation integrates members of society through rights and duties, so it is the legal constitution which determines the coming into existence of legal relations. According to Allott, legal relations embody all impulses of life (necessities, wishes, desires, obligations, etc.).[14] This means that:

> By legal relation in the form of a right, society is considered to confer on the right-holder the benefit, the protection, the assurance, the individuality of the law. By a legal relation in the form of a duty, society is considered to impose on the duty-holder the burden, the order, the universality of the law.[15]

Allott cautions us, however, that focusing on rights and duties in a strict sense hides important aspects of legal relations and may distort our understanding of law, especially international society and law. This is, among others, because rights and duties are diverse; they can be mutually interdependent but serve different purposes, and they are affected by events outside the law. Drawing on knowledge developed by Jeremy Bentham and Wesley Hohfeld, Allott emphasises a number of rights and duties, many of which are well-known to legal scholars: a claim-right, a power-right, a requirement duty, a liability-duty, and a disability-duty.

What is important to Allott to emphasise is that rights are constraining while duties are empowering. Both create a consciousness in the holders that is important for the legal relations and necessary for the social exchange to be productive. Actors in a legal relation become psychologically aware of the need to make choices for the best outcome; they become motivated to achieve certain practical implications; they understand that law has a distributive effect, and thus being actors in a legal relation is educational. Allott argues that participating in legal relations also spills over into the non-legal relationships, such as conventional duties of protocol, politeness and family relations.

Allott interestingly develops a set of principles that embody the legal relation of social exchange:

1. *The principle of integration*, that makes law part of the total social process.
2. *The principle of transformation*, that sees law as dynamic.
3. *The principle of delegation*, that accepts all legal power as delegated power.
4. *The principle of the intrinsic limitation of power*, that accepts that legal power is limited.
5. *The principle of the supremacy of law*, that accepts that all social power is under the law.
6. *The principle of the supremacy of the social interest*, that sees all legal power as power in the social interest.
7. *The principle of social responsibility*, that accepts that all social power is accountable.

Allott's principles make it possible through the social processes of a society to create its own survival through time by allowing the transformation of the future into the past. 'They are the principles without which the structure-system of a

[14] ibid, 159.
[15] ibid, 160.

society could not be a structure-system.'[16] From the perspective of minority rights, Allott's social exchange theory helps us understanding that rights are negotiable and are socially determined. He shows us that 'all legal power is shared power' and that sharing of power must involve all members of society, all humankind.[17] This implies that we must participate in the social exchange on an equal basis. It is not unusual, therefore, that the legal right to equality has become a centre principle of minority rights protection. But how has the principle of equality worked for members of minorities?

4. Equality as Differentiated Difference

The one human right that is always linked to minority protection is the right to non-discrimination. It derives from the principle of equality, which is a liberal value of many faces or dimensions. It is a value that is still developing as our societies grow more diverse, or rather, as we recognise more willingly our human diversity. While the *principle* of equality has adapted to new scopes of diversities, as these get recognised socially and politically, the *concept* of equality has been static when it comes to improving the effect of non-discrimination, or the verifiable equality. This means we have a principle of equality that may have good aims and intentions, but which does not deliver in terms of equity and equal standing. A short review of the principle shows that there are not only diverse opinions as to what the principle must deliver, there is also perhaps an internal contradiction in the principle.

4.1. The Principle of Equality[18]

The principle of equality is one of the most contested and controversial ideas of modern-day social, moral and political philosophy. Having developed from being a rational political tool during ancient times into a moral concept of desirable interhuman relations during the Enlightenment, equality remains contested both as a principle and as a tool. The disagreement among scholars about the principle of equality hinges mainly on its role in a theory of justice. Consequently, both the reach and the function of the principle of equality as an equalising tool remain highly controversial.

[16] ibid, 168.

[17] ibid, 177.

[18] This discussion relies on Tove H. Malloy, 'Conceptualizing Democratic Diversity Management for Multicultural Societies: Theories of Society and Law' (2006/7) *European Yearbook of Minority Issues*, 293–98.

The terms 'equality', 'equal', and 'equally' signify a qualitative relationship.[19] They refer to a connection between different objects, persons, processes or circumstances that have the same characteristics or qualities in at least one respect but not in all respects. Equality should thus be distinguished from 'identical' or similar in terms of sameness. When we say that all men are equal, we are therefore not saying that they are identical or similar. Rather, we presume a difference between the persons compared, and an absolute outcome is thus impossible. Moreover, equality can be both descriptive and prescriptive. Prescriptive equality, which is our main concern here, is not attainable without also applying a descriptive component. Equality consists of a tripartite relation between at least two persons and one or more qualities. Two persons, A and B, are equal in a certain respect C only if they share or enjoy equality in that particular respect. C must thus represent a relevant comparative standard of the desired quality of equality.[20] This quality is the variable that must be predetermined in all cases before we can ascertain or evaluate the extent to which there exists equality between two persons. The quality of equality is the standard that has developed over time, and which is the object of scholars' contesting and controversial debates.

To understand the different types of quality of equality, it is helpful first to note that inequality does not come in only one type. The idea of fundamental equality that we are all of equal worth, as opposed to being treated as equals, requires us to think of our lives and actions as taking place at various levels. This is why Michael Walzer argues that the full package of equality consists of a complex set of equalities that are applied in various spheres.[21] Because of the complexity of life and the plurality of criteria for justice, he argues that we should think of distributive justice in terms of 'complex equality', meaning that our needs for equality may vary from sphere to sphere. This means that for the individual to be able to enjoy equality in all spheres he/she must be made able to access different types of equality as his/her needs require. Inequality happens not only in terms of the quality of life that is required to live a life in human dignity; it also happens because of human characteristics and (lack) of status, including class status. Finally, inequality may be a consequence of both direct and indirect discrimination. Equality is, therefore, of both an empirical nature and a normative nature, although the two are difficult to separate. Hence, the quality of equality is no longer seen as a single variable but rather as a complex group of variables.

4.2. The Concept of Equality – An Index[22]

The idea that everyone should be furnished with the same material level of goods and services has Marxist undertones, although absolute economic equality was

[19] Stefan Gosepath, 'Equality' (2007) in Edward N Zalta (ed), *The Stanford Encyclopedia of Philosophy* www.plato.stanford.edu/entries/equality.

[20] ibid.

[21] Michael Walzer, *Spheres of Justice* (New York, Basic Books, 1983).

[22] Gosepath, 'Equality' (n 19), presents this typology.

not envisioned by Marxism. 'Simple equality' is not supported by many scholars because it raises a number of problems in regard to equality in general. It begs questions about the measurement of the equality of the goods to be distributed, it raises questions of time span, it requires Pareto-optimality, it begs the question of differences, and it removes the individual's freedom of choice. It is egalitarian but not of the type of equality supported by most liberal egalitarians. As it is not difference-sensitive, it would not be desirable as a tool of accommodation of racial and ethnic minorities.

A revisionary conception of simple equality is 'equality of outcome'. This is a form of egalitarianism that seeks to reduce or eliminate differences in material condition between individuals or households, usually through equalising income and/or wealth. It therefore equalises where people end up rather than where or how they begin.[23] This need not only be in an economic sense. Outcome in terms of political representation is an important aspect of gender, race, and ethnic equality. Critics of equality of outcome argue that it disregards the importance of individual responsibility and choice. Moreover, it begs the question as to what we are seeking to equalise, and may actually result in delivering inequality on another or what we call reverse discrimination. However, it is an important aspect of equality when seeking accommodation of identity and structural groups, such as women, racial and ethnic minorities. The reason for this is that equality of outcome can address difference as well as structural disparity.

Related to equality of outcome is the conception of 'equality of result', which postulates that equality should be measured by the results that an institution yields.[24] A social policy that seeks to enhance equality in certain aspects can be judged by the effect it has on the quality of individual people's lives. For instance, a poverty alleviation policy would only be considered equalising if it yielded good results in absolute numbers. Although this seems a conception that is easy to support, liberal egalitarians have rejected it as too narrow and one-sided, since it only allows for measuring the consequences of the policy and not the intentions. In the distribution of justice, they argue, the intentions behind a policy of equality are also important. Like equality of outcome, equality of result is an instrumental conception of equality.

In contradistinction to most egalitarian and instrumental conceptions of equality, libertarians and economic liberals argue for a minimalist view of the distribution of justice that promotes the individual's right to freedom over any redistribution of social goods for the sake of equality.[25] Basically, libertarians assert a strong opposition between equality and freedom, believing that through our acting in the free market we are ourselves responsible for achieving equality. Hence, the idea is that self-accomplishment determines our position in society. According to libertarians, freedom can only be curtailed for the sake of maintaining public order. Libertarians

[23] Anne Phillips, 'Defending Equality of Outcome' (2004) 12 (1) *Journal of Political Philosophy*, 1–19.
[24] Gosepath, 'Equality' (n 19).
[25] Robert Nozick, *Anarchy, State, and Utopia* (Oxford: Blackwell, 1974).

thus view 'equality of accomplishment' normatively as the freedom to act unrestrained. Critics of this conception argued that even a free market cannot generate unrestricted rights over unequal amounts of resources; space and raw materials are not unlimited and thus not available for anyone to possess in unlimited quantities. Moreover, it relies too much on luck, extraordinary natural gifts, inherited property and status.[26] Positive social circumstances are thus likely to be 'favouritised' at the cost of equality. This account is therefore not difference-sensitive.

The conception of 'equality of welfare' is motivated by the moral view that it is desirable that the amount of human goods gained by each person for his/herself over the course of his/her life should be the same.[27] The central criterion for justice must consequently be equalising the conditions of individuals. This conception raises some problematic issues. The core problem is that what is required for one person's well-being may not provide other people with a sense of well-being. Moreover, some people may be in greater need of support to achieve well-being than others. Finally, equality of welfare has been accused of taking away the individual's incentive for feeling responsible for their own well-being, possibly resulting in poor administration of their welfare goods. For our purposes, it is important, however, that equality of welfare can be difference-sensitive, as it is now being applied to Roma communities in some countries.

Many egalitarians prefer 'equality of opportunity', which is based on the moral argument that individuals should be responsible for their own decisions, and that only the opportunity to have the resources, such as welfare, that they feel they need in order to make their decisions, should be the object of equality.[28] Thus, it is not the resources that must be equalised but the opportunity to utilise certain resources in the quest for well-being. Equality of opportunity therefore requires the presence of options for each individual that are similar to the options enjoyed by all other people. Equal opportunity thus prevails when human beings effectively enjoy equality of possibility. Equality of opportunity is defended by scholars on both sides of the aisle, meaning that egalitarians, including the more liberal ones, can argue that, given such resources, the individual's freedom need not be curtailed in the application of those resources, while multiculturalists can argue that arriving at an ideal society where every member enjoys equal opportunities may be a society that respects difference. Hence, the multiculturalist conception of equality of opportunity would have to be difference-sensitive towards the identity of individuals. Some scholars have tried to marry equality of opportunity with welfare equality,[29] while others have sought to augment welfare and opportunity

[26] Gosepath, 'Equality' (n 19).

[27] Richard Arneson, 'Egalitarianism' in Edward N Zalta (ed), *The Stanford Encyclopedia of Philosophy* https://plato.stanford.edu/entries/egalitarianism/.

[28] Richard Arneson, 'Equality of Opportunity' (2002) in Edward N Zalta (ed), *The Stanford Encyclopedia of Philosophy* www.plato.stanford.edu/entries/equal-opportunity.

[29] Richard Arneson, 'Equality and Equal Opportunity for Welfare' (1989) *Philosophical Studies* 56:77; and Richard Arneson, 'Equality of Opportunity for Welfare Defended and Recanted' (1999) 7(4) *Journal of Political Philosophy*, 488–97.

with the dimension of access. Yet again, some argue that equality of opportunity is in fact the measurement by which equality of outcome should be established.[30]

'Equality of resources' requires that persons who are born with unequal innate gifts should be compensated; what applies for social circumstances should also apply for such gifts. This view, according to John Rawls, may be described as a theory of 'primary goods', meaning individuals should have equal initial starting positions. The view of equality that ensues from this is justice as fair play, which makes sure that the fair play favours the most disadvantaged. A 'difference principle' is thus applied, which takes into account the fact that the free market cannot protect certain disadvantaged groups.[31] According to Ronald Dworkin, a view of strict equality of resources distributes resources not according to differentiation but on the basis of personal ambition.[32] A person who has not been ambitious enough and has thus not accumulated enough resources must thus rely on a fictive insurance scheme. The mechanisms of the insurance scheme are beyond the scope of this article; suffice it to note that the scheme would penalise some for their unfortunate circumstances while others may be subsidised for the costs of their choices.[33] This is why equality of resources has been criticised for not taking into account the diversity of tastes and preferences.[34] Clearly, we could also argue that whatever the merits of Dworkin's theory, it does not allow for explicit differentiation.

Multiculturalists and feminists have problems with most of the egalitarian conceptions of equality as they create uniformity. The general tenet of their argument is that cultural difference is a value that most conceptions of equality tend to overlook.[35] Rather, standard conceptions of equality tend to mean assimilation to a pre-existing and problematic male or white or middle-class norm. To overcome this, multiculturalists and feminists call for 'equality of status', which recognises differences without leading to an essentialism grounded in sexual or cultural characteristics. The argument for accepting difference while seeking equality spurred an involved, but somewhat confused, theoretical debate in the last decades of the twentieth century. The confusion arose because some multiculturalists and feminists argued that sexual, racial and ethnic differences should become irrelevant while others held that such differences are highly relevant but should not result in inequality. In essence, the dispute is about how equality is to be attained while valuing difference.

In addition to the tension between equality and difference, or to be more precise, between equality and the freedom to remain different, the equality of status conception brings into the debate the fundamental question of groups versus individuals. This is because not only liberal theory but, more importantly, liberal law is based on

[30] Phillips, 'Defending Equality of Outcome' (n 23), 2.

[31] John Rawls, *A Theory of Justice* (Oxford: Oxford University Press, 1971), 76–90 and 90–5.

[32] Ronald Dworkin, 'What is Equality Part 2: Equality of Resources' (1981) 10 Philosophy and Public Affairs, 228–240.

[33] Will Kymlicka, *Contemporary Political Philosophy* (Oxford: Clarendon Press, 1990), 83.

[34] Phillips, 'Defending Equality of Outcome' (n 23), 1.

[35] Classic texts defending multiculturalism include Will Kymlicka, *Multicultural Citizenship* (Oxford: Clarendon Press, 1995) and David Miller, *On Nationality* (Oxford: Clarendon Press, 1995).

the individual as the core component and rights holder. Minorities seeking equality of status through demands for recognition are thus not easily accommodated as groups in the general paradigms of liberal law. Of course, in practice, individual human rights on a collective notion protect members of such minorities on the basis of a recognition that their members should not suffer discrimination and exclusion. But recognition of difference based on group membership is not easily accepted. Moreover, difference at the group level is one thing, but difference also exists at the individual level. The debate about recognising group difference thus runs the risk of promoting assimilation of the individual to a view of differences based solely on the characteristics of the group identity. This not only violates the rights of the individual but also raises questions of how to reach equality for both the individual and the group. This has become the most difficult aspect of multiculturalism, ie, to accommodate difference while protecting equality. In reality, we may be faced with an internal tension of how to accommodate differentiated difference while promoting equality? To help us find answers to that question, it might be instructive to review the ethical dimension of justice. In order to examine the ethical dimension, it is necessary to understand the difference between rights and obligations.

4.3. Special Rights and Obligations

On obligations, Onora O'Neill has argued that unless obligation-bearers are identifiable by right-holders, claims to have rights amount only to rhetoric.[36] O'Neill's argument is part of a broader discussion of the rivalry between justice and virtue, or one might say between rights and obligations. Her concern is with people's reasoning about action and which principles to follow when taking action; especially in the individual's practical reasoning of how to take ethical consideration of others. So, she is motivated in the same manner as Allott, but seeks to peek into the minds of individuals when they act.

Like Allott, O'Neill divides our world into the universal and the particular. She disagrees with the universalists, who, she argues, accept a degree of abstraction in reaching 'substantive conclusions about justice, rights and obligations'.[37] In O'Neill's view, universalists risk being blind to conditionality. hereon this matter, she points the same way as Waldron. Universalists, she argues, overlook that to achieve justice, we must apply a differential approach based on a critical notion of practical reasoning that prevents us from adopting principles we do not accept. In other words, the universal approach must involve judgement about goals and achievements. This requires that we tackle to the problem of scope.

However, scope is a difficult matter, according to O'Neill. To bridge the gap between the universal scope and the particular scope, she introduces the need for

[36] Onora O'Neill, Towards Justice and Virtue: A Constructive Account of Practical Reasoning (Cambridge: Cambridge University Press, 1996), 129.
[37] ibid, 3.

ethical considerations of the other. Universal principles of justice, she argues, are of no use, if we do not find ways to fix the scope, structure and content of principles.[38] A very common approach, but not her preferred approach, is to seek definite contours of individuals that deserve our ethical considerations. However, this particularist approach will lead to appropriate recognition based on some theoretical, metaphysical claims but will not necessarily guarantee ethical standing, or status and recognition, for all. Rather, O'Neill argues, we need just procedures by which we recognise the other in a universal, open, constructive and practical manner. Granted, such procedures will involve gaps and lack of full knowledge about the other, including inaccurate knowledge, but if we are willing to connect with the other and correct our assumptions, the procedures can be improved. O'Neill admits that this is a cosmopolitan view, but it is a contingent and approximate view that allows for the correction of our relationships with others and thus the option to show our ethical consideration.

The next step for O'Neill is to connect ethical consideration to obligations. If we are able to give ethical consideration to others, we might be willing to accept obligations towards them. O'Neill makes an interesting observation about the relationship between rights and obligations. She notes that in contemporary thinking, the rights focus is usually on the rights-holder or rights-bearer, or the entitlements of subjects, and the notion of obligations becomes a subordinate notion. This is the liberal approach that we are all quite familiar with and which holds that universal rights do not impose obligations on all of us, whereas specific rights only incur rights on some specific duty-bearers. However, according to O'Neill, we must distinguish between universal liberty rights and universal welfare rights. To her, there is a false dichotomy in universal rights. For instance, universal liberty rights may not require ethical consideration, if they represent negative freedom, whereas universal welfare rights (to goods and services), representing positive freedom, do require ethical consideration. This to O'Neill is a false dichotomy regarding obligations because both types of freedoms require institutional structures for enforcement and thus impose obligations on society. What makes them different is that they are genuinely asymmetric in distribution of goods.[39] That means that universal welfare rights are of 'a particular sort of right whose counterpart obligations' are 'distributed according to one or another institutional scheme, hence strictly speaking a special right', and that their vindication as well as their enforcement would have to justify institutional structures of a particular type.[40] O'Neill has in mind international human rights with specific aims, such as social, economic and cultural rights. These rights can cause consternation if they are not understood correctly. 'A premature rhetoric of rights', O'Neill argues, 'can inflate expectations while masking a lack of claimable entitlements'.[41] This is why she argues for taking obligations seriously.

[38] ibid, 91.
[39] ibid, 132.
[40] ibid.
[41] ibid, 133.

Taking obligations seriously, to O'Neill, requires that we learn to understand the structural differences between obligations that either have or lack corresponding rights.[42] The way to spot this is to look for their embodiments in institutions, relationships and lives.[43] O'Neill distinguishes between imperfect obligations and perfect obligations. Imperfect obligations refer to identifiable obligation bearers, but there may not be any corresponding rights-holders. Perfect obligations, on the other hand, exist only between identifiable obligation-bearers and identifiable right-holders. This influences the institutional structures that support the implementation of the relevant rights.

Remembering the asymmetric distinction from earlier, the distribution of universal obligations results, according to O'Neill, in two types of obligations: universal perfect obligations and specific perfect obligations. Universal perfect obligations may not impose positive tasks, but they put obligations on all of us. An example is the right to life; we all have an obligation not to kill. Although such universal perfect obligations are usually institutionalised, they also depend on the virtue and ethical behaviour of the individual. In contrast, specific perfect obligations impose positive tasks because they 'connect specific agents to specified recipients of action, to whom they owe and for whom they are bound to perform, [and] who are the holders of the equivalent special right'.[44] Examples of specific perfect obligations are among other welfare rights, but they may also include contractual rights, promises and family ties. What is important in the case of specific perfect obligations is the ethical questions about relationships, practices, and institutions. Thus, the obligation-bearers have a duty both to guarantee the right and the premises upon which the right is established. Most importantly, the obligation-bearer cannot opt out of the obligation due to lack of virtue or ethical concerns. She or he must take it seriously. In summarising her arguments, O'Neill offers a diagram of types of obligations:

Table 1 Types of obligations

	Universal	**Special**
Perfect	Held by all, owed to all; Counterpart liberty rights; Embodied above all in legal and economic systems.	Held by some, owed to specified others; Counterpart special rights; Fixed by structure of specific transactions and relationships; Can be distributively universal given appropriate institutions.

(continued)

[42] ibid, 141.
[43] ibid, 146.
[44] ibid.

Table 1 ***(Continued)***

	Universal	Special
Imperfect	Held by all, owed to none; No counterpart rights; Embodied above all in character and expressed in varied situations.	Held by some, owed to none; No counterpart rights; Embodied in ethos of specific relationships and practices and in characters; Often, but not exclusively, expressed in action within special relationships.

Source: Onora O'Neill, *Towards justice and virtue. A constructive account of practical reasoning* (Cambridge University Press, 1996).

To clarify, transactions and relationships are philosophical terms for actions that require institutions. O'Neill's normative argument is therefore that:

> Effective limitation of the vulnerabilities that facilitate injury (especially of the vulnerabilities that arise from destitution and disease) needs more than sporadic and unclaimable individual exertion and good will. It needs institutions which allocate responsibilities and create positive rights that will prevent or limit systematic injury of the vulnerable.[45]

These responsibilities are our obligations to each other. However, assuming that we can identify obligation-bearers, how do we make sure that they meet their responsibilities? Or, in more practical terms, how do we institutionalise obligations?

5. Minority Rights Provisions and Obligations

As noted earlier, the European minority rights scheme is a good case study because the guidelines in the Council of Europe instruments are the most developed types of minority provisions, and because instruments are usually accompanied by explanatory reports and thematic commentaries. For a theoretical discussion, the set of guidelines that has made a serious effort at explaining the scope of minority rights provisions, is the FCNM TC4. The TC4 sets out a few fundamental principles regarding the approach that the drafters of the FCNM have chosen and which the Advisory Committee to the FCNM has implemented. One important principle is that:

> Depending on the nature of the minority rights contained therein, the scope of application of the Framework Convention must therefore be established separately for each article, which is why, from its first monitoring cycle, the Advisory Committee has referred to its article-by-article approach.[46]

[45] ibid, 190.
[46] Advisory Committee, The Framework Convention, Thematic Commentary No 4 (n 3), 16.

This has proven a brilliant political move, as it allows states that are party to the FCNM to apply a flexible method of minority protection, but it is also very useful from the perspective of identifying obligations because it allows for distinguishing between perfect and imperfect obligations. Another principle pertains to effective equality, especially with the view to avoid that hierarchies are created between groups of minorities. And a fundamental principle is the obligation to consider integration a two-way, or give-and-take, process. The TC4 even highlights the obligations held by governments that are not 100 per cent in control of all of the territory of the State. In other words, a government cannot opt out of obligations. All in all, there is no doubt that the TC4 considers obligations relevant in all the articles designed to enhance minority protection.

To assist governments in understanding the notion of scope of application, the TC4 divides minority rights provisions into three categories according to scope of application. These are:

1. FCNM provisions that apply to all.
2. FCNM provisions with a broad scope of application.
3. FCNM provisions with a specific scope of application.

The definition of the first category is provided as rights that 'apply to all persons on the territory of states parties, including those not belonging to national minorities, either explicitly or by implication through their specific link with provisions that are applicable to all'.[47] The rights in question are Articles 6 and 12, respectively the right to protection against discrimination through promotion of mutual respect and inter-cultural dialogue, and through education.

The second category, the broad scope category, is not defined explicitly in the TC4, but it argues that a major aim of the FCNM is to 'ensure that minority rights are not arbitrarily withheld from persons belonging to national minorities who should be protected under the Framework Convention'.[48] The rights in question are Articles 4, 5, 7, 8, 9, 10(1), 10(3), 11(1), 11(2), 12(3), 14(1), 14(3) and 15. In other words, the majority of the rights of the FCNM are considered as broad in scope.

The third category, the specific scope category, is linked to the 'particular financial and administrative commitment required in order to give effect to some language rights contained in the Framework Convention', and therefore 'states parties may establish special conditions for their enjoyment'.[49] The rights in question are Article 10(2), right to use a minority language in relations with local administrative authorities; Article 11(3), the right to have topographical indications and signposts also displayed in the minority language; and Article 14(2), the right to learn minority languages or receive instruction in minority languages.

[47] ibid, 19.
[48] ibid, 22.
[49] Advisory Committee, The Framework Convention, Thematic Commentary No 4 (n 3), 27.

Table 2 FCNM provisions according to scope

All persons	Broad scope	Specific scope
Article 6 Article 12	Article 4 Article 5 Article 7 Article 8 Article 9 Article 10(1), 10(3) Article 11(1), 11(2) Article 12(3) Article 14(1) Article 14(3) Article 15	Article 10(2) Article 11(3) Article 14(2)

Source: Derived from TC4 by author.

The *Travaux Preparatoires* of the FCNM also tell us what the drafters had in mind when it comes to obligations. In fact, the issue of obligations was a main assumption, as the drafters saw the instrument as a tool to emphasise mainly State obligations, as opposed to subjective rights provisions. Thus, the drafters discussed the notion of rights, and it was agreed that provisions should not give rise to individuals claiming subjective rights. The notion of State obligations was indeed front and centre to the drafters.[50]

6. Obligations and Institutional Frameworks

Having identified the obligation-holders as all state parties to the FCNM, we must recall, as O'Neill argued, that not all obligations give rise to rights and not all rights impose obligations. Thus, the nature of obligations that the FCNM imposes must also be explained. Moreover, given that the aim is to link obligations to institutional frameworks, the next question is, therefore, what types of obligations require institutional frameworks? O'Neill's typology (see Table 1) can assist us in ascertaining which type of obligations are involved. Are they universal perfect or universal imperfect or are they special perfect or special imperfect? The determination of these relationships will indicate not only what type of right a provision is, but also whether there is a need to establish institutions to secure the implementation of the right. Given that categories 2 and 4 – the imperfect obligations – do not require a

[50] Council of Europe, Ad Hoc Committee for the Protection of National Minorities (CAHMIN), Meeting Report, CAHMIN (94)5 (1 February 1994).

fixed institutional framework, it suffices to focus on categories 1 and 3 – the perfect obligations.

6.1. Perfect Obligations and Institutions

With regard to the FCNM provisions, the assumption is that all FCNM provisions correspond to a right. Article 1 can be excluded as it simply states the key question of our discussion as a fact, namely that minority rights are human rights. In reading Articles 2 through 19, there are no provisions in the FCNM that do not have a counterpart right or are owed to none. Keeping O'Neill's perfect obligation category, one therefore arrives at a typology of FCNM provisions with three categories and a slightly different distribution, as listed in Table 3.

Table 3 FCNM provisions according to obligations and institutions

	Universal rights	**Special rights**	
Perfect obligations	A. Held by all, owed to all; Counterpart liberty rights; Embodied above all in legal and economic systems.	B. Held by some, owed to specified others; Counterpart special rights; Fixed by structures of specific transactions and relationships; ***Can be distributively universal given appropriate institutions.***	C. Held by some, owed to specified others; Counterpart special rights; Fixed by structures of specific transactions and relationships;
	Article 2 ***Article 3*** ***Article 5*** Article 6 ***Article 7*** ***Article 8*** ***Article 9*** ***Article 12*** ***Article 13***	***Article 3*** ***Article 7*** ***Article 8***	Article 4 ***Article 5*** ***Article 9*** Article 10 Article 11 ***Article 12*** Article 14 Article 15 Article 16 Article 17 Article 18 Article 19

Source: Author.

Article 2 refers to values that put obligations on States that are universally applied by the international society. Article 3 imposes rights obligations on States to respect free self-identification because it is universally applied by the international society. Article 4 imposes rights obligations on States to guarantee the right of equality and to set up institutions to that effect. Article 5 refers to cultural values that put obligations on States to take positive measures to build institutions. Article 6 refers to liberal democratic values that put obligations on States to take positive measures to build institutions. Articles 7 and 8 impose rights obligations on States that are universally applied by the international society. Article 9 imposes rights obligations on States to take positive measures to build institutions because they are universally applied by the international society. Articles 10 and 11 impose rights obligations on States to take positive measures to build institutions. Article 12 refers to educational values that put obligations on States to take positive measures to build institutions. Article 13 refers to educational values that put rights obligations on States to respect private education. Article 14 imposes rights obligations on States to take positive measures to build institutions. Articles 15 and 16 refer to liberal democratic values that put obligations on States to take positive measures to build institutions. Articles 17, 18 and 19 impose rights obligations on States to take positive measures to build institutions.

However, some of the FCNM provisions are problematic to fit into O'Neill's typology. They are shown in italics in Table 3. The provisions that pose problems for the O'Neill typology are Articles 5, 9 and 12. The TC4 has Article 5 (in bold) in the broad scope category (A), whereas O'Neill's typology puts it in two categories, the category applying to all with liberty rights (A) and the category imposing perfect obligations on States to create institutions (C). Article 12 (in bold) is also placed in these two categories (A and C). Articles 3, 7, 8 and 9 (in bold) are provisions that are held by all, owed to all as liberty rights and are embodied in legal and economic systems. Thus, they can also be placed in two categories (A and B, but with Article 9 in A and C). Finally, Article 13 (in bold) is not mentioned by the TC4 at all, whereas according to the O'Neill typology it would fit in the category of perfect obligations held by all, owed to all to respect a liberty right (A). What becomes clear is that when we add perfect obligations as a variable, the distribution of FCNM provisions shift. We see many more provisions in category C, the category of special rights fixed by structures of specific transactions and relationships but not able to be distributed universally or found in legal and economic systems. We therefore also see more provisions in category A, the category for liberty rights embodied in legal and economic systems. What is important is that 15 provisions require positive measures to build institutions.

There seems no question that the minority rights provisions of the European regime are provisions that impose perfect obligations of both the universal and the special type. This can only strengthen the argument that minority rights are human rights. Using the categories of the FCNM, one can establish that the scope of application selected by the drafters and identified in the TC4 differ from O'Neill's categories of perfect obligations. In fact, O'Neill's typology allocates more provisions in the universal category, and thus seems to render those provisions closer to human rights. However, O'Neill's perfect universal obligations require institutional frameworks, namely legal and economic systems. The reason why O'Neill has assigned institutional frameworks to perfect universal obligations is explained as follows:

> Universal rights to goods and services, such as welfare rights, are in fact unlike liberty rights. It is true that rights of both sorts need institutional structures for their *enforcement*, but liberty rights do not need institutional structures to be claimable and waivable. By contrast, rights to goods and services can be claimed or waived *only* if a system of assigning agents to recipients has already been established, by which the counterpart obligations are 'distributed'.[51]

The importance here is then whether the rights protected by perfect universal obligations are claimed by the rights-holders. We tend to think that universal rights are liberty rights, or rights that do not impose obligations. But they are in fact claimable. And when someone claims a liberty right, it imposes obligations on others. Special rights, on the other hand, are always considered claim rights because they are linked to someone who accepts the obligation and who makes sure that the special rights are protected.

The final question is which type of institutions will correspond to perfect obligations? O'Neill has described them as 'structures of specific transactions and relationships', in relation to perfect special obligations and as 'legal and economic systems' in relation to perfect universal obligations.[52] 'Structures' always indicate something solid: if not a building, perhaps an organisation with certain powers. 'Specific transactions' would seem to indicate a change of ownership in terms of tangible goods. That could be anything from money to aid and support. 'Relationships' indicate that parties know each other enough to recognise the other as an actor and a human being. 'Legal and economic systems', she describes as the human rights framework of the UN, such as the International Covenant on Economic, Social and Cultural Rights. The TC4, on the other hand, does not provide specific descriptions of institutions but instead refers to policy-making and the obligation to adopt legislation. It also refers to human rights standards, such as the European Convention on Human Rights and UN conventions, as well as mechanisms within the Council of Europe.

7. Conclusions

It would seem that minority rights are still human rights but with a differentiation in that there are two cases in which universality becomes relevant without

[51] O'Neill, Towards Justice and Virtue (n 36), 131.
[52] ibid, 150–52.

impeding on the material outcome. The first is the case of liberty rights, if they are claimed by the rights-holders (category A); and the second is the case of special rights that can be distributed universally (category B). Applying O'Neill's typology to FCNM provisions has shown (Table 3), that there are in fact nine articles or provisions that could fall under these categories and thus may be seen as human rights as well as minority rights (A and B). The other nine are special rights and therefore minority rights (indicated in black in C), and three provisions are both universal and special rights (category B). A simplified view is offered in Table 4.

Table 4 FCNM provisions according to distribution

A	B	C
Universal liberty rights distributed as claim rights	Special rights with potential universal distribution	Special rights with restricted distribution
Nine FCNM provisions of which six overlap with column B and C	Three FCNM provisions overlapping with column A	Nine FCNM provisions of which three overlap with column A

Source: Author.

Granted, O'Neill's typology is not perfect. It was thus necessary to create or add a category (B) by splitting the perfect special obligations into two categories (B and C). Nevertheless, given that the material outcomes in terms of being able to claim a right are key to the successful implementation of minority rights, the above analysis shows that all the FCNM provisions discussed are guaranteed material outcomes because they all have counterpart rights, either liberty rights or special rights. Whether they are human rights or minority rights is perhaps of less importance, assuming that the material outcomes are of greatest importance. It is therefore not the scope that determines whether minority rights are human rights, but rather their application and ability to guarantee material outcomes as envisaged by the intentions of the duty-bearers establishing the institutional frameworks.

2

Minority Rights as Human Rights? Concepts, Doctrine, and Practice

MIODRAG JOVANOVIĆ AND IVANA KRSTIĆ

1. Introduction

Early attempts to protect minority groups can be traced to treaties following the Treaty of Westphalia.[1] After World War I and the establishment of the League of Nations, explicit protections for minorities were included in peace treaties to stabilise newly formed States with diverse ethnic populations. The modern framework for minority rights within human rights began to crystallise after World War II, particularly with the founding of the United Nations and the adoption of the Universal Declaration of Human Rights (UDHR) in 1948, which, according to some authors, laid a foundation for equal rights and non-discrimination, implicitly supporting minority protections.[2] However, minority rights gained more explicit recognition in Article 27 – the core universal human rights instrument – the International Covenant on Civil and Political Rights (ICCPR).

The treatment of minority rights as part of human rights law was also acknowledged in the opening provision of the Council of Europe (CoE) Framework Convention for the Protection of National Minorities, which unequivocally states that '[t]he protection of national minorities and of the rights and freedoms of persons belonging to those minorities forms an integral part of the international protection of human rights'. Thus, it is fair to say that the dominant vocabulary of the relevant international legal doctrine is that minority rights *are* human rights. On the occasion of celebrating twenty-five years of the Framework Convention,

[1] Patrick Milton, 'Guarantee and Intervention: The Assesment of the Peace of Westphalia in International Law and Politics', in Simone Zurbuchen (ed), *The Law of Nations and Natural Law* (Leiden: Brill, 2019) 191.

[2] More on the issue why there was no reference to special protection provisions for ethnic, religious, or linguistic minorities in the UDHR, in Sumedha Choudhury, 'On the 75th Anniversary: Looking Back at the Minority Question in the Making of the UDHR' Twailr: Reflection (15 June 2024) www.twailr.com/on-the-75th-anniversary-looking-back-at-the-minority-question-in-the-making-of-the-udhr/.

the president of the Advisory Committee, Petra Roter, went a step further and stated that this instrument 'has firmly established universal minority rights as human rights and their implementation as a matter of joint international concern'.[3]

There are three conceptual claims lurking behind this dominant rhetoric: 1. that minority rights share the same justificatory grounds as human rights; 2. that, insofar as human rights are by definition individual, the same applies to minority rights, and 3. that in virtue of being an integral part of the family of human rights, minority rights are also universal. In the first part of the chapter, we will demonstrate that none of the three claims seem to be warranted. This finding by no means implies that minority rights are unjustifiable because one may obviously resort to an independent justificatory ground for the protection of minority rights *per se*, through some version of the 'politics of recognition'. Yet, we want to investigate whether there is any justificatory route for the claim that minority rights are (to be treated as) an integral part of human rights. We propose to explore the 'functionalist', ie, 'political conception' of human rights, according to which a distinguishable feature of this type of rights is that they are treated in the global legal and political practice as 'trump-over-sovereignty' rights. Following this line of reasoning, minority rights would be treatable as human rights only to the extent that they can be shown to be part of the respective practice in which they are also taken as 'trump-over-sovereignty' rights. In the remainder of the paper, we inspect, first, whether the evidence for this claim can be found in the widespread anti-discrimination practice. It transpires that the upshot of this avenue for minority protection is the blurring of the very concept of 'minority', which is in itself detrimental to the groups that traditionally enjoy protection in international law. We then move to the question of admissibility and justiciability of minority rights because the strongest indication of treating minority rights as 'trump-over-sovereignty' rights concerns the availability of their direct judicial protection and enforcement. We conclude that current models of minority rights protection largely prioritise State sovereignty over the substantive rights of minorities, thereby seriously weakening the suggested alternative 'political conception' for treating minority rights as human rights.

2. Conceptual Problems of Treating Minority Rights as Human Rights

As was already noted, there are at least three unstated and unelaborated conceptual premises of the dominant international doctrinal stance that minority rights are human rights. We will briefly inspect each of them.

[3] Petra Roter, 'Twenty-five years of the Framework Convention for the Protection of National Minorities' (2023) www.coe.int/en/web/minorities/statement-from-petra-roter-president-of-the-advisory-committee#_ftn1.

2.1. Minority Rights Share the Same Justificatory Grounds as Human Rights

Whatever human rights might be, they are necessarily singled out as extraordinary. That is, insofar as they are first and foremost rights,[4] the fact that they are treated as a distinctive type of rights indicates that there must be something special about them. No wonder, then, that this feature is readily acknowledged in the scholarship. Cranston holds that one of the distinguishable features of human rights is that they are of 'paramount importance',[5] Nickel and Etinson speak of their 'high priority', while in Raz's words, human rights are commonly thought to possess 'exceptional importance'.[6] But if this is so, what is the source of their exceptionality? Put succinctly, the claim of human rights' special status in the legal universe of rights calls for answering the question of what it is that makes it the case that something qualifies as a human right.

The dominant strand of, or 'the orthodox view' in, human rights philosophy addresses this issue by pointing out their particular foundation/ground/justification.[7] Although one may come across various scholarly classifications of human rights,[8] the foundationalist response to the exceptionality dilemma is usually taken as a criterion for grouping the proponents of this view under the umbrella term *Foundationalists*. Raz says that '[t]hey take "human rights" to be those important rights which are grounded in our humanity. The underlying thought is that the arguments which establish that a putative right-holder has a human right rely on no *contingent* fact except laws of nature, the nature of humanity and that the right-holder is a human being'.[9] Irrespective of the clear nuances between different foundationalist theories,[10]

[4] As put by Nickel and Etinson, '[l]est we miss the obvious, human rights are rights'. James Nickel and Adam Etinson, 'Human Rights', in Edward N. Zalta & Uri Nodelman (eds), *The Stanford Encyclopedia of Philosophy* (Fall 2024 Edition), https://plato.stanford.edu/entries/rights-human/.

[5] The other two features for something to pass the test of human rights are that they should be practicable to secure them by legislation, and that they should be genuinely universal as moral rights. Maurice Cranston, 'Human Rights, Real and Supposed' in D D Raphael (ed), *Political Theory and the Rights of Man* (Bloomington: Indiana University Press, 1967) 43–51.

[6] Joseph Raz, 'Human Rights in the Emerging World Order' (2010) 1 *Transnational Legal Theory* 39.

[7] Tasioulas is right in claiming that these terms can be used interchangeably. *ibid*, 45, fn 2.

[8] For instance, Dembour speaks of 'natural scholars', who conceive of human rights as *given*, 'deliberative scholars' who take them as *agreed upon*; 'protest scholars' who thought of them as *fought for*; and 'discourse scholars' who take them as *talked about*. Marie-Bénédicte Dembour, 'What Are Human Rights? Four Schools of Thought' (2010) 32 *Human Rights Quarterly* 1, 1–20. Kirste, on the other hand, distinguishes between approaches which try to ground human rights in their content (historical and anthropological theories) and those that are focused on their form (positivist and procedural theories). Stephan Kirste, 'Das Fundament der Menschenrechte' (2013) 52 *Der Staat* 1, 119–140.

[9] Joseph Raz, 'Human Rights Without Foundations' in Samantha Besson and John Tasioulas (eds), *The Philosophy of International Law* (Oxford: Oxford University Press, 2010) 323.

[10] Tasioulas differentiates, for instance, between meta-ethical and normative foundationalism. In discharging extreme foundationalism, he argues that human rights foundations 'are characterized by a value pluralism that embraces both moral and prudential elements'. In particular, '[h]uman rights are grounded in the universal interests of human beings each and every one of whom possesses an equal moral status arising from their common humanity'. John Tasioulas, 'On the Foundations of Human Rights', in Rowan Cruft, S Matthew Liao and Massimo Renzo (eds), *Philosophical Foundations of Human Rights* (Oxford: Oxford University Press, 2015) 50.

their common denominator is the claim that 'a human right is not something that a person possesses as a result of her membership in any legal, political or social association. Instead, the grounds of human rights are found in a more foundational pre-political substratum of moral thought in terms of which positive institutions may be criticised'.[11]

Under the foundationalist view, the argument that minority rights are human rights implies that just as human rights are possessed by each human being in virtue of the fact of membership in the human species, so minority rights are also possessed by each minority group simply in virtue of the fact of minority status. However, the most obvious problem in drawing an analogy between humans and minorities pertains to the different normative power of the comparable facts.[12] Namely, while the fact of being a human is considered sufficient for triggering the right-holding status,[13] the fact of being a minority is considered necessary but not sufficient for triggering the analogous status. What is additionally required in the latter case is that the social fact of *being* a minority is transformed by the respective legal order's act of recognition into the *legal status* of minority. Put differently, it is not enough for a minority group to be socially identifiable and visible *to* law, it has to be additionally visible as such *in* law.[14]

This is a well-known fact of international legal life. The most often mentioned example is the French reservation on ICCPR minority rights provision, which states that '[i]n the light of article 2 of the Constitution of the French Republic, the French Government declares that article 27 is not applicable so far as the Republic is concerned'.[15] Put differently, although one can socially identify minority groups of, say, Corsicans or Bretons, in the eyes of the French constitution, they are legally non-existent. There are other European 'denial States', unwilling to provide legal recognition of socially identifiable minority groups, such as Belarus, which is not even the member of the Council of Europe, or Greece, which legally recognises only the existence of the Muslim religious minority in Thrace, according to the 1923 bilateral Treaty of Lausanne.[16]

[11] Anthony Robert Sangiuliano, 'Towards a Natural Law Foundationalist Theory of Universal Human Rights' (2014) 5 *Transnational Legal Theory* 2, 219.

[12] This formulation resonates with a famous, yet controversial Georg Jellinek's phrase 'die normative Kraft des Faktischen' (normative power of factual), which we will not discuss here in detail. For an elucidation of this philosophical stance, see, Andreas Anter (ed), *Die normative Kraft des Faktischen – Das Staatsverständnis Georg Jellineks* (Baden-Baden: Nomos, 2020).

[13] To be sure, there is an obvious natural law flavour of this statement, mainly because of the significance of this legal theory for the development of human rights law. See in general, Tom Angier, Iain Benson, and Mark Retter (eds), *The Cambridge Handbook of Natural Law and Human Rights* (Cambridge: Cambridge University Press, 2022).

[14] Miodrag Jovanović, 'Making Social Groups Visible *to* and *in* Law – Essentialisation and Law's Generality', in Jessika Eichler and Kyriaki Topidi (eds), *Minority Recognition and the Diversity Deficit: Comparative Perspectives* (Oxford: Hart, 2022) 21–34.

[15] All declarations and reservations on ICCPR are at www.treaties.un.org/Pages/ViewDetails.aspx?chapter=4&clang=_en&mtdsg_no=IV-4&src=IND.

[16] Tove H. Malloy, 'Dialogue with the Unwilling: Addressing Minority Rights in So-called Denial States' (2014) *ECMI Working Paper* 77, 1–25.

All this is a manifestation of a more general problem – the lack of a universally accepted and binding international legal definition of 'minority'. Some argue that, although '[t]his state of affairs necessarily implies a degree of uncertainty … such uncertainty is to be preferred over the inclusion of a definition that would most likely be based on the lowest common denominator and would, by definition, exclude any evolution'.[17] That this indeed might be so is testified in the definition, adopted by the CoE Parliamentary Assembly's Recommendation 1201 (1993), according to which 'national minorities' refer to groups of persons in a State which, *inter alia*, 'maintain longstanding, firm and lasting ties with that State' and 'are sufficiently representative'.[18] This is but an illustration of uncertainties surrounding the concept of minority, which effectively annul the possibility of grounding the concept of minority rights on the same foundations on which the concept of human rights was built.

2.2. Insofar as Human Rights are Individual, Minority Rights are Individual as Well

In his seminal work *International Law and the Rights of Minorities*, Thornberry concludes that 'the group is "unacknowledged presence" behind the individual rights. Collective rights are a substantive, if not a "formal" aspect of a legal entity. The greater part of this reality is given over to individual rights'. Consequently, it would be fair to say that '"[m]inority rights" are substantive and indirect, not formal and direct'[19] This is an insightful depiction of the dominant doctrinal understanding of minority rights. Namely, most of the international legal instruments, whose explicit or implicit purpose is to provide protection for certain minority groups, predominantly use the language of individual rights, more precisely, the so-called 'persons-belonging-to' formula.[20] That legislative technique was largely triggered by the general post-World War II political sentiment, reflected in a conscious departure from the collective protection rhetoric, so characteristic of the preceding League of Nations.[21] The clear

[17] Frank Steketee, 'The Framework Convention: A Piece of Art or a Tool for Action?' (2001) 8 *International Journal on Minority and Group Rights* 1, 6.

[18] Parliamentary Assembly's Recommendation 1201 (1993), www.assembly.coe.int/nw/xml/XRef/Xref-XML2HTML-en.asp?fileid=15235 This definition, which gives a significant leeway to States in recognising which group should acquire the status of 'minority', is also adopted in the European Parliament resolution of 13 November 2018 on minimum standards for minorities in the EU (2018/2036(INI)), www.europarl.europa.eu/doceo/document/TA-8-2018-0447_EN.pdf.

[19] Patrick Thornberry, *International Law and the Rights of Minorities* (Oxford: Oxford University Press, 1991) 396.

[20] For an instructive comparative survey of the minority protection instruments on European soil, which demonstrates this trend in legal drafting, see, eg, Reiner Hofmann, 'Minority Rights: Individual or Group Rights? A Comparative View on European Legal Systems' (1997) 40 *German Yearbook of International Law*, 356–382.

[21] It is historically confirmed that one of the major incentives for the drafters of the UN Universal Declaration of Human Rights to abandon the language of group protection and collective rights was the fact that Nazi military conquests were largely grounded in the alleged violations of the German minority rights in neighbouring countries.

alternative to such an international legal regime, framed in terms of the rights of certain minority groups, was one of individual rights.[22] Inis Claude wrote in 1955 that '[t]he doctrine of human rights has been put forward as a substitute for the concept of minority rights, with the strong implication that minorities whose members enjoy individual equality of treatment cannot legitimately demand facilities for the maintenance of their ethnic particularism'.[23] Does all this strengthen the claim that minority rights boil down to individual human rights?

Hardly so. It transpires that the removal of minority groups from international law 'was never complete'.[24] In fact, the Sub-Commission on Prevention of Discrimination and Protection of Minorities was set up already in 1946. Two years later, the Convention on the Prevention and Punishment of the Crime of Genocide was adopted. Article 2 of this convention outlaws all the acts 'committed with the intent to destroy, in whole or in part, a national, ethnical, racial or religious group'.[25] Although the aforementioned Article 27 of ICCPR was phrased in the individualist language, it nonetheless preserved the 'unacknowledged presence' of minority groups. Capotorti, for instance, reports about the work of the UN Commission on Human Rights, which since 1978 has been considering a draft Declaration on the Rights of Minorities – a proposal made by the Delegation of Yugoslavia. The initial draft used a collectivist language and spoke of 'the rights of national, ethnic, linguistic and religious minorities'. A subsequent draft, submitted by the same country, changed the vocabulary and referred to 'the rights of persons belonging to national, ethnic, religious and linguistic minorities'. According to Capotorti, '[t]his change helped to overcome criticism arising from the use of a language not coinciding with that used in Article 27 of the Covenant on Civil and Political Rights, which was, after all, the starting point of the Yugoslav initiative'.[26] Although the 'persons belonging to' formula has become dominant in the doctrinal drafting of international legal instruments, conceptually speaking, it could not affect the nature of the stipulated rights.

This becomes evident even from the opening article of the UN Declaration on the Rights of Persons Belonging to National or Ethnic, Religious and Linguistic Minorities. It stipulates that 'States shall protect the existence and the national or ethnic, cultural, religious and linguistic identity of minorities within their respective territories and shall encourage conditions for the promotion of that identity'.[27]

[22] Joel E. Oestreich, 'Liberal Theory and Minority Group Rights' (1999) 21 *Human Rights Quarterly* 1, 113.

[23] Inis Claude, *National Minorities: An International Problem* (Cambridge, Mass: Harvard University Press, 1955) 21.

[24] Patrick Thornberry, 'Minority and Indigenous Rights at "The End of History"' (2002) 2 *Ethnicities* 4, 517.

[25] Convention on the Prevention and Punishment of the Crime of Genocide, 78 U.N.T.S. 277, entered into force 12 January 1951.

[26] Francesco Capotorti, 'Are Minorities Entitled to Collective International Rights?' (1990) 20 *Israel Yearbook on Human Rights*, 352.

[27] Declaration on the Rights of Persons Belonging to National or Ethnic, Religious and Linguistic Minorities, UN Doc. A/RES/47/135, 18 December 1992.

The employed wording clearly suggests that the rights to existence and identity are rights directly vested in the referent minority groups, that is, they are *collective rights*. International legal doctrine, however, tries to shun away from that term as much as possible, even if such deliberate avoidance is conceptually indefensible. Take the Explanatory Report of the Council of Europe's Framework Convention for the Protection of National Minorities. In Article 3, par. 2 of the Framework Convention, it is stated: 'Persons belonging to national minorities may exercise the rights and enjoy the freedoms flowing from the principles enshrined in the present framework Convention individually as well as in community with others'. The Explanatory Report rightly points out that the possibility of joint exercise of certain guaranteed rights and freedoms 'is distinct from the notion of collective rights', but then it does not bother to elucidate this concept.[28]

Just as collective rights cannot be equated with jointly exercised individual rights (eg, right to strike, freedom of assembly, freedom of association), they cannot also be treated as a mere designation for the accumulation of all the individual rights of the group members. Simply put, they are rights directly bestowed on respective minority groups, with a clear rationale of protecting their legitimate interests, which may at times conflict and even override the interests of individual group members.[29] That collectives, and not individuals, are primary right holders of minority rights is probably best graspable in situations when those rights are denied, violated, or repelled. In such cases, it is the group, rather than any particular individual, who is wronged. Drawing from the latest Balkan ethno-national conflicts, Várady comes to the same conclusion: 'It is abundantly clear that the targeted victims are precisely the minority groups, rather than citizens as individuals'.[30] Simply enough, '[t]he denial of bilingual road signs, place names, and minority schools can hardly be conceived as anything but an attitude and a gesture towards a group; it would be quite difficult to structure opposition against such denial on the basis of individual rights'.[31]

2.3. Since Human Rights are Universal, Minority Rights are Universal as Well

The last tacit assumption of the claim that minority rights are human rights concerns their alleged universality. The claim would go as follows: if the same set of human rights is universally held by all humans, then, *mutatis mutandis*, the same set of minority rights is universally held by all minorities. In a famous 1976 article,

[28] Framework Convention for the Protection of National Minorities – Explanatory Report, ETS no. 157, para 37.

[29] For a philosophical grounding of the concept of collective rights, see, Miodrag Jovanović, *Collective Rights – A Legal Theory* (Cambridge: Cambridge University Press, 2012).

[30] Tibor Várady, 'Minorities, Majorities, Law, and Ethnicity: Reflections of the Yugoslav Case' (1997) 19 *Human Rights Quarterly* 1, 38.

[31] ibid, 39.

Dinstein argued that there were 'collective human rights accorded by general international law to every minority everywhere'. These are: the right to physical existence, stemming from the Genocide Convention, and the right to preserve a separate identity, stemming from Article 27 of ICCPR.[32]

The uncontested aspect of Dinstein's argument is that the mentioned rights are enjoyed by *all internationally protected minorities*, insofar as instruments of general international law safeguard them. However, does this amount to the claim that the said minority rights are *universal*? It seems that some of the issues raised in the debate regarding the universality of human rights are applicable here as well. Raz, for instance, challenges the temporal dimension of universality, arguing that if it is understood diachronically, then it would lead to an absurd conclusion that even cave dwellers of the Stone Age had human rights.[33] Accordingly, it is more plausible to argue that human rights are 'synchronically universal, meaning that all people alive today have them'.[34] By way of analogy, one might argue that the synchronic universality of minority rights implies that all minorities existing today enjoy them. However, as we already mentioned, this would be wrong on factual grounds because only *some* socially identifiable minority groups are accorded the status of minorities in the international legal order. Dinstein makes a similar remark: 'Palpably, there are many other types of minorities in the world: there are, among others, a minority of blondes, a left-handed minority and a minority of students. All these, albeit minorities, do not enjoy international human rights on a collective basis. But ethnic, religious and linguistic minorities have a preferred status, and they are the ones that should rivet our attention'.[35]

The universality claim therefore needs to be significantly modified to read as follows: synchronic universality of minority rights implies that all and only those internationally recognised minorities existing today enjoy them. But then, we are faced with yet another problem. As pointed out by Dinstein, '[a] common error is to lump all minorities together and to look upon them as if they were all in the same boat'.[36] There are different types of minorities, and some of the rights on a putative list of minority rights that serve legitimate interests of one minority group (eg, linguistic minority rights for a linguistic minority) would not make much sense in the case of another (eg, linguistic rights for a religious minority). Simply put, international minority rights law consists of 'specific provisions relating to

[32] Yoram Dinstein, 'Collective Human Rights of Peoples and Minorities' (1976) 25 *International and Comparative Law Quarterly* 1, 118ff.

[33] Raz (n 6), 9.

[34] ibid, 10. Tasioulas also speaks of 'a temporally-constrained form of universality'. He says: 'For us, today, human rights are those possessed in virtue of being human and inhabiting a social world that is subject to the conditions of modernity. This historical constraint permits very general facts about feasible institutional design in the modern world, eg, forms of legal regulation, political participation and economic organisation, to play a role in determining which human rights we recognize'. John Tasioulas, 'The Moral Reality of Human Rights', in Thomas Pogge (ed), *Freedom from Poverty as a Human Right: Who Owes What to the Very Poor?* (Oxford: Oxford University Press, 2007) 76–77.

[35] Dinstein (n 32), 112.

[36] ibid.

particular minorities', with the two mentioned rights that are accorded 'to every minority anywhere'.[37] Consequently, if the universality claim is applicable at all to minority rights, it is applicable in a highly restricted form: *synchronic universality of minority rights implies that all and only those internationally recognised minorities existing today enjoy rights to physical existence and preservation of identity.* However, since this modification is a drastic departure from the widely endorsed formula of the human rights universality, insofar as not every minority, in virtue of its minority status, is entitled to an equal set of minority rights, it is safe to conclude that, conceptually speaking, minority rights are not to be considered human rights *stricto sensu*.

3. An Alternative Route for Treating Minority Rights as Human Rights?

Does everything said so far jeopardise the very foundations of the minority rights concept? Certainly not. One may obviously provide an independent justificatory ground for the protection of minority rights through some version of the 'politics of recognition',[38] ie, the normative political theory of 'multiculturalism'.[39] Although the most prominent theories of minority rights try to base them on some classical liberal values, such as liberty,[40] or equality,[41] they do not essentially contribute to the idea that minority rights *are* human rights. Hence, the remaining question is the following: if the traditional foundationalist justificatory route is inapt, is there any other that can ground the mainstream view of international legal doctrine, according to which minority rights are to be treated as human rights?

We argue that an unexplored justificatory route concerns the so-called 'functionalist' or 'political conception' of human rights. The first label is owed to the idea that human rights are not conceived as grounded in some pre-political substratum of moral thought, but in 'its functional role in regulating the conduct of political institutions' at the international level. The second, more common label in the literature stems from the fact that this approach 'takes the existing practice of the human

[37] ibid, 118.

[38] The key postulate of this politics is famously formulated by Taylor: 'Just as all must have equal civil rights, and equal voting rights, regardless of race or culture, so all should enjoy the presumption that their traditional culture has value'. Charles Taylor, 'The Politics of Recognition', in Amy Gutmann (ed), *Multiculturalism: Examining the Politics of Recognition* (Princeton: Princeton University Press, 1994) 68.

[39] For different strands of this political theory, see, eg, Simon Thompson, *The Political Theory of Recognition: A Critical Introduction* (Cambridge: Polity Press, 2006).

[40] This is the case with the most influential version of 'liberal multiculturalism', that of Will Kymlicka, who argues that 'minority rights are not only consistent with individual freedom, but can actually promote it'. Will Kymlicka, Multicultural Citizenship: A Liberal Theory of Minority *Rights* (Oxford: Oxford University Press, 1995) 75.

[41] See, eg, Bhikhu Parekh, Rethinking Multiculturalism – Cultural Diversity and Political Theory (Basingstoke: Palgrave Macmillan, 2000).

rights regime as its point of departure'.[42] The idea was first hinted in Rawls' *The Law of Peoples*, where he speaks of human rights as 'urgent rights' with a 'special role' of 'restrict[ing] the justifying reasons for war and its conduct, and … specify[ing] limits to a regime's internal autonomy'.[43] Raz follows in Rawls' footsteps, arguing that there are no 'principled' but only 'pragmatic' reasons for singling out human rights as some exceptional category of rights.[44] These pragmatic reasons stem from 'the crucial role human rights play in the emerging world order'.[45] This anti-foundationalist, 'political conception' of human rights can be extracted from the dominant trend in human rights practice,[46] which is to treat them as 'trump-over-sovereignty' rights,[47] that is, as rights 'regarding which sovereignty limiting measures are morally justified'.[48]

Without necessarily taking 'political conception' as *the* correct philosophical grounding of human rights,[49] in the remainder of the chapter, we intend to test whether this approach can offer a lifeline for the thesis that minority rights are human rights. Under this conception, *minority rights would be treatable as human rights only to the extent that there is enough evidence that they are part of the respective practice in which they are taken as 'trump-over-sovereignty' rights.*

To determine whether this is indeed the case, we will first investigate whether minority rights can function as 'trump-over-sovereignty' rights through the implementation of broad anti-discrimination clauses that include traditional minority markers, such as ethnicity, religion, or language. We will demonstrate that, while this is an important channel for minority protection, its unwelcome consequence is the further blurring of the criteria for defining 'minority'. Thus, anti-discrimination practices cannot be taken as sufficient to ground the case for minority rights as 'trump-over-sovereignty' rights. *Second*, we will show that the same holds for the present institutional frameworks, primarily focused on human rights protection. Simply put, they do not provide adequate avenues for the admissibility and justiciability of minority rights. *Finally*, we will outline the realistic sovereignty-limiting capacity of minority rights, concluding that even within the alternative 'political conception', it is hardly tenable to speak of minority rights as human rights.

[42] Sangiuliano (n 11), 220.

[43] John Rawls, *The Law of Peoples (with 'The Idea of Public Reason Revisited')* (Cambridge Mass. and London: Harvard University Press, 1999) 79.

[44] Raz (n 6), 42.

[45] This role is evidenced 'first, in expressing the worth of all human beings; second, in placing on the agenda concerns other than those of intergovernmental relations or big business profit; and third, in empowering individuals and voluntary associations in creating an additional channel for exerting influence and affecting the international order'. ibid, 47.

[46] Beitz also defines human rights as 'the constitutive norms of a global practice whose aim is to protect individuals against threats to their most important interests arising from the acts and omissions of their governments (including failures to regulate the conduct of other agents)'. Charles Beitz, *The Idea of Human Rights* (Oxford: Oxford University Press, 2009) 197.

[47] Ronald Dworkin, *Justice for Hedgehogs* (Cambridge Mass. and London: The Belknap Press of Harvard University Press 2011) 333–334.

[48] Raz (n 9), 329.

[49] For some of the criticism of this approach, *see, eg*, Jovanović (n 29), 172ff.

3.1. Anti-discrimination Practice and the Blurring of the 'Minority' Concept

Historically, the anti-discrimination clause has greatly benefited individuals belonging to traditional minorities. Yet, the 1948 UDHR provision already stipulated that 'any characteristic', given the right factual context, could qualify as sufficient 'personal ground' for protection under anti-discrimination law. The subsequent explicit inclusion of different grounds, such as sexual orientation, age, and disability, in the anti-discrimination framework has sparked meaningful discussions about the nature of minority status.[50] In short, the expanded understanding of anti-discrimination practice may lead to the dilution of protections for established minority groups, whose specific rights and historical contexts might be overshadowed by a proliferation of newer classifications. Consequently, although undeniably important, anti-discrimination standards can at best be seen as an anteroom of minority protection and not minority rights themselves.

The evolving jurisprudence of the European Court of Human Rights (ECtHR) provides an illustrative example of how the anti-discrimination practice can contribute to blurring the 'minority' concept. This is particularly vivid in recognising 'suspect' or 'particularly serious' grounds of discrimination, which demand heightened scrutiny and justification compared to other grounds. As Gerrards argues, it is the application of the margin of appreciation doctrine in the context of Article 14 of the ECHR, which is 'an important instrument for the Court to find its way out of the field of tension'.[51] The ECtHR's application of varying margins of appreciation and intensities of review significantly impacts the outcomes of discrimination cases and is not based on the traditional view of minority groups. For example, the ECtHR underlines that differences based exclusively on sex require 'very weighty reasons', 'particularly serious reasons' or 'particularly weighty and convincing reasons' by way of justification.[52] By classifying 'sex' as 'suspect ground', the ECtHR signals the need for strong justifications for any differential treatment and recognises the heightened risk of harm this form of discrimination poses to equality and individual dignity. Conversely, 'religion' is more often upheld under a broader margin, as in *Eweida and Others v United Kingdom*.[53] In that case, the Court balanced the rights of religious individuals with employers' rights to regulate their workplace, illustrating that,

[50] Sandra Fredman, *Discrimination Law* (Oxford: Clarendon, 2022) 168–170. Article 14 of the ECHR and Article 1 of the Protocol no. 12 recognise the following grounds of discrimination: 'sex, race, colour, language, religion, political or other opinion, national or social origin, association with a national minority, property, birth or other status'.

[51] Janneke Gerrards, 'The Margin of Appreciation Doctrine, the Very Weighty Reason Test and Ground of Discrimination', in Marco Balboni (ed), *The Principle of Discrimination and the European Convention of Human Rights*, (Napoli: Editoriale Scientifica, 2017), 2.

[52] See, eg, *Konstantin Markin v Russia*, ECtHR (GC) App No 30078/06, 22 March 2012; *Beeler v Switzerland*, ECtHR (GC), App No 78630/12, 11 October 2022, paras 126-127; para 95.

[53] *Eweida and Others v United Kingdom*, ECtHR, App Nos 48420-10 et al., 15 January 2013.

in cases involving religion, the State has greater leeway to navigate competing rights and interests. Similarly, in *Leyla Şahin v Turkey*, the Court deferred to Turkey's decision to restrict the wearing of headscarves in universities, allowing Turkey to justify its policy by emphasising the importance of maintaining secular principles in its public institutions.[54] Furthermore, even if the ground is considered to be 'suspect', such as in the case of race and ethnic origin, the wide margin of appreciation[55] and the imposition of a high burden of proof on plaintiffs[56] results in an incapacity to address structural or systemic discrimination, which can be more relevant for traditional minorities.[57] The ECtHR's reluctance to robustly protect the rights of certain minorities is particularly evident in cases concerning Roma, where it has frequently shown hesitation to characterise systemic discrimination.[58]

The case law surrounding the application of anti-discrimination provisions also reveals a hesitance to apply a group-based understanding of minority rights. Unlike the International Convention on the Elimination of All Forms of Racial Discrimination (ICERD), which mandates States to adopt special measures for the protection and development of particular racial groups, the ECHR's provisions lack explicit group-based protections.[59] Thus, the Court has often failed to recognise the unique circumstances of 'old' minorities in favour of a more generalised application of anti-discrimination principles, which has not adequately addressed their specific needs. Moreover, the interpretation of Article 1 of Protocol 12, which introduced a broader, free-standing right to equality, further complicates matters of minority protection. Ratified by less than half of the CoE Member States, the limited case law from the ECtHR under this protocol indicates a potential reluctance to expand protections for minorities through this avenue, resulting in a legal landscape that does not necessarily reflect the complexities of minority status and rights.[60]

The challenges faced by 'old' minorities are further exacerbated by the lack of positive obligations in the Court's rulings. While the idea of positive obligations is intended to allow for the proactive protection of rights, especially in cases of racially motivated conduct, the Court's jurisprudence has not consistently upheld

[54] *Leyla Şahin v Turkey*, ECtHR, App No 44774/98, 10 November 2005.

[55] See, for example, *Chapman v UK*, ECtHR, App No 27238/95, 18 January 2001.

[56] See, for example, *Nachova and Others V Bulgaria*, ECtHR, App Nos 43577/98, 43579/98, 6 July 2005.

[57] Structural discrimination can be manifested through laws, policies, and practices that may disproportionately impact minority groups negatively; the struggle to address it effectively limits the ability of established minority groups to seek redress for discriminatory practices. For more on structural inequalities and the need to achieve substantive equality see Sandra Fredman, 'Substantive Equality Revisited' (2016), 14 *International Journal of Constitutional Law* 3, 712–738.

[58] See, for example, *Orsus and Others v Croatia*, ECtHR, App No 15766/03, 16 March 2010.

[59] The ICERD in Article 2, para 2 requires that States take 'special and concrete measures to ensure the adequate development and protection of certain racial groups or individuals belonging to them'. This is therefore the only international human rights treaty that expressly allows special measures to achieve substantive equality.

[60] This Protocol was ratified only by twenty out of 47 States since 2000 when this instrument was adopted.

strong measures or guidelines for practical enforcement.[61] For example, even when ethnic profiling is acknowledged, such as in the *Linguar* case, the Court does not mandate specific training or systemic reforms to address these issues, leaving gaps that potentially jeopardise the protection of established minority groups.[62]

Overall, the concept of 'minority' and the relevant legal frameworks are in a state of flux. The ECtHR's jurisprudence illustrates the challenges of reconciling traditional minority rights with evolving understandings of identity and discrimination. As societal definitions shift, the need for a robust and coherent framework that delineates and protects the rights of all minority groups becomes increasingly imperative to ensure justice and equality across the board.

3.2. Admissibility and Justiciability of Minority Rights

The strongest indication of treating minority rights as 'trump-over-sovereignty' rights concerns the availability of their direct judicial protection and enforcement. It is precisely in this regard that even the most advanced minority protection regime – the CoE Framework Convention – does not rely on such an institutional setup. Both CoE instruments are monitored by expert bodies that conduct State reviews, publish country-specific opinions and recommendations, and issue thematic commentaries. However, despite this structural oversight, the absence of normatively robust enforcement structures means that the Framework Convention's provisions remain primarily aspirational, with their implementation depending on the goodwill of States and interpretative efforts of regional adjudicative bodies. Discussing the challenges posed by the lack of enforceable obligations and the reliance on State discretion, Henrard emphasises the limitations of this 'soft' legal approach. She argues that it weakens the Convention's potential to safeguard minority rights effectively.[63]

In practice, this means that traditional minorities, while protected under specialised frameworks, often return to human rights mechanisms in search of remedies. Given the limited enforceability of minority specific instruments, the ECtHR has become a key forum through which such claims are pursued. Thus, while not expressly mandated to protect minority rights, the ECtHR has established a substantial jurisprudence that resonates with the opinions of the Advisory Committee on the Framework Convention for the Protection of National Minorities. This occurred even though the previously proposed additional 1993 protocol on minority rights that would have pushed the

[61] The ECtHR usually requires an effective investigation, without the need to take all reasonable steps to unmask racially motivated acts and to establish if ethnic hatred or prejudice played a role in the event. See, for example, *Burlya and Others v Ukraine*, ECtHR App No 3289/10, 6 November 2018; *Škorjanec v Croatia*, ECtHR, App No 25536/14, 28 March 2017.

[62] *Linguar v Romania*, ECtHR, App No 48474/14, 16 April 2019.

[63] Kristin Henrard, Devising and Adequate System of Minority Protection: Individual Human Rights, Minority Rights and the Right to Self-Determination (Leiden: Brill-Nijhoff, 2000) 156–158.

ECtHR to confront collective harms was rejected due to insufficient political support from CoE Member States. The ECtHR has developed key judgments on issues central to minority communities; these include the right to register an association;[64] the denial of recognition and registration of a church;[65] the right to education;[66] and the right to identity and religion.[67] The said rights and freedoms are widely regarded as the foundations of democratic pluralism.

In *Gorzelik and Others v Poland*, the Court interpreted Article 11 of the ECHR to support the right of a minority association to register, affirming a form of collective protection.[68] Nevertheless, the ECtHR's reliance on an individualistic human rights framework restricts its ability to address the unique collective needs of minority groups fully.[69] In *Chapman v the United Kingdom*, the Court recognised that some issues faced by Roma communities reflect 'their lifestyle as a minority', yet it ultimately deferred to the State's margin of appreciation concerning land use restrictions, which limited the scope of protection for collective minority interests. Xanthaki also notes this gap, asserting that the Court's focus on individual rights has created barriers to achieving more holistic, systemic protections for minority communities.[70]

This limitation is further illustrated in cases in which the ECtHR declined to consider collective victimhood, such as *Ouardiri v Switzerland*[71] and *Ligue des Musulmans de Suisse v Switzerland*.[72] Here, the Court dismissed claims related to the Swiss minaret ban on the grounds that the applicants failed to prove individual victim status, showing the difficulty in framing collective grievances within the individual rights-oriented ECHR structure. This approach, while facilitating minority rights within an existing framework, often fails to capture collective harms experienced by a minority *qua* group.[73] Scholarly critiques, such as those by Thornberry, highlight that the lack of recognition for collective victimhood undermines the very essence of minority rights, which inherently require the

[64] *Sidiropulous v Greece*, ECtHR, App No 26695/95, 10 July 1998; *Gorzelik and Others v Poland*, ECtHR, App No 44158/98, 17 February 2004.

[65] Metropolitan Church of Bessarabia and Others v Moldova, ECtHR, App No 45701/99, 13 December 2001.

[66] *D. H. and Others v the Czech Republic*, ECtHR, App No 57325/00, 13 November 2007.

[67] *Kokkinakis v Greece*, ECtHR, App No 14307/88, 25 May 1993; *Hofman v Austria*, ECtHR, App No 12875/87, 23 June 1993; *Thlimennos v Greece*, ECtHR, App No 34369/97, 28 June 1996; *Lauci and Others v Italy*, ECtHR, App No 30814/06, 18 March 2011.

[68] *Gorzelik and Others v Poland*, ECtHR, App No 44158/98, 17 February 2004.

[69] See Julie Ringelheim, 'Identity Controversies Before the European Court of Human Rights: How to Avoid the Essentialist Trap' (2002) 3 *German Law Journal*, 7.

[70] Alexandra Xanthaki, 'Against Integration, for Human Rights' (2016) 20 *International Journal of Human Rights* 6, 815–838.

[71] *Ouardiri v Switzerland*, ECtHR, App No 65840/09, 28 June 2011.

[72] Ligue des Musulmans de Suisse v Switzerland, ECtHR, App No 66274/09, 28 June 2011.

[73] For the critique of these judgments see Grégor Puppinck, 'No victim status', said the European Court of Human Rights in the Minarets Cases v Switzerland, ECLJ, *www.eclj.org/no-victim-status-said-the-european-court-of-human-rights-in-the-minarets-cases-v-switzerland*. Nathalie Gunasekera, A Popular Initiative to Ban Minarets and Its Human Rights Implications, Islamic Law Blog, September 15, 2020, *www.islamiclaw.blog/2020/09/15/a-popular-initiative-to-ban-minarets-and-its-human-rights-implications/*.

acknowledgment of group-based identity and protection.[74] Thus, if analysed from a collectivist perspective, which takes the constitutional ban on constructing minarets as a collective infringement on the religious freedoms of the Muslim minority, the outcome could have been markedly different, and the applicants might have been recognised as representatives of a marginalised group.

However, despite these long-standing hurdles, a notable shift emerged in the *Wa Baile v Switzerland* case, where the ECtHR found that the general indications of systemic discrimination are sufficient to shift the burden of proof to the State, relieving the applicant from proving individual racist intent.[75] This case shows a slow recognition of the systemic nature of ethnic profiling, contrary to the *Basu*[76] and *Muhammad*[77] cases, where the ECtHR insisted that the applicants establish intent. This recent shift suggests a possible recalibration of its admissibility and proof standards.

In contrast to the CoE, the European Union (EU) explicitly commits to protecting minority rights in its foundational documents. Article 2 of the Treaty on European Union (TEU) mandates respect for the rights of minorities as a foundational EU value, and Art. 22 of the EU Charter of Fundamental Rights enshrines respect for cultural, religious, and linguistic diversity. The EU Charter also contains a non-discrimination clause (Art. 21), which adds to the list of forbidden personal grounds for discrimination 'membership of a national minority'.

Despite this law-in-books, EU law-in-action often approaches minority protection through a non-discrimination lens, providing only general protection without specific mechanisms to address minority group needs. Thus far, the Court of Justice of the European Union (CJEU) has delivered only nine decisions based on violations of Art. 22, and concerning: ban on slaughter without stunning in light of religious freedoms;[78] knowledge of languages in a call of expression of interests;[79] education allowance;[80] obligation to draft employment contract in a certain language and the use of languages in relations between employers and employees, as well as in company documents and papers;[81] refusal to renew the residence to a migrant, based on private partnership;[82] national rules which provide that a

[74] Patrick Thornberry, *International Law and the Rights of Minorities* (Oxford: Clarendon Press 1991) 63–65.

[75] *Wa Bale v Switzerland*, ECtHR, App No 43868/18, 25883/21, 20 February 2024. See Nazizwe Dube, 'Wa Baile v. Switzerland: An Implicit Acknowledgment of Racial Profiling as Structural Discrimination', *Strasbourg Observers*, 26 March 2024.

[76] *Basu v Germany*, ECtHR, App No 215/19, 18 October 2022.

[77] *Muhammad v Spain*, ECtHR, App No 34085/17, 18 October 2022.

[78] Belgium/Constitutional Court 117/2021.

[79] Case-377/16, Judgment of the Court (Grand Chamber), *Kingdom of Spain v European Parliament*, 26 March 2019.

[80] C-390/17, P: Appeal brought by Irit Azoulay, Andrew Boreham, Mirja Bouchard and Darren Neville, 28 June 2017 against the judgment of the General Court (Eighth Chamber) in Case T-580/16, *Azoulay and Others v European Parliament*, 28 April 2017.

[81] C-202/11, *Anton Las v PSA Antwerp NV*, Judgment of the Court (Grand Chamber), 16 April 2013.

[82] C-187/10, Judgment of the Court (Second Chamber) reference for a preliminary ruling from the Raad van State – Netherlands, 29 September 2011.

person's surnames and forenames may be entered on the certificates of civil status of that State only in a form which complies with the rules governing the spelling of the official national language;[83] and external publications of the vacancy notices for senior management posts in the Official Journal of the European Union would that are to be in English, French, and German only.[84]

The CJEU has, thus, considered minority-related issues in a limited scope, focusing more on procedural than substantive rights. More specifically, in *Runevič-Vardyn and Wardyn v Vilniaus Miesto Savivaldybė Administracija*, the CJEU addressed the issue of language requirements in employment contracts and official documents, reinforcing procedural compliance rather than establishing a clear minority rights framework.[85] Likewise, in cases involving religious slaughter practices, the CJEU has primarily interpreted EU directives, focusing on procedural alignment rather than substantively expanding minority protections. As Hunter-Henin argues, the concept of religious neutrality used by the CJEU 'fails to comply with the overarching values which the concept was initially designed to promote – the autonomy which citizens ought to enjoy in order to decide for themselves what constitutes a good life; the liberty for them to live according to their chosen conception of the good life and the opportunity for citizens and groups to do so on equal terms'.[86] Similarly, in *S.A.S. v France*, the ECtHR upheld France's ban on full-face coverings in public spaces, including the niqab and burqa, citing religious neutrality and 'living together' as grounds for the restriction.[87] The Court accepted France's argument that the ban aimed to promote social cohesion and protect the rights of others, viewing the State's position on religious neutrality as a legitimate interest.

As a result, while the ECtHR and CJEU contribute to minority rights protection, their approaches often lack the depth and direct applicability needed to address minority communities' specific and collective rights. This limitation was underscored in *D.H. and Others v Czech Republic*, where the ECtHR found that systemic discrimination against Roma children in education violated Article 14 of the ECHR but did so within an individual rights framework that lacked provisions for broader collective action. Hannum argues that such frameworks, while offering some protection, are constrained by the absence of collective rights language, leaving many aspects of minority protection unaddressed.[88] The minority rights protection may have certain benefits from this indirect model of protection

[83] C-391/09, *Malgožata Runevič-Vardyn and Łukasz Paweł Wardyn v Vilniaus*, Judgment of the Court (Second Chamber), 12 May 2011.

[84] T-185/05, *Italian Republic v Commission of the European Communities*, Court of First Instance, decision of 20 November 2008.

[85] C-391/09.

[86] Myriam Hunter-Henin, 'Religious Neutrality at Europe's Highest Courts: Shifting Strategies' (2022) 11 *Oxford Journal of Law and Religion* 1: 45.

[87] See also *SAS v France* (GC), ECtHR, App No 43835/11, 1 July 2014.

[88] Hurst Hannum, Autonomy, Sovereignty, and Self-Determination: The Accommodation of Conflicting Rights (Philadelphia: University of Pennsylvania Press, 1996) 107–110.

(eg, the ECtHR developed its jurisprudence even concerning States that are not parties to the Framework Convention), but the drawbacks are heavier. Most importantly, minority rights are admissible and justiciable only to the extent that they are interpretatively translatable into some of the enshrined human rights. This necessarily leaves uncovered significant and genuine aspects of minority protection, typically their collectivist dimension.

The absence of a comprehensive institutional mechanism for minority rights protection in Europe reflects a cautious balance between State sovereignty and minority protections.[89] However, it also means that minorities must often navigate a patchwork of rights that are dependent on reinterpretation within frameworks primarily designed for individual rights. Without a robust, enforceable mechanism, minority rights protection remains piecemeal, limiting the transformative potential of these rights as 'trump-over-sovereignty' rights and perpetuating gaps in the protection of minority identity, culture, and autonomy across Europe.

3.3. The Realistic Sovereignty-limiting Capacity of Minority Rights

The issue of minority rights within international law has garnered significant attention, particularly through instruments that ostensibly safeguard these rights. However, a closer critical examination reveals inherent limitations in their language and implementation. Notably, many of these minority rights instruments incorporate provisions that grant States considerable latitude regarding which articles to accept, thereby undermining the uniformity of protection intended for minorities. For instance, the European Charter for Regional or Minority Languages allows States the discretion to determine which specific languages they choose to protect, diluting the intended protective effect of the instrument. Furthermore, the CoE Framework Convention for the Protection of National Minorities exemplifies this trend through its use of vague language and 'claw-back clauses'.

Illustrative is Article 14, para. 2 of the Framework Convention, which prescribes the following: 'In areas inhabited by persons belonging to national minorities traditionally or in substantial numbers, if there is sufficient demand, the Parties shall endeavour to ensure, as far as possible and within the framework of their education systems, that persons belonging to those minorities have adequate opportunities for being taught the minority language or for receiving instruction in this language'. The language employed in this provision, which includes terms like 'sufficient demand', 'shall endeavour to ensure', 'as far as possible', and 'adequate opportunities' introduces a considerable degree of ambiguity. These drafting devices provide a wide scope for interpretation, thereby endangering the substance of the obligation and leaving unanswered the balance to be drawn

[89] ibid.

between different elements and the criteria for the enjoyment of this right.[90] Such vague drafting starkly contrasts 'hard law' formulations of human rights norms, typically found within treaties, which establish clear obligations for State Parties.

Moreover, limitations on minority rights often arise in practice, as many rights associated with minorities – such as the freedoms of assembly, religion, speech, and privacy – can face restrictions, allowing State Parties to invoke national interests or security concerns as valid justifications. Article 19 of the Framework Convention specifies that limitations should only be 'necessary', but it fails to articulate what constitutes a necessary limitation or how States should reconcile such limitations with their obligations under international law. Moreover, the Framework Convention does not mandate State Parties to ensure the direct applicability of its provisions within their domestic legal frameworks. Hence, rights enshrined in the Convention may not be justiciable, leading to a lack of accountability in enforcing minority rights. Article 2 of the Framework Convention merely recommends that its provisions be applied 'in good faith' and 'in a spirit of understanding and tolerance'. All this is insufficient to ensure enforcement or to address violations effectively.

In summary, while minority rights instruments like the Framework Convention and the European Charter for Regional and Minority Languages establish a framework for protection, their flexible and often vague language, reliance on discretion, and lack of enforceability severely hinder their protective capacity. They reflect an approach that creates a precarious balance, prioritising State sovereignty over the substantive rights of minorities. And for minority rights to be treatable as 'trump-over-sovereignty' rights, it should be the other way around.

4. Conclusion

While minority rights are often recognised within the international human rights frameworks and are viewed as essential to protecting the unique identities of diverse communities, they do not qualify as human rights in practice. First, minority rights lack the enforceable, universal status associated with human rights. Frameworks like the CoE's instruments are normatively aspirational rather than robust, with provisions allowing States significant flexibility and discretion in choosing which obligations to implement. Second, the ECtHR's reliance on an individual rights rather than a collective rights approach prevents comprehensive protection of minority rights as group-based entitlements. This methodology is further restricted by the ECtHR's reluctance to acknowledge collective victimhood. Without a basis for collective rights within these human rights frameworks, minority rights remain secondary to individual protections. While accommodating

[90] Duncan Wilson, 'Educational Rights of a Persons belonging to National Minorities' (2004) 10 *International Journal on Minority and Group Rights* 4, 335.

State sovereignty, this discretionary approach restricts the uniform application of minority rights and introduces inconsistency, thereby weakening their status in contrast to inalienable human rights.

Unlike human rights, minority rights frequently lack direct applicability within domestic legal systems. Instruments like the Framework Convention do not mandate States to incorporate these rights into domestic law, making them less likely to be enforceable and justiciable. This reliance on soft law guidelines, such as the requirement for States to act in good faith, offers limited recourse for minorities to seek legal protection. Finally, the fluidity of the concept of 'minority' itself and its protection by anti-discrimination frameworks complicates the application of minority rights. Expanding definitions of minority groups to include newer identities such as sexual orientation, disability, or age has sparked debates on the prioritisation and scope of these rights, potentially diluting the protections for established ethnic or religious minority groups. This shifting definition does not align with the stable, universally applicable nature of human rights, further underscoring the challenges in treating minority rights as human rights. Consequently, without 'hard law' mechanisms and enforceable standards, minority rights remain secondary, and conditional protections rather than fundamental human rights.

What is needed for minority rights to become 'trump-over-sovereignty' rights? Expanding existing treaties or developing new conventions specifically for minority rights could significantly enhance protection for minorities by formalising their unique rights as a matter of international law. One approach would be to expand current human rights treaties by adding optional protocols or clarifying provisions that address collective rights explicitly. It would be possible to specify the responsibilities of States in preventing discrimination and in actively endorsing the preservation of minority identities, languages, and traditions, as well as in acknowledging that traditional minorities often endure lingering disadvantages as a result of historical injustices. Another approach would be to create a special convention for minority rights on a universal level, which could lay out specific protections for minority groups and address the unique needs of minority communities more thoroughly.[91] For the moment, all these proposals seem unlikely, as some States resist the idea of collective rights, viewing them as a threat to national unity or an infringement on State sovereignty. And without the prospect of functioning as 'trump-over-sovereignty' rights, minority rights could not even through the 'political conception' qualify for the status of human rights.

[91] Art. 27 of the ICCPR does not impose strong obligations on States to proactively protect and support minority identities. It merely ensures that States do not prevent minorities from engaging in their cultural practices.

PART II

Institutional Setting of Minority Rights Protection

3

The Framework Convention for the Protection of National Minorities and the Northern Ireland Peace Process

ELIZABETH CRAIG

1. Introduction

This chapter examines the shift in the role of the Framework Convention for the Protection of National Minorities (FCNM) over the last three decades in the context of the Northern Ireland peace process, demonstrating the ongoing politicisation of language, culture and identity rights to the present day. The United Kingdom became a State Party to the FCNM in 1998.[1] This was also the year of the signing of the Good Friday/Belfast Agreement (GFA),[2] which ostensibly brought peace to Northern Ireland after many decades of conflict. The adoption of the Council of Europe's FCNM was an integral part of the organisation's response to the geopolitics of the early 1990s and it is the only human rights treaty at regional and/or global level focused on minority protection and the rights of minorities. Whilst the idea of an optional protocol to the European Convention on Human Rights stalled, the idea of a 'framework convention' was considered more politically palatable.[3] The FCNM was presented as a human rights instrument but the link between minority rights and peace and security was explicitly recognised in the Preamble and the FCNM itself was discussed in debates over the future of rights protection as part of the peace process in Northern Ireland, as explored further in this chapter.[4]

[1] *Chart of Signatures and* Ratifications *of Treaty No 157* (Council of Europe) www.coe.int/en/web/conventions/full-list?module=signatures-by-treaty&treatynum=157.

[2] This comprises a Multi-Party Agreement between the UK and Irish governments and most of the political parties in Northern Ireland, and British-Irish Agreement between the two governments, published 10 April 1998 www.gov.uk/government/publications/the-belfast-agreement.

[3] On the history, see Geoff Gilbert, 'The Council of Europe and Minority Rights' (1996) 18 *Human Rights Quarterly* 160.

[4] See also Geoff Gilbert, 'The Northern Ireland Peace Agreement, Minority Rights and Self-Determination' (1998) 47 *International and Comparative Law Quarterly* 943.

Much debate in the literature about the FCNM focuses on its application to 'new minorities'.[5] This includes debates about the role of the principle of self-identification[6] and about the challenges that have arisen in particular minority/majority situations.[7] This chapter, by comparison, specifically addresses the recent recognition of Ulster Scots as a national minority in the UK, utilising an original longitudinal perspective to analyse changes in the role and perceptions of the FCNM over time in the context of the Northern Ireland peace process. The chapter provides illustrations of the continued significance and adaptability of the FCNM,[8] as well as discussing the ongoing politicisation over its application in a very specific historical and geopolitical context. In doing so, it makes an important contribution to the debates over the future of minority rights more generally.[9]

The next section (2) explains and justifies the attribution of 'Human Rights Treaty' to the FCNM, arguing that this is significant to the ability of minority rights to develop through the invocation of this 'living instrument'. Section 3 then explains why the timing of the reception of the FCNM in Northern Ireland was so significant. It argues for the importance of recognising the interrelationship of these two legal instruments before exploring the shift in discussions around culture, identity and language issues in Northern Ireland from 2020 onwards towards specific legislative initiatives, considered in section 4. This shift illustrates the power of minority rights to continue to evolve through particularisation, and sections 5 and 6 then use the specific example of the recognition of Ulster Scots to demonstrate ongoing contestations and tensions that have impacted this process.

[5] Eg, Andrei Dragan, 'New Minorities in the States Parties to the Framework Convention: The Importance of Self-Identification and Recognition' (2018) *Pécs Journal of International and European Law* 101; Roberta Medda-Windischer, Caitlin Boulter and Tove H. Malloy (eds), *Extending Protection to Migrant Populations in Europe: Old and New Minorities* (Routledge, 2019) and Timothy Jacob-Owens, 'Immigration and Multicultural Citizenship in Europe: Insights from the Framework Convention for the Protection of National Minorities' (2022) 29 *International Journal on Minority and Group Rights* 167.

[6] Eg, Elizabeth Craig, 'Who Are the Minorities? The Role of the Right to Self-Identify within the European Minority Rights Framework' (2016) 15 *Journal on Ethnopolitics and Minority Issues in Europe* 6.

[7] Eg, Tamás Kiss and others (eds), *Unequal Accommodation of Rights: Hungarians in Transylvania* (Palgrave Macmillan, 2018); Tove H. Malloy, 'Integration and Special Rights: Greenlanders Living in Denmark and the Council of Europe's Framework Convention for the Protection of National Minorities' (2023) 30 *International Journal on Minority and Group Rights* 443; Gagik Chilingaryan, 'Norms of the Council of Europe in the Postsoviet Space: National Minorities in the Republic of Armenia and the Framework Convention for the Protection of National Minorities' (2023) *Pécs Journal of International and European Law* 28; Kiryl Kascian, 'Latvia's Ambiguous Attitude towards the Framework Convention for the Protection of National Minorities: Is Diversity a Threat?' (2024) 9 *Public Governance, Administration and Finances Law Review* (Online) 91 and Nika Potinkara, 'Finland-Swedes and the Concept of National Minorities in Sweden' (2024) 23 *Ethnopolitics* 59.

[8] See also Elizabeth Craig, 'The Framework Convention for the Protection of National Minorities and Internalisation: Lessons from the Western Balkans' (2021) 46 *Review of Central and East European Law* 1.

[9] Eg, Fernand de Varennes, 'Prefatory Remarks: An Inside Perspective from an Outsider: The UN Special Rapporteur's View on Minority Rights at the UN' in Anna-Mária Bíró and Dwight Newman (eds), *Minority Rights and Liberal Democratic Insecurities: The Challenge of Unstable Orders* (Routledge, 2023).

These sections caution against over-simplification and call for recognition of the complexity of the issues, given the wider political and historical context.

2. Minority Rights as Human Rights – The FCNM as a Human Rights Treaty

It is significant that the FCNM was introduced as a human rights treaty, particularly given evolving debates over beneficiaries and its scope of application.[10] This section demonstrates why it is important that the FCNM is seen as a human rights treaty. Particularly relevant here is an emphasis on the collective, and on the idea of the FCNM as a 'living instrument' in line with the practice of human rights treaties.[11] The Vienna Convention on the Law of Treaties 1969, is clear that what legally determines whether an international or regional instrument is a treaty is not nomenclature, but rather whether it is 'an international agreement concluded between States in written form and governed by international law' (Article 2(1)(a)). But what makes a treaty a human rights treaty? Normally this is evident from a preponderance of rights-based provisions or from the intention of the drafters. On the first point, the FCNM is cautious in its use of rights language. For example, the terminology of rights is not used at all in Articles 5 (on cultural identity), 6 (on tolerance and dialogue), 12 (on intercultural and multicultural education), 15 on effective participation, or 18 (on bilateral treaties and transfrontier co-operation). Meanwhile, some of the provisions that do include a formulation of rights in the first paragraph switch to the language of obligations in subsequent paragraphs. However, this is not so unusual in human rights treaties. This includes, for example, Articles 9 (on the right to freedom of expression and the media) and 14 (on the right to learn a minority language). Meanwhile, on the second point and intention, Article 1 explicitly identifies the protection of national minorities and of their rights as 'an integral part of the international protection of human rights'.[12]

The treaty form was that of 'a framework convention specifying the principles which contracting States commit themselves to respect, in order to assure the protection of national minorities'.[13] It is therefore an instrument that reflects the

[10] This contrasts with other instruments, such as the European Charter for Regional or Minority Languages, which is focused on protection of the languages and cultural and linguistic diversity, and the Framework Convention on the Value of Cultural Heritage for Society.

[11] David Keane and Annapurna Waughray, 'Introduction' in David Keane and Annapurna Waughray (eds), *Fifty Years of the International Convention on the Elimination of All Forms of Racial Discrimination* (Manchester University Press, 2017) 14–23.

[12] 'The protection of national minorities and of the rights and freedoms of persons belonging to those minorities forms an integral part of the international protection of human rights, and as such falls within the scope of international co-operation'.

[13] Explanatory Report to the Framework Convention for the Protection of National Minorities (Strasbourg, 1 February 1995) para 5.

dominant liberal democratic conception of human rights at the time as 'agreed upon' rather than as 'given' or 'fought' for, which, according to Dembour, provides guidance for political actors because it suggests limits of rights are seen as subject to 'reasonable debate'.[14]

According to Bantekas and Oette, 'The current international legal framework on minority protection is based on non-discrimination and equality with members of the majority, whilst at the same time safeguarding and promoting through positive action the minority's distinct right to culture'.[15] This is a useful summary also of the FCNM. It was drafted at the same time as Will Kymlicka was developing his liberal theory of minority rights and advocating for greater recognition of the rights of ethno-cultural groups based on individual freedom and the right to access a societal culture.[16] Furthermore, like Kymlicka, the drafters appeared prima facie to distinguish between national minorities and other ethno-cultural groups. However, Kymlicka had argued for the recognition of rights to self-government and representation rights for national minorities, whereas the FCNM watered this down by focusing instead on 'effective participation' (Article 15), alongside a range of cultural, identity and language rights. The FCNM itself does not define the term 'national minority' and a range of different approaches have been adopted in relation to claims based on ethnicity and national identity (or nationality), and the significance of citizenship.[17]

Although the Explanatory Report states that the FCNM 'does not imply the recognition of collective rights',[18] this appears to be a stretch, particularly given the hybrid approach developed at the global level.[19] It is true that, where rights language is used, the terminology used is the rights of persons belonging to national minorities. It is also true that many of the provisions are either focused on highlighting individual human rights, which are significant for people identifying as belonging to a minority (eg, Articles 9 to 11 of the ECHR as highlighted in Articles 7 and 8 of the FCNM), or particularising generic human rights, such as the right to freedom of expression in Article 9 in relation to the media or the right to use a minority language in Articles 10 and 11. Yet there are other provisions with more of a collective dimension that, whilst not explicitly recognising groups themselves

[14] Marie-Bénédicte Dembour, 'What Are the Limits of Human Rights? Four Schools, Four Complementary Visions' in Bardo Fassbender and Knut Traisbach (eds), *The Limits of Human Rights* (Oxford University Press, 2019).

[15] Ilias Bantekas and Lutz Oette, *International Human Rights Law and Practice* (Cambridge University Press, 2024) 493.

[16] Will Kymlicka, *Multicultural Citizenship: A Liberal Theory of Minority Rights* (Oxford University Press, 1995).

[17] One indication of this is the range of approaches adopted in the declarations made by States upon ratification – see *Reservations and Declarations for Treaty No 157 – Framework Convention for the Protection of National Minorities (ETS No 157)* www.coe.int/en/web/conventions/.

[18] Explanatory Report (n 13), para 13.

[19] Gaetano Pentassuglia, 'Introduction: The Unpacking of Ethno-Cultural Diversity' in Gaetano Pentassuglia (ed), *Ethno-Cultural Diversity and Human Rights: Challenges and Critiques*, vol 122 (Brill, 2018).

as rights-holders, do require State action to protect the interests of the group as a whole. This includes Article 4, which provides for full and effective equality between the majority and the minority and Article 5(1), which requires States 'to promote the conditions necessary for persons belonging to national minorities to maintain and develop their culture, and to preserve the essential elements of their identity'.

Jovanović has made a convincing case for recognising minority identities through collective rights and indeed argues that this is required for the current model of minority protection to operate effectively.[20] Meanwhile Jones has argued that the key for the recognition of collective rights as human rights is that 'they are held jointly by individuals by virtue of their status as human beings' and '[t]ypically will include rights to collective goods'.[21] This applies to many of the provisions in the FCNM requiring States to make provision in minority languages subject to there being 'sufficient demand' (eg, Article 11(3) and Article 14(2)) or only in 'areas inhabited by persons belonging to national minorities traditionally or in substantial numbers' (eg, Article 10(2)) or both (eg, Article 14(2)) or other relevant qualifications (eg, Article 11(3)).

There are also the provisions that are focused more on developing better relations between minority and majority groups, and indeed among all persons 'living on their territory'. This is, for example, the case with Article 6, which provides that: 'The Parties shall encourage a spirit of tolerance and intercultural dialogue and take effective measures to promote mutual respect and understanding and co-operation among all persons living on their territory, irrespective of those persons' ethnic, cultural, linguistic or religious identity, in particular in the fields of education, culture and the media.' The use of the terms 'intercultural' and 'mutual respect' however reflect a slightly different normative agenda, as do the references in Article 5(2) to 'general integration policy' (considered to be helpful) and forced assimilation (considered problematic), and which can shift the focus away from the minority and their rights given the wider emphasis on nation-building.[22]

It is significant that the FCNM is treated as a 'living instrument' and 'should be interpreted and applied in the light of the actual situation', with reference also to changing circumstances and dynamics.[23] Recent academic debates have focused on the idea of 'making and unmaking of permanent minorities', recognising how

[20] Miodrag A Jovanović, 'Recognizing Minority Identities through Collective Rights' (2005) 27 *Human Rights Quarterly* 625.

[21] Peter Jones, 'Collective and Group-Specific: Can the Rights of Ethno-Cultural Minorities Be Human Rights?' in Gaetano Pentassuglia (ed), *Ethno-Cultural Diversity and Human Rights: Challenges and Critiques*, vol 122 (Brill, 2018) 57.

[22] Alexandra Xanthaki, 'Against Integration, For Human Rights' (2016) 20 *The International Journal of Human Rights* 815.

[23] Rainer Hofmann, 'Practical Implementation of the Framework Convention for the Protection of National Minorities: Monitoring Reports of the Advisory Committee' (2012), 5 www.zentralrat.sintiundroma.de/en/wp-content/uploads/sites/2/2012/06/5_rainer-hofmann_practical-implementation-of-the-framework-convention.pdf.

minority and majority identities are not fixed, and can evolve over time, and the need to look 'beyond majority-minority narratives', for example in relation to racialised groups such as the Romani people.[24] This is within a wider context of the observed decline of minority protection in Europe over the last two decades.[25] This is significant as it shows that the parameters of the debates are shifting, as explored further below through consideration of the evolving role of the FCNM in Northern Ireland in relation to the Northern Ireland peace process.

3. The FCNM and the Good Friday/Belfast Agreement

Whilst discussions over group rights played a key role in negotiations over the content of the GFA, the parameters of these debates and the perceptions of the role of the FCNM have shifted over time. The GFA itself marked the end of a particularly violent stage of the decades-long conflict between Protestants/Unionists/Loyalists on the one hand and Catholics/Nationalists/Republicans on the other, and human rights featured prominently in the negotiations.[26] However, the peace process in Northern Ireland had started to gain momentum much earlier. For example, around 3000 people contributed to the so-called 'Citizens' Inquiry' organised by Initiative '92 into ways forward.[27] The subsequent Opsahl Report recommended specific legal recognition of the Nationalist community, and of the principle of 'parity of esteem between the two [main] communities'.[28] This reflected a shift away from the earlier focus on this community as a minority group.[29]

It is significant that these discussions were occurring in parallel to developments within international human rights law. This included debates over the recognition of more collective-oriented rights as human rights within both the Council of Europe and the UN.[30] As the only legally binding regional or global instrument on minority rights, the FCNM emerged as the focus of attention, particularly amongst Unionist politicians. It is telling that Dermott Nesbitt, who was chief negotiator of the Ulster Unionist Party (UUP) during negotiations on the GFA, remained over two decades later a strong advocate of the

[24] Tina Magazzini and Martin Fotta, 'Call for Papers on Romani Racialization Beyond Majority-Minority Narratives: Transnationalism, Activism and Solidarity' (Czech Academy of Science and the Prague Forum for Romani Histories, 2024) www.hsozkult.de/event/id/event-150071.

[25] Boriss Cilevičs, 'National Minority as a Right-Holder and an Actor: Why Minority Protection Is in Decline in Europe' in Kyriaki Topidi and Eugenia Relaño Pastor (eds), *Minority Rights and Social Change: Norms, Actions and Strategies* (Routledge, 2024).

[26] Paul Mageean and Martin O'Brien, 'From the Margins to the Mainstream: Human Rights and the Good Friday Agreement' (1998) 22 *Fordham International Law Journal* 1499.

[27] Torkel Opsahl and others, A Citizens' Inquiry: The Opsahl Report on Northern Ireland (The Lilliput Press, 1993).

[28] ibid, 112–113.

[29] Eg, Harold Jackson and Anne McHardy, *The Two Irelands: The Problem of the Double Minority* (3rd edn, Minority Rights Group International, 1984). Meanwhile the Opsahl report itself contains several references to the minority and majority with reference to the two main communities at the time(ibid.)).

[30] On the former, see eg, Gilbert, 'The Council of Europe and Minority Rights' (n 4).

FCNM.[31] The appeal was no doubt linked to the reference in the FCNM to respect for existing territorial integrity[32] and the perception of the framing of the instrument, at least at that time, as cultural rather than as political or socio-economic.[33] In contrast, Mark Durkhan of the Social Democratic and Labour Party (SDLP), which has always had a strong Nationalist base, has observed that the FCNM approach 'did not go down well with a lot of participants due to the language of national minorities, and the overall impression that 'people were trying to assert rights on their own terms'.[34] The references to respect for existing territorial integrity appeared to serve to limit aspirations for further constitutional change and for an eventual united Ireland. Meanwhile, it was becoming clear that for many Nationalists, 'minority' status was not something to be defended and was instead something that needed to be countered as part of the peace process. As a result, by the time the GFA was signed, the emphasis in relation to minority rights had already shifted, as discussed further below.

The new governance structures for Northern Ireland envisaged in the GFA were explicitly based on the right to self-determination, with the emphasis on power-sharing and consociationalism.[35] The group accommodations made in the GFA for the historically oppressed and largest 'minority' (Catholics/Nationalists) therefore went well beyond the requirements of the FCNM.[36] There was, however, clear recognition also of the need to take specific measures to protect and promote the Irish language not just as an indigenous language, but also as a historically marginalised one, as well as the Ulster Scots language. The timing of the discussions was crucial given the coming into force of the FCNM in the UK earlier in the year and ongoing negotiations over the UK's ratification of the European Charter for the Protection of Regional or Minority Languages (the Languages Charter), with a clear synergy developing between developments in European minority (rights) law and the GFA negotiations.[37] For example, additional undertakings included the Republic of Ireland's ratification of the FCNM,[38] as well as those in relation to the Irish language and for Ulster Scots.[39]

[31] Eg, his presentation to the Ad Hoc Committee on a Bill of Rights, Meeting of 15 October 2020. Official Report: Minutes of Evidence.

[32] Art 21 and the Preamble.

[33] However, note the references in Article 15 to effective participation 'in cultural, social and economic life and in public affairs'.

[34] *Report of the Ad Hoc Committee on a Bill of Rights* (4 February 2022) https://www.niassembly.gov.uk/assembly-business/committees/2017-2022/ad-hoc-committee-on-a-bill-of-rights/reports/report-of-the-ad-hoc-committee-on-a-bill-of-rights/ paras 212–213.

[35] *Good Friday Agreement* (Multi-Party Agreement) 'Constitutional Issues' section (Belfast, 10 April 1998) paras 1–3, s 1.

[36] ibid, Strand One, Democratic Institutions in Northern Ireland.

[37] ibid, Economic, Social and Cultural Issues, para 4.

[38] ibid, Rights, Safeguards and Equality of Opportunity, Human Rights, para 9.

[39] ibid, Economic, Social and Cultural issues, paras 3–4. This included the establishment of Foras na Gaelige (Irish) and Tha Boord O Ulstèr-Scotch (Ulster Scots) as part of the new North/South Language Body – see www.northsouthministerialcouncil.org/language-body.

Some of the earlier stages of discussions over the content of a Bill of Rights for Northern Ireland and the wide scope of application of the FCNM adopted by the UK have been explored elsewhere.[40] For now, it suffices to note that the GFA specifically envisaged that the newly established Northern Ireland Human Rights Commission (NIHRC) would be invited

> to consult and to advise on the scope for defining, in Westminster legislation, rights supplementary to those in the European Convention on Human Rights, to reflect the particular circumstances of Northern Ireland, drawing as appropriate on international instruments and experience. These additional rights to reflect the principles of mutual respect for the identity and ethos of both communities and parity of esteem, and – taken together with the ECHR – to constitute a Bill of Rights for Northern Ireland.[41]

The FCNM is not mentioned specifically, and there have been extensive discussions in the decades since about whether the term 'particular circumstances' justifies a wide or narrow approach to the development of new rights protections.[42] Tellingly, more than a quarter of a century later, Northern Ireland still does not have a Bill of Rights. Indeed, the most recent attempt to restart the discussion resulted in a final report but no consensus on a way forward and no further follow-up action.[43] The next section therefore examines the alternative approach that has emerged in recent years and how the underlying principles of the FCNM (and subsequently also the Languages Charter) have been adapted to address the specific concerns generated by the historical and geopolitical context and in light of current political, legal, social and cultural realities.

4. 2020: A New Decade, A New Approach?

The next section illustrates how internal discussions have moved beyond the earlier focus on the text of the FCNM to the trickier task of internalising the underlying goals and principles, and particularisation. Over the course of over a quarter of a century, devolution in Northern Ireland has faced many challenges with a lack of progress on key legislative initiatives. This is partly, but not only, due to regular suspensions of the Northern Ireland Assembly and of devolved government for political reasons. Meanwhile, the last few years have seen significant changes in the political landscape in Northern Ireland in the post-Brexit era. Sinn Féin, historically

[40] Eg, Elizabeth Craig, 'The Framework Convention for the Protection of National Minorities and the Northern Ireland Bill of Rights Process' (2009) 60 *Northern Ireland Legal Quarterly* 201. On the approach of other States, see see eg, Craig, 'Who are the Minorities?' (n 6).

[41] *Good Friday Agreement* (Multi-Party Agreement) 'Rights, Safeguards and Equality of Opportunity' (Belfast, 10 April 1998), para 4.

[42] Eg, Colin Harvey, 'The Implementation of a Bill of Rights in Northern Ireland' (2001) 52 *Northern Ireland Legal Quarterly* 342 and Colin Harvey and Alex Schwartz, 'Designing a Bill of Rights for Northern Ireland' (2009) 60 *Northern Ireland Legal Quarterly* 181.

[43] Report of the Ad Hoc Committee on a Bill of Rights (n 34).

a Republican party, is now the largest party in the Northern Ireland Executive, Unionism has been hit with one crisis after the other and discussions about a border poll have moved from the margins to the mainstream. It is within this wider context that recent changes in the role of the FCNM need to be examined, as Unionists come to terms with losing their majority status and attention shifts to the protection of minorities within a future united Ireland.[44] The UK, meanwhile, continues to be subject to regular monitoring under both the FCNM and the Languages Charter, with both monitoring bodies expressing consistent concern about the lack of progress on language and equality issues.[45]

The New Decade, New Approach (NDNA) deal of January 2020[46] was intended to mark the beginning of a new era and to lead to the restoration of devolution.[47] However, not much progress had been made in implementing the various commitments in the deal before normal operations in the Assembly were suspended again in February 2022. The deal itself was negotiated between the British and Irish governments and the five main political parties in Northern Ireland and included a section (after the section on the programme of government)[48] focused on rights, language and identity.[49] As well as three new legislative bills covering issues of identity and language (for which draft legislation had been produced by the Office for Legislative Counsel in Northern Ireland at the request of the UK government), the NDNA deal also included a commitment by the UK government to the establishment of an Ad-Hoc Committee on a Bill of Rights for Northern Ireland within the Northern Ireland Assembly 'to consider the creation of a Bill of Rights that is faithful to the stated intention of the 1998 Agreement'.[50] However, as had happened with the Northern Ireland Bill of Rights Forum almost 15 years earlier, and with the Commission on Flags, Identity, Culture and Tradition (FICT), which was established in June 2016 under the earlier Stormont House and Fresh Start Agreements,[51] the final report reflected a continued lack of consensus on how best to proceed.[52]

[44] Rory O'Connell and others, *How Could Minority and Women's Rights be Protected in a United Ireland?* (2024)www.pure.ulster.ac.uk/ws/portalfiles/portal/198368970/Report_Women_s_Rights_.pdf.

[45] Detailed documentation on the first five monitoring cycles under the FCNM can be found at www.coe.int/en/web/minorities/united-kingdom with documentation on the first five monitoring cycles under the Languages Charter at www.coe.int/en/web/european-charter-regional-or-minority-languages/reports-and-recommendations.

[46] *New Decade, New Approach* (8 January 2020) https://assets.publishing.service.gov.uk/media/5e178b56ed915d3b06f2b795/2020-01-08_a_new_decade__a_new_approach.pdf.

[47] Sean Haughey, 'Back to Stormont: The New Decade, New Approach Agreement and What it Means for Northern Ireland' (2020) 91 *The Political Quarterly* 134.

[48] New Decade New Approach (NDNA), 8 January 2020 (n 46), paras 19–24.

[49] ibid, paras 25–27, see also Annex E.

[50] ibid, para 28.

[51] Stormont House Agreement (23 December 2014) and A Fresh Start: The Stormont Agreement and Implementation Plan (November 2015); see also Final Report of the Commission on Flags, Identity, Culture and Tradition (1 December 2021) www.executiveoffice-ni.gov.uk/publications/commission-flags-identity-culture-and-tradition-final-report.

[52] Report of the Ad Hoc Committee on a Bill of Rights (n 34).

Neither of the two subsequent reports reflects a particular emphasis or consideration of minority rights. The FCNM is only superficially[53] addressed in the final FICT report, as is the Framework Convention on the Value of Culture Heritage for Society[54] and the European Charter for Regional or Minority Languages.[55] Discussions appear to have been more extensive in relation to the bill of rights, but the summary provided in the final report of the Ad-hoc Committee on a Bill of Rights suggests little change from early Unionist support for the FCNM and greater reticence on the part of Nationalists.[56] Whilst the NDNA deal did include a specific commitment by the UK government to recognise Ulster Scots as a national minority under the FCNM,[57] the FCNM is mentioned only one other time in the 62 page document, alongside the Languages Charter and the UN Convention on the Rights of the Child, an indication as to how perceptions of the potential for European minority rights law to help in providing a framework for moving forward have changed.

It could be argued that the broader spirit of the FCNM is to an extent reflected in the commitment to legislation for the creation of a new Office for Identity and Cultural Expression (OCIE), and for the new roles of Irish Language Commissioner and a 'further such Commissioner …. to enhance and develop the language, arts and literature associated with the Ulster Scots/Ulster British tradition in Northern Ireland.'[58] It is, however, clear that that the commitments do not just replicate the wording of the FCNM. This is, for example, evident from the articulation of two new 'national and cultural identity principles' with paragraph 25 of the NDNA document stating that:

> The parties affirm the need to respect the freedom of all persons in Northern Ireland to choose, affirm, maintain and develop their national and cultural identity and to celebrate and express that identity in a manner which takes into account the sensitivities of those with different national or cultural identities and respects the rule of law. They also affirm the need to encourage and promote reconciliation, tolerance and meaningful dialogue between those of different national and cultural identities in Northern Ireland with a view to promoting parity of esteem, mutual respect, understanding and cooperation. These principles will be reflected in legislation.

The term 'national identity' notably does not appear in the text of the FCNM itself, and the reference to the 'sensitivities' of those with 'different national and cultural identities' is also a very specific expression that has caused some concern, as explored further below. It could further be argued that the three-pronged approach is also more reflective of the 'particular circumstances of Northern Ireland', given desires to move beyond the 'two communities' paradigm.

[53] FICT Report, paras 5.6–5.7 and 8.8–8.10.
[54] ibid, paras 3.5–3.8.
[55] ibid, para 8.11–8.15.
[56] Report of the Ad Hoc Committee on a Bill of Rights (n 34), paras 212–213.
[57] NDNA Annex A: UK Government Commitments to Northern Ireland, para 24.
[58] NDNA, Part 2: Northern Ireland Executive Formation Agreement, para 27.

The original idea was that the legislation envisaged in NDNA would be adopted by the Northern Ireland Assembly and amended as appropriate and as agreed in the Assembly. However, this did not happen due to the collapse of the Assembly in February 2022; consequently, it was Westminster that took responsibility for the Identity and Language (Northern Ireland) Act, which gained royal assent on 6 December 2022, and which combined the three initiatives. Sections 1–3 of the Act made legislative provision for the establishment of the Office of Identity and Cultural Expression, an Irish language Commissioner and a new Ulster Scots and Ulster British Commissioner. The new Office of Identity and Cultural Expression is required to promote awareness of the new 'national and cultural identity principles' and to monitor and promote compliance with the new public authority duty to have due regard to the new principles.[59] In line with NDNA commitments, the Act also provided for the official recognition of the Irish language in Northern Ireland (section 2) and for the repeal of Administration of Justice (Language) Act (Ireland) 1737, which prohibited the use of any language other than English in the courts (section 4). It therefore appears that the process of particularisation of requirements of the FCNM and the Languages Charter is ongoing, albeit with much ongoing political contestation. This is demonstrated further through consideration of the controversies over the recognition of Ulster Scots as a national minority in May 2022[60] and around the new Ulster Scots and Ulster British Commissioner, which merit further consideration in how the use (and power) of the FCNM has evolved over time.

5. Ulster Scots as a Newly Recognised National Minority

The official recognition of Ulster Scots as a national minority marks a significant shift in terms of group identification and the role of minority rights and minority protection frameworks within the wider post-conflict context. The historical roots of the Ulster Scots communities of today can be linked to the migrations that took place from the Scottish Lowlands to Ulster in the early 17th century, with settlements continuing also over the 18th and 19th centuries. According to the Ulster Scots Agency, these 'were ordinary Scottish families, seeking a new life. They were mainly Presbyterian in faith and outlook, and overwhelmingly Scots-speaking in language'.[61] Whilst there are ongoing debates regarding the ongoing legacy of

[59] Identity and Language (Northern Ireland) Act 2022, s 1 (inserting in Northern Ireland Act 1998, ss. 78F(1) on new public authority duty and s. 78H(2) on OICE duties).

[60] See Brandon Lewis MP, Written Statement HLWS55 (25 May 2022) www.questions-statements.parliament.uk/written-statements/detail/2022-05-25/hlws55.

[61] Brandon Lewis MP, Written Statement HLWS55 (25 May 2022) www.questions-statements.parliament.uk/written-statements/detail/2022-05-25/hlws55.

colonialism in Ireland today[62] and the invocation of concepts of 'settlement' and 'indigenousnness', the minority rights framework provides a very different framing and one that can be more easily linked to the framing of the conflict as an 'ethnonational' one.[63] The danger, however, is that dominant self-perceptions and the link to narratives of the past, as future threats to peace, are thereby neglected,[64] with the overall focus on the current situation and reality. This is why the ongoing controversy matters, particularly given what it reveals about shifts in minority identifications and affiliations over time, as demonstrated in the rest of this section about the current position of Ulster Scots.

Although spoken by members of both communities, Ulster Scots is a language, culture and heritage most often associated with the Protestant/Unionist community and Protestant/Unionist majority areas. According to the 2021 census, 10.38% of the population of Northern Ireland declared some ability in Ulster Scots and 12.45% some ability in Irish. Only 1.66% reported speaking Ulster Scots daily (the percentages are highest in the Causeway Coast and Glens and in Mid and East Antrim), compared to 2.37% speaking Irish daily (the percentages here are highest in mid-Ulster and Belfast).[65] However, a key feature of the shift to recognition as a national (or ethnic) minority[66] is moving beyond the primary focus on language in the GFA. Here it is relevant that the 2021 Census was also the first time in the history of Northern Ireland that a greater percentage of residents declared themselves as Catholic (42.31%) than as Protestant or from another Christian background (37.36%), with 17.39% declaring no religion at all.[67]

Strong criticism of the recognition of Ulster Scots as a national minority under the FCNM has come from the Committee on the Administration of Justice (CAJ), a highly influential human rights non-governmental organisation, often perceived as being more engaged in issues of concern to the Nationalist community. This demonstrates the significant ongoing politicisation and contestation around the FCNM and minority rights. For example, the CAJ described the move in a briefing to the Westminster Parliament in 2022 as 'a separate seeming political side deal within

[62] See, eg, SJ Connolly, 'Settler Colonialism in Ireland from the English Conquest to the Nineteenth Century' in Edward Cavanagh and Lorenzo Veracini (eds), *The Routledge Handbook of the History of Settler Colonialism*(Routledge 2017) and on 'old/new settlement histories' see Stephen Howe, 'Northern Ireland and Settler Colonialism to the Good Friday Agreement of 1998' in Edward Cavanagh and Lorenzo Veracini (eds), *The Routledge Handbook of the History of Settler Colonialism*(Routledge 2017). See also R McVeigh and B Rolston, *Ireland, Colonialism and the Unfinished Revolution* (Beyond the Pale Publications, 2021).

[63] Adrian Guelke, 'Northern Ireland's Flags Crisis and the Enduring Legacy of the Settler-Native Divide' (2014) 20 *Nationalism and Ethnic Politics* 133, 134–135.

[64] Guelke argues that this is one of the advantages of the former framing, ibid,148.

[65] Northern Ireland Statistics and Research Agency (NISRA), 'Main Statistics Language' (Census 2021) www.nisra.gov.uk/publications/census-2021-main-statistics-language-tables.

[66] The UK's position at the time was that such recognition [as a national minority] 'is without prejudice as to whether they meet the definition of a 'racial group' under the Equality Act 2010, leaving this for the courts to decide' (Statement made by Brandon Lewis MP, 25 May 2022).

[67] NISRA Main Statistics Religion' (Census 2021) https://www.nisra.gov.uk/publications/census-2021-main-statistics-religion-table.

NDNA to move away from language in the way the UK recognises Ulster Scots under the Framework Convention' and criticised a failure to consult Ulster Scots speakers on whether they self-identify as an ethnic group.[68] The CAJ also raised questions as to 'the extent Ulster Scots in this context will be used as a proxy for the tradition of political unionism'.[69] The next section considers this claim further in light some of the contestations that have arisen in relation to the new Identity and Language (Northern Ireland) Act of 2022. It considers also the future role envisaged for the FCNM in this Act given the ever-changing geopolitical context.

6. The FCNM and the Identity and Language (Northern Ireland) Act 2022

Consideration of some of the debates that preceded the adoption of the 2022 Act further illustrate the dangers of over-simplification and of conflating different identities. This is most evident in relation to the naming of the new 'Ulster Scots' Commissioner. The NDNA document itself envisaged that there would be a Commissioner 'to enhance and develop the language, arts and literature associated with the Ulster Scots / Ulster British tradition in Northern Ireland'.[70] This appears to have reflected concerns within at least some of the Unionist community about an exclusive focus on Ulster Scots, with for example the Orange Order, a Protestant fraternal order,[71] declaring that: 'As British citizens living in the United Kingdom, we have a complex and multi-layered identity which in many areas is wider that simply "Ulster Scots"'.[72]

The title proposed in the draft legislation presented to Parliament was 'Commissioner for the enhancement and development of the language, arts and literature associated with the Ulster Scots and the Ulster British tradition', which the government said better reflected the recognition of Ulster Scots as a national minority.[73] However, this approach was criticised by the Northern Ireland Human Rights Commission (NIHRC), which noted that 'Ulster British' 'is not a term or a linguistic/national minority group presently recognised by human rights treaty bodies. It appears that Ulster Scots culture is at risk of being conflated with a distinct political identity'.[74] This point was also raised with the Advisory Committee

[68] Committee on the Administration of Justice (CAJ), *Briefing Note on Identity and Language (Northern Ireland) Bill* (to the House of Lords, May 2022) para 24.

[69] ibid.

[70] NDNA, para 27(c).

[71] Clifford Stevenson, Susan Condor and Jackie Abell, 'The Minority-Majority Conundrum in Northern Ireland: An Orange Order Perspective' (2007) 28 *Political Psychology* 105.

[72] Grand Orange Lodge of Ireland (@OrangeOrder), 'Response to *New Decade, New Approach*' (Twitter, 10 January 2020, 1:36pm) https://x.com/OrangeOrder/status/1215628463438225414.

[73] HL Deb 6 July 2022, vol 823, col 1021 (Lord Caine).

[74] Northern Ireland Human Rights Commission (NIHRC), *Briefing on the Identity and Language (Northern Ireland) Bill* (2022) para 4.8.

under the FCNM (ACFC), which essentially deferred to the NIHRC's assessment, concluding that 'these proposals further contribute to the sectarianism surrounding cultural questions: the naming of a commissioner for Ulster Scots as for the Ulster Scots and the Ulster British Tradition unnecessarily conflates this minority identity with a distinct political one'.[75]

What was eventually adopted in the Westminster legislation (but notably without the support of the Democratic Unionist Party (DUP)) was a requirement for the appointment of 'a Commissioner for the Ulster Scots and the Ulster British tradition'.[76] The role of the Commissioner is 'to enhance and develop the language, arts and literature associated with the Ulster Scots and the Ulster British tradition in Northern Ireland'.[77] The new Commissioner will be required to 'promote awareness of Ulster Scots services provided by public authorities to the public or a section of the public in Northern Ireland'.[78] This provision makes the significance of the limitation to arts, language and literature clear, as there is a limit to the numbers of public authorities with a relevant remit.[79] Meanwhile, the Commissioner is also required to:

> b) provide or publish such advice, support and guidance as the Commissioner considers appropriate to public authorities in relation to—
>
> (i) developing and encouraging the relevant language, arts and literature (including in relation to facilitating the use of Ulster Scots in the provision of services to the public or a section of the public in Northern Ireland);
>
> (ii) the effect and implementation of the international instruments specified in subsection (3) in relation to the relevant language, arts and literature;[80]

The international instruments referred to include the FCNM, the Languages Charter and the United Nations Convention on the Rights of the Child (UNCRC). The principle of self-identification, recognised in Article 3 of the FCNM, is notably not included in the legislation, nor is there specific a reference to Ulster Scots as a national minority. In preparing such guidance, the Commissioner 'must consult with such public authorities and other persons as the Commissioner considers appropriate', which could presumably include Ulster Scots speakers themselves, although this is not made explicit.[81] There is also a complaints process for when a public authority has failed to show due regard to such guidance,[82] although the duty for them to have such regard is not

[75] Advisory Committee on the Framework Convention for the Protection of National Minorities (ACFC), *Fifth Opinion on the United Kingdom* (adopted 8 December 2022) para 11.

[76] Northern Ireland Act 1998, s 3, pt 7C, new s 78R.

[77] Ibid. new s 78S(1).

[78] ibid. Specifically, this 'means services provided in Ulster Scots or likely to be of particular interest to those with an interest in the relevant language, arts and literature'. (new section 78S(2)).

[79] HL Deb 6 July 2022, vol 823, col 1035 (Lord Morrow).

[80] Northern Ireland Act 1998, new s 78S(2).

[81] Northern Ireland Act 1998, new s 78S(4).

[82] Northern Ireland Act 1998, new s 78T.

explicitly outlined as it is for Irish.[83] It therefore appears that some commitment to the FCNM and its underlying values remains, even if there is still considerable uncertainty about the exact implications of what this means in practice.

Perhaps unsurprisingly, the passage of the Identity and Language (Northern Ireland) Act 2022 through Parliament witnessed continued political divisions and polarisation on language, culture and identity issues. This illustrates the continued complexity of shifting identities and perceptions thereof in an ever-changing geopolitical climate. This was clearly evidenced in the debates on the legislation in the House of Commons. For example, DUP MPs in their contributions during debates in Parliament focused on continued obstacles in relation to the Northern Ireland Protocol post-Brexit and drew comparisons in relation to how Irish and Ulster Scots were being treated,[84] and ended up voting against the Bill.[85] There are, for example, a lot of technical as well as substantive differences with the provisions on the new Irish Language Commissioner, including the duties of public authorities and questions of accountability.[86] The Alliance Party MP Stephen Farry and SDLP MPs by comparison spoke in favour, expressing hope that the Bill would mark a shift away from such 'weaponisation' and 'politicisation' of language.[87] However, there remain questions about whether the 2022 Act goes far enough in relation to the Irish language,[88] with concerns also raised about the extent to which the views of Ulster Scots have been taken on board.[89] There are also concerns about the possibility of the qualification of the national and cultural principles relating to 'sensitivities' in section 1 of the Identity and Language (Northern Ireland) Act being used to deny aspects of culture, or being 'weaponised'.[90] This illustrates the continued complexity and ongoing contestation on issues coming within the ambit of the FCNM, over a quarter of a century after the signing of the Good Friday Agreement and the coming into force of the FCNM.

7. Conclusion

This chapter has examined the shift in perceptions of the FCNM over the last three decades in the context of the Northern Ireland peace process. It provided a clear illustration of how the idea of minority rights as human rights remains

[83] *cf* duty in relation to Irish language to have regard to best practice standards developed (Northern Ireland Act 1998, new s 78O).

[84] Eg, Debate in House of Commons during second reading stage on 12 October 2022, HC Deb 22 June 2022, vol 717, cols 158, 160, 162–163, 171, 173, 189–191, 194 (Jim Shannon, Sammy Wilson, Jeffrey Donaldson, Richard Thomson, Carla Lockhart, Paul Givan).

[85] HC Deb 12 October 2022, vol 720, col 276.

[86] *cf* detail of Northern Ireland Act 1998, ss 2–3, and new ss 78J–78Q and 78R–78U.

[87] Eg, HC Deb 12 October 2022, vol 720, cols 178, 182–184, 372 (Claire Hanna, Stephen Farry, Colum Eastwood).

[88] Eg, HL Deb 7 June 2022, vol 823, col 1100 (Baroness Suttie).

[89] ibid. see also HL Deb 7 June 2022, vol 823, col 117 (Baroness Harris of Richmond).

[90] ibid.

subject to ongoing politicisation and contestation by focusing on the process of particularisation. This is illustrated through consideration of the significance of the recent recognition of Ulster Scots as a national minority under the FCNM as well as recent legislative developments. Since the GFA, most concessions made to Ulster Scots have been in the context of greater protection being either argued for, or granted to, the Irish language, creating the impression of winners and losers and reinforcing a scarcity and 'diminishing majority' mentality. This chapter has, however, illustrated the power of minority rights to continue to evolve through particularisation, as well as the need for caution against over-simplification and conflation of issues and identities in the process. The establishment of three new institutions focused on identity, cultural expression, language, arts and literature more than 25 years after the GFA provides the opportunity for the implementation of a broader interests-based approach that moves beyond the traditional majority/minority paradigm and focuses more on the role of public authorities and their accountability. No recommendations of either the Committee of Experts under the Languages Charter or the ACFC or even of the UK and Irish governments are going to make that happen. Rather, the responsibility now clearly lies with the Northern Ireland Assembly and Executive as well as the relevant officer-holders to take this forward. Perhaps that is the main lesson that can be learnt from this contribution on minority rights as human rights: that human rights as currently understood and applied can only ever provide a set of principles to guide political action, rather than providing concrete answers to complex problems and ever-evolving demographics in very specific historical and geopolitical contexts.

4

25 Years of Implementation of the European Charter for Regional or Minority Languages

VESNA CRNIĆ-GROTIĆ[1]

1. Introduction

The European Charter for Regional or Minority Languages, established by the Council of Europe in 1992, stands as a vital treaty aimed at safeguarding and promoting the linguistic diversity of Europe. It came into force in 1998. Celebrating its 25th anniversary in 2023, the Charter has become a cornerstone of the broader Minority Rights Regime in Europe. The document is an essential framework for the protection of languages traditionally used by national minorities, as well as for fostering intercultural understanding and multilingualism across Europe. Despite its successes in raising awareness and supporting linguistic communities, challenges remain in its implementation, particularly due to the flexibility granted to States Parties and to changing societal and political landscapes. This chapter aims to review the Charter's progress, to evaluate its effectiveness in protecting minority languages, and to explore areas where improvements are still needed.

2. Novel Approach by the Charter

The European Charter for Regional or Minority Languages (hereafter: the Charter) has 25 States Parties today among the 46 Member States of the Council of Europe.[2] The last ratification was made in 2010 by Bosnia and Herzegovina and the last signature was made by Portugal in 2021. It reflects a certain reluctance among

[1] University of Rijeka, Faculty of Law, Committee of Experts, European Charter for Regional or Minority Languages ORCID ID: www.orcid.org/0000-0002-8497-9599.

[2] All information can be found at the official website: www.coe.int/en/web/european-charter-regional-or-minority-languages/home. Access to the Comex case law is via the HUDOC database at hudoc.ecrml.coe.int/.

Member States to fully commit to respecting and promoting regional or minority languages under the Charter, particularly when compared to its 'sister treaty', the Framework Convention for the Protection of National Minorities (FCNM).[3]

The idea behind the Charter was to provide protection and promotion of regional or minority languages, stressing the value of interculturalism and multilingualism without, however, prejudice to the use of the official languages and the need to learn them (Preamble). However, there are several important novelties in this treaty. The protection is based on the concept of 'cultural heritage' and not on the human rights protection or the protection of the members of minorities. Woehrling, as one of the drafters of the Charter, claims that the Charter 'aims to safeguard language forms which are considered to have cultural value in themselves'.[4] Another significant novelty consists of the so-called *menu-system*, which allows States Parties to 'pick and choose' particular undertakings of the Charter for selected regional or minority languages. This approach makes it rather difficult for the States Parties to compare each other's performance, which can be an important tool, especially for the neighbouring or kin-States.

The Charter's protection and promotion of regional or minority languages covers various fields of public life (education, judicial and administrative authorities, media, culture, economic and social life and transfrontier co-operation) including the revitalisation of endangered languages. The languages protected are defined in Article 1 as the languages 'traditionally used within a given territory of a State by nationals of that State who form a group numerically smaller than the rest of the State's population' and that are 'different from the official language(s) of that State'. The emphasis is on the traditional use and on the territory where such languages are used, although the Charter also recognises non-territorial languages, such as Romani or Yiddish in some countries. Dialects of the official language(s) and migrant languages are excluded.[5] States can opt to include their less widely used official language(s), as was done, for example, by Finland with respect to Swedish, or by Switzerland with respect to Romansh and Italian in the Canton of Ticino. Regional languages are not affiliated to any particular minority group but are spoken by populations of a certain part of the State territory, such as Kashub in Poland or Low German in Germany.

One of the key elements in the definition of regional or minority languages is the 'territory in which the regional or minority language is used'. According to the Charter, it means 'the geographical area in which the said language is the mode of

[3] The FCNM has 38 States Parties and protects minority languages as part of the minority protection measures, www.coe.int/en/web/minorities/home.

[4] Jean-Marie Woehrling, The European Charter for Regional or Minority Languages: A Critical Commentary (Council of Europe Publishing 2005) 19–21.

[5] In its monitoring, the Committee of Experts was approached by representatives of the speakers of Silesian in Poland, Ruthenian in Ukraine and Scanian (Skånska) from Sweden, spoken in the province of (Scania) Skåne. Recently, the Committee of Experts was approached by representatives of Elfdalien. The official view was that these are dialects of the official languages. The Committee of Experts asked the authorities to enter into a dialogue with their speakers. Eighth evaluation report on Sweden, Council of Europe, CM(2022)16, paras 35–38.

expression of a number of people justifying the adoption of the various protective and promotional measures provided for in this Charter'. Many States have struggled with determining such territories.

Some States with traditional linguistic policies, such as the United Kingdom, often follow broader administrative boundaries, such as those of Wales or Scotland. In Scandinavian countries, there are traditional administrative units that deal with Sami.[6] Many countries tend to limit their obligations to smaller administrative units, often municipalities, by imposing percentage thresholds. For example, Poland requires that 20 per cent of the population of the relevant municipality belongs to a minority, while Slovakia recently lowered its threshold from 20 per cent to 15 per cent, verified by two rounds of census data. Ukraine had a 50 per cent threshold,[7] as did Croatia, which later reduced it to one-third.

These arbitrary thresholds present several problems. In larger administrative units, even small percentages can conceal significant linguistic communities. Moreover, even a small percentage might represent the highest concentration of speakers of that particular language. In some States, certain languages do not meet the threshold at all, rendering ratification under Part III of the Charter meaningless.[8] Lastly, tying language protection to census results makes it volatile and uncertain, with each new census potentially altering the level of protection.[9] The Committee of Experts has, therefore, been reluctant to agree with the thresholds and percentages. The Committee of Ministers supported this view in its recommendations.[10]

The Charter allows reservations to Article 7.5 with respect to non-territorial languages. So far, only Croatia has used this opportunity thus excluding, for example, Romani Chib from the protection of the Charter.[11] According to the Vienna

[6] In Finland, the area is called Sami Homeland. The Act of National Minorities and Minority Languages in Sweden defines administrative areas where municipalities have specific obligations vis-à-vis persons speaking Finnish, Meänkieli and Sami. These administrative areas cover 84 municipalities and 15 county councils.

[7] Council of Europe, *Application of the Charter in Ukraine: Initial Monitoring Cycle* ECRML (2010) 6. In the 2017 monitoring round the threshold was lowered to 10% with the plans to raise it to 30%. The aggression by the Russian Federation in 2022 interfered with regular monitoring of the application of the Charter.

[8] In a number of States Parties, some regional or minority languages do not reach the threshold anywhere. For example, Croatia ratified for the use minority languages at the level of counties (regional authorities) but no minority reaches one third of the population in any of the 21 counties. There is, however, the possibility to introduce a language in the official use voluntarily. This possibility was used only by the Istrian County for Italian.

[9] In the Croatian town of Vukovar, the Serbian minority's population dropped below one third, to 29.73%, in the 2021 census, prompting local authorities to abolish services in Serbian and the use of the Cyrillic script.

[10] See, eg, Council of Europe, *Recommendation to Romania* CM/RecChL(2023)7; *Recommendation to Poland* CM/RecChL(2023)6; *Recommendation to Croatia* CM/RecChL(2020)7; *Recommendation to Slovakia* CM/RecChL(2019)5.

[11] Roma in Croatia also use Boyash Romanian that the Committee of Experts considered to be a territorial language. Council of Europe, Committee of Experts, *Fifth Evaluation Report on Croatia* (2014) para 14. In its ratification instrument of 19 September 2005, Ukraine also excluded paragraph 5 of Article 7 of Part II but it is unclear whether it is still the case.

Convention on the Law of Treaties, if the reservation is allowed by the treaty no adoption is necessary.[12] Nevertheless, the Committee of Experts has been attempting to negotiate its withdrawal in order to ensure protection of Romani Chib in Croatia.[13]

3. Part II of the Charter

Part II of the Charter concerns objectives and principles and not precise implementing rules. The States Parties are expected to respect these basic undertakings and to build the necessary framework for the preservation of regional or minority languages.

It has been the view of the Committee of Experts, regardless of the ratification instrument, that Part II applies to all regional or minority languages corresponding to the definition in Article 1. Some States interpreted the Charter as providing protection only to languages with some co-official status. In Spain, for example, alongside languages that are co-official or officially recognised in several Autonomous Communities, protection should also extend to minority languages that lack such recognition. Thus, Asturian in the Principality of Asturias does not have a co-official status but is recognised as a cultural wealth and is covered by Part II, unlike Darija in the Autonomous City of Ceuta or Extremaduran in the Autonomous Community of Extremadura that have no protected status under the Spanish legislation.[14] The view of the Committee of Experts is that such regional or minority languages should be protected by (at least) Part II of the Charter.

One of the basic undertakings with respect to minority languages is to recognise them 'as an expression of cultural wealth', however, such recognition must not be confused with recognition of a language as an official language.[15] States should further respect the geographical area of each regional or minority language and should avoid designing administrative units that render the use of the regional or minority languages more difficult. In some cases, the Committee of Experts has been concerned about the potential impact of merging administrative units on minority languages. When such mergers take place, smaller linguistic communities may become part of larger administrative units in which they represent a reduced proportion of the population. This change can lead to diminished access to services, education, and public life in these languages. The Committee of Experts

[12] Vienna Convention on the Law of Treaties (adopted 23 May 1969, entered into force 27 January 1980) 1155 UNTS 331, art 20(1).

[13] Council of Europe, Committee of Experts, *Seventh Evaluation Report on Croatia* (2024).

[14] Even the languages that have the official status in some Autonomous Communities do not enjoy protection in others, like Catalan. It is official in the Autonomous Communities of Catalonia, Balearic Islands and in Valencia (as Valencian). However, it is also traditionally used in Aragon and Murcia (as Valencian) without a co-official status.

[15] Explanatory Report to the European Charter for Regional or Minority Languages (Strasbourg, 5 November 1992) para 58.

has sought assurances from States that such mergers would not undermine the use of regional or minority languages.[16]

Further objectives and principles that States Parties should follow in their policies include the resolute action measures for the protection and promotion of regional or minority languages. In the interpretation of the Committee of Experts: 'Most undertakings under the Charter, however, require more than simply allowing public and private bodies to make use of minority languages. They do not imply merely passive permission to use regional or minority languages, but require positive action from the authorities to promote the use of these languages'.[17] The Charter requires a proactive approach, especially when the language in question is in a precarious situation. Measures should include the encouragement of public and private use of the language and contacts with other groups speaking the same or similar language, including across borders. Resolute action should also include adequate earmarked funding. Finally, the most important aspects of language protection and promotion include education and university research. Unlike Article 8 of Part III of the Charter that contains important and concrete undertakings concerning education at various levels, from pre-school to university education, Article 7 brings a more general duty to provide 'forms and means for the teaching and study of regional or minority languages at all appropriate levels' and to promote their 'studies and research at universities or equivalent institutions'. As emphasised before, Part II and its Article 7 apply to all regional or minority languages and not only to those covered (also) by Part III. The implementation will depend on the size and the needs of the linguistic group and the language in question.

4. Part III of the Charter and the Menu-System

Part III of the Charter is applied to the languages specifically chosen by the State Party, and this list cannot be presumed or altered by any other actor. While States have the freedom to decide which languages will be covered under Part III, this decision should not be made arbitrarily. Typically, States consider factors such as tradition, historical efforts to protect and promote regional or minority languages, as well as the size and development of these languages.

[16] Mergers of municipalities were an issue in Switzerland (Council of Europe, Committee of Experts, *Eighth Evaluation Report on Switzerland* CM(2022)171, paras 48–51) where the Swiss authorities took adequate care that languages remain protected and promoted. Similar concerns were raised in Armenia (Council of Europe, Committee of Experts, *Fifth Evaluation Report on Armenia* CM(2020)156, para 13.); in Finland legislation was amended so that, in the context of a municipal merger, a bilingual municipality shall not become monolingual even if in the newly constituted municipality the number of minority language speakers is lower than the one prescribed by the Act (Council of Europe, Committee of Experts, *Fifth Evaluation Report on Finland* CM(2018)114, para 9).

[17] Council of Europe, Committee of Experts, *Third Evaluation Report on the Slovak Republic* CM(2012)144, para 38.

Moreover, Part III operates under a 'menu-system', in which States select specific undertakings that will apply to some or all of the chosen languages. Over the past 25 years, the Committee of Experts has emphasised that this selection should be tailored to the needs of each language, rather than applying the same level of protection uniformly to all languages. Undertakings, decided by States Parties, should also consider the needs and wishes of the speakers. Nevertheless, the selection should try to be realistic with a view to full and reasonable implementation since the monitoring carried out by the Committee of Experts will look for the promised results. Furthermore, the Charter provides for the upgrade of protection and the extension of the list of languages protected (Article 3.2).[18] There is no mechanism in the Charter that allows States Parties to downgrade their protection.

The menu system allows the possibility to choose among the undertakings of various stringencies. Altogether, the Charter offers 68 different undertakings in Articles 8 to 14 and the States Parties have to select at least 35 in accordance with Article 2.2, including at least three chosen from among articles dealing with education (Art. 8) and cultural activities (Art. 12); and one from articles covering judicial (Art. 9) and administrative authorities (Art. 10), media (Art. 11) and economic and social life (Art. 13).[19] If we take as an example primary education (Article 8.1.b), States can choose between offering education in the relevant regional or minority language, making a substantial part of education available in that language, providing the teaching of the relevant regional or minority languages within the regular education system, or to apply one of these measures to 'at least those pupils whose families so request and whose number is considered sufficient'. Identical provisions apply mutatis mutandis to different levels of education (pre-school, secondary education or technical and vocational education). It is important to emphasise that the use of regional or minority languages in education should be 'without prejudice to the teaching of the official language(s) of that State'. In its practice, the Committee of Experts has identified many problems concerning this provision from both ends – some regional or minority languages speakers want to limit learning of the official language to a minimum while some States want to limit the extent to which teaching of regional or minority languages is present in education.[20]

[18] For example, the United Kingdom extended Part III protection to Manx on the Isle of Man in 2020. Germany extended Part III protection to several minority languages in 2003 and 2021. Norway recognised Kven as a separate minority language in one of its periodical reports and extended the protection under Part III to South and Lule Sami in their declaration in 2021. On 1 July 2024, the Netherlands notified the Council of Europe of the extension of the protection of the Papiamento/Papiamentu language under Part II of the European Charter for Regional or Minority Languages to the European part of the Kingdom of the Netherlands. The language is traditionally spoken on islands in the Caribbean.

[19] There is no obligation to accept Article 14 on transfrontier exchanges.

[20] In the fifth monitoring round in Spain, the Committee of Experts established that the trilingual model (Castilian, Catalan, English) hampered the implementation of language immersion for bilingual education in Catalonia. In Galicia, the legislation did not allow more than 50% of the courses to be offered in Galician in non-university education. In 2015, the Supreme Court of Spain ruled that at least 25% of school subjects at all levels have to use Castilian as teaching language for those parents who ask for it to guarantee that Castilian is not excluded. Council of Europe, Committee of Experts, *Fifth Evaluation Report on Spain* CM(2019)125, para 10.

The Committee of Experts encourages the authorities to provide for continuity in education and not to request high thresholds for the creation of a class. There are additional measures in Article 8 that States can choose to improve the situation of the selected regional or minority languages in the field of education. They can choose to offer university education in such languages and to offer them as subjects of adult education, they can further ensure teaching of the history and the culture reflected by the regional or minority languages in the territory concerned to all students to promote multilingualism or interculturalism as some of the objectives of the Charter. The Committee of Experts also looks at the availability of teachers and teaching materials that are expected to implement the choices made.

This model of different stringencies of undertakings, but also an offer of additional options, is followed throughout the Charter and in all its fields, which results in very different obligations for the States Parties of the same treaty, a feature that is quite unique among treaties. There is no quid pro quo in this treaty, and it makes the comparison between States rather pointless.

5. Monitoring

The monitoring of implementation is carried out by the Committee of Experts, Committee of Ministers and the Secretary General of the Council of Europe that submits biennial reports to the Parliamentary Assembly.

According to Article 15, every State Party has to submit periodical reports on their policies and the measures taken to the Secretary General in one of the two official languages of the Council of Europe (English or French). The first report is due after one year and the subsequent reports should be submitted every three years. However, the Committee of Ministers changed that rule in the 2018 Reform, so the reporting period is now five years with an interim report after two and a half years.[21] Periodical reports are examined by the Committee of Experts, which consists of independent experts from the States Parties (Article 16). The Committee can also receive information from non-governmental organisations established in the State Party. It has been a regular practice to make on-the-spot visits and interview many stakeholders about the situation of regional or minority languages.[22] These visits have proven to be very useful in creating a more complete picture of the protection and promotion measures, and also of the general situation, in the monitored country.

[21] Council of Europe, Committee of Ministers, *Strengthening the Monitoring Mechanism of the European Charter for Regional or Minority Languages* CM(2018)165 (decision, effective 1 July 2019) https://search.coe.int/cm?i=09000016808f22ea.

[22] Committee of Experts of the European Charter for Regional or Minority Languages, *Rules of Procedure*(adopted 2019) art 17. Available at: https://rm.coe.int/minlang-2019-07-comex-rules-of-procedure-final/1680954878.

Based on all the information acquired, the Committee of Experts makes its evaluation report with observations and recommendations to the Party. In particular, this report contains proposals for the recommendations to the Committee of Ministers that this body may direct to the Party concerned. Based on the 2018 Reform, the evaluation report does not have to wait for the decision of the Committee of Ministers to be made public as was the case under the Charter. In the 'old' system, the Committee of Ministers was not allowed to make changes to the Committee of Experts' report, so it was really not justified to keep the reports caught in the Committee of Ministers for months or even years.[23] Under the new system, the State Party has two months to make comments on the evaluation report and to ask for a confidential dialogue if there are factual issues to be corrected. However, no changes to the conclusions or recommendations are possible. Comments made by the Parties will be published together with the Committee of Experts' report.[24]

The monitoring process ends with the adoption of the recommendations by the Committee of Ministers and their publication. In the following reports, the Party has to describe its reactions to these and other recommendations.

6. Evaluation of the Charter Success

The Charter remains the only treaty that specifically deals with the protection of regional or minority languages. Together with the FCNM these two Council of Europe treaties are the only international legally binding treaties on the protection of minorities and their languages.

Over the past 25 years, the Charter has helped to raise awareness about and visibility of regional or minority languages in its States Parties among the general population. However, it has also raised awareness among the speakers of some regional or minority languages about the value of their languages and the possibilities to preserve and promote them.

The application of the Charter brought about the wish by some to have their languages recognised and to provide them with the protection of the Charter. These include Kven in Norway, Meänkieli in Sweden, and Part II languages in Spain or in Croatia (Slovenian, Boyash Romanian, Istro-Romanian).[25] Some languages were given Part III protection, such as Manx on the Isle of Man. In some

[23] One of the extremes concerned the 2nd report on Serbia that was held in the Committee of Ministers for little over two years. Serbia submitted its report on 23.9.2010, the Committee of Experts adopted its evaluation report on 4.5.2011 and the Committee of Ministers adopted the recommendations on 11.6.2013.

[24] Council of Europe, Committee of Ministers, Decision: European Charter for Regional or Minority Languages – Strengthening the Monitoring Mechanism CM/Del/Dec(2018)1330/10.4e, art 1(f).

[25] Recently, the Committee of Experts was approached by representatives of Ume Sami and Pite Sami in Sweden, very small communities with separate and different Sami languages. The number of their speakers, however, seems to be under 100.

States, the administrative areas were extended to enable Part III protection (Lule Sami in Sweden). Many languages were reinforced and given a proper framework for their use in public life.

However, one can also talk about some shortcomings. First of all, after 25 years of implementation a kind of 'glass ceiling' has been reached, meaning that the Committee of Experts often has to repeat its recommendations through several rounds.[26] The Charter also suffers from the deterioration of human rights in Europe where minorities are targeted by extreme parts of societies. The public use of regional or minority languages becomes a visible target for such groups, especially in post-conflict societies.[27] Finally, the Charter may be considered outdated in the field of media. Traditional media face difficulties, electronic media as we know today did not exist in the 1990s, when the Charter was designed. New digital media is therefore not covered *expresis verbis*. To overcome such difficulties the Committee of Experts has a duty to accept interpretation that will make sense in the new circumstances.[28]

The Committee of Experts has by now developed a significant body of case law, which should be used to interpret the Charter and enhance understanding for the benefit of regional or minority languages in Europe.

7. Conclusion

Over the past 25 years, the European Charter for Regional or Minority Languages has played a pivotal role in enhancing the visibility and preservation of minority languages across its States Parties. While the Charter has successfully facilitated greater recognition and protection for various regional or minority languages, its impact has been somewhat limited by evolving political, social, and technological changes. The emergence of new forms of media and fluctuating human rights standards across Europe present fresh challenges to the Charter's relevance and efficacy. As Europe continues to grapple with these issues, it is crucial for the Charter to evolve in its interpretation and application, ensuring that regional and minority languages remain protected and cherished as vital components of Europe's cultural heritage.

[26] Spain ratified to provide that the courts, 'at the request of one of the parties, shall conduct proceedings in the regional or minority languages'. However, the Spanish national legislation (Organic Law on the Judiciary) requests that the other Party does not object to it. Spain has not amended the national legislation since the initial report.

[27] Vesna Crnić-Grotić, 'The Right to Display Place Names in Regional or Minority Languages within the Council of Europe Legal Framework' in Iryna Ulasiuk, Laurenţiu Hadîrcă and William Romans (eds), *Language Policy and Conflict Prevention* (Brill, 2018) 182–196.

[28] The Committee of Experts investigated this problem in: Committee of Experts of the European Charter for Regional or Minority Languages, *New Technologies, New Social Media and the European Charter for Regional or Minority Languages: Report for the Committee of Experts* (2019).

5

Human Rights, Including Rights of Persons Belonging to Minorities, in the External Action of the European Union

JULIA SZELIVANOV[1]

1. Introduction

In this chapter, I present an analytical overview of the policy framework of the external action of the European Union in the field of the protection of the rights of persons belonging to minorities, as part of the general human rights agenda and in the context of the EU's overall approach to human rights as individual rights. I will also give a brief description of other relevant policy tools. I will focus on the global area of action, ie, the multilateral/United Nations context, excluding EU's relations with regional organisations and the complex field of enlargement.

The respect, protection and fulfilment of human rights is a cornerstone of the external action of the European Union and is an essential element of building inclusive and pluralistic societies. Despite the fact that that EU has no competence concerning minorities, in its major policy documents it still refers to this important category of persons and calls on States to respect, protect and fulfil the rights of the persons belonging to minorities, including national, ethnic, religious and linguistic minorities, in accordance with applicable international norms and standards (as per the EU Action Plan on Human rights and Democracy 2020–27).[2] The EU promotes their right to participate effectively in cultural, religious, social, economic and public life. Similarly, the rights of persons belonging to minorities constitute an integral part of the anti-discrimination agenda.

In this article, the term 'minority rights' in the context of EU action, used sometimes for the sake of brevity, should be understood as 'rights of persons belonging

[1] The views expressed are purely those of the writer and may not in any circumstances be regarded as stating an official position of either the European External Action Service or the European Union.

[2] European External Action Service, *EU Action Plan on Human Rights and Democracy 2020–2024* (Council of the European Union, 18 November 2020), which has been extended until 2027.

to minorities, including national, ethnic, religious, and linguistic minorities', as defined in the EU Action Plan on Human Rights and Democracy 2020–27.

2. Human Rights Including Rights of Persons Belonging to Minorities: Legal Framework and Policy Documents of the External Action of the European Union

Upholding human rights has been a long-term cross-cutting issue of internal and external policies and programmes of the European Union. The Preamble of the Treaty of the European Union (TEU) stresses the universal value and the individual character 'of the inviolable and inalienable rights of the human person'. In its external human rights policy documents, the EU, referring to the spirit of the Vienna Declaration and Programme of Action (VDPA), reaffirms 'that human rights are universal, indivisible, interdependent and interrelated, be they civil, cultural, economic, political or social'.[3] In its 2012 Strategic Framework on Human Rights and Democracy and its Action Plan for implementation, the EU aims at enhancing coherence at policy level and states that it will 'promote human rights in all areas of its external action without exception'.[4]

The EU's approach to the rights of persons belonging to minorities is rooted in the general understanding of the individual nature of human rights. The legal systems of some Member States, however, accept the collective aspect of human rights in certain contexts (eg, rights of Indigenous Peoples) and others do not allow groups to be considered as right-holders.[5] The European Treaties do not provide a common legal framework or common standards of rights of persons belonging to national minorities; the European Commission therefore has no competence in questions like the definition or recognition of minorities, their aspirations for autonomy, or the use of regional or minority languages. With the common human rights legal framework provided by the European Convention on Human Rights (ECHR), the competence of establishing and implementing policies on minority issues remained principally the domain of decision of the Member States. Still, the large majority (23 out of 27) of EU Member States ratified the Council of Europe Framework Convention for the Protection of National Minorities (1995).[6]

[3] Council of the European Union, Council Conclusions on EU Priorities in UN Human Rights Fora (2023).

[4] EU Strategic Framework and Action Plan on Human Rights and Democracy (2012).

[5] See, UN Committee on Economic, Social and Cultural Rights, Consideration of Reports Submitted by States Parties under Articles 16 and 17 of the International Covenant on Economic, Social and Cultural Rights: Fourth Periodic Reports of States Parties Due in 2011: France E/C.12/FRA/4 (20 March 2014) www.digitallibrary.un.org/record/707425?v=pdf.

[6] Council of Europe, *Framework Convention for the Protection of National Minorities* CETS No 157. The following 23 EU Member States had ratified this convention: Austria, Bulgaria, Croatia, Cyprus, Czech Republic, Denmark, Estonia, Finland, Germany, Hungary, Ireland, Italy, Latvia, Lithuania, Malta, The Netherlands, Poland, Portugal, Romania, Slovakia, Slovenia, Spain, Sweden. The following 4 EU Member States had not ratified the convention: Belgium, France, Greece and Luxembourg.

According to scholars, the internal standards adopted by a number of Member States are rather low and aim only to preserve the status quo within States).[7] That would mean that this lowest common denominator is also reflected in the external action of the European Union. Nevertheless, the non-discrimination agenda provides a strong common ground for Member States, sufficient to be reflected in a number of EU external policy documents. Also, in the post-Lisbon period, the anti-discrimination or cultural approach to minorities has been gradually added to with a stronger human rights component.[8] In the same vein, the language on minorities has become stronger in the EU's external action policy documents.

3. Prohibition of Discrimination

The prohibition of discrimination is one of the main principles of international human rights law. Since the adoption of the Universal Declaration of Human Rights, this principle has been further emphasised in the human rights instruments that have been developed and incorporated into the national laws of the majority of countries around the world. Similarly, in its major human rights policy documents, the EU states its commitment to fighting all forms of discrimination within its borders and beyond.

In the European Union's founding treaties, in the Charter of Fundamental Rights of the European Union and in the European Convention on Human Rights, the prohibition of discrimination is a core principle, referred to in a number of articles. Article 10 of the Treaty on the Functioning of the European Union, while not singling out minorities, has a clear anti-discrimination reference: 'in defining and implementing its policies, the EU should aim to fight against discrimination' based on racial or ethnic origin, religion or belief, among others. Article 2 of the Treaty on European Union (TEU) refers to 'human dignity, freedom, democracy, equality, the rule of law and respect for human rights, including the rights of persons belonging to minorities' as the EU's founding values. According to Article 3 of the TEU, 'in its relations with the wider world, the Union, shall contribute to [...] the protection of human rights, [...] as well as to the strict observance and the development of international law, including respect for the principles of the United Nations Charter'. Article 21 of the Charter of Fundamental Rights of the European Union prohibits discrimination on a number of grounds, including language or membership of a national minority. Article 21 of the TEU sets the principles that guide the Union's external action, and those are the ones 'which have inspired its own creation, [...], and which it seeks to advance in the wider world', namely 'democracy, the rule of law, the universality and indivisibility of human rights and fundamental freedoms, respect for human dignity, equality and solidarity, and

[7] Tawhida Ahmed, 'The Treaty of Lisbon and Beyond: The Evolution of EU Minority Protection?' (2013) 38 European Law Review 30, 31.

[8] ibid.

respect for the principles of the United Nations Charter of 1945 and international law'. In addition to this, Article 22 states that the Union shall respect cultural, religious and linguistic diversity.

Combating all forms of discrimination was a priority in the 2012 EU Strategic Framework on Human Rights and Democracy, and in the subsequent EU Action Plans for Human Rights and Democracy (2015–19 and 2020–27). Under its human rights-based approach, adopted to guide EU's action in international partnerships, the EU also aims at 'empowering persons belonging to groups that may experience discrimination or inequalities to claim their human rights, such as [...] persons belonging to minority ethnic groups or other minorities and indigenous peoples', among others.[9]

The development of the EU's internal anti-discrimination framework provides a complex set of instruments to directly or indirectly promote the cause of persons belonging to minorities. A number of steps have been taken in different areas to uphold the rights of persons belonging to minorities at EU level, such as prohibiting speech which incite hatred based on racial or ethnic origin, among others,[10] or establishing a framework for combating direct and indirect discrimination on the grounds of racial or ethnic origin.[11] To respond to the needs of Roma people as the largest ethnic minority in the EU, present across most Member States and beyond, the European Commission has adopted the EU Roma strategic framework for equality, inclusion and participation 2020–2030[12] to promote equality, socioeconomic inclusion and meaningful participation, but also to put forward education and employment targets for the Roma. The right of persons belonging to minorities to speak their own languages remains a competence for individual Member States, with the understanding that the principle of non-discrimination must be respected. The Commission's Communication on a New Framework Strategy for Multilingualism aims at promoting linguistic diversity in the EU, including the use of minority or regional languages.[13] The *Charter for Regional or Minority Languages*[14] of the Council of Europe has been ratified by 16 out of the 27 EU Member States.

[9] European Commission, Commission Staff Working Document: Applying the Human Rights Based Approach to International Partnerships – An Updated Toolbox for Placing Rights-Holders at the Centre of EU's Neighbourhood, Development and International Cooperation SWD(2021)338 final, 7.

[10] Council Framework Decision 2008/913/JHA of 28 November 2008 on combating certain forms and expressions of racism and xenophobia by means of criminal law [2008] OJ L328/55 requires the criminalisation of public incitement to violence or hatred based on race, colour, religion, descent or national or ethnic origin.

[11] Council Directive 2000/43/EC of 29 June 2000 implementing the principle of equal treatment between persons irrespective of racial or ethnic origin [2000] OJ L180/22.

[12] European Commission, EU Roma Strategic Framework for Equality, Inclusion and Participation 2020–2030 (2020).

[13] European Commission, *Communication on a New Framework Strategy for Multilingualism* COM(2005)596 final, 22 November 2005.

[14] Council of Europe, *European Charter for Regional or Minority Languages* CETS No 148. The following 16 EU Member States had ratified this convention: Austria, Croatia, Cyprus, Czech Republic, Denmark, Finland, Germany, Hungary, Luxembourg, The Netherlands, Poland, Romania, Slovakia, Slovenia, Spain, Sweden.

The EU has been expanding its policies to counter discrimination against religious minorities. In 2015, the positions of European Commission Coordinators on combating antisemitism and on combating anti-Muslim hatred were created. In 2021, the EU presented its first comprehensive Strategy on Combating Antisemitism and Fostering Jewish Life. Recently, a Joint Communication of the European Parliament and the Council was adopted raising a voice against hatred.[15]

4. Global Context

Globally, the post-World War II period marked a new approach to human rights in general and to minority rights, in particular. On the one hand, the drafting and adoption of the Universal Declaration of Human Rights in 1948; on the other hand, the fresh memory of how the situation of minorities was used as a pretext for war. These largely determined the approach to minority rights and moved it towards the understanding that upholding all human rights would guarantee the protection and promotion of the rights of persons belonging to minorities[16] (ie, these rights, as being exercised in community, are still attributed to individuals as right-holders). The Declaration on the Rights of Persons Belonging to National or Ethnic, Religious and Linguistic Minorities (1992) that remains the only universal document – though a non-binding one – dedicated to specifically minority rights, has been adopted by the UN General Assembly without a vote, which is a sign of a rather consensual approach within the UN membership.[17] It also demonstrated that that the individual character of minority rights was accepted by the wide UN membership, while the State's obligation to protect the group as a whole is based on the fact that the group is formed by persons entitled with those rights.[18] This approach was adopted by the United Nations in the International Covenant on Civil and Political Rights[19] at the time, and in a way the same logic was followed by the European Union.

In this context, we cannot fail to mention the rights of Indigenous Peoples as the other category of 'non-dominant ethno-cultural groups' (though, in a number of countries they actually constitute a majority), whose protection requires a specific regime. Indigenous Peoples have become a standalone category of right-holders in the context of human rights, and not only due to several specificities compared

[15] European Commission and High Representative of the Union for Foreign Affairs and Security Policy, *Joint Communication to the European Parliament and the Council: No Place for Hatred, a Europe United Against the Hate* JOIN(2023)51 final.

[16] Will Kymlicka, *Multicultural Citizenship* (Oxford: Oxford University Press, 1995) 2-3.

[17] UN General Assembly, Declaration on the Rights of Persons Belonging to National or Ethnic, Religious and Linguistic Minorities (adopted 18 December 1992) UNGA Res 47/135.

[18] Dieter Kugelmann, 'The Protection of Minorities and Indigenous Peoples Respecting Cultural Diversity' (2007) 11(1) *Max Planck Yearbook of United Nations Law Online* 233, 244.

[19] International Covenant on Civil and Political Rights (adopted 16 December 1966, entered into force 23 March 1976) 999 UNTS 171, art 27.

to minorities (colonisation in the past, traditional lifestyle, etc.),[20] but also due to the recognition of the collective nature of their rights by relevant UN documents, the most important being the United Nations Declaration on the Rights of Indigenous Peoples (UNDRIP).[21] By now, a regular global discussion on the rights of Indigenous Peoples has become a well-working practice within the UN (including the annual Permanent Forum on Indigenous Issues or the Expert Mechanism on the Rights of Indigenous Peoples (EMRIP), the EU being a participant).

On the contrary, the UN's approach to minorities, has been less efficient. Fernand de Varennes, former Special Rapporteur on minority issues, recently highlighted the 'almost complete failure to mainstream minority rights at the United Nations'.[22] In the same vein, the UN Secretary-General stated that 'thirty years after the UN Declaration, the world is falling short. … We are not dealing with gaps – we are dealing with outright inaction and negligence in the protection of minority rights.'[23] Not only the absence of a legally binding universal document, but also because the lack of definition of minorities makes the realisation of the rights of persons belonging to minorities more challenging. The Working Group on Minorities, until the end of its mandate in 2006, did not manage to become a global venue for promoting the cause of minorities with the same level of success as witnessed in the case of fora discussing indigenous issues. Contrary to the UN minority declaration, UNDRIP was adopted by vote,[24] and a number of States supported it only due to its exceptional nature and a scope that was limited to a very specific category, one that certainly cannot serve as a reference for the minority context.[25] Having said this, the challenges faced by Indigenous Peoples were still part of the UN discussions on minority rights, and the accumulated experience on debates on minority issues became the starting point for a legal analysis of the rights of Indigenous Peoples.[26]

In the external action of the European Union, similar to the evolution of the international law, the development of policy documents on the rights of Indigenous Peoples has been more visible than in the case of the rights of minorities. *Council Conclusions on Indigenous Issues* were adopted in 2017, but

[20] Will Kymlicka 'The internationalization of minority rights' (2008) 6(1 *International Journal of Constitutional Law* 1, 5–13.

[21] UN General Assembly, *United Nations Declaration on the Rights of Indigenous Peoples* (adopted 13 September 2007) UNGA Res 61/295.

[22] United Nations, 'Highlighting a Resurgence of Human Rights Abuses Worldwide, Third Committee Calls on Nations to Urgently Abide by Existing Treaties to Eradicate Them, Rapporteur Underscores Almost Complete Failure to Mainstream Minority Rights at United Nations' (Press Release, GA/SHC/4356, 20 October 2022).

[23] United Nations Secretary-General, 'Commemorating 30 Years of Declaration, Secretary-General Says Countries Promoting Minorities' Rights, Participation in Society More Prosperous, Peaceful' (Press Release SG/SM/21474, 21 September 2022) www.press.un.org/en/2022/sgsm21474.doc.htm.

[24] United Nations, 'General Assembly Adopts Declaration on Rights of Indigenous Peoples; 'Major Step Forward' towards Human Rights for All, Says President' (Press Release GA/10612, 13 September 2007) www.press.un.org/en/2007/ga10612.doc.htm.

[25] Kymlicka (n 18), 18.

[26] Kugelmann (n 16), 233., 236.

no analogous policy document on minority rights has been developed so far. This is despite the fact that the rights of Indigenous Peoples are a priority for only a limited number of EU Member States (notably those Nordic countries that have Indigenous populations), while for others, this either falls out of the scope of their interest, or they would remain vigilant against any formulation that would contradict their own legal system (that might not recognise the collective aspirations of their own ethnic groups).[27] This is demonstrated in the practice of EU policy documents of referring to the rights of Indigenous Peoples only in the context of UNDRIP.[28] While minority and indigenous issues are clearly separated in the EU's documents, in the 2017 Council Conclusions, a reference to minorities is present: 'the European Union is founded on values of respect for human dignity, freedom, democracy, equality, the rule of law and respect for human rights, including the rights of persons belonging to minorities. Furthermore, the prohibition of discrimination on any grounds and the respect for cultural, religious and linguistic diversity are fundamental principles under the Charter of fundamental rights of the European Union'.[29]

5. External Action

Although the EU minority-related legal framework is often characterised as not being proactive enough[30] (in terms of operating mostly within the context of the freedom from discrimination instead of the domain of rights), in its external efforts, the EU has been gradually expanding its advocacy for the rights of national, ethnic, religious and linguistic minorities, in line with the UN declaration. This action is guided by a number of policy documents in which the EU undertakes to respect, protect and fulfil human rights, including the rights of persons belonging to national minorities. The formulations are bound by Member States' political priorities, while based on previously agreed common language of documents adopted on behalf of all 27 EU Member States. Those include Council Conclusions (some of which have been mentioned above); statements delivered on behalf of the EU in international human rights fora, for instance in the Human Rights Council (HRC) or the Third Committee of United Nations General Assembly; but also statements made by the High Representative of the Union for Foreign Affairs and Security Policy (HRVP) on behalf of the EU.

[27] Décision du Conseil Constitutionnel n° 99-412 DC du 15 juin 1999, para 6.

[28] See eg: European Union, Action Plan for Human Rights and Democracy 2020–2024 (2020) 12; Council of the European Union, Council Conclusions on EU Priorities in UN Human Rights Fora in 2023(2023) 23; Council of the European Union, Council Conclusions on EU Priorities in UN Human Rights Fora in 2024(2024) 33; European Union, 'EU Statement – UN General Assembly 3rd Committee: Rights of Indigenous Peoples' (9 October 2023).

[29] Council of the European Union, *Council Conclusions on Indigenous Peoples* (2017) art 1.

[30] Tawhida Ahmed (n 5), 32.

Complementing a discrimination-oriented approach with a rights-based vision is reflected in the most relevant external policy documents. The 2012 Strategic Framework on Human Rights and Democracy explicitly mentions the rights of persons belonging to minorities, though at this stage the reference was framed around freedom of religion or belief, fighting discrimination in its widest terms, and was mentioned together with indigenous peoples: 'the EU will promote freedom of religion or belief and to fight discrimination in all its forms through combating discrimination on grounds of race, ethnicity, age, gender or sexual orientation and advocating for the rights of children, persons belonging to minorities, indigenous peoples, refugees, migrants and persons with disabilities'.[31] Among foreseen actions, it proposes to pay a special attention to rights of persons belonging to minorities in bilateral dialogues with third countries, using best practice and existing EU instruments to support those efforts.[32] The 2015–19 Action Plan on Human Rights and Democracy added an element of not only supporting partner countries' efforts, but also 'relevant initiatives by the UN, as well as regional organisations aimed at protecting and promoting the rights of persons belonging to minorities and engage with their representatives'.[33]

In 2020, the Council adopted the third EU Action Plan on Human Rights and Democracy, which is the most recent overarching document in the field of human rights of the EU, setting out the its priorities for the 2020–27 period.[34] It is framed around five main areas of action (protecting and empowering individuals; building resilient, inclusive and democratic societies; promoting a global system for human rights and democracy; new technologies: harnessing opportunities and addressing challenges; delivering by working together). It calls on 'all states to respect, protect and fulfil the human rights of persons belonging to minorities, including national, ethnic, religious, and linguistic minorities in accordance with applicable international norms and standards'.[35] The same chapter further contains a reference to the rights of Indigenous Peoples, with the traditional clause referring to the UNDRIP. The Action Plan aims at promoting inclusive, participatory and representative decision-making for persons belonging to minorities and other persons in vulnerable situations.[36] The most recent Council Conclusions on EU priorities in UN Human Rights fora (2023, 2024) that guide EU action in the United Nations Human Rights Council and the UN General Assembly's Third Committee dedicated a whole standalone and rather

[31] Council of the European Union, Strategic Framework on Human Rights and Democracy (2012) 2.

[32] ibid. Outcome V/ 28.

[33] Council of the European Union, Action Plan on Human Rights and Democracy 2015–2019 (2015) 26.

[34] Originally adopted for the period of 2020–27, but extended till 2027, see Council of the European Union, Council Conclusions on the Alignment of the EU Action Plan on Human Rights and Democracy 2020–2024 with the Multiannual Financial Framework 2021–2027 (2024).

[35] Council of the European Union, *Action Plan on Human Rights and Democracy 2020–2027* (2020) para 1.1(f).

[36] ibid, para 2.2.f).

detailed paragraph to respecting, protecting and fulfilling the human rights of persons belonging to minorities as per the UN Declaration; their right to freedom of expression; opposition to hate speech; and a reference their effective participation not only in cultural, religious, social, economic or public life, but also in relevant international fora, in which the EU undertakes 'to continue to address issues of persons belonging to minorities where their representatives have no or limited access to speak themselves'.[37] Member States agree that defending the rights of persons belonging to minorities is critical. Individual Member States' initiatives often help to promote the cause of minorities in UN human rights fora (see the priorities of the 2024 Hungarian EU presidency,[38] Austria's priorities for its Human Rights Council membership 2019–21,[39] or the HRC resolution on the rights of persons belonging to national or ethnic, religious and linguistic minorities, led by Austria and Slovenia, together with Mexico).[40]

Though this chapter does not focus on regional aspects, it is useful to briefly mention the Council Conclusions on EU priorities for cooperation with the Council of Europe (CoE) 2023–24, that foresees continued cooperation between the EU and the CoE on freedom of religion or belief, 'including the rights of persons belonging to minorities to express their religion through specific cultural, traditional and religious practices or their right not hold religious beliefs, in line with the Charter of Fundamental Rights'.[41] Similarly, the Council Conclusions on EU priorities at the Organization for Security and Cooperation in Europe urge 'for the full implementation of all Human Dimension commitments by all participating States, in full compliance with human rights law, […] and the respect, protection and fulfilment of all human rights, including those of persons belonging to national minorities'.[42] The EU also supports the High Commissioner on National Minorities.

In addition to the Conclusions, the Council has adopted a series of thematic guidelines on human rights. They provide practical instructions for EU action with third countries, international organisations and civil society on a number of priority areas, including action against the death penalty; promoting the rights of the child; protecting human rights defenders; and others (thirteen in total). The EU Guidelines on Non-discrimination in External Action are intended to reinforce other EU human

[37] Council of the European Union, Council Conclusions on EU Priorities in UN Human Rights Fora in 2023(2023) para 22.

[38] Council of the European Union, *Programme of the Hungarian Presidency of the Council of the European Union in the Second Half of 2024* (2024) 9 www.hungarian-presidency.consilium.europa.eu/media/32nhoe0p/programme-and-priorities-of-the-hungarian-presidency.pdf.

[39] Austrian Federal Ministry for European and International Affairs, 'Austria in the UN Human Rights Council' (BMEIA, undated) www.bmeia.gv.at/en/austria-in-the-un-human-rights-council.

[40] United Nations Human Rights Council, *Resolutions adopted at the 55th session* (27 February–31 March 2024) www.hrcmeetings.ohchr.org/HRCSessions/RegularSessions/55/Pages/resolutions.aspx.

[41] Council of the European Union, Council Conclusions on EU Priorities for Cooperation with the Council of Europe (CoE) 2023–2024 (2023) para 24.

[42] Council of the European Union, conclusions on EU priorities at the OSCE (2023) para 13.

rights policy documents, enhancing the effectiveness and visibility of action of combatting discrimination (including on the basis of belonging to minority groups), as well as supporting the participation of civil society in multilateral forums where discrimination-related issues are discussed.[43] Similarly, Annex I of the EU Guidelines on Freedom of Expression Online and Offline, provides examples of actions that may violate or undermine the enjoyment of the right to freedom of opinion and expression, and which include blasphemy laws, persecuting persons belonging to religious or other minorities, or hate speech aimed at inciting hatred against a group or a member of a group.[44]

6. Other Elements of EU's Engagement

6.1. Multilateral Engagement

On multilateral fora, the EU has focused on several UN resolutions aimed at improving the situation of minorities worldwide, including those addressing persistent cases of violations of their rights. Thus, the EU (together with the Organization of Islamic Cooperation) has been leading the United Nations General Assembly (UNGA) Third Committee resolution on the situation of human rights of Rohingya Muslims and other minorities in Myanmar, which has been adopted consensually. Similarly, the HRC resolution on the situation of human rights in Afghanistan refers to the rights of persons belonging to minorities, including Hazaras. The EU regularly participates in interactive dialogues with the UN Special Rapporteur on minority issues in the sessions of the UNGA Third Committee and Human Rights Council, and draws attention to different aspects of the rights of persons belonging to minorities, including their role in conflict prevention and ensuring sustainable peace, but also to emerging threats such as those coming from artificial intelligence.[45] At the 2023 UN Forum on Minority Issues, which was focused on the challenges that persons belonging to minorities face in terms of social and economic participation, the EU addressed discrimination and marginalisation, advocating for strengthened checks and balances, institutional frameworks, and a bigger role for independent national human rights institutions and support for human rights organisations. The EU also underlined the importance of addressing practices that maintain inequality, especially for women and girls belonging to minorities.[46] As underlined in the 2022 Forum, the EU sees the support of independent National Human Rights Institutions

[43] European Union, EU Guidelines on Non-Discrimination in External Action (2010) 15, 30.

[44] European Union, EU Guidelines on Freedom of Expression Online and Offline (2014) 17.

[45] European Union, 'EU Statement – UN General Assembly 3rd Committee: Interactive Dialogue on Minority Issues' (26 October 2023). www.eeas.europa.eu/delegations/un-new-york/eu-statement-%E2%80%93-un-general-assembly-3rd-committee-interactive-dialogue-minority-issues_en.

[46] European Union, 'EU Statement – UN Human Rights Council, Forum on Minority Issues' (30 November–1 December 2023) hrcmeetings.ohchr.org/HRCMechanisms/ForumMinority/Pages/16th-session.aspx.

and of human rights defenders as an important tool in combating discrimination and marginalisation.[47]

6.2. Bilateral Engagement

Besides policy documents, a number of additional tools exist that help EU human rights action at the country level. The EU's *human rights and democracy country strategies* are based on EU human rights guidelines and other policy documents and were drafted with active engagement with civil society, to take account of the specificities of each country and provide tailor-made solutions. In the context of the *human rights dialogues* with third countries (currently over sixty), the rights of persons belonging to ethnic, religious and linguistic minorities are regularly mentioned (for example, the EU recalled the particularly vulnerable situation of persons belonging to religious, ethnic and linguistic minorities across China, including Uyghurs and Tibetans in China;[48] it pointed out that measures to 'protect religions' often violate the freedom of religion or belief of minorities in Indonesia;[49] and the rights of persons belonging to minorities and vulnerable groups were discussed with regards to India).[50] The EU's action also implies financial engagement in supporting the rights of persons belonging to minorities, for example, in 2023, in Namibia, Sri Lanka or Vietnam.[51] The challenges faced by Roma people continue to be an important element of the EU's action, to assist partner countries to meet the commitments of the 2020–2030 Strategic Framework. In 2023, the EU supported central and local public authorities and Roma civil society organisations in the Western Balkans and Türkiye, focusing in the fields of education, employment and the reintegration of returnees.[52] To mention enlargement countries briefly, a pre-accession conditionality mechanism that requires the development of strong democratic institutions, respecting rule of law and fundamental rights, including protection of minorities, has been established for those. In this context, the EU continued to support the alignment of Ukraine's legislative framework on the protection of persons belonging to minorities with international standards. In 2023, the 2022 Law on National

[47] European Union, 'HRC Forum on Minority Issues 2022 – EU Intervention – Item 4. Reform: Filling the Gaps in the Implementation of the Declaration' www.eeas.europa.eu/delegations/un-geneva/hrc-forum-minority-issues-2022-eu-intervention-item-4-reform-filling-gaps-implementation-declaration_en.

[48] European Union, 'China: 39th Human Rights Dialogue with the European Union Took Place in Chongqing' (Press Release, 17 June 2024) www.eeas.europa.eu/eeas/china-39th-human-rights-dialogue-european-union-took-place-chongqing_en.

[49] European Union, 'Indonesia: 10th Human Rights Dialogue with the European Union Takes Place in Brussels' (Press Release, 17 July 2024) www.eeas.europa.eu/eeas/indonesia-10th-human-rights-dialogue-european-union-takes-place-brussels_en.

[50] European Union, '10th EU-India Human Rights Dialogue' (Press Release, 15 July 2022) www.eeas.europa.eu/delegations/india/10th-eu-india-human-rights-dialogue_en.

[51] European Union, Annual Report on Human Rights and Democracy in the World 2023 123, 217, 223.

[52] ibid, 33.

Minorities (Communities) was amended in close consultation with representatives of national minorities, upon the recommendations of the Venice Commission.[53]

In terms of trade, all beneficiary countries of the General System of Preferences (GSP), have to abide by the principles of fifteen core conventions on human rights and labour rights. Via its GSP+ mechanism, the EU offers tariff reductions to vulnerable countries that have ratified and implemented relevant international human rights conventions.[54] Bilateral trade agreements and the various associations and cooperation agreements between the EU and non-EU countries or regional organisations include a key human rights clause that foresees limiting cooperation in case of grave violations of human rights. However, persistent discrimination on the basis of belonging to minority groups remains a problem in a number of GSP+ beneficiaries.[55]

7. Other Tools

In December 2020, the Council established a *global human rights sanctions regime* that allows the EU to target individuals, entities and bodies – including State and non-State actors – responsible for, or otherwise associated with, serious human rights violations and abuses worldwide. As of September 2024, the Council has imposed restrictive measures on a total of 117 individuals and 33 entities. Some of those individuals have also been listed for violations of rights of persons belonging to including individuals for violating the rights of the Crimean Tatar community.[56]

In addition to legal and policy framework, the EU has at its disposal *financing instruments* to promote human rights in third countries. The Neighbourhood, Development and International Cooperation Instrument (NDICI)– Global Europe, supports human rights and democracy in the world via its thematic human rights pillar, in addition to geographic pillars. Areas for cooperation for geographic programmes and areas of intervention for thematic programmes and global challenges focus on human rights, including rights of persons belonging to national minorities.[57] An important asset of this instrument is that the consent of the government of the given country is not required.

The EU Special Representative (EUSR) for Human Rights has a specific role to enhance the effectiveness and visibility of EU human rights action. His broad

[53] ibid, 34.

[54] European Commission, *Generalised Scheme of Preferences Plus (GSP+)* (Access2Markets summary, updated 2025) www.trade.ec.europa.eu/access-to-markets/en/content/generalised-scheme-preferences-plus-gsp.

[55] European Commission, Second Report on the Effects of GSP and the Special Incentive Arrangement for Sustainable Development and Good Governance (GSP+) (COM(2008) 252 final, 2008) 3.

[56] See, Official Journal of the European Union L 221I, 8 September 2023, Annex.

[57] Regulation (EU) 2021/947 of the European Parliament and of the Council of 9 June 2021 establishing the Neighbourhood, Development and International Cooperation Instrument – Global Europe, amending and repealing Decision No 466/2014/EU and repealing Regulation (EU) 2017/1601 and Council Regulation (EC, Euratom) No 480/2009, Annex II, paras 1(c), 2(f); Annex III, paras 1.1(a), 1.7(d).

mandate permits the Representative to raise their voice on the most diverse human rights issues, including on minority rights. Former EUSR, Eamon Gilmore, delivered a statement on behalf of the EU at the UN General Assembly High-Level Week on the occasion of the 30th anniversary of the UN Minority Rights Declaration in 2022, which drew attention to the violation of rights of Rohingya, Uyghurs, Yazidis and others.[58]

The European Parliament not only contributes to the development of the EU's human rights via its relevant resolutions, but also by the means of policy proposals, raising awareness about violations and supporting civil society and human rights defenders, as well as via country visits. The Parliament's annual resolution on human rights and democracy in the world and the European Union's policy on the matter takes stock of the results of the past year. The resolution of 28 February 2024, encouraged persons belonging to minorities to participate in electoral processes, and paid attention to the particular vulnerability of certain categories of persons, such as women, belonging to minorities.[59] The Subcommittee on Human Rights (DROI) of the European Parliament is responsible for the promotion of democratic values and human rights, including the rights of persons belonging to minorities in third countries, evaluating the implementation of relevant EU instruments and providing a venue for dialogue with civil society.

8. Conclusion

While the absence of a common legal framework for the protection and promotion of the rights of persons belonging to minorities within the EU is reflective of the highly diverse positions of Member States, the EU's external action both via its policy documents as well as its country-based activities, including in the context of enlargement, prove that the rights of persons belonging to national minorities remain high on the EU's agenda in terms of its external human rights engagement. This commitment has been renewed on a yearly basis via the Council Conclusions on EU priorities in UN human rights fora, expressed in EU statements and the action of EU in the field all over the world. In policy documents, EU Member States underline the rights aspect of the minority issue and go beyond the non-discrimination framework. The high variety of norms and practice of Member States makes it impossible to foresee any substantial change in developing common policy documents dedicated to minority rights; however, the existing political instruments work in favour of the promotion of those rights and provide an adequate basis for action in both in multilateral and bilateral settings.

[58] European Union, 'Statement by Eamon Gilmore, EU Special Representative for Human Rights, at the UN General Assembly High-Level Week – Minority Rights' (Press Statement, 21 September 2022) www.gilmore.ie/un-general-assembly-high-level-week-minority-rights/.

[59] European Parliament, Resolution of 28 February 2024 on Human Rights and Democracy in the World and the European Union's Policy on the Matter – Annual Report 2023 (28 February 2024).

PART III

Spectrum of Minority Rights Protection

6

'Battling' Nations and Minorities' Fundamental Educational Rights before the ECtHR: *Valiullina*'s Promises and Missed Opportunities

KRISTIN HENRARD

1. Introduction: Minorities, States and Fundamental Rights

With the emergence of nation states in the 19th century, a tense relationship developed between the nation states on the one hand and other ethnic groups, defined as national minorities, on the other.[1] For the nation state, the minorities' demands for the protection of their distinct identity generates political unrest as too much focus on the distinct identity of the minority is perceived to harm the project of nation building, and maybe even chip away at the State's territorial integrity, thus threatening States' much cherished sovereignty.[2] Nation states' unease about minorities, their claims and implications, manifests itself in a variety of ways: States at times deny the presence of minorities on their territory,[3] argue that there is no need for minority specific rights, or define the latter in a way that leaves them a lot of discretion (and thus also possibilities to read these rights down).[4]

[1] Linda S Bishai, 'Sovereignty and Minority Rights: Interrelations and Implications' (1998) 4(2) *Global Governance* 157.

[2] See also ibid 176; Franzisca Zanker, 'Integration as Conflict Prevention: Possibilities and Limitations in the Experience of the OSCE High Commissioner on National Minorities' (2010) 21(3) *Security and Human Rights* 220, 222.

[3] France is well known to emphasise the central importance of the right to equal treatment, which would imply that there are no minorities in France: Jeremie Gilbert and David Keane, 'Equality versus fraternity? Rethinking France and its minorities' (2016) 14 *International Journal of Constitutional Law* 883.

[4] Minority-specific rights instruments tend to include many conditional clauses and escape clauses, such as 'where such a request corresponds to a real need', 'the Parties shall endeavour to ensure', and 'as far as possible' See art 10, para 2 Framework Convention for the Protection of National Minorities (FCNM).

Relatedly, States tend to aim for an integrated and cohesive society and their idea of integration is often one that expects the minorities to 'fit in' and leave their distinctiveness behind.[5] Persons belonging to minorities envisage substantively equal and effective participation in all realms of society, without necessarily giving up their distinct identity. The latter's understanding of integration is one that does not go hand in hand with forced assimilation,[6] but rather sees integration as a two-way process, expecting both the minority and the majority members to make some adjustments, towards the greater good of an integrated society.[7]

States' sensitivity about minorities and their claims is obviously amplified in post-occupation contexts, where the persons claiming minority protection are part of the group that used to occupy the territory and adopted assimilationist policies, as seen in the case of ethnic Russians in the Baltic States.[8]

The relationship between persons belonging to minorities on the one hand and fundamental rights on the other, has shifted drastically over time. It has been argued elsewhere more extensively, that minorities, their concerns and protection needs actually triggered the emergence of fundamental rights, and continued to steer the development of fundamental rights until and including the League of Nations and its Minorities treaties.[9] After the second World War, the UN abandoned the focus on minority specific rights, and instead focused on human rights, as rights for every human being.[10] The latter were, by their nature, initially considered to be sufficient to address minorities' problems; this was supported by the idea that human rights supposedly constrain pure majority rule, and are thus counter majoritarian. Nevertheless, already early on the acknowledgement grew that minorities need special attention;[11] and also some special rights that are minority-specific.[12]

This can be understood in a broader framework: in addition to general human rights, certain groups have special protection needs that merit the development of additional, tailored, category-specific rights. While this understanding has resulted in the development of several conventions with rights specific to, for example racial

[5] Dora Kostakopoulou, 'The Anatomy of Civic Integration'(2010) 73(6) *Modern Law Review* 933, 945–47.

[6] See also art 5 FCNM.

[7] Inter alia Council of Europe, *Les Mesures et Indicateurs d'Intégration* (Council of Europe 1998) 11; Joseph H Fichter, *Sociology* (University of Chicago Press 1971) 229.

[8] The Baltic States encompass Latvia, Estonia and Lithuania.

[9] Kristin Henrard, *The Ambiguous Relationship between Religious Minorities and Fundamental (Minority) Rights* (Eleven Publishers International 2010).

[10] The Universal Declaration of Human Rights, proclaimed by the UN General Assembly on 10 December 1948 (GA Res 217 A (III), 10 December 1948), does not contain any minority-specific rights.

[11] As visible in the creation of the UN Sub Commission on the Prevention of Discrimination and the Protection of Minorities (1947), see inter alia John P. Humphrey, 'The United Nations Sub-Commission on the Prevention of Discrimination and the Protection of Minorities' (1968) *The American Journal of International Law* 869, 870.

[12] Article 27 was included in the *International Covenant on Civil and Political Rights* (adopted 16 December 1966, entered into force 23 March 1976) 999 UNTS 171.

groups,[13] women[14] and children,[15] for persons belonging to minorities the norm development at the UN level halted in 1992 with a not legally binding Declaration.[16]

The violent ethnic conflicts in the early 1990s in Europe informed a vision of minority specific rights and the related protection of minorities as key for the maintenance of peace and security, and for the survival of the existing States.[17] This in turn facilitated the 1995 adoption of the Council of Europe Framework Convention for the Protection of National Minorities (FCNM). The FCNM not only emphasised that minority rights are part and parcel of the human rights paradigm,[18] it also corroborated as core tenets of minority protection (substantive) equality (article 4), respect for the distinct minority identity (article 5) and inclusion/integration (article 6). The FCNM furthermore confirmed the complementary nature of general human rights and minority specific rights, as it includes both typical general rights such as the freedom of expression, association and the freedom of religion,[19] and typical minority specific rights such as those regarding language use.[20] At the same time, the formulation of the minority specific rights, and particularly the many vague clauses and conditionalities,[21] confirm States' unease about granting such rights and provide them ample opportunities to read down what is expected from them. As the rights in the FCNM do not have a complaints procedure, it remains useful and important to use the route of general human rights, while arguing for an interpretation of these rights that is inspired by minority specific rights and their core tenets.[22] In Europe, complaints in terms of general human rights before the European Court of Human Rights result in judgments that are legally binding on the State against which they are pronounced. The Court has actually acknowledged that the FCNM represents a European consensus on the need to protect minorities' security, identity and lifestyle.[23]

As the title reveals, this chapter focuses on fundamental rights concerning education in the jurisprudence of the ECtHR. Education is of crucial importance both for the State at large and for minorities, because of the double function of education. Education on the one hand has a dominant qualification function in

[13] Convention on the Elimination of All Forms of Racial Discrimination (New York, 7 March 1966).

[14] Convention on the Elimination of All Forms of Discrimination against Women (New York, 18 December 1979).

[15] Convention on the Rights of the Child (New York, 20 November 1989).

[16] The UN General Assembly adopted the Declaration on the Rights of Persons Belonging to National or Ethnic, Religious and Linguistic Minorities (GA Res 47/135, 18 December 1992).

[17] At first agreement was reached at the OSCE, as is visible in the *Document of the Copenhagen Meeting of the Conference on the Human Dimension of the CSCE* (Organization for Security and Co-operation in Europe, 29 June 1990) paras 30–40.

[18] Art 1 FCNM.

[19] ibid, arts 7–9.

[20] ibid, arts 10, 11, 14.

[21] See the example in n 4.

[22] Important arguments to steer that can be drawn from the foundational values of minorities' fundamental rights as captured in FCNM, arts 4, 5, 6, and 15, namely substantive equality, identity and integration.

[23] *Chapman v UK* A no 27238/95 (ECtHR, 18 January 2001) para 93.

that it prepares students to obtain the necessary qualifications to be able to fully participate in society. On the other hand, education has a socialisation function, which is important not only for socialisation in the national society through the teaching of its values and mores but also for learning about minority identities, their languages and traditions.[24]

When considering the various ways in which education is important towards the building of a nation, it comes as no surprise that it is one of the key means for oppressors to try to assimilate groups through the imposition of their language through education (as medium of instruction). In the post-occupation phase, education is particularly sensitive for the re-established State, when the previous oppressor claims minority language rights in education, particularly the right to be educated in their (now minority) language. It is in any event striking that the few cases before the ECtHR on language as medium of instruction all concern 'battling nations', several of which have an element of actual or past occupation. The ECtHR reasoning in the recent case(s) on language in education regarding the Russian minority in Latvia invite further reflection on the status of minority rights as human rights, and the way in which minority specific rights (can/could/should) influence the interpretation of general human rights (through systematic or contextual interpretation).[25]

The chapter starts with three sections that set the scene for the analysis of the ECtHR case law regarding language rights in education. A first section discusses the basic principles regarding the interpretation of general human rights and what issues are considered more closely when analysing judgments of the ECtHR. A second section lays out general developments in the ECtHR jurisprudence concerning minorities, and the extent to which this contributes to minorities' identity and substantive equality. The third section elaborates on the different ways in which education matters to both the State (from an integration perspective) and minorities (from a substantive equality, identity and integration perspective). It furthermore discusses the various reasons why education in one's mother tongue is important (for minorities' substantive equality, identity and integration). The fourth section then proceeds with the analysis of the case law of the ECtHR regarding language in education. While the Court seemed to move towards an accommodation of parents' wishes (in favour of the protection and promotion of the minority identity) in this respect, particularly in the *Catan* case, the more recent judgments against Latvia paint a more ambiguous picture. The fifth section zooms in on these judgments, with special attention on the first judgment, *Valiullina*,[26] the principles of which are followed and relied upon in the

[24] See text to n 65-67 on the social and cultural integration dimension.

[25] See art 31 Vienna Convention on the Law of Treaties (adopted 23 May 1969, entered into force 27 January 1980) 1155 UNTS 331, paras 1–2. The context that needs to be considered when interpreting a particular human rights convention; can be another human rights convention or other instruments reflecting customary international law. See also Odile Ammann, *Domestic Courts and the Interpretation of International Law* (Martinus Nijhoff 2020), more particularly the chapter 'Interpretative Methods of International Law: What are they and Why use Them' 204–205.

[26] *Valiullina et al v Latvia*, A no 56925/19 (ECtHR, 14 September 2023).

later cases. Having discussed *Valiullina*'s promises and missed opportunities, the Chapter concludes by urging the ECtHR to refine its *Catan* jurisprudence and to enhance its proportionality analysis while incorporating minority-specific rights through systematic interpretation.

2. General Human Rights, and Minorities and the Interpretation by International Courts

In terms of setting the scene, this section starts with a succinct discussion of the general characteristics of fundamental rights and the concomitant State obligations. A reflection on the characteristics of minorities and of the overarching goals of minority protection then allows for the identification of guiding principles for the interpretation of fundamental rights of persons belonging to minorities.

Human rights are called fundamental rights because they concern rights that one is entitled to simply because one is a human being and one needs these rights to have a dignified life.[27] This fundamental character of rights has implications for the way these rights should be interpreted, in the sense that the scope of application of fundamental rights should be interpreted broadly or generously.[28] Notwithstanding their fundamental nature, most fundamental rights are not absolute and thus allow States under certain conditions to impose limitations on their enjoyment to reach certain (other) public interests or to protect the rights of others.[29] Since such limitations can be conceived as exceptions (to the rule), a restrictive interpretation is called for. The limitation clauses tend to require that limitations need to serve one of a number of legitimate aims (representing public interests) and need to be proportionate to that aim.[30] While these legitimate aims tend to concern general concepts with a potential broad scope,[31] a limitation to fundamental rights presupposes concrete and serious reasons.[32] The criterion that

[27] See also Jerome J. Shestack, 'The Philosophical Foundations of Human Rights' (1998) 20 *Human Rights Quarterly* 205–215.

[28] See also Alastair Mowbray, 'Between the Will of the Contracting Parties and the Needs of Today: Extending the Scope of Convention Rights and Freedoms beyond what could have been foreseen by the drafters of the ECHR' in Eva Brems and Janneke Gerards (eds), *Shaping Rights in the ECHR: The Role of the European Court of Human Rights in Determining the Scope of Human Rights* (Cambridge University Press, 2014) 69–70.

[29] The ECHR and ICCPR have similar limitation clauses; cf arts 8-11 ECHR and arts 17–19, 21–22 ICCPR. See also the provisions concerning civil and political rights in the African Charter on Human and Peoples' Rights and the American Convention on Human Rights.

[30] The exhaustive list of legitimate aims is not identical between the respective fundamental rights. Article 9 of the ECHR, regarding freedom of religion, has fewer legitimate aims than Article 8's right to respect for private, family life and home.

[31] Typical examples are national security or public safety, public order (ordre public), the protection of public health or morals or the protection of the rights and freedoms of others.

[32] Inter alia Sébastien Van Drooghenbroeck and Cecilia Rizcallah, 'The ECHR and the Essence of Fundamental Rights: Searching for Sugar in Hot Milk?' (2019) 20 *German Law Journal* 904.

tends to trigger the most elaborate analysis, contestation and differences of opinion is the proportionality requirement, which invites a balancing of the respective interests, taking into account all relevant circumstances.[33] Nevertheless, also here it can be argued that the rule that limitations need to be interpreted narrowly calls for the grant of a narrow discretion (margin of appreciation) and thus a high level of scrutiny by the international Court.

The concern for the effective enjoyment of fundamental rights has entailed the identification of an expanding range of positive State obligations, also in relation to civil and political rights.[34] The proportionality principle has a significant role to play in delineating these positive State obligations: what can reasonably be expected from the State in the given circumstances? The nature of positive obligations also implies that States never have absolute positive obligations, even when it concerns absolute rights. Even more so than in the case of negative State obligations, there are often many ways to satisfy one's positive State obligations. Put differently, differences of opinion can also emerge here about the question as to whether the State has done 'enough'. Given the distinct nature of positive State obligations, States tend to obtain a broader margin of appreciation.[35] Nevertheless, the overarching goal of an effective protection of fundamental rights calls for sufficient supervision (level of scrutiny) by international courts.

When evaluating (international) courts' interpretation of the fundamental rights of persons belonging to minorities, it is important to keep in mind the typical characteristics of minorities. There may not be a generally accepted (let alone a legal) definition of 'minorities',[36] but this concept refers to groups that have a distinct ethnic, religious and or linguistic identity, that they wish to hold on to, notwithstanding their non-dominant and numerical minority position.[37] An effective protection of the fundamental rights of such groups requires, on the one hand, a sufficient protection against invidious discrimination, and on the other, the grant of special measures aimed at the protection of their distinct identity.

[33] See inter alia Jonas Christoffersen, *Fair Balance: Proportionality, Subsidiarity and Primarity in the European Convention On Human Rights* (Martinus Nijhoff Publishers, 2009) 227ff.

[34] Whereas social and economic rights typically generate positive State obligations, civil and political rights were originally considered mainly to trigger negative State obligations. The increasing focus on the need for human rights to be effective has resulted in the identification of ever more detailed and demanding positive State obligations, also in relation to civil and political rights. Regarding the ECHR, see inter alia Vladislava Stoyanova, 'Framing Positive Obligations under the ECHR law: Mediating between the Abstract and the Concrete' (2023) 23 *Human Rights Law Review* 1–34.

[35] Inter alia Vladislava Stoyanova, *Positive Obligations under the ECHR within and beyond boundaries* (Oxford University Press, 2023). See also Jean-François Akandji-Kombe, *Positive obligations under the European Convention on Human Rights: A guide to the implementation of the European Convention on Human Rights* (Council of Europe, 2007).

[36] This is most strikingly visible in the absence of definition of the concept minority in the Framework Convention for the Protection of National Minorities (see Art. 3 FCNM).

[37] See inter alia the chapter dedicated to this definitional question in Kristin Henrard, *The Interrelation of General Human Rights, Minority Rights and the Right to Self Determination for an Adequate Minority Protection* (Martinus Nijhoff, 2001).

The overarching concerns and goals of minorities (and the core tenets of minority protection) are thus (substantive) *equality* and respect for the distinct *identity*.[38] In view of States' concerns and fears that minorities' would not (want to) integrate, and thus threaten their goal of an integrated society, it is important to confirm[39] that minorities are not against integration, quite the contrary. In so far as integration concerns full and (substantively) equal participation in society and all its institutions, *integration* is one of the overarching goals of minorities as well.[40] However, their vision of integration is one that does not require forced assimilation but respects their individual identities.[41] Once again, it is obvious how crucially important interpretation is, whether it concerns the interpretation of concepts or of legal rules.

The preceding paragraphs imply that at least two important points matter to ensure that fundamental rights provide an adequate protection for persons belonging to minorities. First, the way human rights are interpreted should be in line with their counter majoritarian nature. The ECtHR often emphasises that 'democracy does not simply mean that the views of a majority must always prevail: a balance must be achieved which ensures the fair treatment of people from minorities and avoids any abuse of a dominant position'.[42] In this respect it has been noted that the European Convention on Human Rights (ECHR) embraces a notion of inclusive democracy,[43] implying that minorities should not be forcibly assimilated. Secondly, as general rights are not explicitly aligned to the specific protection needs of minorities, the principle of systematic or holistic interpretation invites the ECtHR to be influenced and guided by the minority specific rights of the FCNM.[44] The latter would imply an interpretation of the ECHR that is more geared towards minorities' substantive equality and right to respect for the minority identity. Such interpretation also favours an interpretation of the scope of application of fundamental rights that embraces identity dimensions of these rights.

When evaluating limitations to fundamental rights of minorities, it is especially important for international courts not to leave too much discretion to States, and to adopt a sufficiently high level of scrutiny, going hand in hand with sufficient

[38] This is nicely reflected in the core articles of the FCNM, more particularly article 4 on the right to equal treatment (clearly opening to substantive equality), article 5 on the right to identity and article 6 which de facto seems to concern several facets of an integrated society, by State duties to promote mutual respect, understanding and cooperation among all persons living in the territory. See also the Permanent Court of International Justice's (PCIJ's) reasoning in *Minority Schools in Albania, Advisory Opinion*, PCIJ Series A/B no 64 (PCIJ, 6 April 1935).

[39] See the introduction.

[40] For a detailed analysis of the visions of integration in the FCNM, see Kristin Henrard, 'Tracing Visions on Integration and/of Minorities: An Analysis of the Supervisory Practice of the FCNM' (2011) *International Community Law Review* 333.

[41] See text to n 63-67 the discussion on the concept of integration.

[42] *SAS v France* A no 43835/11 (ECtHR, 1 July 2014) para 128.

[43] See also Robert Spano, 'Inclusive Democracy and the ECHR' [2023] *E.H.R.L.R.* 112.

[44] The ECtHR's Guide to Protocol No 1, Article 2 specifies in para 10 that 'Article 2 of Protocol No 1 must be interpreted in harmony with other rules of international law', so the principle of systematic interpretation is accepted.

guidance by the court. However, international courts' awareness of States' sensitivity about minorities and their claims, particularly when these are perceived as contrary to States' nation building ambitions, makes several courts prefer to take a step back, and to grant States a broad margin of appreciation (or more radically, to limit the scope of application of particular fundamental rights). Put differently, international courts' concern that high levels of scrutiny may jeopardise their political legitimacy in the eyes of the States, at times may induce them to lower their scrutiny and sacrifice their supervisory role.

3. Developments in the Interpretation of Human Rights by the ECtHR

Before zooming in on educational human rights and the ECtHR jurisprudence in this respect, the overall approach of the Court in relation to minorities and their fundamental rights claims is painted in broad strokes. Initially, the ECtHR was not open towards teleological interpretations that embraced the protection of the distinct minority identity, and particularly for language rights it adopted an a contrario reasoning. The Court noted that the Convention only has explicit language rights in the criminal law sphere (arrest and criminal court cases in articles 5 and 6 respectfully), that are furthermore restricted to a language one understands. According to the Court, this would imply, a contrario, that other fundamental rights would not enshrine additional language rights in official contexts, which would presuppose extensive positive State obligations.[45]

In combination with the increased attention for the predicament of minorities and the development of minority specific rights in the Council of Europe, from the 1990s onwards the ECtHR has been offering more firm protections to persons belonging to minorities, both protecting them against invidious discrimination, and ensuring that the exercise of their human rights would not be limited simply because they manifest a distinct identity.[46] A next important development in the ECtHR case law happened in two landmark cases in 2000 and 2001, namely *Thlimmenos* and *Chapman*. Each of these judgments contained immensely important statements of principle about States' positive State obligations in relation to minorities.

In *Thlimmenos*, the Court clarified that the prohibition of discrimination also encompasses duties of differential treatment, more particularly that when

[45] See inter alia *Inhabitants of Leeuw St Pierre v Belgium* A no 2333/64 (Eur Comm HR, 15 July 1965); *Fryske Nasjonale Partij et al v the Netherlands* A no 11100/84 (Eur Comm HR, 12 December 1985); *Mathieu, Mohin and Clerfayet v Belgium* A no 9267/81 (ECtHR, 2 March 1987) para 52; *Inhabitants of Alsemberg and Beersel v Belgium* A no 1474/62 (26 July 1963). See also Fernand de Varennes, *Language, Minorities and Human Rights* (Brill, 1996).

[46] See inter alia *Sidiropoulos v Greece* A no 26695/95 (ECtHR, 10 July 1998) para 41; *United Communist Party of Turkey et al v Turkey* A no 19392/92 (ECtHR, 30 January 1998) para 57; *Kurt v Turkey* A no 24276/94 (ECtHR, 25 May 1998) paras 133–134.

individuals find themselves in significantly different situations, the State has to treat them differently to accommodate these distinct characteristics and related protection needs and ensure *substantive equality*.[47] While the Court's pronouncements were not minority specific, the case did concern a member of the Jehovah's Witnesses and thus a religious minority. *Thlimmenos* thus added an important dimension to the prohibition of discrimination that could lead to the recognition of State duties to adopt special measures for minorities, thus protecting their substantive equal treatment.

In *Chapman*, the ECtHR went even further and recognised that article 8's right to respect for private life, family life and home also entail a positive State obligation to facilitate the minority way of life, a crucial dimension of the minority *identity*.[48] The Court did specify that belonging to a minority does not imply immunity from general laws to safeguard community assets as a whole.[49] Nevertheless, the Court added that 'the vulnerable position of … a minority means that some special consideration should be given to their needs and their different lifestyle both in the regulatory framework and in reaching decisions in particular cases'.[50]

Particularly interesting for the argument developed in this chapter is the Court's explicit engagement in (and since) *Chapman* with the implications of the FCNM (and its core tenets of substantive equality, respect for the minority identity and inclusion/integration) for the interpretation of rights in the ECHR, thus engaging in systematic interpretation.

While the Court acknowledged that the adoption of the FCNM reveals a European consensus about the need to protect minorities and their distinct identity, the European consensus would only be present at the level of general principles and is not sufficiently concrete to identify far-reaching State obligations.[51] The Court could thus grant the state a broad margin of appreciation in relation to the matter of enabling Roma to live in their caravans, particularly in the context of general planning decisions. The promising principles are thus undermined by the grant of a broad margin of appreciation to the State and do not lead to much actual protection for the way of life of Roma.[52]

Unfortunately, the ECtHR case law since *Thlimmenos* and *Chapman* has not revealed many developments towards the identification of either duties of differential treatment aimed at putting persons belonging to minorities in a substantively equal situation, or of more concrete positive State obligations to facilitate the

[47] *Thlimmenos v Greece* A no 34369/97 (ECtHR, 6 April 2000) para 44.
[48] *Chapman v UK* A no 27238/95 (ECtHR, 18 January 2001) para 96.
[49] ibid.
[50] ibid.
[51] ibid, paras 93–94.
[52] This line of reasoning is visible in subsequent cases: *Partei Die Friesen v Germany* App No 65480/10 (ECtHR, 28 January 2016) para 43; but see how this can still lead to a critical analysis and finding of violation in *Bakirdzi and EC v Hungary* App Nos 49636/14 and 65678/14 (ECtHR, 10 November 2022) para 58. Note however that in *Tasev v North Macedonia* App No 9825/13 (ECtHR, 16 May 2019) para 33 that the right to self-identification is a cornerstone of international law on the protection of minorities, especially in regard to the right not to avail yourself of your minority status and related rights.

minority way of life, not even gradually. The Court's Research Division in its report on *Cultural Rights in the case law of the ECHR*, reveals how few relevant cases there are. Furthermore, the example highlighted by the report[53] clearly shows the interplay of the Court's legitimacy concerns. The judgment in the *Muñoz Diaz* case[54] reveals the contrasting approach for the more neutral question about the availability of a survivor's pension as compared to the more controversial question about criteria under which Roma marriage as such should be recognised by a State. For the former, the Court does establish a violation of the prohibition of discrimination, while acknowledging 'the importance of the beliefs that the applicant derives from belonging to the Roma community – a community which has its own values that are well established and deeply rooted in Spanish society'.[55] For the latter, the Court ducks the question by claiming that the religious marriages (that had been recognised by Spain) and Roma marriages are not comparable.[56] In this way, the Court avoids treading on the more sensitive issue of dictating to States what type of non-civil marriages they should recognise officially.

4. Education, its Critical Functions and its Relevance Towards the Realisation of Minorities' Equality, Identity and Integration

This third 'preparatory' section towards the analysis of the ECtHR case law on language rights in education zooms in on education, elaborates on its critical functions and related importance to both the State and minorities.[57] A distinct subsection focuses on language rights in education. The discussion of the minority perspective is informed by the overarching principles of substantive equality and the right to respect for identity, while clarifying the multiple and complementary dimensions of integration.

[53] Research Division, *Cultural Rights in the Case Law of the ECHR* (Council of Europe 2011) para 14.
[54] *Muñoz Díaz v Spain* App No 49151/0 (ECtHR, 8 December 2009).
[55] ibid, para 56, 59–65, 69, and 71.
[56] ibid, para 80–81.
[57] The importance of education and educational rights for minorities is confirmed inter alia by the fact that the FCNM has dedicated no less than three articles to educational matters, highlighting the importance of an inclusive curriculum and of equal access to education (Art. 12 FCNM), of possibilities for minorities to set up and manage their own private educational institutions (Art. 13 FCNM) for teaching in and of the minority languages, while ensuring that minorities have an adequate knowledge of the official language (Art. 14 FCNM). See also the choice of topic of the first *Thematic Commentary* of the FCNM's Advisory Committee (AC), and of the first thematic recommendations of the Organization for Security and Co-operation in Europe (OSCE)'s High Commissioner on National Minorities. Interestingly, the AC has published a much longer and revised *Thematic Commentary on Education Rights of National Minorities*, warranted by the striking developments of minorities' educational rights over the past 20 years. The AC thus puts in evidence the dynamic nature of fundamental rights (of minorities), including the possible shifts in interpretations thereof.

Education is crucially important for the State and for minorities because it has both a qualification and a socialisation function. Through education, students obtain the necessary skills and knowledge that prepares them for higher education and eventual employment. The question of *equal* opportunities as regards access to education at all levels for persons belonging to minorities is key here,[58] also because it translates into equal opportunities to personal development; access to higher education and successful careers.[59]

The education socialisation function concerns the passing on of values and mores. Regarding the State's aim of an integrated society, the focus is on the transmission of national values, mores, and the national language. Persons belonging to minorities tend to be interested in becoming proficient in the national language and becoming familiar with the national values to optimise their full participation and inclusion in the national society.[60] For them it is equally important that also the minority values and languages are included in the curriculum, to protect the minority *identity*.[61] The FCNM does require States to adopt an inclusive curriculum that also reflects the histories, cultures, languages and religions of minorities.[62] The 2024 *Revised FCNM Thematic Commentary on Education* under the FCNM explicitly acknowledges, taking into account the developments of the last years, the emerging understanding of 'the right to education as a right to inclusive education, which on the one hand does impart the values of the State but on the other hand also ensures the development of respect for the children's and their parents' cultures, identities and religions'.[63] Similarly, the 2013 Organization for Security and Co-operation in Europe (OSCE) *Ljubljana Guidelines on Integration of Diverse Societies*[64] highlights the significance of education for an integrated society and for the promotion of respect for diversity (encompassing several identities).

Some further thoughts are warranted about the notion of '*integration*' since the preceding text already noted that minorities and States seem to retain an understanding of 'integration' that is not identical. The biggest point of discussion is of course the degree to which integration would require minorities to give up their identity versus an understanding of integration as ruling out forced assimilation and rather conceiving integration as a two-way process, presupposing both sides

[58] See art 12, para 3 FCNM.

[59] See text to n 63–68 on the conceptual definition of integration, including the recognition of the vital role of the prohibition of discrimination and participatory rights for a project of integration.

[60] See inter alia Klaus D. Beiter, *The Protection of the Right to Education in International Law* (Martinus Nijhoff, 2005) 100, 562–563.

[61] Francesco Capotorti, *Study on the Rights of Persons belonging to Ethnic, Religious and Linguistic Minorities* (UN 1991) 60; Julie Ringelheim, 'Between Identity Transmission and Equal Opportunities: The Multiple Dimensions of Minorities 'Right to Education' in Kristin Henrard (ed), *The Interrelation between the Right to Identity of Minorities and their Socio-Economic Participation* (Martinus Nijhoff 2013) 91–95.

[62] Art 12, para 1 FCNM.

[63] AC/FCNM, Thematic Commentary No 1 on Education under the FCNM (Council of Europe 2024).

[64] www.osce.org/hcnm/ljubljana-guidelines. These Guidelines have been developed under the auspices of the OSCE's High Commissioner on National Minorities, are used in the practice of the HCNM and thus have authoritative value.

to make some adjustments and accommodations.[65] The FCNM reflects a vision of integration both in its text and the supervisory practice that rules out forced assimilation and rather aims at the full and equal inclusion of minorities, while respecting their distinct identity.[66]

The extensive integration literature confirms that equality and the right to equal treatment, including the effective protection against discrimination, is a foundational value of integration.[67] Beyond this, in social sciences a useful distinction has been made between four interrelated dimensions of integration, which further enriches one's understanding of the complex and multifaceted nature of 'integration'. These dimensions also clarify why integration is so important for minorities as well.[68] The literature distinguishes between structural, social, cultural and identificational integration dimensions.[69] Structural or legal integration is an important *conditio sine qua non* for the integration of population groups, as it ensures equal, non-discriminatory access to rights, and effective access to essential services and to the labour market, housing, education, etc.[70] Social integration refers to relationships between the other population groups, thus reflecting the actual inclusion of the group into national society. The underlying interaction between groups will further enhance cultural integration, which refers to the cognitive, attitudinal and behavioural adaptations of the respective groups. Ultimately, identificational integration points to a sense of belonging of a group and its commitment to and identification with the national society.

There is an obvious connection between these dimensions in the sense that when one has equal access to education and jobs, this will enhance one's interaction with persons of the other groups, which will in turn facilitate cultural integration. Relatedly, when the different groups are being taught together, following an inclusive curriculum, this potentially enhances social and cultural integration. Finally, when one has equal access to society's respective domains, and effectively builds relationships with persons from other groups, one is bound to feel included in the national society which in turn can generate a stronger sense of belonging.[71]

[65] See several articles referenced above in n 5 and 7.

[66] See arts 4-6 and 12 FCNM. See also Henrard, 'Tracing Visions of Integration and/of Minorities' 347; Tom Hadden, 'Integration and Separation: Legal and Political Choices in Implementing Minority Rights' in Ghanea and Xanthaki (eds) *Minorities, Peoples and Self-Determination* (Martinus Nijhoff, 2005) 174–175.

[67] Jan Niessen and Thomas Huddleston (eds), *Legal Frameworks for the integration of Third-Country Nationals* (Martinus Nijhoff, 2009).

[68] Roberta Medda-Windischer, *Old and New Minorities: Reconciling Diversity and Cohesion* (Nomos, 2008) 247–248; Zanker, 'Integration as Conflict Prevention' 223.

[69] Victor Armony, 'Multiculturalism, Interculturalism and the Effects of a Weak Ethnos' (2012) 9 *Canadian Diversity* 2.

[70] Han Entzinger & Renske Biezeveld, *Benchmarking in Immigrant Integration* (European Commission Report, August 2003) 3–4.

[71] It has been claimed, though, that integration processes do not necessarily develop at the same speed for the respective dimensions. See the literature on segmented integration, inter alia A Portes and M Zhou, 'The New Second Generation Segmented Assimilation and Its Variants' (1993) 530 *The Annals* 74–96.

The foundational principles of minority protection concerning (substantive) equality, respect for identity and integration clearly supports teaching the different populations groups together, following an inclusive curriculum, providing equal access and equal opportunities.

4.1. Language in Education: The Importance of Instruction in the Minority Language and its Operationalisation

These foundational principles of substantive equality, respect for the distinct minority identity and integration also support the importance of education in one's mother tongue. There are at least five interrelated reasons why it would be problematic not to teach persons belonging to minorities in their mother tongue.[72]

First, sociolingual data have shown that instruction in the mother tongue is essential to actually grasp what is being taught, which means that one has no equal access to the educational material and to education in general when one is educated in a different language.[73] While this is particularly the case for the first few years of education, some teaching in the minority language should remain throughout one's educational trajectory.[74] A closely related second equality argument concerns the importance of mother tongue education for one's cognitive and one's emotional development in the sense that if one is not taught in one's mother tongue this hampers one's cognitive and emotional development, and thus jeopardises one's equal opportunities.[75]

A third argument rather speaks to the right to respect for the distinct minority identity. Education through the minority language is important to ensure the preservation and development of the minority language and the tradition of the minority culture conveyed through it.[76] A fourth argument combines the equality with integration rationales when it is noted that being educated in one's mother tongue, strengthens one's linguistic skills in the national language, and will thus have positive repercussions for one's success in education and later in the job market. The fifth argument considers the interaction between education in the minority language and various integration dimensions. The preceding equality arguments already speak to structural integration, equal access to education, and to equal opportunities more generally.[77] In addition, the preference to teach the

[72] The AC/FCNM has underscored the vital importance of education in the minority languages in its renewed *Thematic Commentary on Education* (2024) highlighting 'the obligation to adopt a clear legal framework that ensures that minority language education is and remains effectively available and to remove all undue obstacles hampering access to such education' para 89.

[73] AC/FCNM, Thematic Commentary No 3 The Language Rights of Persons Belonging to National Minorities Under the FCNM (Council of Europe 2012) para 72.

[74] ibid para 12, see also para 21.

[75] See also HCNM, *The Hague Recommendations Regarding the Education Rights of National Minorities* (OSCE 1996) para 11.

[76] ibid para 1; AC/FCNM, *Thematic Commentary on Education* (2024) para 87.

[77] See also HCNM, The Ljubljana Guidelines on Integration of Diverse Societies (OSCE 2012) para 45.

different groups together coupled with a certain level of education in the mother tongue favours multilingual education, which is considered to be 'conducive to genuine (social) integration'.[78] Last but not least, when one receives education in one's minority language, it sends a strong message of inclusion towards the group concerned, which is conducive to identificational integration.

Turning to the *operationalisation* of education in the minority languages, the following discussion first turns to the relevance of the context to determine the appropriate approach and then identifies relevant parameters. Discussing the relevance of context is particularly apt, given the setting of the ECtHR cases on language in education. The FCNM's Advisory Committee (AC) underscores in its 2024 *Thematic Commentary on Education* both the justifiable need for language revitalisation after years of forced assimilation and the problematic surge of nationalism, especially in post-conflict situations.[79] In the end, the AC opines that notwithstanding any nation-building concerns, there should always be room for minority language education.[80] The AC confirms both the importance of learning the official language for one's effective socioeconomic and political participation and access to equal opportunities and the fact that integration does not only depend on the learning and knowledge of the official language.[81] In other words, when a State introduces measures to promote the official language, this should go hand in hand with measures to protect, develop and use national minority languages.[82]

When one considers the supervisory practice in relation to the multiple qualifiers that are included in article 14 of the FCNM, it is obvious that the intention of the AC is to reduce State sovereignty and to strengthen the right to education in one's mother tongue also when this concerns minority languages. The AC underscores that the condition of traditional settlement and territorial concentration are two distinct conditions that are not cumulative. Put differently, 'the criterion of traditional settlement applies regardless of the number of persons belonging to national minorities, encompassing also cases of numerically smaller minorities or minorities who live geographically dispersed … traditional presence of the given minority therefore requires adapted solutions to fit the specific context'.[83] When States rely on the criterion of substantial numbers, the AC actually invites States not to work with thresholds. If thresholds are in place, the Committee often requests a lowering of the threshold, while avoiding an overly strict or inflexible

[78] AC/FCNM, *Thematic Commentary on Education* (2024) para 22. See also HCNM, *Ljubljana Guidelines* (2012) para 45.
[79] AC/FCNM, *Thematic Commentary on Education* (2024) paras 8–9.
[80] ibid, para 11.
[81] ibid, and see also para 51 and 88.
[82] ibid, para 84.
[83] AC/FCNM, Thematic Commentary on Education (2024), para 93.

approach.[84] According to the Committee, the most important criterion should be 'sufficient demand' rather than numbers involved.[85] The AC regularly highlights the State obligation to encourage parents to request education in the minority language and to make them aware of the benefits involved.[86]

Overall, the supervisory practice under the FCNM confirms the essential contribution of education in the minority language to both the distinct minority identity and substantively equal treatment of persons belonging to minorities, and it strengthens State obligations to this effect accordingly.

5. ECtHR, Minorities and Language in Education: Shifts in Interpretation Prior to *Valiullina*

As the ECHR is not minority specific, the formulation of the rights therein does not explicitly speak to minority concerns about the medium of instruction or the content of the curriculum in public education. Interpretation by the Court is thus decisive for the extent to which these concerns are actually protected. Article 2 protocol 1 of the ECHR consists of two sentences. The first concerns the student's access to education ('no person shall be denied the right to education'), the second concerns parents' rights to have their 'philosophical and religious convictions' respected by the State 'in the exercise of any functions that it assumes in relation to education and teaching'. As the following analysis will demonstrate, the interpretation of both sentences of article 2 protocol 1 has potential implications for the medium of instruction.

Throughout its jurisprudence, the Court has acknowledged that education is a matter of great interest to the State and 'by its very nature calls for regulation by the State'.[87] The Court also grants States a certain margin of appreciation in this regard, and even a broad margin in relation to curriculum matters.[88] Nevertheless, for certain curriculum matters, the Court has been willing to de facto reduce that margin of appreciation, as is visible in its close scrutiny of the actual content of courses on religion.[89] The ECtHR has also been ready to identify ever more demanding and concrete positive State obligations to prevent and counter segregated (and inferior) education for Roma students.[90] Put differently, the Court has already combined a recognition of a certain margin of appreciation for States with

[84] ibid paras 94 and 97. Similarly, the 'as far as possible' qualifier should be interpreted narrowly and restrictively (para 98).

[85] ibid, para 95.

[86] ibid, para 96.

[87] *The Belgian Linguistic case* (No 2), A no 1474/62 (ECtHR, 23 July 1968) para 5 of 'the Law' part.

[88] *Folgerø et al v Norway* A no15472/02 (ECtHR, 29 June 2007) paras 84 and 89.

[89] This is exactly visible in the Folgerø, see paras 90-95 and 102.

[90] See inter alia *Szolcsán v Hungary*, A no 24408/16 (ECtHR, 30 March 2023).

de facto increasing scrutiny in certain educational matters, also some that States may consider intertwined with sovereign choices.[91]

As was already flagged above, in relation to language in education, the handful of relevant cases have always been set against a background of nationalism battles or battling nations. In the *1968 Belgian linguistics case*, the Court set off with a rather restrictive take on language in education rights, while already opening the door for a more extensive reading in light of the need for rights to be effective. This case concerned a complaint of parents of children living in the Dutch speaking community of Belgium regarding the lack of provision of education in French. This setting is the outcome of a tensed 'battle' between the Flemish and the Walloons in Belgium that was managed with a major constitutional reform and the introduction of a federal system, including a division of the country in three monolingual and one bilingual parts. The families concerned are French speaking but live in the monolingual Flemish part. Against this background of 'battling nations' that was settled by a carefully balanced constitutional system, it is obvious that a finding of violation of the ECHR would not be well received by Belgium, and other federal States.[92]

Regarding the right of access to education (sentence 1), the Court was not willing to accept that this would encompass 'education in the language of choice'. On the basis of the effectiveness principle, the ECtHR was willing to go beyond the text and 'read in' the requirement that the education should be provided 'in the or one of the official languages of the state, in order to draw profit of it'. However, the Court did not have regard for the socio-linguistic data on the importance of instruction in the mother tongue in order to effectively have access to the curriculum content taught.[93] Regarding the second sentence on parents' rights, the Court was not willing to accept that 'philosophical and religious convictions' – to be respected by authorities in their educational rules and policies – encompass linguistic preferences.

In two later cases, 2001 and 2012 respectively, in settings of disputed territories, and actual occupied territory, with the occupying forces imposing their language as medium of instruction, the Court was willing to recognise that the Convention's education right has some further linguistic dimensions. Maybe this distinct setting, implying a violation of basic principles of international law by the occupying forces, also enabled the ECtHR to make bolder pronouncements.

[91] It seems indeed that the Court is willing to scrutinise States' educational standards, policies and actions more strictly in relation to the content of the curriculum on religion, and to oblige States to ensure that the ethnic minorities are not put in segregated and inferior education.

[92] Most of the complaints were not upheld. Only the narrow complaint of discrimination due to lack of access to French schools in municipalities with facilities, because the parents were not living in these municipalities, was upheld: *Case Relating To Certain Aspects Of The Laws On The Use Of Languages In Education In Belgium* (Merits), A nos 1474/62, 1677/62, 1691/62, 1769/63, 1994/63, 2126/64 (ECtHR, 23 July 1968).

[93] See inter alia Gulara Guliyeva, 'Education; Language and Linguistic Minorities in the EU: Challenges and Perspectives' (2013) *ELJ* 229.

It should be noted though that the Court did not link or limit its reasoning to situations of occupation, thus pointing to a broader validity thereof.[94]

In *Cyprus v Turkey* (2001) the Court evaluated the Turkish occupation of Northern Cyprus, and also of relevance for the discussion here, it evaluated the regulation and provision of education in Greek. While the Turkish occupying forces maintained basic education in Greek, they closed the only secondary school that provided education in Greek. The Court's reasoning in at least two respects recognised the relevance of a linguistic dimension to the right to education under the ECHR. First, it recognised that the medium of instruction matters for the effective access to education, where it establishes a 'denial of the substance of the right' due to the 'failure of the TRNC authorities to make continuing provision for (Greek Language schooling) at the secondary level'.[95] Second, the Court acknowledged that parents' preferences in terms of the medium of instruction also matter when evaluating a possible violation of article 2 protocol 1[96] with the reference to the wishes of parents pointing to the second sentence. To be sure, the Court did not explicitly acknowledge that linguistic preferences qualify as philosophical conviction, and it does not explicitly identify a State duty to respect these linguistic preferences.

Catan et al van Moldova and Russia (2012) concerned the situation of the region of Transnistria in Moldova, where pro-Russian rebels, backed-up by Russia, took over and tried to secede. Here, the rebels also imposed a different medium of instruction, namely Russian, while the few schools that maintained Moldovan were harassed in many ways and were obliged to use Moldovan in Cyrillic script. As regards the right to access to education, the Court again emphasised the importance that the substance of the right should not be injured. Also, in this case, this is connected to the question of the medium of instruction: the Court confirms its reasoning in the *Belgian linguistics case* that the right to education would be meaningless if it would not be in the or one of the official languages of the State.[97] In this respect, the Court was critical about the various ways in which education in Moldovan is de facto made impossible; also due to the obligation to use Cyrillic script, which is a combination for which no proper textbooks exist.[98] The Court's conclusion was that 'these measures amounted to an interference with the parents' rights to ensure their children's education and teaching in accordance with their philosophical convictions'.[99] In other words, the Court in this case acknowledged

[94] See also Jacqueline Mowbray, *Linguistic Justice: International Law and Language Policy* (Oxford University Press, 2012) 37-38.

[95] *Cyprus v Turkey*, A no 25781/94 (ECtHR, 10 May 2001) para 278.

[96] ibid para 278: 'the authorities must no doubt be aware that it is the wish of the Greek-Cypriot parents that the schooling of their children be completed through the medium of the Greek language'.

[97] *Catan et al v Moldova and Russia*, A nos 43370/04, 8252/05, 18454/06 (ECtHR, 19 October 2012) para 137.

[98] ibid, para 141-143.

[99] ibid, para 143.

that linguistic preferences of parents amount to philosophical convictions that need to be respected by the State (in principle).

Interestingly, while the Court's reasoning does point to the grossly disproportionate nature of interferences, it did not explicitly engage in any proportionality considerations. Instead, it emphasised the lack of legitimate aim, because the sole purpose of the respective measures is said to be entrenching a separatist ideology.[100] Put differently, the Court's reasoning in *Catan* left many questions open: what are relevant proportionality considerations in relation to these positive State obligations, for example when a country has many dispersed linguistic groups? What if authorities do not have a secessionist agenda? What if there are no abrupt changes but gradual ones? Sadly, in the three cases against Latvia over 2023–24, the Court did not further develop this line of reasoning by adding proportionality parameters, instead it chose to reverse the clock.

6. *Valiullina et al v Latvia:* About Promises and Missed Opportunities

Of the three cases against Latvia concerning the medium of instruction, the first one, *Valiullina et al v Latvia*[101] regarding public education, covering primary and secondary education, sets the scene and is heavily relied upon by the Court in the two subsequent cases, which concern private education (*Dzibuti et al v Latvia*)[102] and preschool education (*Djeri et al v Latvia*)[103] respectively. In the latter two cases, the Court follows the reasoning of the Latvian government that these form part of the State educational system, and that thus similar principles apply.[104] Hence, the following in depth analysis focuses on the *Valiullina* case and reveals how an account of the Court's actual reasoning translates as a mix of, on the one hand, promising pronouncements (some of which are a leap forward), and on the other hand, making pronouncements that constitute a leap backward, going hand in hand with missed opportunities.

The case concerns complaints by parents and children who identify as part of the Russian speaking minority in Latvia, about legislative changes that reduce the use of Russian as medium of instruction in primary and secondary public schools in Latvia. It certainly qualifies as a situation of 'battling nations'; in view of the fact that Russia had, for decades, occupied Latvia, during which time it had imposed Russian as the default medium of instruction and also more generally in public life. Since Latvia regained independence, it has been eager to restore Latvian as the only official language, actively promoting its use in public life and certainly in the

[100] ibid, para 144.
[101] *Valiullina et al* (ECtHR, 14 September 2023).
[102] *Dzibuti et al v Latvia*, A no 225/20 (ECtHR, 16 November 2023).
[103] *Djeri et al v Latvia*, A no 50942/20 (ECtHR, 18 July 2024).
[104] *Dzibuti et al* (ECtHR, 16 November 2023) para 149; *Djeri et al* (ECtHR, 18 July 2024) paras 146–147.

education system. The Russian speaking minority has been vigorously claiming the right to be educated in Russian.

Valiullina clearly represents a challenging case for the ECtHR with its complex constellation and questions about the position and rights of a group that was an assimilationist oppressor in the pasts and that now claims the protection of minority rights, and the acceptable reach of a nation building exercise and related measures.

6.1. The Court's Reasoning in *Valiullina*

The Court starts its analysis with the complaint in terms of the right to education under article 2 of protocol 1, to proceed with the discrimination complaint in terms of article 14 junctio article 2 protocol 1. The Court confirms its reasoning in the *Belgian linguistics case* that the right of access to education implies the right to be educated in the or one of the national languages of the State.[105] In this regard, it emphasises that its critical assessment in *Catan* was triggered by the fact that the authorities no longer allowed education in the Romanian language in Latin script, which was the national language (and not the Romanian language in Cyrillic script).[106] The Court furthermore presents its preceding jurisprudence as clearly denying that parents linguistic preferences would be 'philosophical conviction'.[107] The ECtHR acknowledges that the FCNM could be the basis for an evolutive interpretation of the ECHR but points out that while the majority of Council of Europe States have ratified the FCNM, not all did so.[108] In any event, article 14 of the FCNM on language in education would be framed in such a way that it leaves a very broad margin of appreciation to States. According to the Court, ultimately there is 'no sufficient international material to warrant the conclusion that article 2 protocol 1 would enshrine the right to access education in the language of one's choice, as there is no European consensus on minorities' educational rights in this regard'.[109]

Importantly, the Court accepts for the first time a discrimination complaint about not being educated in one's mother tongue, as falling within the scope of application of article 14 junctio 2 protocol 1.[110] As the Court identifies a differential treatment in terms of being educated in one's mother tongue or not (in comparable settings)[111] it continues with the analysis of the 'reasonable and objective

[105] *Valiullina et al* (ECtHR, 14 September 2023) para 122.
[106] ibid, para 130.
[107] ibid, para 125.
[108] *Valiullina et al* (ECtHR, 14 September 2023) para 134.
[109] ibid, the Court goes on to conclude that the complaint is inadmissible ratione materiae.
[110] *Valiullina et al* (ECtHR, 14 September 2023) para 147.
[111] *Valiullina et al* (ECtHR, 14 September 2023) para 194. Interestingly, several paragraphs later, in the midst of the proportionality assessment, there is suddenly a statement about a possible indirect discrimination that needs to be explored: the legislative measures may apply to students in all public

justification' test. The Court easily acknowledges that measures to protect one's national language serve a legitimate aim for the State.[112] Having regard to the supervisory practice of the CJEU and the Council of Europe's Venice Commission, the Court considered this aim as being especially weighty, considering the history of suppression.[113] The ECtHR also identifies two further legitimate aims, following the argument of the Latvian constitutional court, namely first, about having sufficient knowledge of the State language 'to be able to participate in the life of democratic society',[114] and second, to offer all students equal chances while also countering the consequences of segregation during the Soviet regime.[115]

In its assessment of the proportionality principle, the ECtHR highlights that the legitimate aim of correcting factual inequalities and restoring the status of the Latvian language needs to be pursued while respecting the State obligation to ensure that the Russian minority could still learn and preserve its language.[116] In the remainder of its reasoning, the ECtHR returns several times to this historical background of suppression of the Latvian language during the Soviet regime, which now needs to be remedied[117] and which also justifies the need to improve the knowledge of the Latvian language among pupils.[118] The Court further emphasises that the change of language of instruction was a very gradual and even flexible one, since there is still some education in Russian in primary and partially in secondary education in Latvia.[119] Having regard to the broad margin of appreciation that the FCNM leaves to States as regards minority languages in education, the related lack of European consensus and the clear need for redressing the status of the Latvian language in the context of the Russification policies during the Soviet occupation,[120] the Court concludes that Latvia did not overstep its broad margin of appreciation.[121]

6.2. The Analysis of the Court's Reasoning in *Valiullina*

A brief analysis focusing on the central question in *Valiullina* is followed by a more drawn-out evaluation of the reasoning of the Court, identifying remarkable leaps forward, and a major leap backward.

schools; there may be a disproportionate impact on the claimants. The Court does not return to this line of reasoning in the subsequent analysis though.

[112] ibid, paras 187–188.
[113] ibid, paras 199–200.
[114] ibid, para 198.
[115] ibid, para 201.
[116] ibid, para 204.
[117] ibid, paras 210–211.
[118] ibid, para 208.
[119] ibid, paras 206–207.
[120] ibid, paras 210–211.
[121] ibid, paras 212–213.

Throughout its reasoning, the Court is eager to demonstrate its understanding of the underlying complexities, more particularly its understanding of the history of the Soviet occupation, during which the Latvian language was severely restricted, and the ensuing legitimacy of the desire of the Latvian State to re-establish Latvian as the official language. While the Court does acknowledge a State obligation to ensure that the Russian minority could still learn and preserve its language (identity), from the start, the Court tilts towards a finding in favour of the Latvian State. On the one hand, the Court minimises the reduction in terms of instruction in Russian, while emphasising that it is also for the Russian speakers important to learn the Latvian language when they want to optimise their participation in Latvian society (integration). On the other hand, the ECtHR focuses on the text of the FCNM and not on the (entire) supervisory practice of the AC, which has added considerable 'bite', reducing the discretion of the States concomitantly, while strengthening the positive State obligations to provide education in the minority language.

In several respects, *Valiullina* develops promising lines of reasoning that can be considered a progressive shift leap forward in the jurisprudence of the ECtHR regarding language rights, and the prohibition of discrimination. First of all, it is immensely important that the Court goes beyond the formal equality argument that there cannot be a problem if all are taught in the same language. Indeed, in *Valiullina* the Court acknowledges that there *is* a relevant difference in terms of being taught in one's mother tongue or not. This is an important step towards recognising the substantive equality argument in favour of education in the minority language, which also contributes to the right to respect for the minority identity. Secondly, the Court develops an extensive reasoning in relation to the discrimination complaint, both regarding the legitimate aim requirement and the proportionality one. Unfortunately, the Court's further reasoning strongly tilts towards Latvia's arguments about the need for affirmative action and the re-establishment of the status of the Latvian language. Notwithstanding the Court's explicit engagement with the claimants' arguments, it is obvious that the Latvian State's interests are accorded more weight than the Russian speaking minority's interests to further their substantive equality, and respect for their distinct identity.

In some respects, the Court's reasoning in *Valiullina* amount to missed opportunities. The Court acknowledges that even groups that used to be the dominant groups may, following a change in government, become minorities, entitled to minority rights. It would have been welcome to see further considerations about the (strength of the) rights of such minority groups, in view of overall substantive equality concerns. The ECtHR does hint at the relevance of the historical context, several times, but does not really provide further parameters. Relatedly, the Court notes that in a setting of post-occupation, developing policies of nation building is legitimate, as long as these are reasonable (not disproportionate). In this respect, no further indications are provided as to how this proportionality requirement will be assessed, particularly in relation to minorities' equality and identity interests.

Unfortunately, the Court also takes two leaps back, more particularly in its interpretation of Article 2, Protocol No. 1 sentence 2 and its de facto undermining of any guiding value of minority specific rights for the interpretation of general human rights.

Regarding Article 2 of Protocol No. 1 the Court actually rewrites the *Catan* judgement's explicit acceptance that the linguistic preferences of parents do amount to philosophical convictions that need to be respected by the authorities. In *Catan*, the ECtHR had furthermore connected the conclusion about a denial of the substance of the right 'with disregarding the wish for parents that their children be taught in the official language which is also their mother tongue'.[122] However, in *Valiullina*, the Court represents its preceding jurisprudence as if it had focused throughout on limiting the first sentence to a right to education in (one of) the national languages. As was highlighted above in the discussion of the *Catan* case, the Court had omitted to combine its explicit recognition that linguistic preferences of parents qualify as philosophical convictions (that need to be respected by public authorities in the way they organise education) with nuances informed by proportionality considerations. The Court could have used *Valiullina* as an opportunity to refine its *Catan* jurisprudence through the addition of relevant proportionality parameters. In this regard, it could have referred to article 14 of the FCNM's criteria and the related supervisory practice.

Unfortunately, in *Valiullina*, the Court takes a second leap back by almost erasing any guiding value of the minority specific rights under the FCNM. The promising opening towards an engagement with the discrimination complaint went hand in hand with the Court's dismissive assessment of the potential relevance of minority specific rights and their supervisory practice towards the interpretation of rights enshrined in the ECHR. To be sure, since *Chapman*[123] the ECtHR has acknowledged that the FCNM reflects a European Consensus about the need to respect minorities' distinct identity and way of life.[124] Admittedly, when turning to concrete measures and related positive State obligations, the Court tends to summarily point out that the consensus is not sufficiently concrete to provide guidance, which translates into the grant of a broad State discretion.[125]

In *Valiullina*, the Court develops an extensive reasoning about minority specific rights, but only to undermine their possible value, by focusing almost exclusively on the wide discretion that the FCNM leaves to States, ultimately discrediting its

[122] *Catan et al* (ECtHR, 19 October 2012) para 134.
[123] *Chapman* (ECtHR, 18 January 2001).
[124] ibid, para 93.
[125] ibid, para 94. See for further references n 49.

interpretative guidance through systematic interpretation.[126] It seems promising that the ECtHR has regard for the AC's Thematic Commentary, however the Court refers to Commentary no 3 on Language Rights whereas the most appropriate one is Commentary no 1 on Education Rights of National Minorities, as recently revised.[127] What is more, the Court chooses not to have regard to the supervisory practice of the AC that still acknowledges the many qualifiers in article 14 of the FCNM but has been urging States to adopt a generous approach towards the provision of education in the minority language, thus reading down the impact of these qualifiers (traditional presence of territorial concentration).[128] The AC even urges States to raise awareness amongst parents about the importance of education in the mother tongue.[129] In other words, the Court's exclusive focus on references to a broad discretion that is left to the contracting States does not do justice to the full picture.[130]

Furthermore, this onslaught on the value of minority specific rights was not necessary at all to reach a finding of non-violation in the cases against Latvia: the reasoning of the Court shows that it could have easily concluded to a non-violation because the differential treatment would be proportionate to the legitimate aim, having regard to the arguments about the gradual and flexible implementation of the measures.[131] Put differently, the Court's reversal of *Catan's* recognition that parent's preferences about the medium of instruction are philosophical convictions that need to be protected (in principle), and the dismissal of the relevance of minority specific rights for the interpretation of the ECHR, can be considered as 'overkill'. These aspects of the Court's reasoning in *Valiullina* exemplify the fragile position of minorities' rights, especially when international courts are confronted with a determined nation-building exercise after years of illegitimate occupation, and their own ensuing legitimacy concerns.

[126] Similarly, the Court brushes Recommendations of the High Commissioner on National Minorities of the OSCE off the table as 'just recommendations' (para 210) and thus not legally binding, again dismissing their significant political authority towards Member States of the OSCE: see also Natalie Sebanadze and Vincent de Graaf, 'Are Some States And Minorities More Equal Than Others? Double Standards And The Work Of The OSCE High Commissioner On National Minorities' in Kristin Henrard (ed), *Double Standards pertaining to Minority Protection* (Martinus Nijhoff, 2010) 117–120.

[127] ibid, para 3.

[128] ibid, paras 93–98.

[129] AC/FCNM, *Thematic Commentary on Education* (2024).

[130] AC/FCNM, *Thematic Commentary on Education* (2024) para 3: The appropriateness of a systematic interpretation in which minority specific rights influence the interpretation of general human rights is confirmed in the 2024 Thematic Commentary on Education of the AC/FCNM, where it underscores that 'minority rights form an integral part of human rights, and as such are a matter of joint international concern'.

[131] For a more critical assessment, based on a more in-depth assessment of the laws and practice in Latvia, see the blog by Sarah Ganty and Dimitry V Kochenov 'Hijacking Human Rights to Enable Punishment by Association: Valiullina, Dzibuti and Outlawing Minority Schools in Latvia' (*Strabourg Observers*, 23 November 2023). See also Sarah Ganty, Dimitry Kochenov and Ignatius Nugraha, 'Constitutional Identity vs. Human Rights: the ECtHR's Bizarre Turn in Three Latvian Cases' (*VerfBlog*, 21 December 2023).

7. Conclusion: How to Move Forward

The concerns of States regarding nation building and territorial integrity go hand in hand with the lack of political will for strong minority specific rights. Nevertheless, the development of the human rights paradigm since World War II, at the level of the UN and especially of the Council of Europe, recognises that persons belonging to minorities have additional protection needs. This is also reflected in the FCNM's core values of substantive equality, respect for minorities' distinct identity and inclusion/integration.

The chapter demonstrates that the ECtHR in several respects is willing to interpret the ECHR non-specific rights in a way that embraces substantive equality and respects minorities' identity, thus confirming the FCNM's core values. At the same time, the preceding analysis has revealed that these developments have ultimately been minor, due to the strong focus on a broad margin of appreciation of States, allegedly informed by the Court's legitimacy concerns towards the contracting States.

The case law on language in education rights demonstrates the critical importance of education in general and the medium of instruction in particular in situations of battling nations, due to the important socialisation role of education. The few cases and the shifts between them also nicely demonstrate the ECtHR's legitimacy concerns towards the contracting States. The Court's case law is wavering indeed, revealing leaps forward in cases of illegal occupation, and, as visible in the cases against Latvia, leaps backwards in a post-occupation phase where the minority claiming rights is the same population group that previously occupied the country. Does this reveal that not all minority rights are under threat but rather the rights of particular minorities that are linked to illegal expansionism? Unfortunately, the Court's dismissal of the value of minority rights and their possible contribution to the human rights paradigm risks having broader ramifications. This reasoning, in any event, also entailed that the Court's significant recognition in *Valiullina* of the relevance of the medium of instruction in terms of the prohibition of discrimination, ultimately resulted in a finding of non-violation.

The chapter thus urges the ECtHR to re-evaluate the value of minority specific rights and the underlying core values of substantive equality, the right to respect for the minority identity and minorities' inclusion, and the way in which these can influence the (systematic) interpretation of the ECHR. More particularly regarding the medium of instruction, acknowledging and applying the proportionality checks implicit in the minority specific rights could also assist the Court in fine-tuning the strong principle it has put forward in *Catan*, instead of throwing it out entirely.

7

Minorities' Participation in Public Affairs: A Human Rights Norm or a Conflict Prevention Technique?

MILICA V. MATIJEVIĆ* AND ANA KNEŽEVIĆ BOJOVIĆ**

1. Introduction

If we tried to parallel the evolution of international minority rights as human rights after the Second World War with the main stages of human life, we would probably say that they are now in an early adulthood phase. The inclusion of Article 27 in the International Covenant on Civil and Political Rights[1] could be seen as the moment when they were born as a part of international human rights law; the different attempts to develop them, which were crowned in the United Nations Declaration on Minorities,[2] as a long childhood; and the entering into force of the Framework Convention for the Protection of National Minorities (FCNM)[3] – the first legally binding multilateral instrument devoted to minority protection – could represent their coming-of-age.

One can observe in that picture that the 'adolescence' of international minority rights passed in the blink of an eye. Their meteoric maturing was a consequence of the outburst of ethnic violence on the European continent. It is known in the history of minority rights that their quick evolution was a reaction to the proliferation of violent conflicts that followed the collapse of the Soviet Union and the Socialist

* Senior Research Fellow, Institute of Comparative Law (Belgrade, Serbia); m.matijevic@iup.rs; ORCID: 0000-0002-2459-9201. This work was conducted as part of the research project implemented in 2025 by the Institute of Comparative Law, with financial support from the Ministry of Science, Technological Development and Innovation of the Republic of Serbia (Contract No. 451-03-136/2025-03/200049).

** Senior Research Fellow, Institute of Comparative Law (Belgrade, Serbia); a.bojovic@iup.rs; ORCID: 0000-0002-3746-5747.

[1] International Covenant on Civil and Political Rights (16 December 1966) 999 UNTS 171.

[2] Declaration on the Rights of Persons Belonging to National or Ethnic, Religious and Linguistic Minorities (3 February 1992) UNGA Res 47/135.

[3] Framework Convention for the Protection of National Minorities (1 February 1998) ETS No 157. Hereinafter, 'FCNM', 'Framework Convention' or 'Convention'.

Federal Republic of Yugoslavia.[4] Less known is that this development was also propelled by the progress in the understanding of ethnic conflict.[5] By the last decade of the twentieth century, conflict resolution theory was already a fully grown field of peace studies, based on the postulate that addressing the needs of ethnic groups was a key to resolving violent ethnic conflicts.[6] In the 1990s, these theoretical insights were incorporated into the conflict resolution strategies pursued in the European war-torn countries through the peacebuilding efforts of the United Nations (UN), the European Union (EU), and other international organisations.[7]

The postulates of conflict resolution theory, and conflict prevention as such,[8] are clearly reflected in the vision of minority rights as 'guarantees of stability, security and peace' on which the FCNM is based.[9] However, the ambition of the drafters of the FCNM was not only to prevent the re-emergence of old (or the emergence of new) ethnic conflicts, but also for the Convention to serve as a source of legally binding principles. These principles were to be developed into fully-fledged minority rights norms through their transposition into national legal frameworks.[10] The Advisory Committee on the FCNM[11] has been given the most

[4] See, for instance: Will Kymlicka, '*The Evolving Basis of European Norms of Minority Rights: Rights to Culture, Participation and Autonomy*' in Marc Weller, Denika Blacklock and Katherine Nobbs (eds), *The Protection of Minorities in the Wider Europe* (Basingstoke, Palgrave Macmillan, 2008) 12–13; Kirsten Shoraka, *Minority Rights in the EU* (London, Routledge, 2010) 95–96; David Galbreath and Joanne McEvoy, *European Minority Rights Regime* (Basingstoke, Palgrave Macmillan, 2012) 112.

[5] According to the definition found in the Routledge Handbook of Ethnic Conflict, ethnic conflict is 'a form of group conflict in which at least one of the parties involved interprets the conflict, its causes, and potential remedies along an actually existing or perceived discriminating ethnic divide (Karl Cordell and Stefan Wolff, 'The Study of Ethnic Conflict: An Introduction' in Karl Cordell and Stefan Wolff (eds), *The Routledge Handbook of Ethnic Conflict* (London, Routledge, 2016) 4).

[6] For a brief overview of the main conflict resolution theories: Milica V Matijević and Vesna Erić Ćorić, 'Peacebuilding and the Conflict Resolution Theories' in Ivica Đorđević, Marina Glamotchak, Svetlana Stanarević, Jasmina Gačić (eds), *Twenty Years of Human Security: Theoretical Foundations and Practical Applications* (Belgrade, Faculty of Security Studies of the University of Belgrade, Institut Français de Géopolitique Université Paris, 2015) 8.

[7] See, for instance, Florian Bieber, 'Power Sharing after Yugoslavia: Functionality and Dysfunctionality of Power Sharing Institutions Post-War Bosnia, Macedonia and Kosovo' in Sid Noel (ed), *From Power Sharing to Democracy: Post-Conflict Institutions in Ethnically Divided Societies* (Montreal: McGill-Queen's University Press, 2005).

[8] There is not a commonly accepted definition of conflict prevention (Erik Melander and Claire Pigache, 'Conflict Prevention: Concepts and Challenges' in W Feichtinger, Predrag Jureković (eds), Konfliktprävention: zwischen Anspruch und Wirklichkeit (Wien, Austrian National Defence Academy 2007) 11). For the purpose of this chapter, we define it as the theory and practice concerned with addressing latent, underlying, or structural features of a society that can lead to a conflict, whether a new one or a re-occurrence of the earlier conflict (Dina Carment and Mary Fischer, 'Conflict Prevention: A Policy in Search of a Theory or a Theory in Search of a Policy?' in Karl Cordell and Stefan Wolff (eds), The Routledge Handbook of Ethnic Conflict (Routledge, 2016) 170). Some authors, on the other hand, define it by the stage of conflict and confine it to the pre-conflict stages (Mats Lund, 'Conflict Prevention: Theory in Pursuit of Policy and Practice', in Jacob Bercovitch, Vlad Kremenyuk and Ira William Zartman (eds), *The Sage Handbook of Conflict Resolution* (London, Sage, 2009) 289).

[9] FCNM, Preamble. See, also, the preamble of the UN Declaration *on Minority Rights*. Shoraka argues that the creation of minority protection systems has been always driven by security concerns (Shoraka, *Human Rights and Minority Rights* (n 4) 96).

[10] Council of Europe, *Explanatory Report to the Framework Convention for the Protection of National Minorities*, ETS No 157 para 13.

[11] Hereinafter 'Advisory Committee' or 'Committee'.

important role in that process, not only as the body in charge of monitoring the implementation of the Convention, but also by being entrusted with the task of fleshing out the normative content of these principles.[12]

This chapter examines the relationship between human rights and conflict prevention objectives in European minority rights practice by analysing the monitoring work of the Advisory Committee. The chapter's main question is whether and to what extent the work of the Committee has been influenced by the conflict prevention objectives. The initial impetus came from our earlier research when we observed palpable differences between the Advisory Committee's supervisory practice in different States Parties.[13] From that, an idea was born that these variations might be explained by the different stages of the EU accession process/the EU membership of the monitored countries. We hypothesised that the Advisory Committee pushed harder for the implementation of the minority rights principles in those States Parties that are or have been subject to the minority rights conditioning during accession to the EU.

The literature on the development of the European minority rights standards points to the strong interrelatedness between EU enlargement and the implementation of the FCNM.[14] It is often argued that the integration of minority rights protection into the EU accession criteria turned the accession process into an important form of leverage for the enhanced implementation of the FCNM.[15] At the same time, it is evident that the inclusion of minority rights among the accession requirements was not motivated by a commitment to secure their uniform legal regulation and implementation across the Member States, given the absence of an unequivocal normative basis for the protection of minority rights in the European Union.[16] Rather, the rationale for such a role of minority rights appears to lie in their perceived relevance for preventing the spillover of

[12] See: Marc Weller, 'Creating the Conditions Necessary for the Effective Participation of Persons Belonging to National Minorities' (2004) 10(4) *International Journal on Minority and Group Rights* 266.

[13] Milica V Matijević, 'Adequate Representation of Persons Belonging to National Minorities in Public Sector: The Nature, Content and Scope of Obligations in the Comments of the Advisory Committee for the Framework Convention' (2020) 64(4) *Strani pravni život* 55–68.

[14] Galbreath and McEvoy, *The European Minority Rights Regime* (n 4) 80. Wilkinson even argues that the EU has been relying on the Council of Europe in encouraging the accommodation of the special needs of national minorities as a conflict resolution tool (Steven I Wilkinson, 'Conditionality, Consociationalism, and the European Union' in Sid Noel (ed), *From Power Sharing to Democracy: Post-Conflict Institutions in Ethnically Divided Societies* (Montreal: McGill-Queen's University Press, 2005) 239).

[15] Bernd Rechel, 'Introduction' in Bernd Rechel (ed), *Minority Rights in Central and Eastern Europe* 54 (Routledge, 2009) 4.

[16] Tove H. Malloy and Balázs Vizi, 'Introduction to the Research Handbook on Minority Politics in the European Union' in Tove H. Malloy and Balázs Vizi (eds), *Research Handbook on Minority Politics in the European Union* (Edward Elgar Publishing, 2021) 2. Many authors have been highly critical of such 'double standards' situation. See, for instance: Wojciech Sadurski, 'Minority Protection in Central Europe and Accession to the EU' in Marc Weller, Denika Blacklock and Katherine Nobbs (eds), *The Protection of Minorities in the Wider Europe* (Palgrave Macmillan, 2008) 211; Carter Johnson, 'The Use and Abuse of Minority Rights: Assessing Past and Future EU Policies Towards Accession Countries of Central, Eastern and South-Eastern Europe' (2006) 13(1) *International Journal on Minority and Group Rights*; James Hughes and Gwendolyn Sasse, 'Monitoring the Monitors: EU Enlargement Conditionality and Minority Protection in the CEECs' (2003) 1 *Journal on Ethnopolitics and Minority Issues in Europe*.

ethnic disputes from candidate States into the European Union.[17] In that sense, if a correlation between the EU enlargement process and the monitoring of the FCNM is established, it could offer valuable evidence for the thesis that the Committee's work has been influenced by conflict prevention objectives and, consequently, that these objectives continue to shape European minority rights practice.

To test this hypothesis, we conducted a small-scale analysis of the Advisory Committee's country-specific opinions concerning States Parties that have joined the EU during various enlargement waves, including the EU founding members and countries that are still in the pre-accession phase. The analysis was about identifying the main similarities and differences in these opinions by using the EU membership/accession status of a country as the primary point of reference. The research framework developed in this way was to shed light on whether and to what extent conflict prevention goals may have influenced the Advisory Committee's approach to monitoring.

The investigation focused specifically on how the Advisory Committee evaluated the implementation of an aspect of the principle of effective participation of persons belonging to national minorities in public affairs. This aspect concerned the level of representation of persons belonging to national minorities in public bodies, as envisaged under Article 15 of the FCNM. Since the beginning, the Advisory Committee has interpreted Article 15 as embracing not only the political participation of national minorities but also their right to be adequately represented in the workforce of civil administration and other public bodies of States Parties.[18] The ethnic composition of civil administration and other public bodies was also under scrutiny in the European Commission's progress/country reports.[19]

According to the Advisory Committee, Article 15 is a central provision of the FCNM and key to the full enjoyment of other minority rights.[20] Many authors also

[17] Gwendolyn Sasse adds to these democratisation concerns (Gwendolyn Sasse, 'Tracing the Construction and Effects of EU Conditionality' in Bernd Rechel (ed), *Minority Rights in Central and Eastern Europe* (Routledge, 2009) 17).

[18] cp with Joseph Marko, *Effective Participation of National Minorities: A Comment on Conceptual, Legal and Empirical Problems*, Report prepared for the Committee of Experts on Issues Relating to the Protection of National Minorities DH-MIN(2006)014 (Strasbourg, 20 October 2006) 7.

[19] At this stage of the research, the authors were aware that the European Commission, on several occasions, scrutinised the implementation of the standard of adequate representation in Croatia, as well as in-progress reports on Serbia, North Macedonia and Montenegro. e.g. For Croatia, see European Commission progress reports for 2006 (at 11), 2007 (at 12), 2008 (at 13), 2009 (at 14) and Comprehensive monitoring report on Croatia's state of preparedness for EU membership (p 7). For Serbia, see, Reports for 2020 (at 39), 2021 (at 40), 2022 (at 46), 2024 (at 43). For North Macedonia, see, Reports for 2020 (at 35), 2022 (at 36) 2023 (at 38). For Montenegro, see Report for 2020 (at 41).

[20] Advisory Committee on the Framework Convention for the Protection of National Minorities, Commentary No. 2: The Effective Participation of Persons Belonging to National Minorities in Cultural, Social and Economic Life and in Public Affairs, ACFC/31DOC(2008)001 (27 February 2008), in *Compilation of Thematic Commentaries of the Advisory Committee* (Council of Europe Publishing 2013), para 3; Advisory Committee, *Thematic Commentary No.* 3: The

point to this right as the basic tenet of contemporary minority protection.[21] As an attempt to address both the recognition and the redistribution-related needs of national minorities, Article 15 also strongly resonates with some of the basic assumptions of conflict resolution theory about destructive social conflict. John Burton, one of the pioneers in the field of conflict resolution, in the 1980s, developed the 'human needs theory', later called the 'generic theory of conflict', in which he argued that denial of basic human needs, among which identity and distributive justice have a particularly important role, is at the root of violent conflict.[22] Their fulfilment, according to him, is a prerequisite for sustainable peace. During the 1990s, the ideas of Burton and other peace researchers were materialised in conflict resolution and conflict prevention techniques for addressing identity and distributive justice needs in ethnically divided societies through different power-sharing mechanisms, including proportional representation of ethnic groups in administrative bodies.[23] In that sense, this segment of Article 15 represents an important link between the human rights and the conflict prevention approaches to minority rights.[24]

The chapter is structured in the following way. First, we provide an outline of our research methodology. A brief overview of the main elements of the standard of adequate representation, as we named the selected aspect of Article 15, is then provided. In the third section, we present the main findings of our investigation. Finally, we analyse these findings and offer conclusions about the role of conflict prevention and human rights as two distinct, though overlapping, approaches within European minority protection practice.

Language Rights of Persons Belonging to National Minorities under the Framework Convention, ACFC/44DOC(2012)001 rev (24 May 2012), in Compilation of Thematic Commentaries of the Advisory Committee (Council of Europe Publishing 2013) para 84.

[21] Eg, Annelies Verstichel, 'Elaborating a Catalogue of Best Practices of Effective Participation of National Minorities: Review of the Opinions of the Advisory Committee Regarding Article 15 of the Council of Europe Framework Convention for the Protection of National Minorities' (2004) 2 *European Yearbook of Minority Issues* 175; Marc Weller, 'Article 15' in Marc Weller (ed), *The Rights of Minorities: A Commentary on the European Framework Convention for the Protection of National Minorities* (Oxford University Press 2005) 429; Kristin Henrard, 'Challenges to Participation in the Name of 'Integration': Participation, Equality and Identity as Interrelated Foundational Principles of Minority Protection' in William Romans, Iryna Ulasiuk and Anton Petrenko Thomsen (eds), *Effective Participation of National Minorities and Conflict Prevention* (Leiden, Brill Nijhoff, 2020) 79.

[22] See, for instance, John Burton, *Resolving Deep-Rooted Conflict: A Handbook* (University Press of America, 1987) 29. For a generic analysis of Burton's 'human needs theory' and his contribution to the conflict resolution theory and practice, see: Richard E Rubenstein, 'Basic Human Needs: The Next Steps in Theory Development' (2001) 6(1) *International Journal of Peace Studies*.

[23] See, for instance, Carnegie Commission on Preventing Deadly Conflict, *Preventing Deadly Conflict: Final Report* (New York, December 1997) Box 4.9, 100. More on the various conceptions and institutional manifestations of powers-sharing in the post-conflict societies in: Sid Noel (ed), *From Power Sharing to Democracy* (McGill-Queen's University Press, 2005).

[24] For a general introduction to the relevance of Article 15 for conflict prevention, see: William Romans and Iryna Ulasiuk, 'Introduction: Effective Participation of National Minorities from a Conflict Prevention Perspective' in William Romans, Iryna Ulasiuk and Anton Petrenko Thomsen (eds), *Effective Participation of National Minorities and Conflict Prevention* (Brill Nijhoff, 2020).

1.1. Methodological Considerations

The Advisory Committee is an independent expert body created to evaluate the level of implementation of the FCNM in States Parties.[25] Through the monitoring procedure, which involves examination of State reports, gathering of information from other relevant sources, and on-site visits, the Advisory Committee adopts detailed country-specific opinions.[26]

In the research, we analyse country-specific opinions on twelve States Parties. A choice was made to form three distinct groups of countries. The first group consists of Western European democracies that recognise the existence of minorities on their territories and that were not subject to EU external conditionality, or their accession requirements did not include minority rights. This group comprises Germany, as one of the 'twin engines' of the European Union; the United Kingdom, which joined the European Community in its first enlargement cycle in the 1970s; Spain, as a representative of the so-called 'Mediterranean enlargement', which joined the European Community in 1986; and Sweden, an EU Member State since 1995, representing the fourth round of enlargement.[27]

The second group consists of countries that have joined the EU as part of the so-called 'Eastern enlargement' and were subject to EU conditionality, which specifically included the 'respect of minority rights' criterion.[28] This group comprises Slovakia and Estonia, which joined the EU along with eight more countries in 2004,[29] and Romania, which joined the ranks of EU Member States in 2007.[30] Finally, this group includes Croatia, which became an EU Member State

[25] Framework Convention, Art 26, para 1. For an overview of the beginnings and the first decade of the Advisory Committee's activities see: Gaetano Pentassuglia, 'Monitoring Minority Rights in Europe: The Implementation Machinery of the Framework Convention for the Protection of National Minorities– With Special Reference to the Role of the Advisory Committee' (1999) 6(4) *International Journal on Minority and Group Rights*; Alan Phillips, 'The Beginning' in Tove H. Malloy and Ugo Caruso, *Minorities, Their Rights, and the Monitoring of the European Framework Convention for the Protection of National Minorities* (Leiden, Brill Nijhoff, 2013) 13–42.

[26] For rules regulating its monitoring activities see: Resolution (97) 10 of the Committee of Ministers of the Council of Europe (17 September 1997).

[27] Treaty of Accession of Denmark, Ireland, Norway and the United Kingdom [1972] OJ L 73; Treaty of Accession of Spain and Portugal [1985] OJ L 302; Treaty of Accession of Norway, Austria, Finland and Sweden, [1994] OJ C 241.

[28] In 1993, the European Union established the Copenhagen criteria for accession to the European Union. They were further strengthened by the Madrid European Council in 1995. (Accession criteria (Copenhagen criteria), at www.eur-lex.europa.eu/legal-content/EN/TXT/?uri=legissum:accession_criteria_copenhague). The Copenhagen criteria include: the stability of institutions guaranteeing democracy, rule of law, and protection of human and minority rights, coupled with a functioning market economy and the ability to take on the obligations of membership, including the capacity to effectively implement the body of EU law.

[29] Treaty of Accession of the Czech Republic, Estonia, Cyprus, Latvia, Lithuania, Hungary, Malta, Poland, Slovenia and Slovakia [2003] OJ L 236.

[30] Treaty of Accession of Bulgaria and Romania [2005] OJ L 157. Romania, along with Bulgaria, was subject to a dedicated Cooperation and Verification mechanism aimed to address shortcomings identified in their EU accession process vis-à-vis judicial independence, organised crime, corruption and integrity in the public sector.

in 2013, following an accession process marked with even stricter conditionality with added focus on human rights.[31]

The third group consists of candidates for EU membership: Albania, Montenegro, North Macedonia, and Serbia. The four countries are all subject to comprehensive EU conditionality, marked by the 'fundamentals first' approach.[32] Their EU enlargement is currently directed by the revised EU enlargement methodology,[33] in which progress on the fundamental reforms, including minority protection, sets the overall pace of accession negotiations. The minority rights protection is, therefore, for these countries at the forefront of the EU accession negotiations, which also require the sustained return of refugees and the pursuit of transitional justice and inter-ethnic reconciliation in a post-conflict setting.[34]

The selection of countries was driven by the need to secure representation of all enlargement waves, as well as by our own familiarity with the minority situation and institutional set-up of a country. Until now, all countries under consideration passed through five monitoring cycles, apart from Montenegro and Serbia, who were subject to one less, which means that we have analysed a total of 58 country-specific opinions.[35] Given that countries from the second group became EU Member States during the second (Estonia and Slovakia), third (Romania), and fourth monitoring cycle (Croatia), the changes in the Advisory Committee's monitoring practice before and after their membership admission were an important aspect of the analysis.[36]

In the research, we compared both substantive and procedural aspects of the monitoring process. Although the analysis was focused on the sections of the opinions that deal with the level of representation of persons of minority origin in public sector bodies, as an aspect of Article 15's right to participation in public affairs, at times we also looked at the sections on other provisions of the Convention. There is a mutually reinforcing relationship between the level of implementation of Article 15 and a number of other provisions of the FCNM, which makes its

[31] Treaty of Accession of Croatia [2012] OJ L 112.

[32] The so-called 'fundamentals first' approach was set to push the candidate countries to deal with issues of judicial reform, human rights and fight against organised crime and corruption early in the accession negotiations coupling it with a benchmarking system (Wolgang Nozar, *The 100% Union: The Rise of Chapters 23 and 24* (Netherlands Institute of International Relations, 2012).

[33] The new methodology was introduced in 2020 through the Communication to the European Parliament, the Council, the European Economic, and Social Committee, and the Committee of Regions with a proposal for 'Enhancing the accession process – A credible EU perspective for the Western Balkans' COM(2020) 57 (5 February 2020). More on this in: Ana Knežević Bojović and Vesna Ćorić, 'Challenges of Rule of Law Conditionality' (2023) 7 *Bratislava Law Review*.

[34] These conditions are an integral part of the Stabilisation and Association Agreements (SAAs). See, for instance, Stabilisation and Association Agreement between the European Communities and their Member States, on the one part, and the Republic of Croatia, on the other part [2005] OJ L26/1, Art 4.

[35] The States Parties shall submit their reports every five years calculated from the date on which the previous report was due (Resolution (97) 10 of the Committee of Ministers of the Council of Europe (17 September 1997) para 21).

[36] This aspect was also considered with regard to the Advisory Committee's opinions on the United Kingdom, having in mind its specific situation of having joined the EU in 1972 and formally left it in 2020.

implementation a precondition for the realisation of other minority rights. At the same time, the level of implementation of these other rights reflects the level of implementation of Article 15.[37] This is particularly observable in the relationship of Art. 15 with Art. 6, para. 1, Art. 9, para. 4, Art. 10, para. 2, and Art. 14, para. 2 of the FCNM, given that these provisions require the presence of persons of minority origin in specific segments of the public sector, respectively in police, media, educational institutions, and public administration. For that reason, the share of persons of minority origin/with the command of minority languages in these public bodies was used as an indicator of the degree to which national minorities make up part of the public sector workforce when such analysis was absent from the Article 15 considerations.

2. Adequate Representation of National Minorities in Public Bodies

The participation of persons belonging to national minorities in public affairs through their adequate representation in the workforce of public bodies represents the most novel dimension of participatory rights enshrined in Article 15.[38] While the contours of this aspect of the right to participation in public affairs have also been shaped through the monitoring work of the Human Rights Committee[39] and in the international soft law created under the auspices of the Organization for Security and Cooperation, it is the Advisory Committee that has most significantly contributed to its normative elaboration.[40]

Since the first monitoring cycle, the Advisory Committee has interpreted Article 15 as embracing not only the right to political participation of national minorities but also their right to be adequately represented in public administration and other public bodies of States Parties. Since adequate representation is

[37] Verstichel speaks of the participation of minorities in decision-making processes, taken in broadest sense, 'as a precondition for a sound minority protection'. Verstichel, 'Elaborating a Catalogue of Best Practices' (n 21) 175.

[38] That aspect is not mentioned in the Explanatory Report, which places an accent on the political representation of persons of minority origin. Its novelty is also visible in the fact that, according to Weller, and our own findings, in the first monitoring cycle no State Party met the standard. See: Weller, 'Creating the Conditions' (n 12) 289.

[39] In Article 25 of the ICCPR, access to public service positions is regulated in a separate subparagraph (Art 25, para c). In its General Comment No. 25, the Human Rights Committee interprets the conduct of public affairs broadly as the exercise of power in the legislative, executive and administrative branches (General Comment No. 25: The Rights to participate in public affairs, voting rights and the right of equal access to public service (Art 25, para 5). For the monitoring practice, see, for instance, the Human Rights Committee's concluding observations from 2014, where it expressed its concern over underrepresentation of Israeli citizens of Arab origin in the civil service (Human Rights Committee, *Concluding Observations on the Fourth Periodic Report of Israel* UN Doc CCPR/C/ISR/CO/4 (28 October 2014) paras 7, 8).

[40] OSCE High Commissioner on National Minorities, *The Ljubljana Guidelines on Integration of Diverse Societies & Explanatory Note* (2012) 46–47.

a precondition for the realisation of several other minority rights, the Advisory Committee's reflections on the scope and content of this standard frequently appear in its pronouncements on other provisions of the Convention. The Committee's views on the right to adequate representation are also found in its thematic commentary of Article 15.[41]

Although the Committee employs different terms to distinguish this element of Article 15 from the political representation, its core meaning remains consistent. Regardless of whether a public body is political, administrative, or entrusted with specific mandates, persons of minority origin should be adequately represented within its workforce.[42] The proportion and the qualitative aspects of their presence should be sufficient to ensure that the participation of national minorities in the work of public institutions is effective. These quantitative and qualitative components together form what we have elsewhere defined as the 'standard of adequate representation of persons belonging to national minorities in public bodies'.[43]

In the interpretation of the Advisory Committee, a few basic rules determine what constitutes adequate representation. While the share of persons of minority origin should approximate their share in the overall population, the measures aimed at arriving at 'rigid, mathematical equality in the representation' should be avoided.[44] The duty of adequate representation applies to all territorial levels of public sector bodies. In other words, it concerns not only public bodies situated in areas with a more substantial minority population but also the central-level public bodies. The standard pertains to all segments of the public sector and not only to bodies dealing with matters of particular importance to national minorities. Representation in public administration is just one element of the standard, with other equally important elements being the representation in police, judiciary, and executive bodies, all the way down to public enterprises.[45] To enable effective participation, the representation of persons of minority origin should not be confined to entry-level positions but should also include the senior grades.

Like the majority of the FCNM's provisions, Article 15 is a programmatic norm that sets out the objectives the State Parties are expected to pursue by taking into account the specific circumstances of their minority groups. Beneath its rhetorical and often vague references to concepts such as diversity, social inclusion, and good governance, the Advisory Committee's interpretation of the standard of adequate

[41] Advisory Committee, *Thematic Commentary No. 2*, paras 120–128.

[42] In other words, among persons who occupy a position within the organisational structure of a public body, not as representative of a political party or an interest group but based on their skills and expertise.

[43] Milica V Matijević, *Adequate Representation of Persons Belonging to National Minorities in Public Bodies* (Belgrade, Institute of Comparative Law 2024) Pt I. The Committee primarily uses the term 'adequate representation', but it also employs some other expressions, such as 'reasonable representation' (*Fourth Opinion on Serbia*, para 123), and 'equitable representation' (*Second Opinion on North Macedonia*, para 195).

[44] Advisory Committee, *Thematic Commentary No. 2*, paras 120 and 123.

[45] For the sake of simplicity, in the chapter we use the term 'public bodies', or 'public sector' as general terms denominating all levels of public administration (local, regional, central-level) and all types of public bodies, including public enterprises.

representation reveals three distinct yet interrelated objectives: the elimination of prejudice and employment discrimination, equal access to public services, and the accommodation of identity-related needs of national minorities.[46]

That implies that States Parties are obliged to establish normative and institutional conditions for adequate representation of persons of minority origin within the public sector. Where these ordinary methods fail to bring about the desired outcome, more proactive interventions are warranted. Such measures would typically be concerned with enhancing the employment opportunities for underrepresented minority groups, including through targeted recruitment and specialised training programmes. The States Parties are also expected to ensure the stability of their employment and career progression on par with those available to members of the majority population.[47]

Owing to its relatively novel character, this particular aspect of Article 15 has so far attracted limited attention from scholars, and its doctrinal analysis is rarely found in the literature. Among the few notable scholarly contributions is the monograph by Annelies Verstichel dedicated to participatory minority rights. There, Verstichel provides an overview of the basic characteristics of the Advisory Committee's approach to the standard.[48] Similarly, Mark Weller, through his examination of the Advisory Committee's work, affirms that adequate representation of persons of minority origin in public bodies, or as he calls it, 'executive representation', is an important element of the right to participation that extends to all territorial and functional levels of the public sector.[49] Kristin Henrard, in her analysis of participatory rights in the international hard and soft law instruments, highlights the concept of 'mirror representation' as a core component of the Advisory Committee's normative elaboration of the right to adequate representation.[50] Henrard argues that the Committee's evaluations operate on the premise that a public body is representative when its composition, in approximate terms, mirrors the demographic composition of the country's population.[51] As part of her commentary on Article 15, Tove H. Malloy characterises adequate representation as a form of direct participation in public affairs. She points to inequalities in access to public sector employment and the persistent lack of disaggregated data as recurrent issues raised by the Advisory Committee as barriers to the realisation of this standard.[52]

[46] More on this in: Matijević, *Adequate Representation* (n 43) 24–34.

[47] Fourth Opinion on the UK, para 129; Second Opinion on Estonia, para 186.

[48] Annelis Verstichel, *Participation, Representation and Identity: The Right of Persons Belonging to Minorities to Effective Participation in Public Affairs–Content, Justification and Limits* (Intersentia, 2009) 318–320.

[49] Weller, 'Creating the Conditions' (n 12) 282–284.

[50] Kristin Henrard, '"Participation", "Representation" and "Autonomy" in the Lund Recommendations and Their Reflections in the Supervision of the FCNM and Several Human Rights Conventions' (2005) 12(2) *International Journal on Minority and Group Rights* 136–138.

[51] Henrard, 'Participation, Representation and Autonomy' (n 50) 158, 160.

[52] Tove H. Malloy, 'Commentary of Article 15 of the Framework Convention for the Protection of National Minorities' in Rainer Hofmann, Tove H. Malloy and Detlev Rein (eds), *The Framework Convention for the Protection of National Minorities: A Commentary* (Leiden, Brill Nijhoff, 2018) 278–282.

Following this brief overview of the standard of adequate representation of persons of minority origin in public bodies – both in theory and in the Advisory Committee's practice – we now turn to the main findings of our analysis.

3. The Findings

When the Advisory Committee began its role of evaluating the implementation of the FCNM, none of the countries covered by the analysis had public bodies that could be deemed representative in terms of minority participation. Where the Committee analysed the matter under Article 15, the conclusion was obvious. In other country-specific opinions, such conclusion ensued from the inadequate number of civil servants with the knowledge of minority languages, identified under Art. 10, para. 2 of the Convention, or the sub-performance in the implementation of other closely related provisions. Another important characteristic of the milieu in which the monitoring started was the unavailability of data. The absence of data on ethnic composition of the public sector workforce has been a steady feature of all the countries under analysis, apart from the UK.[53] During further monitoring cycles, partial datasets became available in some of the countries.

3.1. The General Characteristics of the Advisory Committee's Monitoring Approach

The most obvious feature of the Advisory Committee's evaluations concerning the representativeness of public bodies in the selected countries is an absence of the systematic approach to the matter. This is firstly evident in the variations of section headings addressing minority representation in the public sector. For example, in its fifth opinion on Albania, the Committee employed a broad title – 'Socio-economic participation – employment and regional development (Article 15)'[54] – while in the fifth opinion on Croatia, a more specific heading was used: 'Effective participation in public affairs and decision-making process – public administration (Article 15)'.[55] Although most country-specific opinions distinguish between participation in public affairs and participation in socio-economic life by addressing them under separate headings, there are instances where these two aspects of Article 15 are merged into a single section, which also covers the issue of public body representativeness.[56] This

[53] Advisory Committee, *Thematic Commentary No. 2*, para 29.

[54] *Fifth Opinion on Albania*, 37 in relation to paras 199, 201. On the other hand, in the second opinion, the Committee used the section title 'Participation in the public administration and economic life' (*Second Opinion on Albania*, 36, in relation to paras 208, 211).

[55] Fifth Opinion on Croatia, para 35.

[56] In the second opinion on Montenegro, for instance, the Committee used a generic heading 'Effective participation of persons belonging to minorities in social life and in public affairs', under

lack of consistency is observable not only across countries but also in relation to the same country over different monitoring cycles.[57]

The absence of the systematic approach to the matter is further reflected in the discontinuity of evaluations. Specifically, when the Advisory Committee identified the underrepresentation of certain minority groups within the public sector, that did not automatically result in the follow-up on the matter in the subsequent monitoring cycle. In many instances, the Advisory Committee would examine representation in one opinion, neglect the topic in the following one, just to return to similar conclusions in later opinions.[58] Looking back at the first monitoring cycle, it is difficult to discern a clear rationale for the Committee's attention to the representation in some countries from the outset, in contrast to others where it only begun to investigate the matter at later stages of the monitoring process.[59] The most illustrative in this regard is the example of Spain, where the question of adequate representation was only raised in the fifth opinion, when the Committee called on the authorities to 'improve the representation of Roma in the public bodies at all levels, central, regional and local levels, in the media, in executive bodies and the judiciary through positive measures'.[60] As a result of this lack of consistency in the monitoring, it has been difficult to gain a linear understanding of the developments in this field for the majority of analysed countries.

3.2. The Advisory Committee's Monitoring Approach and EU Enlargement

Although the literature points to a strong interrelatedness between EU accessions and the process of monitoring, and despite our initial hypothesis that the

which it addressed several aspects of implementation of Article 15, including the level of participation of persons of minority origin in the public sector workforce. *Second Opinion on Montenegro*, 3 in relation to paras 177, 184.

[57] For instance, in the *Third Opinion on Slovakia*, the Committee uses a very specific title 'Participation in public services and the law enforcement agencies' (*Third Opinion on Slovakia*, 42), while in the fourth opinion it goes back to the general title 'Participation in public life and decision-making processes' (*Fourth Opinion on Slovakia*, 26).

[58] eg, The Committee started investigating the matter already in the first opinion on Romania, when it asked the authorities to collect the data (para 71), it identified underrepresentation in the second opinion (para 187), in the third, fourth and fifth opinion it did not evaluate the matter, even though in the fifth opinion the need to increase the minority language speakers among the public sector employees was among the recommendations for immediate action (para 11).

[59] In Slovakia, for instance, the Advisory Committee did not look into the level of representativeness of public bodies in the first opinion, when it only identified an inadequate number of civil servants with the knowledge of minority languages under Art. 10, para 2. (*First Opinion on Slovakia*, para 36). On the other hand, in the case of Romania, a country belonging to the same group, the evaluation of the presence of minorities in public sector bodies found its place already in the first monitoring cycle (*First Opinion on Romania*, para 71).

[60] Fifth Opinion on Spain, para 89.

Advisory Committee conducted more scrupulous evaluations in the States Parties that were, or are still, subject to the minority rights conditioning, our findings did not support the correlation between the two. The variations observed in the Advisory Committee's supervisory practice across the country-specific opinions cannot be explained by the EU membership or accession status of the countries in question. In other words, the investigation revealed that the more systematic and in-depth evaluations found in some country-specific opinions did not coincide with the phases of EU enlargement during which the implementation of minority rights was a formal accession requirement. This conclusion ensues both from the comparison of the three groups of countries selected for analysis and from the examination of the differences between the countries from the same group. Let us first look at the variations in the Advisory Committee's approach to monitoring across the three groups of countries.

While the Advisory Committee did not evaluate the level of inclusiveness of public bodies at all in the two countries from the first group, Germany and Sweden, it did enquire on this matter in Spain and in the UK, even though they were not subject to formal minority conditioning during their EU accession.[61] The monitoring process concerning the UK is a particularly salient exception to the low prominence of this matter when it comes to the first group of analysed countries, as Article 15 considerations include the question of adequate representation in all of the Committee's opinions.

In the second group of countries, i.e., countries which have joined the EU through the enlargement process that included the formal 'minority rights' criterion, we observed a more sustained Committee's interest in adequate representation. However, the identified variations could not be ascribed to the individual EU accession paths of the countries in question. In Slovakia, the Advisory Committee started addressing the question of representativeness of the public sector only in the second opinion, which was adopted after Slovakia joined the EU. This despite the fact that, already in the first opinion on Slovakia, the Advisory Committee found that minority languages could not be effectively used before public administration due to the lack of civil servants who are proficient in minority languages.[62] Conversely, with regard to Croatia, the Advisory Committee showed a sustained interest in the matter of adequate representation both before and after 2013, when the country became an EU Member State.[63]

[61] While their negotiations on joining the EU did not feature minority protection as an important factor, it should be noted that the requirements for democracy and the rule of law were addressed within the accession context in the case of Spain, through a general commitment of the Member States to safeguard the principle of rule of law. See: Marko Kmezić, *EU Rule of Law Promotion: Judiciary Reform in the Western Balkans* (Routledge, 2018) 15.

[62] *First Opinion on Slovakia*, para 36. On the other hand, as noted, the Committee delves into the matter already in the first monitoring cycle on Romania and Croatia, which are from the same group of countries.

[63] Starting from the first monitoring cycle, when it found that the situation in Croatia vis-à-vis the presence of minorities in the public sector workforce was incompatible with Article 15, the Advisory Committee evaluated the matter under Article 15 in all opinions adopted by now.

The case of Estonia represents an even more telling illustration of our findings about the lack of correlation between the Advisory Committee's monitoring approach and the country-specific EU enlargement trajectories. In the first opinion on Estonia, which was published two years before the country became an EU Member State, the Committee briefly analysed the question of adequate representation under Article 15. In the opinion, it also referred to barriers to the public sector employment of persons of minority ethnicity, such as the high bar regarding proficiency in the State language and the citizenship-related difficulties. In the second opinion, published one year after Estonia became an EU Member State, the Advisory Committee identified underrepresentation of persons of minority origin in the public sector,[64] as well as a generally low unemployment rate of the Russian minority ensuing from the direct and indirect employment discrimination affecting its members.[65] Eventually, among all the countries in the second group, only the monitoring practice regarding Romania sustained our hypothesis, as the Committee investigated the implementation of this segment of Article 15 merely in the opinions that were adopted before the country joined the EU in 2007.[66]

The third group, which is made up of the candidate countries whose EU accession path is to an even greater degree conditioned by the effectiveness of their minority rights regimes, provides further arguments against our initial hypothesis. While the analysis of the opinions on Montenegro, North Macedonia, and Serbia demonstrated a steady attention being devoted to the public sector representation through a scrupulous and detailed analysis of this particular aspect of Article 15 in all monitoring cycles, the situation is different when it comes to Albania. There, the Advisory Committee's approach was less systematic, even though this country has been participating in the EU integrations under the same conditions as the other three countries, albeit with a later start of the process. The Advisory Committee undertook the evaluation in the first and second cycles; it dropped it from the third and fourth ones to address it again in the fifth monitoring cycle but only to a limited extent because of the persistent lack of data on the presence of minorities in the public sector.[67] At the same time, the Committee's pronouncements on the related aspects of other minority rights, such as, for instance, the

[64] Second Opinion on Estonia, para 58.

[65] ibid, para 160. The Advisory Committee also shows that, among else, the legal provisions on the use of minority languages were not in accordance with the Article 10 standards (paras 96, 97).

[66] ie, in the first and second opinion, which were adopted in 2002 and 2006; ie, before the country became an EU Member State in 2007. In the subsequent opinions, the Advisory Committee analysed only the political participation of minorities, the consultative mechanisms, and the general level of participation of persons of minority origin, in particular of Roma, in the economic and social life of the country. At the same time, the level of realisation of some other provisions of the Convention pointed to the continuous underrepresentation of persons of minority origin in certain segments of the public sector (*Third Opinion on Romania*, para 188; *Fourth Opinion on Romania*, para 133; *Fifth Opinion on Romania*, para 11).

[67] First Opinion on Albania, paras 75, 76; Second Opinion on Albania, para 211; Fifth Opinion on Albania, paras 199, 201.

presence of minorities in the police force, demonstrated the continuous relevance of this question in Albania.[68]

3.3. Monitoring in the Ethnic Conflict Settings

Even though the investigation did not confirm the validity of our initial hypothesis about the correlation between the EU accession and the Advisory Committee's monitoring practice, the research findings have pointed to another potential link between the conflict prevention objectives and the Committee's approach to the standard of adequate representation. Throughout the research, we have observed several important similarities in the Advisory Committee's evaluations of the matter in the opinions that concerned five countries. These countries come from all three groups covered by the research: the UK (first group), Croatia (second group), Montenegro, North Macedonia, and Serbia (third group).

The most obvious feature shared by all five countries is that they have had an ethnic conflict experience in their recent past.[69] Four out of five countries on the list were party to the conflicts that led to the dissolution of the Socialist Federal Republic of Yugoslavia. There is ample literature explaining in detail these civil wars and their role in the adoption of the FCNM. Here we shall just briefly note that the break-up of the Socialist Federal Republic of Yugoslavia gave rise to three major armed conflicts: in Croatia (1991–1995), Bosnia and Herzegovina (1992–1995), and Kosovo*[70] (1998–1999). Serbia and Montenegro, at the time making up the Federal Republic of Yugoslavia, were directly involved in all three ethnic conflicts. Some smaller conflicts were also waged, including the one in North Macedonia (January-August 2001).[71] All four conflicts ended with peace settlements that included extensive minority rights guarantees. In the United Kingdom, decades of ethnic cleavages in Northern Ireland, known as the *Troubles*, gave rise to a lengthy peace process that finished with the signing of the so-called 'Good Friday Agreement' in 1998.[72]

[68] For instance, the Advisory Committee invited the authorities to promote recruitment of the members of this minority group into the police force (*Third Opinion on Albania*, para 101), and noted that members of Roma and Egyptian communities were hit by an unemployment rate five times higher than for the rest of the population (*Fourth Opinion on Albania*, para 152).

[69] In other words, in the period that shortly preceded or coincided with the adoption and entering into force of the Framework Convention.

[70] This designation is without prejudice to positions on status, and is in line with the UN Security Council Resolution 1244/99 and the International Court of Justice Opinion on the Kosovo Declaration of Independence.

[71] A that time known under the name 'The former Yugoslav Republic of Macedonia'.

[72] The Good Friday Agreement of 10 April 1998, also known as the Belfast Agreement, is in fact a set of two agreements: an agreement reached in the Multi-Party Talks between the British and Irish governments and the eight participating political parties, and an agreement between the British and Irish governments, where the former Agreement is one of the annexes to the latter. Rober Montgomery, 'The Good Friday Agreement and a United Ireland' (2021) 32(2) *Irish Studies in International Affairs* 83–110. See, also: Ian McBride, 'Ethnicity and Conflict: The Northern Ireland Troubles' (2023) 62 *Journal of British Studies* 618–39.

The similarities in the Advisory Committee's approach to the duty of adequate representation in the five countries were observed in relation to both the procedural and the substantive aspects of the monitoring. The principal similarity concerns a more systematic approach to monitoring. In these opinions, a special section was often dedicated to the level of participation of persons of minority origin in public bodies; conversely, in other opinions, these considerations were more often found under generic headings.[73] Another easily observable characteristic of these country-specific opinions is that the sections dealing with adequate representation were more detailed.[74] They included analysis of the ethnic composition of the staff of various public bodies, including those that were rarely or never under evaluation in other country-specific opinions, such as defence sector bodies or public enterprises.[75] Additionally, the Committee paid more attention to the level of representation in the senior grades and managerial structures.[76]

In contrast to the sporadic character of evaluations in other opinions, here the Committee monitored the implementation of the standard within the Article 15 section in each monitoring cycle. The Committee was evaluating the level of representation in the five countries since the first monitoring cycle, whereas such considerations were found in the first opinions of only three other countries.[77] In these opinions, the Committee was not discouraged by the lack of official statistics, unlike in the opinions on other countries, where it often decided not to investigate the matter for the lack of official data.[78] In the second opinion on Slovakia, for instance, the Committee noted the lack of data and invited the authorities 'to ascertain whether the persons belonging to national minorities, particularly to numerically smaller minorities, are adequately represented in the civil service'.[79]

[73] In Serbia, for instance, the Committee used very specific headings, such as 'Participation in public administration and in the judiciary' (*Second Opinion on Serbia*, 42; *Third Opinion on Serbia*, 44), or 'Representation of national minorities in public administration' (Fourth Opinion on Serbia, 36). In the fourth opinion on North Macedonia, the Committee used the heading 'Representation in civil service and administration', although under the same heading it also analysed the level of minority representation in police (*Fourth Opinion on North Macedonia*, 35 and para 88).

[74] As noted, in those country-specific opinions not rarely an entire sub-section under the Article 15 considerations was devoted to the matter of adequate representation (see the ft above). cp with, for instance, *Second Opinion on Estonia*, paras 158, 160.

[75] See, for instance, the *Third Opinion on Croatia*, para 203 and *Third Opinion on Serbia*, para 183.

[76] See, as an illustration, the Committee's pronouncement on North Macedonia, in which it addressed the level of representation of minorities in 'all sectors of the public administration (including in the defence sector)', and also in relation to more senior grades (*First Opinion on North Macedonia*, para 98); the level of presence of minorities in the managerial structures of the public bodies (*Second Opinion on North Macedonia*, para 195); the representation of persons belonging to numerically smaller minorities (*Fifth Opinion on North Macedonia*, para 128).

[77] The considerations of adequate representation are not present in the first monitoring cycle of the other three countries from the first group (Germany, Sweden, Spain). When it comes to the second group, they are not found in the opinion on Slovakia, and in the opinion on Albania, as the remaining country from the third group.

[78] Second Opinion on Slovakia, paras 116, 118.

[79] ibid, para 118.

Conversely, despite the chronic lack of ethnic data in Serbia, the matter was evaluated since the very first opinion.[80]

Speaking about the ethnic data, as already noted, their absence has been the principal problem for evaluations. In all analysed countries apart from the UK and, to a certain extent, Croatia and North Macedonia, the data on the ethnic composition of the public sector workforce have been either non-existent or only partially available. In Germany, for instance, the Advisory Committee was generally considerate of the historical reasons that caused a broad societal opposition to the collection of ethnic data. Only in the last opinion on Germany has the Committee more vigorously addressed the problem, stating that it was not possible to have an understanding of the position of minorities without at least qualitative research that would correlate equality indicators with ethnic affiliation.[81] On the other hand, in the ex-ethnic conflict settings, the Advisory Committee addressed the lack of data with greater resoluteness and persistence. There, the Advisory Committee often insisted on a more comprehensive and systematic data collection. For instance, an outstanding issue under Article 15 in the second opinion on Serbia was that only the data on mother tongue and proficiency in other languages of civil servants were available regarding central-level institutions. This was accompanied by an observation that data on the ethnic belonging of civil servants were needed in order to reach conclusive findings on the level of participation of national minorities.[82] In Montenegro, the Advisory Committee reproached the authorities for the fact that the data on the level of representation were collected through a survey that did not cover the entire State administration and did not display the fields and the professional ranks of positions held by persons of minority origin.[83] Then again, when it comes to Romania, it seemed that the Committee would have been content if at least data on the minority language speakers among the civil servants in the local administrative bodies were available.[84]

It was also observed that the absence of data was less of an impediment to the Advisory Committee's investigations of the level of representation in countries with an ethnic conflict experience.[85] While in some other analysed countries the lack of official data represented a barrier to the evaluation of the matter,

[80] Even though 'the authorities were not in a position to submit quality data on the present situation in this field', already in the first opinion on Serbia and Montenegro, which then formed a State Union of Serbia and Montenegro, the Committee evaluated the situation at a greater length and invited the authorities 'to review and monitor the situation with increased vigour and to take additional measures' (*First Report on State Union of Serbia and Montenegro*, para 103).

[81] *Fifth Opinion on Germany*, paras 78, 83. An earlier, but more modest attempt to address this matter is also found in the third opinion, para 54.

[82] *Second Opinion on Serbia*, para 239. See, also the 'recommendations for immediate action' in the *Fourth Opinion on Serbia*, 2.

[83] Fourth Opinion on Montenegro, para 153.

[84] Fifth Opinion on Romania, para 146.

[85] This observation does not apply to the UK, as this State Party, with some exceptions, regularly and in a systematic manner collected the ethnic data.

in ex-Yugoslav countries the Committee did not seem discouraged. Instead, it relied extensively on other sources, such as circumstantial evidence, reports of State bodies and civil society organisations, and statements of the representatives of national minorities.

Eventually, the analysis showed that in the States Parties with an 'ethnic conflict' background, the Advisory Committee often assigned special importance to the standard of adequate representation. Starting from the second monitoring cycle, the Committee has emphasized the most pressing issues in a separate section entitled, in the beginning, 'issues of concern' and later 'issues for immediate action'. In eight of the total of 23 opinions on the countries with experience of ethnic conflict, the low representation of persons of minority origin was given the status of an 'issue of concern/for immediate action',[86] while in three opinions it was singled out as an 'issue of concern following two or more cycles of monitoring'.[87] In contrast, out of 34 analysed opinions concerning the remaining seven countries, this matter was assigned such rank in only two opinions.[88] Even though in Estonia, for instance, the Committee found in the fifth opinion that the number of persons of minority origin among the staff of public bodies was three times lower than their share in the population and that conditions for the use of minority languages, including before the civil administration, raised 'grave concerns' as to their compatibility with Article 10, this problem was among the issues of concern in only one earlier opinion.[89]

Interestingly enough, our findings on the Committee's approach to the matter of adequate representation in the countries with a background of ethnic conflict are to some extent paralleled in the scholarly literature and practice-oriented texts. A precursory literature review showed that the greatest number of papers and studies on the ethnic composition of the public bodies' workforce and on the legal regulation of this matter comes from these five countries.[90]

[86] The representation of persons of minority origin was given the status of an issue of concern/for immediate action or of 'recommendation for immediate action' in the following country-specific opinions: *Second Opinion on Serbia*, para 283; *Third Opinion on Serbia*, 2; *Fourth Opinion on Serbia*, 2, 41; Second *Opinion* on North Macedonia, para 229; *Third Opinion on North Macedonia*, 2, 34; *Fourth Opinion on North Macedonia*, 2, 40; *Second Opinion on Croatia*, para 185; *Third Opinion on Croatia*, 3, 38.

[87] The representation of persons of minority origin was given the status of an 'issue of concern following two or more cycles of monitoring' in the following country-specific opinions: *Third Opinion on Serbia*, para 231; *Third Opinion on Montenegro*, para 192; *Third Opinion on North Macedonia*, para 197.

[88] The representation of persons of minority origin was given the status of an issue of concern in the *Second Opinion on Estonia*, para 186. The representation of persons of minority origin was given the status of an 'issue of concern following two or more cycles of monitoring' in the *Third Opinion on Slovakia*, para 215.

[89] Second Opinion on Estonia, para 186.

[90] See, for instance: Tijana Vukojičić Tomić, 'Suvremeni pristupi i modeli zapošljavanja društvenih manjina u javnoj upravi' (2017) 17(3) *Hrvatska i komparativna javna uprava* 365–388; Natalija Shikova and Marina Andeva, 'Analysis of the Systems for Representation of Minorities in Public Administration: The Case of the Republic of North Macedonia' (2023) 22(1) *Journal on Ethnopolitics and Minority Issues*

4. The Analysis

In this section, we will try to summarise the findings and discuss some of the factors that might explain them. We also explore what our findings can say about the broader inquiry that has steered the present research, that is, about the relationship between the conflict prevention and the human rights trajectories of the European minority rights regime.

The research showed that the differences in the monitoring approach of the Advisory Committee to the selected countries cannot be explained through the differences in their individual EU accession routes.[91] Instead, the research identified another potential explanation for the variations in the Committee's approach to the standard of adequate representation. We have observed that in the countries that had an ethnic conflict experience in the recent past, the Committee's approach exhibits several common traits, which also represent the main difference between these country-specific opinions and other opinions covered by the research. Put succinctly, the findings testify to a more systematic approach of the Committee to this specific segment of Article 15 in the countries with an 'ethnic conflict' background and a greater vigour in investigating the matter and overcoming the barriers to its evaluation.

Our view is that this difference is closely linked to the significance of participatory minority rights, including the representation of national minorities in public bodies, for conflict prevention. Before elaborating on this point, however, we will also consider some other possible explanations.

A simple explanation – one that would cut short our attempts to identify deeper theoretical implications of the findings – is that public sector employment has played a more important role in securing the socioeconomic equality of national minorities in the five countries in terms of their participation in economic and social life. In other words, a reason could be that in these countries, as compared to others, a position in a public body carries more value due to the bleak situation of their job markets. Of course, such reasoning falls flat once we remember the vast economic differences between the five countries (UK, Croatia, Montenegro, North Macedonia, and Serbia), as well as their economic similarities and differences with the other analysed countries.

in Europe 94–125; Jelena Džankić, 'Montenegro's Minorities in the Tangles of Citizenship, Participation, and Access to Rights' (2012) 11(3) *Journal on Ethnopolitics and Minority Issues in Europe* 40–59; For the studies, see: Elise Uberoi and Helena Carthew, *Ethnic Diversity in Politics and Public Life* (House of Commons Library, No 01156, 2 October 2023); Neli Demireva, 'Ethnic Minority Representation in the Public Sectors of the UK, France, Germany, Sweden and the US' (Equalsoc Reports, 2009); Inicijativa mladih za ljudska prava and Institut za otvoreno društvo, *Zastupljenost etničkih zajednica u državnim organima u Crnoj Gori* (Podgorica, 2010).

[91] However, we do not argue that the Advisory Committee did not rely on the EU accessions as a leverage for the more effective implementation of the Framework Convention. On the contrary, in many opinions, the Committee invokes concrete activities of the States Parties undertaken within the EU accession process. See, for instance, *Third Opinion on Albania*, para 89.

This leads us to another potential explanation, which concerns the practices of structural or systemic discrimination of national minorities.[92] It could be argued that the Advisory Committee was more attentive to the matter in the countries where national minorities were exposed to systemic discrimination in access to public sector employment. There are two principal problems with this argument. Not only would it have been difficult to prove the existence of continuous discriminatory practices against minorities in all five countries,[93] but the argument also collapses once we bring into the picture the position of the Roma minority across Europe and the lack of identical attention to the issue of its adequate representation in the opinions on many other analysed countries.

However, the argument is valuable because it points to an important link between Article 15 and its standard of adequate representation, on the one hand, and the conflict prevention objectives, on the other. In its commentary on Article 15, the Advisory Committee construed the link by emphasising that '[i]n post-conflict situations, particular attention should be paid to the socio-economic situation of persons belonging to minorities who have been discriminated against on account of their national minority background and were barred from employment'.[94] One of the main goals of the standard of adequate representation, as we have already noted, is the elimination of discriminatory practices and the ensuing inequality of ethnic minorities. It is not hard to link this goal to the conflict prevention strategy of addressing the root causes of conflict, embodied in the systematic denial of the basic needs of a group, as its principal approach to violent conflict. In other words, the relationship between the two is quite straightforward.

The third possible explanation of our findings is that the Advisory Committee placed greater attention on the monitoring of this aspect of Article 15 because the five countries had specific legal guarantees of adequate representation. One of the characteristics of the monitoring is that the Advisory Committee mostly reflects on the existing legal and institutional arrangements. According to Annelies Verstichel, this is the main reason why so few of its comments deal with the representation in public bodies.[95]

Although the investigation of the national regulation of adequate representation goes beyond the scope of this chapter, there is no doubt that the legal frameworks of the five countries guarantee adequate representation of persons belonging to minority communities in the public sector in a very concrete way.

[92] More about the concept of structural or systemic discrimination in: Milica V Matijević and Ana Zdravković, 'Breaking the Invisible Cage: Limits of Law in Structural Discrimination' (2024) 3 *Diritto, Immigrazione e Cittadinanza* 1–18; Milica V Matijević, 'Navigating Through the Substantive Equality Doctrine: Anti-Discrimination Law and Social Change' (2024) 15 *Pravni zapisi* 101–103.

[93] Apart from Croatia, where the Committee found in the first monitoring cycle that the situation is not compatible with Article 15 (*First Opinion on Croatia*, para 57), and Serbia and Montenegro, where the Committee, under Art. 4, pointed during the first monitoring cycle to the past discriminatory practices as the reason behind the underrepresentation of minorities in some public sectors (*First Opinion on State Union of Serbia and Montenegro*, para 38).

[94] Thematic commentary No. 2, para 46.

[95] Verstichel, Participation, Representation and Identity (n 48) 332.

In the four ex-Yugoslav countries (Croatia, Montenegro, North Macedonia, and Serbia), adequate representation provisions are laid down in constitutions and constitutional laws,[96] and their implementation is upheld by the constitutional courts.[97] Similarly, in the UK, the presence of persons of minority origin in the public sector is mandated by its equality laws.[98] On the contrary, in most of the other analysed countries, this issue is not regulated by law or is not regulated at all.[99]

The same argument could be used with regard to the observed differences in the Advisory Committee's approach to the collection of ethnic data in the five countries. It could be argued that the Committee has so persistently insisted on the collection of data on the ethnic composition of their public sector workforce simply because such requirement stemmed from their own legal frameworks. In particular, the attentiveness with which the Committee evaluated the matter in the UK could be ascribed to the availability of official data, which has been regularly collected pursuant to the UK equality laws.

The problem with this explanation is that its main argument is only partly valid since, in some of the five countries, specific legal guarantees were adopted after the monitoring process commenced, while the evaluation of the standard took place already in the first monitoring cycle.[100]

However, this hypothetical explanation is very useful because it points to another important link between conflict prevention and the supervisory mechanism embodied in the Advisory Committee. By the time the Advisory Committee started to carry out its monitoring role, the participation of national minorities in public affairs, including through their representation in the public sector

[96] The Constitution of the Republic of Serbia (Official Gazette of the Republic of Serbia 98/2006) includes a provision establishing the obligation of public bodies to take care of the appropriate representation of persons belonging to national minorities in public administration (Art. 77, para 2). In Montenegro, the Constitution adopted in 2007 (Constitution of the Republic of Montenegro (Official Gazette of the Republic of Montenegro, No. 1/2007)) guarantees to the persons of minority origin 'the right to proportionate representation in public services, State authorities and local self-government bodies' (Art 79(10)). The right to adequate representation is in Croatia granted in Art. 22, para 3 of the Constitutional Law on the Rights of National Minorities (Official Gazette No. 155/2002). The Constitution of North Macedonia, as amended further to the Ohrid Agreement (para 4.2), contains several provisions on participation by persons belonging to national minorities in the work of non-elected public bodies (eg, Art. 8).

[97] eg, Constitutional Court of Serbia, Decision IУ-171/2002 of 5th June 2003. cp with the Decision No. 6324/2013 of the Romanian High Court of Cassation and Justice (Decizia nr. 6324/2013), where the court held that the condition to speak the Hungarian language as a part of the job description for a position of a general-secretary of a village hall in a municipality where 70% of the residents belonged to the Hungarian minority was discriminatory.

[98] Equality Act 2010, s 149.

[99] In Albania, for instance, the matter was addressed only in relation to the Roma minority in a policy document (National Action Plan for the Equality, Inclusion and Participation of Roma and Egyptians 2021–2025 of the Republic of Albania (2021), activity 5.7.1, at 107.

[100] In Serbia, for instance, the specific legal regulation of the matter took place in 2002 (Art 21 of the Law on the Protection of the Rights and Freedoms of National Minorities before amendments (Official Gazette of the Federal Republic of Yugoslavia No. 11/2002)), ie, in the year when the monitoring cycle was completed.

workforce, had already become an important conflict resolution technique and a component of the peace accords that brought an end to the main ethnic conflicts in Europe.[101] These peace accords precipitated the legal regulation of the matter in the five countries.[102] It seems that such legal developments, in synergy with the specificities of the Advisory Committee's *modus operandi*, ie, its focus on the existing mechanisms, have entrenched the conflict prevention considerations in the Committee's monitoring practice.[103]

Let us now return to the absence of consistency and coherence as the main characteristic of the Advisory Committee's monitoring practice concerning other countries. We have observed that the Advisory Committee's approach to the standard was not systematic, apart from its opinions on the five countries with ethnic conflict experience. What does that mean for our considerations of the role of conflict prevention and human rights as two distinct, although overlapping, approaches to minority rights? To answer this, we need to briefly go back to the basic postulates of the two approaches.

By its very nature, conflict prevention is concentrated on situations characterised by a higher potential for violent ethnic confrontations. Consequently, the conflict prevention approach to minority rights is necessarily one of selective focus, in which attention is primarily directed to the implementation of minority rights in such contexts where the antagonism between the majority and the minority exhibits an ethnic conflict potential of a certain degree. The short-term goal of conflict prevention is to eliminate factors that can lead to the recurrence of violence, while in the long term it strives towards the transformation of violent conflict into 'peaceful (non-violent) processes of social and political change'[104]

[101] See: Framework Agreement (Ohrid Peace Agreement) (signed 13 August 2001, Skopje), paras 4.1–4.3; The Belfast (Good Friday) Agreement: An Agreement Reached at the Multi-Party Talks on Northern Ireland (Cm 3883, April 1998), para 3, at 16, para 4. at 17; General Framework Agreement for Peace in Bosnia and Herzegovina (Dayton Peace Agreement) (signed 14 December 1995, Paris), Article IX: General Provisions, para 3. However, the link between the power sharing mechanism, including the adequate representation guarantees in the peace accords, and the Advisory Committee's monitoring practice should be further examined in the future research.

[102] For instance, as a consequence of the Belfast (Good Friday) Agreement, the Government of the United Kingdom and devolved Executives have taken a number of steps to secure the rights of minorities in Wales, Scotland and Northern Ireland. In North Macedonia, the sections on equitable representation in the Ohrid Peace Agreement gave rise to a series of legislative activities for the further elaboration of this principle. For a brief overview of the contemporary peace agreements see: Alexia Solomou, 'Comparing the Impact of the Interpretation of Peace Agreements by International Courts and Tribunals on Legal Accountability and Legal Certainty in Post-Conflict Societies' (2014) 27 *Leiden Journal of International Law* 496–499.

[103] Another finding closely related to this one, which is common to all country-specific opinions covered by the analysis and that we found worthy of further examination, is related to the fact that the Advisory Committee in its evaluations places particular emphasis on the level of representation of persons of minority origin in the police and the judiciary, as the segments of the public sector that have special significance in conflict prevention strategies. See, for instance, *Fourth Opinion on Croatia*, para 90; *Second Opinion on Romania*, para 195; *First Opinion on Serbia*, para 103; *Third Opinion on Albania*, para 101.

[104] Hugh Miall, Oliver Ramsbotham and Tom Woodhouse, *Contemporary Conflict Resolution: The Prevention, Management and Transformation of Deadly Conflicts* (Polity Press, 2011) 32.

that would lead to the creation of a more just society. Justice is, in that sense, vital for conflict prevention, but its realisation at times can be sacrificed to the realisation of other, short-term objectives, such as security and stability.

On the other hand, in the human rights approach, the pursuit of justice is above all other considerations. The realisation of justice is both the foundation and the ultimate goal of human rights. They are the trump cards because 'the rights secured by justice are not subject to political bargaining or to the calculus of social interests'.[105] At the same time, this pursuit of justice, as in other fields of law, is shaped by the need to secure legal certainty, as the main *differentia specifica* between law and other normative frameworks.[106] Predictability is a classical criterion for a definition of legal certainty, commonly taken to signify consistency and coherence.[107]

The short comparison of the conflict prevention and the human rights approach shows that, no matter whether the lack of coherence and consistency of the Advisory Committee's monitoring is explained by the limitations of its mandate, the broad margin of appreciation of the States Parties in implementing Article 15, or the vagueness of the standard of adequate representation, this trait brings the monitoring closer to a conflict prevention technique than to its human rights ideal.[108]

No doubt, the two paths are compatible and can work in synergy. Yet, which one of the two prevails could have practical consequences for the European minority rights regime. The balance sheet of more than twenty years of elaboration and monitoring of the standard of adequate representation shows that no country included in the analysis has arrived at the adequate level of ethnic representation of persons of minority origin by the last monitoring cycle.[109] The situation has been even deteriorating in some of them.[110] In the five countries where the monitoring was more systematic, only some of those legal guarantees that were stipulated in the peace accords were implemented.[111] In the meantime, new problems in the implementation

[105] John Rawls, *Theory of Justice* (Belknap Press, 1999), 3–7.

[106] Legal certainty, in the words of Mark Fenwick et al, is 'a normative ideal that has structured legal debates, both at the national and transnational level'. Mark Fenwick, Mathias Siems and Stefan Wrbka, 'The State of the Art and Shifting Meaning of Legal Certainty' in Mark Fenwick, Mathias Siems and Stefan Wrbka (eds), *The Shifting Meaning of Legal Certainty in Comparative and Transnational Law* (Oxford, Portland, Oregon: Hart Publishing, 2017) 17.

[107] For an overview of the definitions of the concept of legal certainty in different jurisdictions in Fenwick et al, 'Legal Certainty' (n 106) 2–9.

[108] Kristin Henrard, for instance, observes that 'allowing states a margin of appreciation regarding the way in which they implement human rights carries the risk of negating the need for uniformity and the related concerns of legal certainty, as well as predictability' (Kristin Henrard, 'A Critical Appraisal of the Margin of Appreciation Left to States Pertaining to 'Church–State Relations' under the Jurisprudence of the European Court of Human Rights', in Kristin Henrard (ed), *The Interrelation between the Right to Identity of Minorities and Their Socio-Economic Participation* (Leiden, Brill Nijhoff, 2013) 237).

[109] In some countries and in some respects, the situation has been deteriorating. See, for instance: *Fourth Opinion on Croatia*, para 90; *Fourth Opinion on the UK*, para 129.

[110] See, for instance: Fourt Opinion on Croatia, para 90; Fourth Opinion on the UK, para 129.

[111] See, for instance, the arrangements for the adequate representation of the members of the Albanian ethnic minority into the police forces in South Serbia (*Second Opinion on Serbia*, para 238; *Third Opinion on Serbia*, para 185), as addressed in the Demilitarisation Statement signed in 2001 in Konculj

of the standard have started to loom: the chronic under-representation of smaller minorities and majority in minority positions,[112] politicisation of ethnicity,[113] and the misuse of the right to adequate representation.[114]

5. Conclusion

In the chapter, we examined the relationship between the human rights and the conflict prevention objectives in the European minority rights regime by analysing the monitoring practice of the Advisory Committee on the FCNM. Specifically, we compared the Committee's approach to the right to effective participation in public affairs across twelve countries with the different EU integration trajectories. The investigation focused on the Committee's evaluations of the representation of persons of minority origin in the workforce of public bodies, as a distinct segment of Article 15 that has emerged from the Committee's monitoring and interpretative practice.

Our initial hypothesis was that more systematic evaluations of the matter in certain country-specific opinions coincided with EU enlargement phases, during which minority rights formed part of the accession requirements. We assumed that the primary rationale for incorporating minority rights into EU accession conditions was to prevent an outbreak of ethnic confrontations within an expanded European Union. Accordingly, the presumed correlation between the EU enlargement process and the Committee's supervision practices was supposed to indicate the influence of conflict prevention objectives on the evolution of European minority rights.

However, the research findings did not confirm our initial hypothesis. Instead, they revealed another potential link between the conflict prevention objectives and the Committee's approach to the standard of adequate representation. Throughout the research, we observed several important similarities in the Advisory Committee's evaluations of the matter in the countries that had an ethnic conflict experience in the recent past. These country-specific opinions exhibited

(Serbia); the equitable representation of persons of Albanian origin in the public sector in North Macedonia, as enshrined in the 2001 Ohrid Agreement (*Fourth Opinion on North Macedonia*, para 86), and the similar arrangements for the representation of protestants in the police in Northern Ireland. When it comes to other countries with ethnic conflict experience, a number of scholars have pointed out, mostly in the context of EU integrations, that the results in the sphere of minority protection were mostly limited to the adoption of laws and policies, without due attention being paid to their effective implementation (eg, Kristina Beretka and Margarita Andeva, 'The Non-Existing EU Standards in National Minority Protection as Prerequisites for Successful European Integration: The Case of Macedonia and Serbia' 2018 13(1) *AICEI Proceedings*; Sanja Vasiljević, 'EU Minority Conditionality and the Rule of Law: The Case of Croatia' in Mario Krešić, Damir Banović, Alberto Carrio Sampedro and Janis Pleps (eds), *Ethnic Diversity, Plural Democracy and Human Dignity* (Springer, 2022) 223–252; Ana Knežević Bojović, Vesna Ćorić and Aleksandra Višekruna, 'Spoljašnje uslovljavanje uslovljavanje Evropske unije i regulatorni odgovori Srbije' (2019) 3 *Srpska politička misao*).

[112] Fourth Opinion on the UK, para 129; Second Opinion on North Macedonia, para 25.

[113] Fourt Opinion on North Macedonia, para 87; Fifth Opinion on North Macedonia, para 128.

[114] Fourt Opinion on Croatia, para 89.

more systematic and persistent monitoring of the standard, in contrast to the general lack of consistency and coherence in the Committee's evaluations vis-à-vis other countries.

We argue that the observed variations in the Committee's approach are closely linked to the relevance of participatory minority rights – including the representation of national minorities in public bodies – for conflict prevention. By the time the Advisory Committee began its monitoring role, the inclusion of national minorities in the public sector workforce had already become a key conflict resolution strategy and, as such, a component of the peace accords that ended major ethnic conflicts in Europe. The peace accords led to the legal regulation of the issue in the countries with an ethnic conflict experience. In turn, these legal developments, combined with the specific character of the Advisory Committee's approach – namely, its focus on existing mechanisms – have embedded the conflict prevention considerations into the Committee's monitoring practice.

This interpretation is further supported by the inherent differences between conflict prevention and human rights approaches to minority rights. While these approaches can and often do operate in synergy – given that the conflict prevention draws its normative framework from the contemporary human rights standards – the influence of the conflict prevention objectives on the Advisory Committee's monitoring practice leads to an instrumental approach to minority rights. As a result, their protection becomes largely directed at achieving practical outcomes, such as stability, rather than at securing the realisation of legal standards. Such an instrumental approach to minority rights may partly explain the low level of implementation of the standard of adequate representation in the analysed countries.

Further research is needed to test the robustness of our findings and explore their broader relevance. It should encompass other minority rights standards that are routinely deployed as conflict prevention tools and broaden the analysis to include other States Parties with a past ethnic conflict experience.[115] For now, we may conclude that the early adulthood phase of international minority rights still reflects an impulse to use them as a shield against new ethnic cleavages – an impulse which twenty years ago catalysed their transformation into legally binding standards.

[115] It would be interesting to analyse the Advisory Committee's approach to the matter in Moldova, as well as in Slovenia and Bosnia and Herzegovina, as the other two ex-Yugoslav countries not covered by the present research. Apart from the questions raised in this chapter, another important direction for future research is the impact of technological development on the standard of adequate representation and its recognition and redistributions related objectives.

8

Assessing Non-Territorial Autonomy to Protect Minorities in the Digital Age and Digital Minorities

ANTONI ABAT I NINET

1. Epistemological Questions of Minorities

1.1. Epistemological Components

The process of deconstruction starts with an analysis and decomposition of the different connotations that the conceptualisation of 'minority' has in the sense of *logos*. At the heart of its essence, the concept of a minority inherently carries with it the reciprocal presence of a majority. This symbiotic relationship is an embodiment of the dialectical principles famously elucidated by Hegel. When we explore the epistemological foundations of how the political and legal constructs of minority-hood are shaped, we find a compelling exemplification of Hegelian dialectics. The normative understanding and development of the concepts relies on a contradictory process despite the fact that majority and a minority are parts of a political unit.

The contradiction, inherent in the normative interpretation of 'minority', emerges seemingly as a response to the compelling necessity of bestowing recognition and rights upon a group which in the numerical minority, constitutes coexist, cohabit, and share a shared territorial expanse with the 'other', the majority. The normative discourse on 'minority' arises from a fundamental tension in seeking equilibrium between the numerically smaller but territorially significant group and the more abundant majority.

The adversarial nature of 'minority' seems to respond to the need of imposing recognition; it also connotes alterity, the theory about the other who alternates with me – implies two poles: I and you or I and it,[1] which entails the most appropriate way to speak of it, us. In this sense, minority implies alterity (otherness)

[1] Martin Buber, *I and Thou* (Simon & Schuster, 1970).

in a personal and social perspective. 'Alter' is a Latin pronoun formed from the noun 'alius' –other, distinct, different–, to which the suffix –ter is added, which distinguishes one element from another within a pair. Thus, 'alter' is opposed to 'ego', the other to the self, but both categories are defined relationally; they refer to each other to the extent that individual identity is not conceived without including in that definition.[2] Levinas inspires us on how to approach the topic of alterity, seeking to preserve the otherness of the other and to respect the difference that distinguishes the other from the self,[3] in our case, the minority of the majority.

There are no minorities without majorities, and vice versa. At the same time, we are all members of minorities and majorities, a fact that should predispose us to have a better understanding of the recognition of rights of minorities. As an example, I am a Catalan speaker, therefore a member of a linguistic minority in Spain, but at the same time, a member of a majority in my town. Let's say that I am a voter for social-democratic parties (also a majority in my town, a minority in my autonomous community, and a majority in the State). Probably, this is also evidence of the inability to see territory in its true sense, or as Connolly remarked, the nostalgic and anachronistic modern system of States that does not reflect reality.[4]

The first idea that comes to mind regarding the concept of minority/majority relations is that it has two core elements: 'territory' and the numerical aspect. In common sense, a majority always implies at least 50 per cent plus one of a specific population within a defined territory. However, this is not always the case. Taking the previous example, as a white male, I am also a member of a majority in all these territorial spheres (local, sub-State and State), despite that in the gender dimension, numerically there are more women than men.[5] Malloy is correct when she states that territory, or the desire to control it, is a primary reason for both in inter and intra-State conflicts. The allure of territory on the individual's psyche evokes feelings of homeland, nation, community, belonging, etc.[6]

However, this trend is changing and territory is losing its hegemony in the generation of these feelings and in many other political and legal domains. Certainly, territory remains a part of the Sancta Santorum of States and international relations, but globalisation and the current digital era are questioning this prominence. And, as advocated in this chapter, the conceptualisation of 'minorities' and its territorial dependence is not escaping this trend.

[2] Olaya Fernández Guerrero, 'Levinas y la alteridad: cinco planos' (2015) 39 *Brocar. Cuadernos de Investigación Histórica* 423–443. See also Emmanuel Levinas, *Altérité et transcendence*, (Fata Morgana, 1995).

[3] Brian Treanor, Aspects of Alterity: Levinas, Marcel, and the Contemporary Debate' (Fordham University Press, 2006) 54.

[4] William E. Connolly, *The Ethos of Pluralism*, (Minnesota University Press, 1995) 22 and chapter 5 as cited by Tove H. Malloy, 'Introduction' in Francesco Palermo and Tove H. Malloy (eds) *Minority accommodation through Territorial and non-Territorial Autonomy* (Oxford University Press, 2015) 1.

[5] Statista, 'Población de España por género' (Statista, 2025) https://es.statista.com/estadisticas/627691/evolucion-de-la-poblacion-de-espana-por-genero/.

[6] Tove H. Malloy (n 4). See also Francesco Palermo, 'Owned or Shared? Territorial Autonomy in the Minority discourse' in Francesco Palermo and Tove H. Malloy (n 4).

Recently, there has been profound debate on the other constitutive element of minorities, namely whether the term 'minority' refers to groups that make up less than 50 per cent of the national or local population. Gay McDougall worked extensively to decouple the definition of minorities from numerical quantum, and included under the definition communities such as people of African descent in Brazil, that is persons who may be in the majority of the population, but are systematically marginalised.[7] On the other hand, the current UN Special Rapporteur on minority issues has sought to re-establish or reinvigorate earlier understandings, whereby a minority refers to a group that is smaller in number than the majority population(s).[8]

In the case of gender, women are considered, sociologically, legally and politically as a minority. This is aimed at favouring the enactment of affirmative action or positive discrimination measures and public policies to mitigate the inequality and discrimination that women, due to their gender, have always suffered. In this concrete case, a teleological interpretation of the term 'minority' supersedes, for good reasons, a literal interpretation of the numerical element by introducing an external and determinant element to the conceptualisation of minorities.

These 'good reasons' are, according to US sociologist Louis Wirth, what justifies the conceptualisation of a group of persons as a minority. In his words, a minority group is any group of people who, due to their physical or cultural characteristics, are subjected to discrimination in comparison to other minorities within the society in which they live.[9] Therefore, even if Black people were in a numerical majority (in the US), they would still unquestionably be considered as a minority due to their position of social, political, and economic subordination.[10] A thorough investigation of the origins of the term minority, of how it came to be applied as a general term for all groups subjected to prejudice and discrimination, and of the meanings currently assigned to it may accomplish more than merely an understanding of its shortcomings.

This definition of minority, based on inferior status rather than statistical representation, allows for a sociological and normative approach to minorities.[11] This presents a paradox, in which a minority group need not necessarily constitute a minority of the population in a specific territory. Such recognition often elicits discomforts and objections, leading to critical characterisations, yet the term continues to be used. Furthermore, it enables political and legislative engineering with the ultimate objective of protecting and preventing discrimination against

[7] Office of the High Commissioner of United Nations, *Practical Guide to Developing Comprehensive, Anti-Discrimination Legislation* (6 December 2022) 128, www.ohchr.org/en/publications/policy-and-methodological-publications/protecting-minority-rights-practical-guide.

[8] Report of the Special Rapporteur on Minority Issues, Effective promotion of the Declaration on the Rights of Persons Belonging to National or Ethnic, Religious and Linguistic Minorities, UN Doc A/74/160 (15 July 2019), www.ap.ohchr.org/documents/E/GA/report/A_74_160.pdf.

[9] Louis Wirth, *The problem of minority groups* (Bobbs-Merrill Company Incorporated, 1945).

[10] ibid, 349.

[11] Raquel Osborne, '¿Son las mujeres una minoría?' (1996) 14 *Isegoría (Revista de Filosofía Moral y Política)* 79–93.

minorities. However, simultaneously, it assumes an ideological connotation of the term, its application.[12] As Meyers remarks, to speak of ideology is to recognise that ideas reflect biases intrinsic to the sociohistorical context from which they emerge. More specifically, it is to acknowledge that ideas embody values and interests and may be constrained by the social and political forces that characterise a particular society.[13]

Some authors have proposed, for example in the case of gender, the suppression of gender distinctions to avoid discrimination. Jule Goikoetxea, also analysing various types of power: political, economic, cultural, etc., concludes that men have more cultural, economic, social, and symbolic power than women. according to these authors, equalising those powers would therefore imply the disappearance of men and women because if we were two beings with the same powers, the concepts of man and woman would not exist. Accordingly, the goal for women is to build societies in which those concepts do not exist.[14]

What seems clear is that non-numeric dependence in considering a group as a minority introduces an ideological component into the definition, classification, and identification of minority groups, subject to ongoing debate and complexity, with nuances that extend beyond mere demographic representation. While consensus remains elusive, certain defining characteristics are frequently cited as indicators of minority status, inviting scrutiny, and often subjecting these groups to unjust treatment. Among these defining traits, race, religion, language, and culture emerge as prominent factors that shape minority group identity, highlighting the significance of shared beliefs, linguistic heritage, and cultural practices in fostering a sense of distinctiveness and vulnerability within broader society.[15]

These elements not only shape group cohesion but also serve as targets for discrimination and marginalisation. The multiplicity of identities within these categories reflects the intricacies of social stratification and underscores the fluidity of minority group dynamics.[16] Beyond the commonly cited characteristics, there exist lesser-known groups and traits whose inclusion in the minority designation warrants exploration. Intersectional identities, such as those defined by gender, sexuality, disability, or socioeconomic status, introduce additional layers of complexity that challenge traditional understandings of minority status and privilege. In essence, the classification of minority groups transcends mere demographic metrics, encompassing a complex interplay of historical, cultural, and socio-political factors.[17]

[12] Barton Meyers, 'Minority group: An ideological formulation' (1984) 32(1) *Social Problems* 1–15.
[13] ibid, 1.
[14] Jule Goikoetxea, *Democracia patriarcal: Euskal Herria, Estado español, Europa* (Txalaparta, 2022).
[15] Meyers (n 12).
[16] ibid.
[17] ibid.

1.2. Normative Definition

This ideological factor makes the normative accommodation / codification (*Normalisierung*) crucial from an epistemological-conceptual standpoint. And here again, the normative understanding and development of the concept rely on a contradictory process, despite that majority and a minority are parts of a same political unit. As we can observe, the normative definition, as always, implies a dose of pretended rationalisation that also determines the conceptualisation and understanding of minorities. The approach can be defined as a pragmatic conceptual proposal. The idea that the law itself governs can be understood as the idea that legal provisions authorise officials to act in a manner entailed by a gasp of the legal provisions.[18] Pragmatic conceptualism rejects the idea that the function of the law necessarily exhausts its content, it does not deny the significance of a functional analysis of the law in legal theorising or in legal interpretation.[19] This section focuses on the main international and regional actors in standard-setting on minority protection, namely the United Nations and the Council of Europe.

In the sphere of the United Nations, the normative standards for the definition and protection of minorities are found in Article 27 of the International Covenant on Civil and Political Rights, which refers to ethnic, religious or linguistic minorities, as does Article 30 of the Convention on the Rights of the Child (remarking in this case persons of indigenous origins) and The United Nations Declaration on the Rights of Persons Belonging to National or Ethnic, Religious and Linguistic Minorities, which is the document that sets essential standards and offers guidance to States in adopting appropriate legislative and other measures to secure the rights of persons belonging to minorities. In its general comment No. 23 (1994), the Human Rights Committee sets out that 'the persons designed to be protected' under Article 27 'are those who belong to a group and who share in common a culture, a religion and/or a language'.[20]

The Declaration also refers to the prohibition of discrimination on the basis of a list of categories such as race, colour, religion, language, nationality and ethnicity or working descent. Through respect for these two principles, the enjoyment of many human rights can be secured, including the right to effective participation in decision-making by minorities and, in particular minority women. In fact, despite that no article refers to different minorities other than those announced in the title, at least the Preamble includes sex among the elements that does not admit distinction to when promoting respect for human rights and fundamental freedoms. Article 1 of the Declaration codifies the obligation for States to protect the existence of national or ethnic, cultural, religious, and linguistic identities of

[18] Benjamin C Zipursky, 'Pragmatic Conceptualism' (2000) 6 *Legal Theory* 475.
[19] ibid, 476.
[20] Human Rights Committee, General Comment No. 23: The Rights of Minorities (Art 27) (1994) para 5.1.

minorities, referring the co-substantial element of territoriality to prescribe this obligation. However, it crucially omits recognition and protection for minorities based on gender, sexuality, disability, or socioeconomic status. The exclusion of these elements from protection may overlook their significance as fundamental aspects of individual and collective identity. In many cases, these omitted elements may represent the most pivotal or transcendent identity traits for certain groups of individuals, surpassing in significance those considered by the Declaration.

The omission may also be due to a lack of agreement or political will among the contracting States to recognise some of the omitted groups as minorities. This lack of consensus could stem from differing perspectives on what constitutes a minority, as well as varying levels of prioritisation of minority rights among the States involved. Additionally, political considerations, such as concerns about sovereignty or internal stability, may influence States' reluctance to formally recognise certain groups as minorities.

Overall, the omission reflects the complexities and challenges inherent in addressing minority rights within the framework of international agreements. It must also be noted that the Convention on the Elimination of All Forms of Discrimination against Women does not mention, nor consider, women as a minority.[21] Similarly, neither the Convention on the Rights of Persons with Disabilities,[22] nor the LGTBI+ people are defined as minority groups. Despite the fact that discrimination against these groups undermines the human rights principles outlined in the Universal Declaration of Human Rights, it does not mention them as minorities. Consequently, it can be argued that the normativisation of Women and LGTBI+ people is more related to 'oppressed groups' as advocated by Meyers than to minority groups.

The second standard-setting and international normative power in relation to the conceptualisation of minorities is the Council of Europe, specifically, Article 14 of the European Convention of Human Rights (ECHR) and the Framework Convention for the Protection of National Minorities, which aims to protect the existence of national minorities within their respective territories.[23] Note that the territorial element dominates the field of action of the Convention. The text, as in the case of United Nations, makes explicit reference to minorities limited almost exclusively to ethnic, cultural, linguistic and religious identities.[24] This time, Article One of the Convention avoids establishing a definition of minorities (national) by doing a referral to 'rights and freedoms of persons belonging to those minorities forms an integral part of the international protection of human rights'.[25]

However, this referral which includes Article 14 of the ECHR 'on the prohibition of discrimination', does include other grounds for securing non-discrimination,

[21] United Nations, Convention on the Elimination of All Forms of Discrimination against Women (18 December 1979) 1249 UNTS 13.

[22] United Nations, Convention on the Rights of Persons with Disabilities, 12 December of 2016.

[23] Preamble of the Framework Convention for the Protection of National Minorities, 1.II.1995.

[24] ibid, Preamble.

[25] ibid in art 1.

including association with a national minority.[26] On the other hand, the ECHR does not enshrine the general principle of equality but rather establishes the prohibition of discrimination solely in the enjoyment of the rights recognised therein. The Venice Commission also follows these lines when it distinguishes between women and minorities, without making any comment on the fact that Article 4.19 of the Election Law of the Former Republic of Macedonia mentions minority gender candidates.[27]

The fact is that there is no universally accepted definition of minorities. Indeed, the 'absence of consistency in understanding who is a minority', as the UN Special Rapporteur on minority issues notes, 'is a recurring stumbling block to the full and effective realisation of the human rights of minorities'.[28] Despite the United Nations Practical Guide to Developing Comprehensive Anti-Discrimination Legislation, which was edited by the Office of the High Commissionerthe stating that 'the existence of a minority group is a matter of fact, not of law nor official policy or decision',[29] the semantic indeterminacy projects a decisive influence on normativisation and political decision-making in considering what constitutes a minority.

International normative powers have delineated which elements determine the constitution of a minority and which do not. Furthermore, these treaties still echo the Westphalian era, particularly concerning the safeguarding of (national) minority rights, which remain embedded within the overarching framework of the State. Consequently, the acknowledgment and protection of minority rights are inextricably intertwined with the concept of statehood and its foundational elements, including territory, as outlined by Article 1 of the Montevideo Convention on Rights and Duties of States.[30] This linkage is particularly pronounced when focusing on the context at hand, specifically concerning the concept of territory. Central to our exploration is an examination of the novel facets that the contemporary landscape has introduced into the realm of defining 'minority' and its interconnected concepts.

[26] Article 14 of the European Convention of Human Rights and Protocol No. 12 to the ECHR.

[27] See European Commission for Democracy Through Law (Venice Commission), *Compilation of Venice Commission Opinions and Reports Concerning Gender Equality* CDL-PI(2021)002, point 103: 'These training programs may include a system of mentoring for inexperienced new members (including women and minorities) as well as gender-sensitive training courses for new members to promote non- discriminatory working …'; in 105: 'Political parties are also associations, and have been recognised as integral players in the democratic process and as 'foundational to a pluralist political society'. In particular, legislation on political parties can promote and support the full participation and representation of women and minorities in political processes and in public life'. See European Commission for Democracy Through Law (Venice Commission), *Joint Opinion on the Electoral Code of 'the former Yugoslav Republic of Macedonia'* CDL-AD(2006)022, adopted by the Venice Commission at its 67th Plenary Session, (Venice, 9–10 June 2006) (para 120). Article 4.19 of the Election Law requires that every list of candidates shall contain a certain number of minority gender candidates.

[28] Office of the United Nations High Commissioner for Human Rights, *Practical Guide to Developing Comprehensive Anti-Discrimination Legislation* (6 December 2022), www.ohchr.org/en/publications/policy-and-methodological-publications/protecting-minority-rights-practical-guide.

[29] ibid.

[30] United Nations, Convention on Rights and Duties of States (26 December 1933) 165 LNTS 19.

The Montevideo Convention, adopted in 1933, establishes four criteria for statehood: a defined territory, a permanent population, a government, and the capacity to enter into relations with other States. While the convention is primarily concerned with statehood, its emphasis on territory has significant implications for understanding minority rights within the context of the modern State system. In contemporary discourse, the notion of territory extends beyond physical land borders to include digital territories, such as cyberspace, and cultural territories, such as linguistic and ethnic domains. Consequently, the safeguarding of minority rights encompasses not only physical territories but also virtual and cultural spaces where minority groups reside and assert their identities.

In an evolving landscape, the conceptualisation of 'minority' extends beyond numerical representation to encompass diverse dimensions such as cultural identity, socioeconomic status, and intersectional identities. Moreover, the recognition of non-traditional minority groups, including women, LGBTI+ communities and persons with disabilities, emphasises the need for a more inclusive and nuanced approach to minority rights that transcends conventional territorial boundaries.

Once the deconstruction of the genealogical historical approach of the logos is concluded, the chapter proposes to analyse whether the current conceptualisation of the minority can be applied to emerging cases of non-territorial minorities that arise because of the globalisation and the digital era. After the process of deconstruction of the meaning of the term 'minority', it becomes apparent that despite allegations that suggest minorities are essentially factual, the numeric factor and the old-fashioned Westphalian orientation dependent on territory serve to limit and jeopardise its potential applicability. It also reveals that the normative sense, which has been considered essential epistemologically, does not provide the necessary clarity to achieve a universally accepted definition; on the contrary, it exposes further uncertainties regarding fundamental elements in defining minorities.

Once the deconstruction of the genealogical historical approach of the logos is concluded, the chapter proposes to analyse whether the current conceptualisation of minority can be applied to emerging cases of non-territorial minorities that arise due to globalisation and the digital era.

2. Minorities in the Digital Age and Digital Minorities

Through the lens of the terminology of Palermo, with 'territory' as a central focal point, this section endeavours to unearth the constraints posed by this rationale within the present epoch characterised by rapid technological advancement and globalisation. It becomes increasingly evident that while the State continues to hold primacy as the principal actor within international law, the evolving stage now encompasses a cast of non-State actors and nascent legal and political entities. Consequently, these emergent entities must also be considered as binding recipients of the protective umbrella extended to minority groups.

It is a matter of fact that the digital era has caused holistic legal, political, and social transformations in our *Lebenswelt*. The digital era has transformed the Homo Videns,[31] into a new sort of human, the Homo Digitalis, a Sapiens surrounded and dependent on Information Technology devices: smartphones, internet computers, e-Books, tablets, the Global Positioning System (GPS), the universal serial bus (USB) and the internet are not simply accessories but necessary elements of our lives. This Homo Digitalis lives permanently connected to an imaginary network. The internet age has incited new social movements characterised to be more horizontal and deliberative and including virality (as the tendency to circulate rapidly and widely from one internet user to another) as one of their main elements.[32]

New sorts of crowds, peoples and minorities are now at the heart of digital networks, as evidenced by the multiplicity of their appearances and aspects, such as in 'flash mobs' that are gatherings of individuals connected by mobile terminals. Citizens are concerned about political matters and want to defend their interests, influence the behaviour of authorities, look for like-minded others, or simply express their opinion in a public manner.[33]

The Homo Digitalis comprises a new form of collective identity, which allows different voices to be represented across borders, while also creating an adverse effect on the individuals' psyche, particularly because of the all-encompassing role of the Internet of Things.

From a social perspective, new non-territorial identities, minorities, and social classes – though not in a strict Marxist sense – are emerging and encompassing the social internet networks as spaces of autonomy, largely beyond the control of governments. People of all generations consume and share all kinds of audiovisual content generated by people from all over the world, on platforms from China, Japan, the EU or the United States. Millions of people communicate on social media platforms, forming (virtual) friendships with whom they share, discuss, and sometimes insult, in what is becoming a new public space. It must be taken into consideration that globalisation and new technologies question the very foundations of national identity,[34] majority groups,[35] minority cultures,[36] social classes,[37] and the definition of minority is not an exception at all.[38]

[31] Giovani Sartori, *Homo Videns: Televisione e post-pensiero* (Editori Laterza, 1997).

[32] Elena Gill Moreno, 'Nuevos abismos sociales en la era digital: de las masas al crowd' (2015) *Política y Sociedad* 192.

[33] Yannis Theocharis and Jan W Van Deth, Political Participation in a Changing World. Conceptual and Empirical Challenges in the Study of Citizen Engagement (Routledge, 2018) 19.

[34] Gal Ariely 'The Nexus Between Globalization and Ethnic Identity: A View From Below' (2019) 19(5) *Ethnicities* 763–783.

[35] Eric P Kaufmann, 'Introduction' in Eric P Kaufmann (ed), *Rethinking Ethnicity Majority Groups and Dominant Minorities* (Routledge, 2004) 1–19.

[36] Sophie Croisy 'Globalization and "Minority" Cultures: The Role of "Minor"' in Sophie Croisy (ed) *Cultural Groups in Shaping Our Global Future* (Brill, 2015).

[37] Catherine Rhein, 'Globalisation, Social Change and Minorities in Metropolitan Paris: The Emergence of New Class Patterns' (1998) 35(3) *Urban Studies* 429–447.

[38] United Nations Declaration on the Rights of Persons Belonging to National or Ethnic, Religious and Linguistic Minorities, UNGA Res 47/135 (18 December 1992).

It is important not only to inquire how this new reality generated by the digital era affects traditional minorities (national or ethnic, religious, and linguistic minorities) and those not included in the list (such as gender, LGBTI+, persons with disabilities, etc) in terms of their own self-understanding and self-awareness, but also the actual effectiveness and virtuality of already recognised rights. Consequently, these emerging digital minorities require special protection of their right in their 'territory' – the digital spectrum.

Self-determination, as expressed by Malloy and Salat, involves the ability of members of a group to come together and muster collective agency to manage their own affairs in a responsible manner under circumstances that are acceptable to all in the group, as well as increasingly acceptable to the society of which the group is a part.[39] This includes self-decision-making; having the freedom to issue decisions, plan, and strategise about their own NTA (non-territorial autonomy) institutions within regulative, normative, cognitive, and imaginary frameworks; as well as self-administration and self-management.[40]

On the other hand, there is a need for protection of *minorities in the digital sphere*. It is a fact that there is a rise in hate speech, xenophobia, racism, and populist nationalism on social media platforms, which has been fuelling violence and attacks against minorities worldwide.[41] In this sense, as Fernand de Varannes, Special Rapporteur on minority issues, remarks, hate speech on social media is spreading and strengthening. Minorities are overwhelmingly the main victims of hate speech, incitement to violence, and discrimination. Where disaggregated data are available on hate speech on social media or on hate crimes, approximately 70 per cent or more of those targeted tend to belong to minorities.[42]

These global, tangible, and systemic challenges demand a coordinated international approach. The utilisation of social media platforms as conduits for promoting extreme populist nationalism, inciting genocide, perpetuating racism, fostering intolerance, and marginalising minorities, coupled with their destabilising impact on numerous societies, is exacerbated by the operational strategies of prominent internet and social media corporations. Operating as private entities, these companies often amplify and incentivise hate speech and extremism due to their prioritisation of profit – characteristics that have propelled them to become some of the most lucrative entities globally.[43]

[39] Tove H. Malloy and Levente Salat 'Towards new Paradigms?' in Tove H. Malloy and Levante Salat (eds), *Non-Territorial Autonomy and Decentralisation. Ethno-cultural diversity governance* (Routledge, 2021) 244.

[40] ibid.

[41] OHCHR, 'Minorities and their rights matter to prevent conflict, says expert' (3 April 2022) www.ohchr.org/en/stories/2022/04/minorities-and-their-rights-matter-prevent-conflict-says-expert.

[42] Report of the Special Rapporteur on minority issues, Fernand de Varennes, A/78/195 presented at the United Nations General Assembly, 16 August 2023, www.ohchr.org/en/documents/thematic-reports/a78195-minority-issues-report-special-rapporteur-minority-issues. For the case of Europe, see also www.commission.europa.eu/strategy-and-policy/priorities-2019-2024/europe-fit-digital-age/digital-services-act_en.

[43] Report of the Special Rapporteur on minority issues, Fernand de Varennes, A/HRC/46/57 presented at the United Nations General Assembly, 03 March 2021, at https://www.ohchr.org/en/documents/thematic-reports/ahrc4657-minority-issues-report-special-rapporteur-minority-issues.

Minorities face heightened vulnerability and disadvantage in their engagement with online platforms. Besides being primary targets of hate speech on these platforms, they are also disproportionately impacted by restrictions and removal measures in content moderation systems. This disparity arises from biases inherent in the notification systems among users and third parties, as well as in the algorithms utilised in content moderation tools, as these algorithms are ultimately developed and overseen by humans.[44] As Fernand de Varennes alerts, the dark side of social media is now impossible to ignore, as these spaces have become a breeding ground for dangerous tropes, propaganda, conspiracy theories, misinformation, disinformation, racism and scapegoating of minorities.[45]

It is crucial to consider the response provided for the protection of minorities in the digital sphere. As seen previously, individuals may simultaneously belong to majorities and minorities depending on the space they occupy, typically territorial. However, the virtual world, with its social networks and audiovisual content platforms, creates a new, non-territorial but nevertheless real space where users may find themselves as minorities. Consequently, they must be safeguarded, following Levinas' example.

3. Protection of Digital Minorities and Minorities in the Digital Age

As previously introduced, by 'digital minorities', I refer to the new emerging minorities in the digital space, which cannot be derived almost exclusively from the multiple existing jurisdictions. Such subjection, besides being legally unviable, would result in unequal treatment, responses, and consequences depending on the individual's place of residence within the minority or their economic capability to sue someone in another State. Moreover, both the minority exposed in the digital network itself (which must be protected) and its protection, being virtual, generate significant issues of competence and jurisdiction attribution, for an offence that can also be universal.

This section of the chapter tests whether the theory of NTA can be applied to protect traditional minorities and emerging minorities in digital spaces. In no case is it considered to replace the possibilities provided by legal systems, albeit immensely challenging, or the more creative option of creating an ad hoc and specific international tribunal with competence, jurisdiction, and effectiveness in protecting emerging virtual and non-territorial minorities. The proposal here aims to complement those tools and propositions and to shed light on a phenomenon that, so far, does not seem to have received the necessary attention.

[44] ibid.
[45] ibid.

Since NTA could be understood as the self-rule of a group through a non-State entity in matters considered vital for the maintenance and reproduction of their culturally distinctive features, it is quite reasonable that NTA arrangements (non-State bodies) should have certain roles in relation to language as one of the features of the communities they represent.[46] If, as it seems entirely certain, group self-regard in the digital world deepens disengagement from a particular State, and digital interaction becomes vitally important for maintaining and reproducing distinctive aspects of the community, all indications suggest that the NTA, including non-State bodies, would be perfectly applicable to protect these transcendent elements of the minority and their rights.

Additionally, as NTA is a concept that includes several distinct forms, including consociationalism, cultural autonomy, juridical autonomy for religious communities, among others,[47] it is also very plausible that the digital exposition of minorities may affect these forms. If the main rationale behind the NTA is to provide a channel for self-rule of dispersed minorities,[48] it also seems appropriate to explore the application and adaptation of NTA to the digital sphere.

Concerning its scope, it is 'a means for the diffusion of powers in order to preserve the unity of a State while respecting the diversity of its population. Technically and legally, these models are structured around individual rights collectively exercised by members of the beneficiary group and overseen by institutions whose authority is determined by numerical representation'.[49]

It is indeed accurate to state that the term NTA encompasses a broad spectrum of meanings and interpretations. There is no singular standardised NTA model, and this lack of specificity allows NTA to manifest in diverse forms, including cultural, personal, and functional autonomy. As previously stated, the comprehension of these NTA types or modalities varies, with conceptual nuances in approaches, yet certain fundamental characteristics can be identified.[50] However, as Nimni remarks, the definition of NTA as a generic form of collective rights and collective representation across non-territorial lines, allows for minority communities to be collectively represented in governance, while sharing a territorial space with other communities that are equally represented.[51]

[46] Vladimir Đurić and Vasilije Marković, 'The Role of Law and Non-Territorial Autonomy Arrangements in the Implementation of Linguistic Rights: A Comparative Perspective' in David J. Smith, Ivan Dodovski and Flavia Ghencea (eds), *Realising Linguistic, Cultural and Educational Rights Through Non-Territorial Autonomy* (Palgrave Macmillan, 2023) 9.

[47] Tove H. Malloy, 'A new research agenda for theorizing non-territorial autonomy?' in Tove H. Malloy and Levente Salat (eds), *Non Territorial Autonomy and Decentralisation: Ethno-cultural Diversity Governance*, (Routledge, 2021) 3.

[48] ibid.

[49] ibid, 4.

[50] Ljubica Djordjević, 'The Many Faces of Minority Non-Territorial Autonomy' in Marija Andeva, Balázs Dobos, Ljubica Djordjević, Börries Kuzmany and Tove H. Malloy (eds) *Non-Territorial Autonomy* (Palgrave Macmillan, 2023).

[51] Ephraim Nimni, 'Minorities and the Limits of Liberal Democracy: Democracy and Non-Territorial Autonomy' in Francesco Palermo and Tove H. Malloy (eds) *Minority Accommodation through Territorial and Non-Territorial Autonomy* (Oxford University Press, 2015) 68.

Nothing seems to be deterrent for the application of NTA for new non-territorial (digital) emerging minorities. This parallels offline NTA, which contrasts with territorial models centred on collective rights upheld solely through the authority of institutions governing specific territorial jurisdictions, independent of resident population size. In its online application, NTA is also perceived as fostering personal autonomy and may be viewed as less disruptive to State unity, offering a promising paradigm for maintaining stability while addressing ethno-cultural demands.[52]

The application of NTA for digital minorities and minorities in the digital realm does not alter these prospects; instead, it opens a different scenario that reinforces the promising paradigm concerning State unity and political stability. The digital era presents unprecedented opportunities for decentralisation (in the case of traditional minorities),[53] and new digital minorities are not State related. Simultaneously, digitalisation situates NTA within what Malloy and Salat defined as new paradigms – new approaches that challenge the monopolistic systems of the State by emphasising interaction between State and non-State actors, suggesting the possibility of competing claims for authority, and questioning the state-centric view of governance regarding the devolution or diffusion of power.[54]

An effective protection of minorities in digital social media necessarily requires the interaction of States and the operators of the specific social media platforms. As an example of this practice, the US Justice Department and Meta Platforms (the non-State actor in the NTA) reached a key agreement to prevent discriminatory advertising in violation of the Fair Housing Act.[55] As a result of this agreement, Meta developed a new system to address algorithmic discrimination. Meta will be subject to court oversight and regular reviews of its compliance with the settlement until June 27, 2026, and the US Justice Department will continue to hold Meta accountable by ensuring that the Variance Reduction System addresses and eliminates discriminatory delivery of advertisements on its platforms.[56]

Regarding the social media platform 'X' (formerly 'Twitter'), there was a nearly 500 per cent increase in use of the N-word in the 12-hour window immediately following the shift of ownership of the platform to Elon Musk. Within the following week, tweets including the word 'Jew' had increased fivefold since

[52] ibid, 4.

[53] See, eg, the case of the Irish Gaeltacht, Steve Coleman and Éamon ó Ciosiáin 'The Irish Gaeltacht as a trans-local phenomenon', in Tove H. Malloy and Levente Salat, *Non-Territorial Autonomy and Decentralisation: Ethno-cultural diversity governance* (Routledge, 2021), 162.

[54] Malloy and Salat (n 39) 243.

[55] See Press Release, U.S. Department of Justice, 'Justice Department and Meta Platforms Inc. Reach Key Agreement as They Implement Groundbreaking Resolution to Address Discriminatory Delivery of Housing Advertisements' (Office of Public Affairs, 9 January 2023), www.justice.gov/opa/pr/justice-department-and-meta-platforms-inc-reach-key-agreement-they-implement-groundbreaking.

[56] ibid.

before the ownership transfer. Tweets with the most engagement were overly antisemitic. Likewise, there has also been an uptick in misogynistic and transphobic language.[57] In response, Musk announced the creation of a 'Content Moderation Council' that failed miserably and was pulled from the site as users created fake accounts for companies and political leaders.[58] Collectively, recent changes to and at X disrupt the ability of marginalised people to find community, produce useful discourse to share ways to foster equality, and protect themselves from hate speech and trauma.

In all of this, it is evident that minorities require protection, and there are compelling arguments supporting the feasibility of applying NTA to safeguard both digital minorities and minorities within the digital realm. These arguments arise from the increasing vulnerability of marginalised groups in digital spaces, where they face unique challenges and risks due to their minority status. Implementing NTA principles can provide a framework for addressing these challenges and ensuring the rights and dignity of all individuals, irrespective of their digital or offline identities. Thus, advocating for the application of NTA serves as a crucial step towards fostering inclusivity, equity, and respect for diversity in the digital landscape.

4. Conclusion

Following Derrida's theory,[59] the process of deconstruction of 'minority' in this chapter has ended without proposing an alternative, thus a re-constructive theory will denaturalise the methodology. However, the chapter does not aim to reconstruct the logos but to value a pure legal dimension, one autonomous to the moral, ethical, and spiritual domains that transform minority into a polysemic term.

A version of this chapter was delivered to the conference hold in Belgrade (Serbia) with the title: 'Are minorities rights (still) Human Rights?' This chapter does not answer the question; however, it points out the nuances of the term 'minority' that are not resolved by its normative accommodation, may stress the concept's inability to respond to the challenges that minorities are suffering in the digital era. To overcome this issue, we can either determine the concept of minority in a general manner (even if it is restrictive), as suggested by Fernand de Varennes, or we can transcend the concept and introduce a variant that allows not only for the protection of the rights of minority groups but also those who are minoritised (regardless of their number or territory). The aim, therefore, is

[57] Rashawn Ray and Joy Anyanwu, 'Why is Elon Musk's Twitter Takeover Increasing Hate Speech?' *Brookings Institution* (23 November 2022) www.brookings.edu/articles/why-is-elon-musks-twitter-takeover-increasing-hate-speech/.

[58] ibid.

[59] Jacques Derrida, Force de Loi: Le Fondement mystique de l'autorité (Galilée, 1994).

not to establish a utilitarian justification for the applicability of the concept but to propose fair solutions to these groups while respecting their identities as parts of a whole, not as counterparts of nothing. In this endeavour, the chapter delves into the exploration of the feasibility of employing an NTA framework to address the challenges encountered by minority groups, both present and anticipated, amidst the evolving landscape of the digital era.

PART IV

Society, Culture, Diversity: Old and New Minorities

9

New Minorities as a New Frontier for Minority Rights Regimes

*The Case of Non-EU Citizens in the Context of EU Member States**

ROBERTA MEDDA-WINDISCHER AND KATHARINA CREPAZ

1. Introduction

'Even though I may not have a definition of what constitutes a minority, I would dare to say that I know a minority when I see one.' This often cited yet contentious statement by Max van der Stoel, the first Organization for Security and Co-operation in Europe (OSCE) High Commissioner on National Minorities, underscores a central and unresolved dilemma concerning minority rights: the identification and delineation of minority groups. What or who constitutes a minority? Which individual and group rights should arise from this status? This issue prompts questions about the entitlements, duties and rights accorded to individuals and groups classified as minorities. Within the realms of policymaking, academia, and public discourse, there persists significant uncertainty regarding the definition of minorities – be they 'minoritised' or perceived as a 'distinct group' – not to mention the complexities surrounding 'new' migrant minorities, their legal standing, and the specific rights inherent to their status. Despite ongoing controversies and discussions about the conceptualisation and characterisation of minorities, particularly those categorised as 'new', clarity regarding fundamental rights remains elusive. Although fundamental rights are ideally regarded as universal and applicable to all, variations persist across different dimensions of these rights concerning various individuals and groups.

* This chapter draws from Roberta Medda-Windischer and Katharina Crepaz, 'Fundamental Rights and Non-EU Minorities: From an Ambiguous Concept to an Integrated Society?' in Tove H. Malloy and Balázs Vizi (eds), *Research Handbook on Minority Politics in the European Union* (Edward Elgar, 2022).

It is widely acknowledged that States bear the primary responsibility for safeguarding minority rights, encompassing the enforcement and realisation of pertinent international agreements and the rights they confer upon individuals belonging to minority groups. However, leaving the determination of who qualifies for minority protection solely to the discretion of States is deemed unsatisfactory, as it may result in inconsistent implementation across different minority groups. International agreements should provide a universally accepted, legally binding definition of minorities to prevent varying interpretations among Member States. Yet, as of now, no consensus has been reached regarding the precise definition or defining characteristics of minorities.

The ambiguity surrounding the term 'minority' is also a notable issue within European law. For instance, the Treaty on the European Union (EU) (Article 2) emphasises the importance of respecting the rights of persons belonging to minorities: 'The Union is founded on the values of respect for human dignity, freedom, democracy, equality, the rule of law and respect for human rights, *including the rights of persons belonging to minorities*'.[1] The EU Charter of Fundamental Rights prohibits discrimination based on belonging to a minority (Article 21 – EU Charter). Despite these provisions, there remains a lack of a clear, legally binding definition or comprehensive conceptualisation of which groups qualify as minorities, allowing Member States considerable discretion in implementing minority protection mechanisms.[2]

However, what may initially seem like a drawback could potentially offer advantages. The absence of a binding definition of minorities, and thus no predetermined limitation to minority groups consisting solely of citizens of EU Member States, opens the possibility of extending protection measures to non-EU minorities, particularly migrant communities, for certain rights. Nonetheless, the question arises: Is citizenship a necessary criterion for membership in a minority group?

Furthermore, there remains a notable absence of a comprehensive framework dedicated to safeguarding the rights of new minorities, notably concerning the right to identity and the right to societal participation, including political engagement. This chapter seeks to illuminate the diverse nature of linguistic, religious, and/or cultural new minorities and to examine the fundamental rights afforded to various types of 'new' minorities, especially those outside the European Union, given the concerns of EU Member States. It also discusses whether new (non-EU) minorities even strive for protection mechanisms similar to those in place for 'old' minorities.[3] Ultimately, it explores potential pathways toward fostering inclusive

[1] Consolidated Version of the Treaty of the European Union [2012] OJ C326/13; emphasis added; Roberta Medda-Windischer and Andrea Carlà, 'European Civic Integration and Common Values: The Experience of a Board Game' (2021) 5(1) *Peace Human Rights Governance* 65–86.

[2] Katharina Crepaz, 'Overcoming Borders: The Europeanization of Civil Society Activism in the "Refugee Crisis"' (2020) 48(6) *Journal of Ethnic and Migration Studies* 1448–1461.

[3] The so-called 'old' minorities (also referred to as 'historical' or 'traditional' minorities) are communities whose members have a distinct language, culture or religion, as compared to the rest of the population. Many have become minorities through the redrawing of international borders, having

and cohesive societies that honour the rights of all minority groups, proposing the 'Tree Mode' as a promising framework for diversity governance encompassing human and minority rights.

2. New (Non-EU) Minorities: Relevance of a Concept in the EU Member States

The term 'new (non-EU) minorities' encompasses a vast and diverse population, necessitating clarification of two key concepts before exploring fundamental rights further. Firstly, the term 'minority' itself lacks a universally binding definition, as discussed earlier, leaving the possibility to include within the concept of minorities also individuals without the citizenship of their country of residence. Secondly, the term 'non-EU' encompasses individuals without EU citizenship, which spans a wide array of groups, including recent third-country nationals (TCNs) arriving through labour migration, TCNs with special status due to bilateral or EU agreements,[4] long-term residents holding residence permits akin to 'civic citizenship', and refugees and asylum seekers, who are protected by specific provisions of international law.[5]

seen the sovereignty of their territories shift from one country to another. Among these communities there are also ethnic groups that, for various reasons, have not achieved statehood of their own, and have now become part of a larger country (or several countries). In many, but not all cases, their co-ethnics may be numerically or politically dominant in another State, which they therefore regard as their 'external national homeland' or kin-State. 'New' minorities consist of migrants and refugees, and their descendants, who are living in a country other than that of their origin, on a basis that is more than merely transitional. Their reasons for migrating encompass a wide range of situations, ranging from acute refugee situations to economic migrants and their family members. For an analysis of the difference between 'old' and 'new' minorities, see Roberta Medda-Windischer, 'Changing Paradigms in the Traditional Dichotomy of Old and New Minorities' in Kristin Henrard (ed), *Double Standards Pertaining to Minority Protection* (Brill-Nijhoff, 2010); Roberta Medda-Windischer, 'The Nexus of Old and New Minorities' in Tove H. Malloy and Claire Boulter (eds), *Minority Issues in Europe: New Ideas and Approaches* (vol 2, Frank & Timme, 2019).

[4] It is beyond the scope of this chapter to go into the details of bilateral and EU collective agreements granting special rights to citizens of certain non-EU countries; for an overview of the special provisions in place in this regard, see European Commission, 'Non-EU nationals' (Employment, Social Affairs and Inclusion 2025) www.ec.europa.eu/social/main.jsp?catId=470&langId=en; for an analysis of bilateral agreements in South-Eastern Europe and their impacts on minorities, see Emma Lantschner and Roberta Medda-Windischer, 'Protection of National Minorities through Bilateral Agreements in South Eastern Europe' (2001) 1(1) *European Yearbook of Minority Issues* 535.

[5] Since 1999, the EU has been working to create a Common European Asylum System (CEAS). Between 1999 and 2005 several legislative measures harmonizing common minimum standards for asylum were adopted. Three pillars underpin the development of the CEAS: bringing more harmonisation to standards of protection by further aligning the EU States' asylum legislation; effective and well-supported practical cooperation; increased solidarity and a sense of responsibility among EU States, and between the EU and non-EU countries. In September 2020, the European Commission has proposed the EU Pact on Migration and Asylum as the next step towards 'striking a new balance between responsibility and solidarity' European Commission, *A Fresh Start on Migration: Building Confidence and Striking a New Balance Between Responsibility and Solidarity* (Press Release 2020) www.ec.europa.eu/commission/presscorner/detail/en/ip_20_1706.

With regard to the first point, the perspective that citizenship is not a prerequisite for inclusion in a minority group suggests that individuals can freely identify with and seek protection and advancement within a minority community if they choose to do so. This viewpoint has received validation from various international entities and nations. As advocated by the UN (United Nations) Human Rights Committee in 1994, the criterion of citizenship, typically employed by States to confine the applicability of international instruments on minorities to specific historical groups, can be substituted with the criterion of presence.[6] Similarly, both the EU Fundamental Rights Agency and the Council of Europe adopt a comparable understanding of minorities: 'Persons belonging to linguistic, ethnic or national minorities, third-country nationals who immigrate to the EU, or immigrants who are long-term residents [and who] may all perceive that they belong to a minority group';[7] or when defining a minority as being composed of 'persons, including migrants, belonging to groups smaller in numbers than the rest of the population and characterised by their identity, in particular their ethnicity, culture, religion, or their language'.[8] The definition proposed by the former UN Special Rapporteur on Minority Issues, Fernand de Varennes, further emphasises that citizenship is not a prerequisite for minority status, affirming that 'a person can freely belong to an ethnic, religious, or linguistic minority without any requirement of citizenship, residence, official recognition, or any other status'.[9]

In this chapter, that has a focus on EU Member States, we propose defining 'new (non-EU) minorities' as third-country nationals who have migrated to the EU, and to consider them as members of new migrant minorities. These migrant minorities encompass individuals from both European and non-European countries, whose legal status may vary depending on bilateral agreements with Member States or the EU as a whole, thereby influencing public perception. However, the term 'new minorities' has encountered challenges and criticism as it appears to imply that individuals with a migrant background occupy a minority position, suggesting their status is inherently 'minoritised'.[10] Contrary to this critique, the term underscores the diverse nature of these groups and the potential for protection and advancement should they desire it. Moreover, it encompasses not only first-generation migrants but also their descendants, including second and third generations born in their country of residence who cannot be simply classified

[6] United Nations, Human Rights Committee, *CCPR General Comment No 23: Article 27 (Rights of Minorities)* (8 April 1994) CCPR/C/21/Rev.1/Add.5 www.refworld.org/docid/453883fc0.html.

[7] European Union, Charter of Fundamental Rights of the European Union [2012] OJ C326/02 eur-lex.europa.eu/legal-content/EN/TXT/HTML/?uri=CELEX:12012P/TXT.

[8] Council of Europe, Committee of Ministers, *White Paper on Intercultural Dialogue: Living Together as Equals in Dignity* (2008) www.coe.int/t/dg4/intercultural/source/white%20paper_final_revised_en.pdf.

[9] United Nations, Special Rapporteur on Minority Issues, Effective Promotion of the Declaration on the Rights of Persons Belonging to National or Ethnic, Religious and Linguistic Minorities, Report to the UN General Assembly 18 (15 July 2019) UN Doc A/74/160 www.undocs.org/A/74/160.

[10] On this point, see Roberta Medda-Windischer and Federica Maino, 'Vulnerabilities, minoritizing processes and concerted solutions for rural scarcities. Learning lessons and tackling marginalisation in Northern Italy' in Antonio Montañés Jiménez, Camila Ferreira Marinelli and Stavroula Pipyrou (eds), Minorities, Scarcity and Conflict (Routledge, 2025).

as 'migrants'. Expanding the scope of minority rights to include 'new minorities' could address existing gaps, particularly in rights pertaining to identity and diversity, which are often ambiguously addressed in international instruments on migrants' rights. Incorporating proven policies for 'old' minorities to accommodate 'new minorities' could represent a significant step forward, especially as many European States and the EU lack robust integration instruments for these populations.[11]

As regards the second point, it has to be acknowledged that with increasing migration and a growing TCN population residing in EU Member States for significant durations, the EU has had to adapt to this evolving demographic landscape. Striking a balance between migrant inclusion and stringent citizenship requirements, EU instruments ranging from the Charter of Fundamental Rights to the Long-Term Residents Directive (LTRD) have introduced the concept of 'civic citizenship'. This notion aims to align the legal status of Member-State nationals and long-term TCN residents, based on residency duration (typically five years), ensuring equal opportunities and treatment. Consequently, migrant and minority integration can be assessed in terms of substantive citizenship rights rather than nominal citizenship status, as articulated by Rainer Bauböck.[12] Furthermore, immigration, globalisation, and subsequent nation-state adaptations have spurred additional changes, including shifts in citizenship regimes from *ius sanguinis* to *ius soli* and *ius domicilii*, increased acknowledgment of multiple citizenship, the rise of supranational governance models such as EU citizenship, and a transition from assimilation to pluralism in national integration policies.

Despite these changes, the pivotal criterion for obtaining EU citizenship still remains citizenship of a Member State, meaning that around 21 million EU residents, constituting approximately 4.7 percent of the EU population,[13] who hold citizenship from non-EU countries, are precluded from EU citizenship. EU citizenship is envisioned to foster closer ties between the EU and its inhabitants, imbuing it with a fresh political and social dimension. However, tying EU citizenship exclusively to Member-State citizenship effectively excludes third-country nationals, many of whom have resided within EU borders for their entire lives, from various rights. Several rights remain accessible only to those in possession of full national citizenship. Firstly, the right to vote and stand for election in national elections holds significant sway. Non-citizens, despite being permanent residents and longstanding contributors to the workforce, face limited opportunities to engage in the democratic process at the national level,

[11] Roberta Medda-Windischer, 'Integration of New and Old Minorities: Beyond a Janus-faced Perspective' (2017) 14(1) *European Yearbook of Minority Issues* 1; Medda-Windischer, 'The Nexus of Old and New Minorities' (n 3).

[12] Rainer Bauböck, The Integration of Immigrants, Report of the 7th Meeting of the Joint Group of Specialists on Migration, Demography and Employment, 15–17 March, CDMG(94) 25 (Council of Europe 1994), para 3.1.

[13] European Commission, *Communication on a New Pact on Migration and Asylum*, COM(2020) 609 final, 23 September 2020, 1, https://eur-lex.europa.eu/legal-content/EN/TXT/?uri=celex:52020DC0609.

thereby lacking influence over migration policy, which is primarily conducted at the national level. Secondly, while citizenship generally bears little relevance to most private-sector employment, it remains crucial in sectors such as the judiciary, military, and law enforcement. For instance, in Germany, a substantial portion of governmental service positions is restricted to German or EU citizens.[14] Within the EU itself, while EU citizens can seamlessly reside and work in another EU Member State, third-country nationals are only granted the right to reside and work in a different EU country after five years of continuous residency and fulfilment of specific integration criteria, as outlined in the Council Directive 2003/109/EC, commonly known as the Long-Term Residents Directive.[15]

To address the deficiency in civic, political, and social inclusion of TCNs in Europe, two potential remedies have been proposed: either national-level reforms aimed at easing the acquisition of national citizenship for TCNs or an extension of the scope of EU citizenship. The former could entail either deregulatory measures to liberalise naturalisation rules or EU-induced harmonisation of national laws governing citizenship acquisition and loss.[16] While long-term harmonisation may be desirable, its feasibility is significantly constrained by the preservation of national sovereignty intertwined with the concept of citizenship. Given the prevailing political climate in Europe, characterised by the ascent of far-right parties and nationalism that frame migration as a threat – a scenario unlikely to shift soon – the prospects for expanding naturalisation opportunities for TCNs appear bleak.[17]

3. Do New Minorities Even Strive for Protection Measures?

Similar to traditional or historical groups, new minorities also assert certain fundamental claims that can be categorised into four main areas, applicable to both old and new minority groups, within the EU and beyond. These categories encompass the right to existence, the right to equal treatment and nondiscrimination,

[14] Government service positions include financial and tax officers, public administration officials, criminologists, judges, prosecutors, bailiffs, police officers, criminal technicians, teachers, judiciary officers and officers of the Federal Office for the Protection of the Constitution.

[15] There are exceptions to this situation due to bilateral agreements between non-EU countries and individual EU Member States or the EU collectively. There are agreements with candidate countries (eg, Albania, Kosovo, Montenegro, North Macedonia, Serbia, Ukraine) as well as with countries that are not aiming for EU accession – for example, Switzerland participates in the Schengen Area for the free movement of people and goods, and Swiss nationals are free to live and work in the EU. For further information, refer to www.ec.europa.eu/social/main.jsp?catId=470&langId=en.

[16] Andrew Evans, 'Third Country Nationals and the Treaty on European Union' (1994) 5(2) European Journal of International Law 199.

[17] Katharina Crepaz, 'The Minority Safepack Initiative: A European Participatory Process Supporting Cultural Diversity' (2020) 17 *European Yearbook of Minority Issues* 23.

the right to identity and diversity, and the right to effective participation in public life.[18]

The right to existence entails protection against physical harm, including genocide, ethnic cleansing, forced population transfers, demographic alterations, and collective expulsions. The principle of equality mandates treating similar situations equitably while recognising the necessity for special measures to ensure substantial equality for minorities, striking a balance between nondiscrimination and the need for specific norms. The right to identity encompasses the freedom to use one's language, express opinions without constraint, practice religion without infringing on others' rights, and safeguard cultural identity while maintaining a sense of belonging in the broader national society. Effective participation involves equal engagement in the electoral process, proportional representation in legislative bodies, establishment of consultative mechanisms, involvement in cultural, social, and economic spheres, and enhancement of economic opportunities for minority members.

Upholding these rights is crucial for fostering trust and loyalty toward the State and society, they thus help to 'avoid the feeling by persons belonging to minorities that they should use other, less acceptable means for their opinions to be considered'.[19] Improving inter-ethnic relations requires policies that nurture a sense of belonging and trustworthiness, fostering a common identity while preserving the distinct characteristics of various groups. The categorisation of these rights serves as a guiding framework for the development of policies and instruments aimed at protecting minority rights, while, at the same time, fostering social cohesion in the broader community. But do new minorities even hold analogous claims and strive for protection mechanisms similar to those in place for 'old' minorities?

A comparative case study investigated precisely whether 'new' minorities hold similar claims, opinions, and desires to 'old' minority groups.[20] Examining the

[18] For an analysis of these categories as applicable to old and new minorities, see Asbjørn Eide, 'Protection of Minorities' (UN Sub-Commission on Prevention of Discrimination and Protection of Minorities, Forty-fifth session 1993) UN Doc. E/CN.4/Sub.2/1993/34 www.documents.un.org/doc/undoc/gen/g93/145/23/pdf/g9314523.pdf; Roberta Medda-Windischer, 'Changing Paradigms in the Traditional Dichotomy of Old and New Minorities' in Kristin Henrard (ed), *Double Standards Pertaining to Minority Protection* (Brill-Nijhoff, 2010).

[19] Francesco Palermo and Jens Woelk, 'No Representation Without Recognition: The Rights to Political Participation of (National) Minorities' (2003) 25(3) *Journal of European Integration* 225, 241–241.

[20] The Project 'MinMig – Accommodating Linguistic, Religious and Cultural Diversity Through a Comparative Analysis of Minorities' and Migrants' Claims' (March 2020-December 2021) investigated whether 'new' minorities hold similar claims, opinions, and desires to 'old' minority groups. Based in the European Region Tyrol – South Tyrol – Trentino (Austria/Italy), 213 CAPI (Computer-Assisted Personal Interviewing) online and telephone interviews were conducted across the interested Austrian and Italian provinces; additionally, qualitative in-depth interviews with 'new' minority representatives (eg, from NGOs or other migrant organizations) were carried out. The project then compared the survey results to protection measures for 'old' minorities outlined in international protection documents. For a more detailed analysis of the project findings, see Katharina Crepaz, *"Old" and "New" Minorities: Regional Synergies, Differences and Perspectives', Final Project Report: MinMig – Accommodating Linguistic, Religious and Cultural Diversity Through a Comparative Analysis of Minorities' and Migrants Claims* (2021) www.zenodo.org/records/5656645.

assertions articulated by 'new' minorities in a survey conducted in the *European Region Tyrol – South Tyrol – Trentino* alongside those of 'old' minorities, drawn from international protection documents, revealed both parallels and distinctions. Remarkably, the majority of assertions put forth by the respondents aligned with the concept of 'legitimate claims' (claims bolstered by specific contextual factors) for 'new' minorities as delineated by Roberta Medda-Windischer, thereby falling within the realms where protective measures designed for 'old' minorities could potentially be extended to benefit 'new' ones, given requisite political resolve.[21] This suggests two conclusions: Firstly, respondents are cognisant of their societal status and position, and they do not advocate for protective measures as comprehensive as those afforded to 'old' minorities, which often seem detached from their daily experiences. Secondly, there exist thematic domains in which a collaborative approach to protecting 'old' and 'new' minorities could be viable and implementation feasible if politically desired. However, it is essential to recognise that the project findings reflect solely the perspectives of respondents at a particular juncture; as emphasised by Boulter, Medda-Windischer and Malloy, '[…] just as the external categorisation of groups changes over time, so too do the aspirations of those groups within the nation-state.'[22] Conducting a comprehensive longitudinal panel study on the assertions of 'new' minorities could potentially address this migrant data gap.

In the realm of education, discernible disparities outweigh similarities between 'old' and 'new' minorities across the three case study regions. For 'old' minorities, primary language education stands as a cornerstone claim, whether through a comprehensive curriculum in the minority language or through supplementary afternoon classes, particularly pertinent for smaller minority languages. Conversely, while respondents with a migratory background also value maintaining proficiency in their or their family's native tongue, they perceive it more as a personal rather than a public obligation. A shared aspect lies in the significant role of language for individual identification, yet the interviewees belonging to 'new' minorities viewed this responsibility as personal, regarding the opportunity to learn migrant languages in schools as potentially advantageous but not a fundamental entitlement as 'old' minorities do.

In contrast to 'old' minorities, whose identity often hinges on distinguishing themselves from the majority population, respondents aspire to integrate into the broader populace, particularly the younger second-generation who emphasise their 'hybrid identity' and their role as mediators between cultures and social groups – a trend also observed in a study on Austria by Haller and

[21] Roberta Medda-Windischer, 'Migration in Sub-State Territories with Historical Linguistic Minorities: Main Challenges and New Perspectives' (2018) 14 *Acta Univ Sapientiae, European and Regional Studies* 57, 28.

[22] Caitlin Boulter, Roberta Medda-Windischer and Tove H. Malloy, 'Introduction: What's in a name?' in Roberta Medda-Windischer, Claire Boulter and Tove H. Malloy (eds), *Extending Protection to Migrant Populations in Europe: Old and New Minorities* (Routledge, 2020).

Berghammer.[23] The aspiration for inclusion is also reflected in their attitudes towards political participation, a significant concern for both 'old' and 'new' minorities, as it affords them a voice in decision-making processes. However, while 'old' minorities are typically citizens of their host countries (with some exceptions, such as stateless Roma) and therefore automatically included in the democratic process, 'new' minorities, often not yet citizens, find themselves partially or completely excluded from voting, such as EU citizens who may vote in local and European Parliament elections but not in national ones. Bauböck and Valchars also explore whether citizenship acquisition or expanded voting rights offer a more viable solution to enhance the political participation of individuals with a migratory background, framing it as a 'chicken or the egg' dilemma – the feasibility of each approach may depend on the prevailing political context. With over 70 per cent of survey respondents deeming voting rights 'important' or 'very important', policymakers face the imperative of ensuring migrants' political engagement.[24]

In their endeavour to uphold cultural and religious customs, both 'old' and 'new' minorities exhibit similarities. However, a distinction emerges once again, reminiscent of the linguistic rights scenario: for 'old' minorities, the visibility of traditions holds significance, whereas for 'new' minorities, these traditions appear to be more private and family-centric, as emphasised by numerous respondents. Many participants expressed a desire to maintain traditions from their or their family's country of origin alongside local regional customs, while also discerning between traditions they wish to preserve and those they may not. Regarding religious traditions, the landscape is even more diverse, with individuals noting that these customs evoke memories of their childhood and are therefore upheld – a sentiment not dissimilar to why many residents without a migratory background celebrate Easter or Christmas. Representatives of migrant associations noted challenges in engaging young people, attributing this difficulty to their weaker ties to their or their family's country of origin, resulting in less interest in preserving cultural traditions. It would be intriguing to explore whether 'old' minority communities encounter similar trends among their youth,[25] where alternative perspectives or cultural influences supersede minority identification, or if this phenomenon is specific to persons with a migratory background, influenced by the stronger pull of the majority culture. Haller and Berghammer observe a 'tendency towards increased structural, social, and cultural integration and identification with the host society' among migrants in Austria, a trend likely mirrored

[23] Caroline Berghammer and Max Haller, 'Sprache und soziale Integration: Die Deutschkenntnisse der Zugewanderten' in Wolfgang Aschauer and others (eds), *Die Lebenssituation von Migrantinnen und Migranten in Österreich: Ergebnisse einer Umfrage unter Zugewanderten* (Springer VS, 2019) 72.

[24] Rainer Bauböck and Gerd Valchars, *Migration und Staatsbürgerschaft* (Österreichische Akademie der Wissenschaften, 2021).

[25] For an analysis of increased regional identification in national minority groups, see Katharina Crepaz, 'Europeanization and the "Regionalization" of National Minority Identity' (2019) 18(3) *Journal on Ethnopolitics and Minority Issues in Europe* 1.

among survey respondents.[26] The concept of flexible identification holds significance, enabling 'new' minorities to embrace their diversity and view intercultural identification as enriching rather than conflicting. These young, multilingual, and often well-educated individuals warrant greater inclusion in the political process, offering valuable role models for their communities, epitomising the ethos of 'if you can see it, you can be it'.

4. Are EU Instruments an Adequate Basis of Protection for New (non-EU) Minorities?

After having outlined the classification of fundamental minority rights, as well as the rights and protection measures desired by persons with a migratory background, we will utilise these categories as a framework for examining fundamental rights pertaining to new (non-EU) minorities within the EU context. Our analysis will distinguish between two types of instruments: Firstly, we will examine EU standards concerning fundamental rights, particularly focusing on non-discrimination, which applies to both EU and non-EU minorities. This examination will concentrate on directives such as the Racial Equality Directive and the Employment Framework Directive. Secondly, we will delve into fundamental rights and instruments specifically tailored for non-EU citizens, with a special focus on migrants or 'new' non-EU minorities. This segment of the analysis will spotlight directives such as the LTRD and the Council Directive on Family Reunification. This analysis will serve as a basis to assess the capabilities, opportunities and shortcomings of the instruments and mechanisms adopted in the EU to protect and promote the cultural diversity of new (non-EU) minorities.

4.1. EU Legal Instruments Applicable to All, Including New (non-EU) Minorities

In addition to legal instruments such as the European Charter of Fundamental Rights,[27] the Employment Framework Directive and the Racial Equality Directive

[26] Berghammer and Haller (n 23) 75.

[27] It must be noted that Title V of the European Charter of Fundamental Rights on 'Citizen's Rights' is generally not applicable to non-EU citizens. However, one provision within Title V applies entirely independently of citizenship: Article 41 concerning the right to good administration. In particular, Article 41(4) widens the personal scope of EU citizens' right to communicate with the EU institutions foreseen in Article 24(4) TFEU (2008) by stating that the right applies to '[e]very person'. In addition, three of the remaining seven provisions give rights to some groups of TCNs: the rights of access to documents, to appeal to the EU ombudsman and to petition the European Parliament, which also apply to 'any natural or legal person residing or having its registered office in a Member State'. Finally, another provision recognizes that, while EU citizens have the right to move, 'freedom of movement

serve as instruments to combat discrimination, prohibiting four primary forms: direct discrimination, indirect discrimination, harassment, and instructions to discriminate. Direct discrimination occurs when 'one person is treated less favourably than another is, has been or would be treated in a comparable situation on grounds of racial or ethnic origin'.[28] For instance, a hotel manager refusing entry to an individual associated with a minority group exemplifies direct discrimination. Indirect discrimination arises when 'an apparently neutral provision, criterion or practice would put persons of a racial or ethnic origin at a particular disadvantage compared with other persons, unless that provision, criterion or practice is objectively justified by a legitimate aim and the means of achieving that aim are appropriate and necessary'.[29] An example could be a requirement for street-cleaning job applicants to pass a written language test, disadvantaging certain communities whose native language differs from the official one. In the context of the Employment Framework Directive, an instance of indirect discrimination might occur if a department store bans employees from wearing hats while serving customers, thereby excluding individuals whose religious beliefs require head coverings, such as Muslim women.

Both directives, however, present significant gaps: the Employment Framework Directive prohibits discrimination across various grounds, but it applies only in employment and vocational training, and the Racial Equality Directive is broader in terms of scope of application, but it does not extend protection to discrimination based on religion or nationality. In this regard, it should be noted that in some cases it might be difficult to determine if nationality, or the lack of EU citizenship, is the exclusionary/discriminatory criterion or if it is the distinguishing features of a person that caused the discrimination, which would then be race-based and covered by the provisions of the Directive.[30]

It is important to note that in the EU context, non-EU citizens from certain European countries (eg, Switzerland, Norway or Serbia) may enjoy more favourable treatment due to bilateral or EU agreements and perceived cultural proximity.[31] For instance, the treatment of the EU Roma minority highlights how certain European minorities may face discrimination despite being citizens. Additionally, it must be

and residence may be granted, in accordance with the Treaties, to third-country nationals legally resident in the territory of a Member State' (Art 45 EU Charter). See Roberta Medda-Windischer and Katharina Crepaz, 'Fundamental Rights and Non-EU Minorities: From an Ambiguous Concept to an Integrated Society?' in Tove H. Malloy and Balázs Vizi (eds), *Research Handbook on Minority Politics in the European Union* (Edward Elgar 2022) 62.

[28] Racial Equality Directive, 2000, Article 2(2)(a).

[29] Racial Equality Directive, 2000, Article 2(2)(b).

[30] Sonia Morano-Foadi, 'Third Country Nationals Versus EU Citizens: Discrimination Based on Nationality and the Equality Directives' (2010) *Social Science Research Network*, 20.

[31] European TCNs who are long- or short-term residents may be perceived differently from those coming from non-European countries. For instance, a Norwegian living in Italy for just a few months may be viewed as less foreign than a Pakistani who has been a resident for 15 years. These differences stem from perceived cultural distance and internalised racism, and they particularly affect visible minorities.

underlined that not all non-citizens are migrants: there are stateless minorities, such as Roma or the Russian-speaking minority in Baltic countries.[32] Despite these nuances, most instruments in this context are particularly relevant for new minority groups resulting from recent migration. While the directives mentioned above are broadly applicable to all individuals residing in the EU, specific legal instruments are also in place to safeguard the rights of non-EU citizens. The next section will explore EU standards specifically tailored for non-citizens, with a focus on migrant workers who encounter discrimination due to their lack of citizenship status.

4.2. EU Legal Instruments Specifically Designed for New (non-EU) Minorities

In the years leading up to 2003, the European Commission consistently advocated for the free movement rights of TCNs. Finally, in 2003, an agreement was reached on the LTRD, which was officially adopted in January 2004 (Council Directive 2003/109/EC of 25 November 2003 concerning the status of third-country nationals who are long-term residents).[33] The LTRD addresses issues of non-discrimination, labour market participation, and free movement for TCNs. However, several limitations may be imposed on the scope of the Directive: Member States have the authority to implement labour market tests limiting movement within the EU based on economic grounds, impose overall quotas on third-country nationals, establish special rules for seasonal or cross-border workers, exceptions regarding social assistance and protection, distinctions among long-term residents based on employment status, and expulsion on grounds of public policy or security. Although the Directive grants the right to move between Member States under specific conditions, this represents a significant new right with practical and symbolic importance for TCNs. The concept of 'long-term resident status' is particularly appealing to residents who are unable or unwilling to obtain nationality due to stringent naturalisation requirements or the potential consequences under their country of origin's laws. However, the limitations and conditions placed upon acquiring long-term resident status and the right to move to another Member State diminish its value in promoting equality between long-term resident TCNs and EU citizens.

In addition to the LTRD, in 2023 the European Commission introduced a directive on the Right to Family Reunification.[34] The primary aim of the Family

[32] There are also approximately 500,000 stateless persons in Europe, many of whom are Roma from the Western Balkans, but also ethnic Russians in the Baltic States (see Council of Europe, European Committee on Legal Co-operation, *Statelessness and Access to Nationality* (2024) www.coe.int/en/web/cdcj/statelessness.

[33] Council Directive 2003/109/EC of 25 November 2003 concerning the status of third-country nationals who are long-term residents [2004] OJ L16/44 https://eur-lex.europa.eu/eli/dir/2003/109/oj/eng.

[34] Council Directive 2003/86/EC of 22 September 2003 on the right to family reunification [2003] OJ L251/12 https://eur-lex.europa.eu/LexUriServ/LexUriServ.do?uri=OJ:L:2003:251:0012:0018:en:PDF.

Reunification Directive is to establish conditions for exercising the right to family reunification by third-country nationals lawfully residing in EU Member States. However, the Family Reunification Directive sets relatively stringent requirements for family reunification, including accommodation meeting certain standards, sickness insurance, and stable resources. Furthermore, Member States retain significant discretion regarding integration measures and 'reception capacity' considerations, including residency requirements and the timing of family member reunification (Family Reunification Directive, 2003, Article 7).[35] The main positive aspect of the Family Reunification Directive is that national rules cannot be more restrictive than those provided for in the Directive. As Groenendijk notes: 'The Directive will act as an implicit standstill-clause against efforts to make the national rules even more restrictive'.[36] Apart from this aspect, the level of protection provided for in the Directive is rather low while the requirements remain high.

Upon analysing the instruments pertaining to non-citizens, particularly migrant workers, it becomes evident that they may not adequately serve as the basis for protecting 'new' (non-EU) minorities with their distinct language, religion, and culture. Likewise, instruments such as the UN Migrant Workers Convention – potentially useful for this purpose – are primarily ratified by emigration countries and therefore lack significance in protecting 'new' (non-EU) minorities. While instruments such as the LTRD introduce the concept of integration measures to enhance migrants' participation in their new home country's society, they do not adequately protect or promote the cultural distinctiveness of non-EU minorities. Consequently, devising policies that safeguard the rights and freedoms of non-EU minorities while fostering trust, belonging, and social cohesion poses a considerable challenge.

5. Reconciling Diversity and Unity: The Human and Minority Rights Inclusion Model

Navigating the intricate balance between social cohesion, unity, and diversity poses a formidable challenge for policymakers. Regardless of the chosen policy approach or combination thereof, difficult trade-offs and substantial policy dilemmas must be addressed. While societies must tailor their inclusion models to suit their unique historical, traditional, demographic, and political contexts, their decisions should be guided by two overarching principles: recognising diversity and nurturing a sense of collective belonging and unity. Striking a balance between these seemingly conflicting principles presents a significant contemporary societal challenge.

Should societies prioritise unity, there is a risk of marginalising minorities, eliciting resistance, and undermining the very unity they seek. Conversely, prioritising

[35] Council Directive 2003/86/EC of 22 September 2003 on the right to family reunification [2003] OJ L251/12 https://eur-lex.europa.eu/LexUriServ/LexUriServ.do?uri=OJ:L:2003:251:0012:0018:en:PDF.

[36] Kees Groenendijk, 'Legal Concepts of Integration in EU Migration Law' (2004) 6 *European Journal of Migration and Law* 111, 118.

diversity may hinder the accommodation of divergent community demands and impede the pursuit of common objectives, potentially leading to disintegration. The quest to reconcile the demands of cultural diversity and political unity – creating a cohesive and stable political community that also addresses the legitimate aspirations of minorities – has been a topic of extensive debate since the emergence of the modern State, particularly in recent decades.[37]

To address this dilemma of diversity governance, it is essential to establish minority and human rights as foundational elements for fostering a cohesive and stable community that respects the legitimate aspirations of minorities. However, achieving this aim poses a significant challenge. We propose a human and minority rights model for diversity governance, termed the 'Tree Model', as a potential pathway for advancing fundamental rights for both majority and minority communities.[38]

In the Tree Model (Figure1), the tree symbolises the ongoing dialogue between minority and majority groups within society. The roots represent the diverse groups present in society, while the branches and foliage symbolise the resultant society where unity and diversity coexist harmoniously. Sustaining the crown of the tree – an integrated yet diverse society – is the trunk, embodying the full spectrum of human rights, including minority rights as outlined, for instance, in the European Convention on Human Rights (ECHR) and its jurisprudence, binding all European nations. The human rights trunk serves as a filter, allowing only those minority and majority claims, practices, or traditions that align with human rights standards to be acknowledged and recognised in society.

Figure 1 The Tree Model

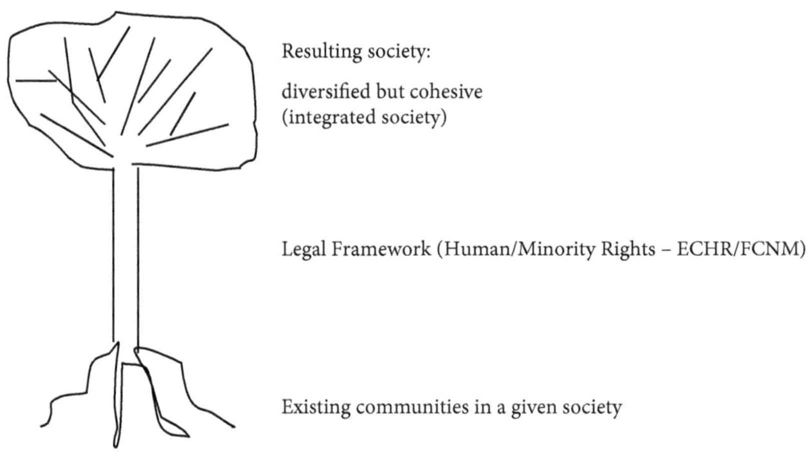

[37] Among the vast literature see Tove H. Malloy, 'Conceptualizing Democratic Diversity Management for Multicultural Societies: Theories of Society and Law' (2008) 6 *European Yearbook of Minority Issues* 281; Joseph Marko and Sergiu Constantin (eds), *Human and Minority Rights Protection by Multiple Diversity Governance: History, Law, Ideology and Politics in European Perspective* (Routledge, 2019) www.taylorfrancis.com/books/oa-edit/10.4324/9781315544724.

[38] Medda-Windischer (n 11), 1.

This model comprises two robust components: (a) the acknowledgment of diversity, encompassing the recognition of religious, ethnic, linguistic, and cultural identities and the groups aligning with them, achieved by broadening the application of certain provisions typical of historical minority protection, such as those outlined in the Council of Europe Framework Convention for the Protection of National Minorities (FCNM), to encompass all minority groups, including new minority groups emerging from international migration flows; (b) the maintenance of unity and cohesion by safeguarding a core set of shared values rooted in the universal human rights framework, contextualised and elaborated, particularly within the European context, by the European Court of Human Rights and its legal precedents. Accordingly, under this model, only minority and majority assertions that adhere to human and minority rights standards will be deemed legitimate and valuable for fostering a stable and cohesive society. The Tree Model, integrating human and minority rights alongside both general and specific integration measures, potentially embodies, to echo Leibniz and his concept of the 'best of all possible worlds', the most optimal model of diversity governance – at least within the European context.

6. Conclusions

The increasing diversity within national communities has prompted the need for the development of new and more robust approaches to accommodate both social cohesion and diversity. While consensus on preventing and penalising genocide, which forms the bedrock of the right to existence, and on eradicating racial discrimination was relatively straightforward, attaining agreement on the right to identity and participation appears more challenging, particularly when considering the inclusion of 'new' minorities. As evidenced by the examination of existing instruments for safeguarding the fundamental rights of new (non-EU) minorities, significant disparities persist between the rights and protective mechanisms available to minority populations who hold EU citizenship and those who do not. These discrepancies are further compounded by variations that stem from bilateral agreements individual EU Member States have forged, predominantly with neighbouring non-EU nations, or agreements collectively entered into by the EU. Alongside legal distinctions, sociopolitical differences in how European citizens perceive European and non-European third-country nationals also exist: except for the Roma, European TCNs tend to be viewed more favourably than their non-European counterparts, who frequently face various forms of discrimination, particularly due to their status as visible minorities.[39] Finally, empirical evidence suggests that new (non-EU) minorities themselves

[39] European Social Survey, 'Attitudes Towards Immigration and Their Antecedents: Topline Results from Round 7 of the European Social Survey' (2016) https://www.europeansocialsurvey.org/sites/default/files/2023-06/TL7-Immigration-English.pdf.

generally differ in their claims and opinions towards minority protection measures, classifying many of the core concerns for 'old' minorities as more personal than public matters. Establishing belonging in their new home country through language proficiency and workplace participation as well as social and political inclusion through voting rights are more pressing concerns.

Flexibility is therefore a core criterium for new frontiers in minority protection. Hence, we have put forth the Tree Model, a framework for diversity governance, which integrates both human and minority rights as a potential pathway to foster an inclusive environment while upholding a shared set of core values. In this model, fundamental rights – both human and minority rights – serve as the common foundation, akin to sturdy roots, from which diverse groups and their unique characteristics can flourish and be nurtured. The Tree Model also provides a common yet diversified framework for different minority and majority groups, and for the different claims and opinions, including those held by 'old' and 'new' minorities. Through the Tree Model, tailor-made solutions to societal challenges across different contexts can be provided.

Implementing the Tree Model for diversity governance presents, however, its own set of challenges. It envisions a society where various communities interact with one another on equal terms, fostering a rich, pluralistic, and tolerant environment. This process imposes burdens on both minority and majority groups. Minorities are encouraged to adopt a forward-looking perspective beyond mere defensive protection, seeking alliances and fostering cooperation with other groups, including the majority, rather than fostering polarisation and divisions. Conversely, majorities must recognise that minority rights are integral to human rights standards and are essential for achieving social cohesion and prosperity for society as a whole, not just for minorities. Nonetheless, realising this vision is complex and fraught with difficulties. Some groups may resist openness and experimentation, while others may staunchly guard their inherited identities. Ultimately, the success of any model hinges on the genuine willingness of both majority and minority groups to engage in continuous interaction, mutual adaptation, and accommodation.

10

Indigenous Peoples' Rights and the European Courts

A Category under Construction

JESSIKA EICHLER

1. Introductory Remarks: Indigenous Rights and European Court Cultures

From the perspective of human rights and decolonising thought, there is much merit in recognising (indigenous) collective rights as a new legal category, both in international human rights law and domestic constitutionalism, but also concerning the regional *ius commune*. Often considered as a '3rd generation' of rights,[1] collective rights give rise to novel questions on damage and attribution, relatedly on duty bearing but also concerning the definition of new legal subjects, that is, rights holder groups. Indigenous 'collective rights' could possibly be considered as one of the most powerful claims being made in contemporary law across judicial orders, and also as one of the most contentious and contested legal regimes given the persisting weight that is given to State sovereignty, territoriality and political autonomies but also as they come to challenge third party interests such as infrastructure and, most essentially, extractive projects. In Europe, this concerns the continent's North to significant degrees where we witness dislocation practices affecting the Sami people, and respectively, a lack of understanding towards the communitarian use of property[2] but also towards indigenous self-governance structures.[3]

[1] Christian Tomuschat, *Human Rights: Between Idealism and Realism* (Oxford University Press, 2014). The term was first coined by Karel Vasak, 'A 30 Year Struggle: The Sustained Effort to Give the Force of Law to the Universal Declaration of Human Rights' (1977) 3(11) *UNESCO Courier*.

[2] See cases on 'contentious' indigenous land claims in Europe's north.

[3] Rebecca Lawrence and Ulf Mörkenstam, 'Indigenous Self-Determination through a Government Agency? The Impossible Task of the Swedish Sámediggi' (2016) 23 *International Journal on Minority and Group Rights* 105–127.

Now, legal responses are provided by different legal frameworks, with indigenous rights not being recognised in any founding document[4] (as in '*sui generis* framework') at regional level, nor in any other legislative attempt. We are thus facing the challenge of a fragmented legal landscape that includes only sporadic jurisprudential trends to respond adequately to violations perpetrated against indigenous peoples in Europe. Far from representing a uniform trend though, we shall instead understand the problem of legal unresponsiveness as an order-specific dilemma.

More specifically, we may witness an institutional reluctance to deal with indigenous rights under the umbrella of the Council of Europe, which is owed to a largely individualised rights approach, including the Framework Convention for the Protection of National Minorities (FCNM), which merely allows rights to be exercised 'in community with others'. Despite progressive trends under the FCNM, which broadly embraces positive obligations, two critical remarks are to be made here: firstly, the FCNM is not submitted to the jurisdiction of the European Court of Human Rights (ECtHR), hence preventing any claims to be brought under the FCNM; and secondly, it has been argued that domestic courts face difficulties in enforcing the FCNM in the absence of States' implementing legislation.[5] It is further referred to the nature of framework treaties, granting State Parties a wide margin of discretion and being supported by somewhat weak monitoring bodies.[6]

Somewhat relatedly, the Court grants wide discretion to the Member States in fulfilling conventional obligations which, inevitably, allows States to protect property rights and to prioritise economic value over the cultural value of lands.[7] It is further maintained elsewhere that both minority groups and indigenous peoples – as collective units – are excluded from the protective realm of the European Convention on Human Rights (ECHR) while general discrimination law (as in Article 14) do provide some safeguards, including a specific mentioning of 'national minorities' as a protected ground.[8] Art.14 is to be interpreted in conjunction with other rights protected by the ECHR such as the right to private life, while Article 1 of Protocol 12 provides for a general anti-discrimination norm which, however, inevitably, only applies to those States having ratified the protocol.[9] Put very boldly, the '*ECHR is essentially designed to protect a range of individual rights,*

[4] Notably, the European Convention for the Protection of Human Rights and Fundamental Freedoms and the Lisbon Treaty including the Charter of Fundamental Rights of the European Union.

[5] Giovanna Gismondi, 'Denial of Justice: The Latest Indigenous Land Disputes Before the European Court of Human Rights and the Need for an Expansive Interpretation of Protocol 1' (2016) 18 *Yale Human Rights and Development Law Journal* 199–227.

[6] Timo Koivurova, 'Jurisprudence of the European Court of Human Rights regarding Indigenous Peoples: Retrospect and Prospects' in Malgosia Fitzmaurice, Panos Merkouris and Phoebe Okowa (eds), *The Interpretation and Application of the European Convention of Human Rights: Legal and Practical Implications* (Martinus Nijhoff, 2013).

[7] Gismondi (n 5).

[8] ibid.

[9] For a more detailed debate see Stefan Kirchner, 'Conceptions of Indigenousness in the Case Law of the European Court of Human Rights' (2016) 38(2) *Loyola of Los Angeles International and Comparative Law Review* 289–309.

not collective rights'.[10] Hope may be placed in the fact that the Court has opted for a fair balance between general community interests and individual human rights where the enjoyment of possessions was infringed upon.[11] The scant scholarly attention the ECtHR has received in the context of indigenous rights may also be derived from the fact that hardly any landmark cases exist in the field, while the Court could be considered as occupying a central position in protecting indigenous rights.[12] It has also been argued the Court would follow an economic rationale through its margin of appreciation doctrine, allowing it to either defer to the State or to establish a pretext for deference, materialising, for instance, where minority rights are subjugated to economic interests associated with public works, and hence public interest.[13]

In the EU context, even more strongly, we are confronted with a persisting influence of a market rationale coexisting at an equal, yet undefined, level alongside fundamental rights protection. We would expect indigenous rights to have been addressed under general equality and non-discrimination provisions in both cases. Given that indigenous rights somewhat depart from classical human rights approaches, the EU order has been proven largely inadequate as far as its distinct collective demands are concerned, commonly being limited to trading or other economic interests, infringements with health and safety regulations or the governance of natural resources. Such framework-specific context would, inevitably, render cultural or identity-related matters into a neglected question, also thereby ignoring the holistic approach on human rights as it is commonly defended by indigenous peoples. It is, however, through exterritorial obligations (including corporate social responsibility) that indigenous rights find some recognition; further conclusions may be drawn from minority rights including, famously, the rights of persons belonging to Roma communities.

Indeed, viewed from a transversal perspective, indigenous rights only enjoy peripherical recognition in Europe, with emphasis being placed on agricultural, resource and land rights, and often finding articulation in relation to conflicts between economic operations and indigenous traditional livelihoods, the protection of traditional territories or as relating to forced relocations. It is also commonly maintained that the Courts have traditionally paid little attention to indigenous human rights and have instead placed emphasis on 'national', ethnic, or linguistic minorities instead, with the exception of – sporadically – the question of climate change in the Arctic.[14] Interestingly, indigenous peoples in Europe have come to enjoy greater levels of protection afforded by international human rights

[10] Gismondi (n 5), 14.

[11] *Broniowski v Poland* App No 31443/96 (ECHR, 22 June 2004) 40 EHRR 21, see for further debates on the matter: Koivurova (n 6).

[12] ibid.

[13] Elisa Ruozzi, 'Indigenous Rights and International Human Rights Courts: Between Specificity and Circulation of Principles' (2011) *APSA Annual Meeting Paper*.

[14] Francesca Ippolito and Sara Iglesias Sánchez, *Protecting Vulnerable Groups: The European Human Rights Framework* (Oxford: Hart Publishing, 2015).

mechanisms than regionally, this concerns Article 27 of the International Covenant on Civil and Political Rights (ICCPR) principally, protecting ethnic, religious or linguistic minorities' right to their own culture, to practise their own religion or use their own language, which has been expanded to explicitly include indigenous peoples. Indeed, the Human Rights Committee has been receiving and has successfully dealt with a number of applications from indigenous communities.[15] Another notable provision lies in Article 15 of the International Covenant on Economic, Social and Cultural Rights (ICESCR), establishing the right to take part in cultural life which is, however, open to all potential victims, not establishing the threshold of belonging to a (minority) group; the same needs to be said about the Convention Again Torture (CAT).[16] In fact, the ICESCR reference resembles what has been established by the Council of Europe Framework on 'National Minorities' in its second thematic commentary on the 'effective participation of persons belonging to national minorities in cultural, social and economic life and in public affairs', basing itself on Article 15 of the FCNM that requires States to create the conditions necessary for such effective participation. Nevertheless, the ECtHR system has been praised for its power to issue enforceable judgments, as a fully operating mechanism, and the possibility for Non-governmental Organisations (NGOs) to file complaints.[17] We shall, in the following section, develop a comparative perspective on the two European Courts in their dedicated dealing with indigenous rights, and relatedly, conflicts of rights issues, the scarcity of hard law sources, and the limits imposed by narrow non-discrimination provisions or the legal recognition of collective rights.

2. Indigenous Rights, Minorities and Collectivity under the Council of Europe Framework

The 'national minority' rights framework, established by the Council of Europe, takes an individualistic stance on minority rights by holding in its Article 3(2) (FCNM) that members belonging to 'national minorities' are to exercise their rights individually or in community with others. While the Explanatory Report to the Convention allows interpreting the notion 'in community with others' widely,

[15] Kirchner (n 9); see the following cases in particular: *Ilmari Länsman et al v Finland*, Communication No 511/1992, UN Doc CCPR/C/52/D/511/1992 (1994); *Jouni E Länsman et al v Finland*, Communication No 671/1995, UN Doc CCPR/C/58/D/671/1995 (1996); *Kitok v Sweden*, Communication No 197/1985, UN Doc CCPR/C/33/D/197/1985 (1988); *Kalevi Paadar, Eero Paadar and his family, Veijo Paadar and Kari Alatorvinen and his family v Finland*, Communication No 2102/2011, UN Doc CCPR/C/110/D/2102/2011 (2014); *Äärelä and Näkkäläjärvi v Finland*, Communication No 779/1997, UN Doc CCPR/C/73/D/779/1997 (2001); *Hopu and Bessert v France*, Communication No 549/1993, UN Doc CCPR/C/60/D/549/1993 (1997).

[16] *Flor Agustina Calfunao Paillalef v Switzerland*, Communication No 2465/2014, UN Doc CCPR/C/126/D/2465/2014 (2019).

[17] Gismondi (n 5).

it does not go as far as to stipulate any collective rights – that would carry procedural implications. Hope may be placed in the First Protocol to the European Convention on Human Rights and Fundamental Freedoms, which refers to any 'natural or legal person' as a claimant.[18]

Also substantially, broader conclusions may be drawn, starting with a largely individualistic idea of property. The ECtHR has been relying on the doctrine of 'eminent domain', the presumption of State monopoly over land.[19] In other words, the ECtHR has been embracing a narrow interpretation of the 'right to peaceful enjoyment of possessions' (Article1, Protocol 1, ECHR), which misses out on recognising the importance of collective rights for the cultural survival of indigenous communities as well as their socioeconomic and spiritual integrity and well-being.[20] Indeed, expropriating or depriving one's property in the name of the public interest is viewed as standing in conformity with the Convention, applying the principle of proportionality, and also granting broad discretion in determining public interest goals if reasonably founded.[21] Yet an eventual solution that favours indigenous rights has been found by placing traditional subsistence activities under the subject-matter jurisdiction in conforming with Article 1, Protocol 1.[22] It may also be generally argued that those ancestral rights now embraced flow from customary indigenous law, not recognised under State law.[23] Some have argued the right to respect for one's possessions is to be considered an autonomous regime, firstly, to establish a *jus commune* given the absence of equivalent protection in the Convention and the persisting heterogeneity of domestic laws.[24] Yet another solution was actively sought by the Court as early as in 1983 when it declared that a minority group would be in the position to claim the right to 'respect for the particular life style it may lead'[25] as falling under 'private life', 'family life' or 'home' under Article 8 of the Convention. The Commission further maintained that the consequences of the construction of a hydroelectric plant in the case at hand did indeed constitute an 'interference with their private life, as members of a minority'.[26] At a broader level, traces of the Court's collective rights tradition may be found in the Commission's case-law, reaching back to the *Taxed Mountains* case and reaffirmed in the *Könkämä* case that declared that Sámi villages had a 'better right than the State to certain

[18] Elena Abrusci, 'Judicial Fragmentation on Indigenous Property Rights: Causes, Consequences and Solutions' (2017) 21(5) *The International Journal of Human Rights* 529–551.

[19] ibid, 17.

[20] Gismondi (n 5).

[21] ibid.

[22] Koivurova (n 6); see the following decision in particular: *Könkämä and 38 other Saami villages v Sweden* App No 27033/95 (ECHR, 25 November 1996).

[23] Ghislain Otis and Aurélie Laurent, 'Indigenous Land Claims in Europe' (2013) 4(2) *Arctic Review on Law and Politics* 206–225.

[24] ibid.

[25] *G and E v Norway* App No 9278/81 (Commission, 3 October 1983) 35.

[26] ibid, 36.

areas',[27] hence making concessions to public interest and also pronouncing itself, explicitly, on the importance of collective rights. Also, elsewhere the Commission refers to the possibility for Sámi villages to initiate proceedings against the State in the ordinary courts, 'requesting these courts to declare that the Sámi, rather than the State, have the rights which they claim'.[28]

Certain limits may be noted however regarding the application of the Convention's non-discrimination provision, its Article 14, which may only be understood as complementing other conventional substantive provisions and may not be invoked independently, as was the case in *Johtti Sapmelaccat Ry and Others v Finland* in which indigenous representatives considered a domestic act discriminatory 'on the basis of their race and their association with a national minority'.[29] Indeed, Article 14 has been described as being of ancillary nature only.[30] Once the provision finds application however, hope may be placed in its positive discriminatory approach, for discrimination to be understood as such where States 'fail to treat differently persons whose situations are significantly different'.[31] The Court unequivocally maintained that Article 14 would not prohibit unequal treatment whose objective was to correct factual inequalities.[32] Instead, the Court maintains that 'Art.14 does not prohibit a Member State from treating groups differently in order to correct "factual inequalities" between them; indeed in certain circumstances a failure to attempt to correct inequality through different treatment in itself gives rise to a breach of the Article'.[33] It further relates such protection to the particular case of minority groups in such situation by holding that 'when such measure disproportionately or even (…) exclusively affected members of a specific ethnic group, then appropriate safeguards have to be put in place'.[34] Safeguards are hence not to be directed to those measures targeting particular groups but also those demonstrating a disproportionately disadvantaging impact on such groups.[35] We may indeed witness 'an emerging international consensus among

[27] Könkämä and 38 Other Sami Villages v Sweden (n 22), 8.

[28] ibid, 9.

[29] *Johtti Sapmelaccat ry and Others v Finland* App No 42969/98 (ECHR, 18 October 2005) 20.

[30] Roman Lehner, 'Artikel 14' in Jens Meyer-Ladewig, Martin Nettesheim and Stefan von Raumer (eds), *Europäische Menschenrechtskonvention: Handkommentar* (Nomos, 2017).

[31] Christoph Grabenwarter, *European Convention on Human Rights: Commentary* (C H Beck, Hart, Nomos 2014) 347.

[32] Heiko Sauer, 'Artikel 14' in Ulrich Karpenstein and Franz C Mayer (eds), *Konvention zum Schutz der Menschenrechte und Grundfreiheiten: Kommentar* (C H Beck, 2012); see also *D H and Others v Czech Republic* App No 57325/00 (ECHR, 13 November 2007) 47 EHRR 3.

[33] Case relating to *Certain Aspects of the Laws on the Use of Languages in Education in Belgium v Belgium* (Merits) App Nos 1474/62, 1677/62, 1691/62, 1769/63, 1994/63 and 2126/64 (ECHR, 23 July 1968) Series A No 6, para10; *Thlimmenos v Greece* App No 34369/97 (ECHR, 6 April 2000) 31 EHRR 411, para 44; *Stec and Others v United Kingdom* App Nos 65731/01 and 65900/01 (ECHR, 12 April 2006) 43 EHRR 47, para 52.

[34] *Oršuš and Others v Croatia* App No 15766/03 (ECHR, 16 March 2010) 51 EHRR 7, para 157; *Buckley v United Kingdom* App No 20348/92 (ECHR, 25 September 1996) 23 EHRR 101, para 76.

[35] *D H and Others v the Czech Republic* (n 32), para 175; *Hugh Jordan v United Kingdom* App No 24746/94 (ECHR, 4 May 2001) 37 EHRR 2; *Hoogendijk v Netherlands* App No 58641/00 (ECHR, 6 January 2005).

the Contracting States of the Council of Europe recognising the special needs of minorities and an obligation to protect their security, identity and lifestyle'.[36] These latter developments may be indicative of an approach favourable to positive discrimination as far as ('national') minorities are concerned, which is more distinctly embraced by the FCNM.

The case of discrimination on ethnic grounds is dealt with as a special case, as 'treating racial violence equally to other acts of not racially motivated violence, constitutes a violation of art.1'.[37] Instead, violence committed for racial motives is to be understood as a particularly serious attack on a person's human dignity, requiring the use of all possible means to combat such violations:[38] to be sure 'no difference in treatment which is based exclusively or to a decisive extent on a person's ethnic origin is capable of being objectively justified in a contemporary society built on the principles of pluralism and respect for different cultures'.[39] Resultantly, procedural duties are established as flowing from the provision in question, also including the State's obligation to investigate based on Articles 2 and 3.[40] Also elsewhere it is stated that discrimination on grounds of race or skin colour, 'national' or ethnic background is to be considered a particularly serious case of an Article 14 violation as it detrimentally affects a person's human dignity.[41] Respectively, the Court calls for dedicated safeguarding obligations that arise in the context of racist forms of violence: in that sense, respective obligations arising from Articles 2, 3, 9, 10 or 11 but also duties related to the investigation of the motives for a crime have been understood in the Article 14 context.[42] It further refers to the need to 'reassert continuously society's condemnation of racism and to maintain the confidence of minorities in the authorities' ability to protect them from the threat of racist violence'.[43] Somewhat relatedly, the Court has ruled on positive discriminatory measures to be adopted in cases of racist violence: it would establish respective obligations under Article 2 as relating to the Roma minority, notably to thoroughly investigate on the racist motivation of such crimes and their unequivocal persecution.[44] It may be interesting to note here that the Court assumes for Article 14 to apply to minorities such as Sinti and Roma 'without giving convincing reasons for the violation of Article 14 in the individual case'.[45]

[36] *D H and Others v the Czech Republic* (n 32), para 181; *Chapman v United Kingdom* App No 27238/95 (ECHR, 18 January 2001) 33 EHRR 18, paras 93–94.

[37] ibid, 362-363; see also: *Turan Cakir v Belgium* App No 44256/06 (ECHR, 10 March 2009).

[38] Lehner (n 30).

[39] *D H and Others v the Czech Republic* (n 32), para 176; *Timishev v Russia* App Nos 55762/00 and 55974/00 (ECHR, 13 December 2005) 44 EHRR 37, para 58; *Nachova and Others v Bulgaria* App Nos 43577/98 and 43579/98 (ECHR, 6 July 2005) 2005-VII ECHR 255, para 157.

[40] ibid.

[41] Wolfgang Peukert, 'Artikel 14' in Jochen Abr Frowein and Wolfgang Peukert (eds), *Europäische Menschenrechtskonvention: EMRK-Kommentar* (Kehl am Rhein, N P Engel Verlag, 2009).

[42] Lehner (n 30).

[43] ibid, 363.

[44] Sauer (n 32); Nachova v Bulgaria.

[45] Grabenwarter (n 31), 363. see also *Nachova v Bulgaria*; *Šečić v Croatia* App No 40116/02 (ECHR, 31 May 2007) 2007-VI ECHR 295.

As a response, the very Convention requires the authorities to use all available means to combat racial discrimination.[46] Indeed, what is at stake here concerns firstly, the possibility to invoke positively discriminatory measures, and secondly, for them to actually be required.[47] The Court further refers to indirect forms of discrimination that have proven relevant as far as minority groups were concerned, holding that no explicit intention was needed, for the applicants to merely provide prima facie evidence, and for the State to prove that no discrimination had been committed (reversal of the burden of proof).[48] This also plays out to the advantage of the victim who might face difficulties to prove such disproportionate effect on herself/himself/x-self.[49] Overarchingly, relevant scholarship hence notes that the discrimination provision would constitute an important foundation for developing effective minority safeguards.[50]

Another regressive trend lies in a somewhat conservative reading of indigenous land and cultural rights, notably to be found in *Hingitaq 53 and Others v Denmark*, in which the Court would consider the displacement of the communities concerned as an instantaneous measure only that could be compensated for by a specific amount of indemnity, and would hence not raise any questions on further-reaching impacts on the communities' cultural identity or traditional practices as well as other adverse effects. A certain autonomy exercised by the communities permits ancestral property to be recognised, for applicants not needing to establish title or to have rights over such land as recognised under the domestic legal order.[51] Scholarly commentary has also referred to international developments in the Article 1 ECHR context, which recognised the social function of property, referring also to the individual and collective needs that are served where land is allocated, used or regulated.[52] Yet another consequence may be derived from the recognition of property: notably, by recognising the autonomy of possessions, different legal cultures have been placed on equal footing.[53] We may however be mindful of the fact that most applications have been dismissed.[54] What may be noteworthy regarding the Sami situation in particular concerns a reindeer herding right that the Court at least makes mention of: established in the Reindeer Husbandry Act, the reindeer herding right refers to winter grazing based on prescription from time immemorial, areas that have not been geographically demarcated in the Act.[55] Sami people in particular follow a Nomadic life style, hence requiring at least usage rights to be respected beyond territorially marked lands.

[46] Lehner (n 30).
[47] ibid.
[48] D H and Others v Czech Republic (n 32).
[49] Lehner (n 30).
[50] Sauer (n 32); *Oršuš v Croatia*.
[51] Otis and Laurent (n 23).
[52] William A Schabas, *The European Convention on Human Rights: A Commentary* (Oxford: Oxford University Press, 2015).
[53] ibid.
[54] Gismondi (n 5).
[55] *Handölsdalen Sami Village and Others v Sweden* App No 39013/04 (ECHR, 30 March 2010).

A valid starting point possibly lies with definitional questions on indigenous identity and its formalisation through the law. The Court develops a wide understanding of indigenous identity: alongside indigenous peoples as such that are to be defined according to subjective/self-determined criteria,[56] the Court also refers to broader power relations and predominance over specific population groups,[57] representing a recurring issue in indigenous worlds. It has also referred to officially recognised minorities such as Kurdish identity as constituting an 'indigenous racial group as well as distinct national minority'.[58] The Court further refers to self-identified groups without however pronouncing itself on the matter let alone recognising these as indigenous peoples.[59] It has been argued elsewhere that the Court largely relies on Member States' definitions.[60]

A landmark decision on the question of indigenous rights was issued with *Handölsdalen v Sweden*.[61] An ever-current matter concerns traditional land use rights, as established by this same decision, 'their historical use of the land has given rise to a special right'. In a partly dissenting opinion, Ziemele specifies: 'with the stated purpose of guaranteeing their cultural identities and other cultural rights, these special steps include the right of indigenous peoples to own the land which such groups have traditionally used and to engage in traditional economic activities', hence unequivocally establishing a particular indigenous right to land. Rather typically, cultural rights and indigenous identity find further contextualisation in relation to economic activities and territorial rights, which corresponds with the approach assumed by the Inter-American Court of Human Rights (IACtHR).[62] Land rights do indeed represent one of the most prominent indigenous claims to this day, also materialising in what has become known as prior consultation and free, prior and informed consent (FPIC).[63]

This inevitably comes with considerable procedural implications, returning to basic questions on equality of arms in accessing justice.[64] Indeed, indigenous

[56] Könkämä and 38 Other Sami Villages v Sweden (n 22); Johtti Sapmelaccat Ry. and Others v Finland (n 29), Handölsdalen Sami Village and Others v Sweden (n 55).

[57] *Andrejeva v Latvia* App No 55707/00 (ECHR, 18 February 2009) 2009-II ECHR 103.

[58] *Avşar v Turkey* App No 25657/94 (ECHR, 10 July 2001) 2001-VII ECHR 253.

[59] *Dmitriyevsky v Russia* App No 42168/06 (ECHR, 3 October 2017); *Vatan v Russia* App No 47978/99 (ECHR, 7 October 2004); *W H v Sweden* App No 49341/10 (ECHR, 8 April 2014); *M Y H and Others v Sweden* App No 50859/10 (ECHR, 27 June 2013).

[60] Koivurova (n 6).

[61] On relevant jurisprudential developments also see, for instance: Koivurova (n 6).

[62] Notably in *Sarayaku v Ecuador* (Merits and Reparations) Inter-American Court of Human Rights Series C No 245 (27 June 2012).

[63] See, for instance, Cathal M Doyle, Indigenous Peoples, Title to Territory, Rights and Resources: The Transformative Role of Free, Prior and Informed Consent (Abingdon, Routledge, 2017); Claire Wright and Alexandra Tomaselli, The Prior Consultation of Indigenous Peoples in Latin America: Inside the Implementation Gap (Abingdon, Routledge, 2019); David Szablowski, 'Operationalising Free, Prior and Informed Consent in the Extractive Industry Sector? Examining the Challenges of a Negotiated Model of Justice' (2010) 30 Canadian Journal of Development Studies/Revue Canadienne d'études du développement 111–128.

[64] César Rodríguez-Garavito, 'Ethnicity.gov: Global Governance, Indigenous Peoples, and the Right to Prior Consultation in Social Minefields' (2011) 18(1) *Indiana Journal of Global Legal Studies* 263–305; see also: Koivurova (n 6).

peoples commonly find themselves in situations of considerable disadvantage in accessing expert knowledge, language particularities, economic means for lawyers but also in terms of general participation procedures that tend to be imposed by the State, and companies to some extent, without considering indigenous particular decision-making practices but also indigenous laws at large. In that sense, Ziemele emblematically revisits procedural guarantees in such particular context:

> the standard is that parties are afforded a reasonable opportunity to present their case under conditions that do not place them at a substantial disadvantage with respect to the adversary. In cases where one party by definition is disadvantaged, proper access to court is ensured by adopting such procedures and safeguards as indeed enable that party to enjoy the same opportunities. This is what the CERD meant when criticising the fact that the burden of proving the right rests exclusively(!) with the Sami, because the whole system presumes that the landowners have the right and they do not have to prove anything. There is therefore no doubt in my mind that the applicants' access to court was not effective. It could not be effective until and unless the entire approach to land disputes of this kind is revised to take account of the rights and particular circumstances of indigenous peoples. The excessive legal costs and the fact that the applicants had to borrow money from their own Fund are elements of the overall unfairness (para. 10).

Much in fact lies in the procedural conditions when it comes to guaranteeing indigenous land rights. Certain constraints are set by the ECHR framework, which limits applications to persons, groups of individuals and non-governmental organisations, with the latter entity having to prove that a given measure has been negatively affecting its missions, goals or objectives.[65] It may be noted here that indigenous villages have come to be regarded as non-governmental organisations[66] which might bring certain advantages as to the question of legal personality and *locus standi*. What was back then the European Commission of Human Rights embraced a generally favourable approach towards indigenous collective rights, specifically in terms of representation: accordingly, the Sámi villages were not only considered to be representing their members in relevant matters, reindeer herding principally, but also accorded the rights designated in a pertinent act to be exercised exclusively by a Sámi by virtue of being a community member.[67] As a consequence, the Commission understands the applicant villages as victims of violations claimable under the Convention and Protocol 1.[68] Another procedural particularity concerns the duration of the proceedings: the ECtHR clearly considers such procedural detail as falling within 'the responsibility of the courts to see to it that the proceedings were conducted expeditiously, especially in view of the fact that the matter examined was of great importance to the parties, not least

[65] Gismondi (n 5).
[66] Könkämä and 38 Other Sami Villages v Sweden (n 22).
[67] ibid.
[68] ibid.

the applicant Sami villages'.[69] The specific situation the Sami found themselves in when making collective land claims hence carried noteworthy procedural consequences. Generally, it has been reported that the Court's admissibility criteria have become stricter over the years with a Court facing a considerable workload.[70]

Indeed it has been maintained that the Court has been following a restrictive approach when determining the status of an association, expecting the claim made and the association's objectives to completely coincide, and for rights to be exercised by individuals, hence disregarding the collective dimension of, for instance, indigenous culture.[71] What remains to be observed as to the particular form of organisation concerned, relates to the potential limits that may arise with the right to assembly and association under Article 11. Often considered under a certain legitimate aim such as 'national security' or 'public safety', the rights of an association may be placed limits on. Relevant scholarly Commentary however points to the 'fact that an association committed to raise awareness to the existence of ethnic minorities and to support their interests alone cannot be seen as a risk to the democratic order of a State'.[72] Rather, States are called upon to recognise the existence of minorities and cultural diversity as 'not only hav[ing] to tolerate this [but] hav[ing] to protect and encourage it according to the principles of international law',[73] hence clearly suggesting a positively discriminatory positioning on the matter. Putting safeguards in place for protecting the rights of indigenous associations may also fall within the broad rationale that places the freedom to associate in the general context of 'democratic society'. Following this line, pluralism, tolerance and a certain openness towards minorities are to be considered foundational for democratic society, hence attributed special significance.[74] Relatedly, the Court considers the significance of associations for the overall functioning of democracy, for instance, when undertaking any proportionality assessment on the rights concerned: in such context, the Court has been attentive to those institutional objectives directed to protecting cultural heritage, ethnic identity or strengthening a (communal) sense of belonging to a minority.[75]

We may, however, also be wary of certain positive trends, starting with a rather conservative reading of the Convention and its Protocols in the *Alta* case and culminating in a more progressive attitude promoted by the Court in the *Handölsdalen* decision: firstly, by being more explicit and open towards minority rights despite the founding instrument being of general applicability, (ie, the Convention); secondly, the Court would first prioritise economic and spatial

[69] Handölsdalen Sami Village and Others v Sweden (n 55) para 65.

[70] Kirchner (n 9).

[71] Ruozzi (n 13).

[72] Grabenwarter (n 31), 311.

[73] ibid.

[74] Felix Arndt and Anja Schubert, 'Artikel 11' in Ulrich Karpenstein and Franz C Mayer (eds), *Konvention zum Schutz der Menschenrechte und Grundfreiheiten: Kommentar* (C H Beck, 2011); see also: *Bączkowski and Others v Poland* App No 1543/06 (ECHR, 3 May 2007) 2007-VI ECHR 221.

[75] ibid; see also *Gorzelik and Others v Poland* App No 44158/98 (ECHR, 17 February 2004) 2004-I ECHR 261.

terms in relation to a minority's private life and then actually go on to consider the detrimental effects on culture; and thirdly, it would reverse its approach that considered the traditional use of territories for subsistence activities as not falling under the right to property.[76] New possibilities may also arise with the view that the Convention is to be treated as a 'living instrument',[77] adopted to new societal trends, and also in view of progressive international standards that may spill-over to European legal orders, becoming most visible in the case of the UN Human Rights Committee and also the UN Declaration on the Rights of Indigenous Peoples.[78] The jurisprudence developed by the Human Rights Committee proves relevant here given that all ECHR States parties are parties to the UN Convention, and also owing to the Committee's invoking of the 'peoples' category, enabling indigenous peoples to access additional rights as established in Common Article 1(2) ICCPR and ICESCR.[79] Very emblematically, the United Nations Convention on the Elimination of All Forms of Racial Discrimination (CERD)'s understanding and recognition of ancestral indigenous lands including collective land tenure has formally been approved by means of ratification of the instrument by almost all Council of Europe members.[80] Respective cross-fertilising effects may be observed as far as a progressive reading of property rights are concerned, borrowing from UN treaty bodies but also the IACtHR.[81] Respective international developments on indigenous rights were also invoked by Judge Ziemele in the *Handölsdalen* decision, referring to the specific situation of indigenous peoples to be considered, in the case at hand, eventually finding a violation of the right to access the courts.[82]

3. The EU Human Rights Order and its Accommodating Potential?

Indigenous rights may be protected under ordinary non-discrimination law, notably Article 21 (EU Charta of Fundamental Rights),[83] including relevant grounds such as ethnic or social background, race, colour, language, religion or belonging to a 'national minority'. Respective safeguards to be considered also concern those established under Article 22 protecting cultural, religious and linguistic diversity. We may however also refer to several ad-hoc attempts to pay due consideration

[76] Koivurova (n 6).
[77] eg *Tyrer v. United Kingdom*, Series A no 26 (1978) 2 EHRR 1.
[78] Koivurova (n 6).
[79] ibid.
[80] Otis and Laurent (n 23).
[81] ibid.
[82] ibid.
[83] For an overview of relevant EU Treaty Law as applicable to the situation of indigenous peoples, see Louise Corselli, 'A Sami Right to Free, Prior and Informed Consent under EU Law? Indigenous Rights from an EU Law Perspective' (Master's thesis, Uppsala Universitet, 2021).

to indigenous rights, including a resolution on deforestation[84] or as it becomes apparent in the field of social corporate responsibility,[85] or relatedly, the EU's external action policies generally.[86]

Another main area worthy of further consideration regarding indigenous peoples' rights lies with the EU's arctic policies, the Arctic Council in particular, which not only allows for intergovernmental collaboration among the eight Arctic States but also importantly permits indigenous representatives to act as permanent participants; issues of relevance impacting on indigenous peoples are addressed in the Council's work.[87] We may want to refer to the role of Arctic indigenous groups that are transnational, including the Inuit Circumpolar Council, which is constitutive of Inuit groups from Russia, Greenland, Alaska and Canada, and that issued the 'Circumpolar Inuit Declaration on Sovereignty in the Arctic', promoting indigenous participation in inter-State matters relating to sovereignty disputes.[88] Indigenous peoples living in the Arctic find themselves in the situation in need of particular rights, including, essentially, the right of use of land and resources;[89] with the right of use also being addressed in *Chiragova and Others v Armenia.*

[84] European Parliament, 'European Parliament Resolution of 22 October 2020 with Recommendations to the Commission on an EU Legal Framework to Halt and Reverse EU-Driven Global Deforestation' (2020).

[85] See, for instance, UN Special Rapporteur on the Rights of Indigenous Peoples, 'European Companies in Indigenous Territories in Latin America: From Conflict to Understanding through Prior Consultation' (2017).

[86] Relevant EU policies on indigenous peoples or touching upon indigenous rights include the following: European Parliament, 'European Parliament Resolution on Transparent and Accountable Management of Natural Resources in Developing Countries: the Case of Forests' (2018); European Parliament, 'European Parliament Resolution on Violation of the Rights of Indigenous Peoples in the World, including Land Grabbing' (2018); European Parliament, 'The Situation of Indigenous Children with Disabilities' (Study, 2017); European Union, 'The New European Consensus on Development' (2017); Council of the European Union, 'Council Conclusions on Indigenous Peoples' (2017); European Commission, 'Joint Staff Working Document – Implementing EU External Policy on Indigenous Peoples' (2016); European Union, 'An Integrated European Union Policy for the Arctic' (2016); European Union, 'Annual Reports on Human Rights and Democracy in the World' (various years); European Parliament, 'Indigenous Peoples, Extractive Industries and Human Rights' (Study 2014); European Union, 'EU Guidelines on Human Rights Defenders' (2008); European Commission, 'Report from the Commission to the Council of 11 June 2002: Review of Progress of Working with Indigenous Peoples' (2002); Council of the European Union, 'Council Resolution of Development Ministers of the European Member States' (November 1998); European Commission, 'Communication from the Commission to the European Council of 27 May 1998 on a Partnership for Integration: A Strategy for Integrating the Environment into EU Policies' (1998).

see also: UN Permanent Forum on Indigenous Issues, 'The EU and Indigenous Peoples' Issues' www.un.org/esa/socdev/unpfii/documents/UNPFII%20European%20Commission%20submission.pdf and recommendations on relevant EU action: Julian Burger, 'Indigenous Peoples, Extractive Industries and Human Rights' (Directorate-General for External Policies of the Union, Directorate B Policy Department 2014).

[87] Jelena Beqiraj, 'Indigenous Peoples' Cultural Identity under EU Law and the ECHR: A Non-Trade Interest or a Human Right?' in Francesca Ippolito and Sara Iglesias Sánchez (eds), *Protecting Vulnerable Groups: The European Human Rights Framework* (Hart Publishing, 2015).

[88] Michael Byers, 'Arctic Region' (2019) Max Planck Encyclopedias of Public International Law.

[89] Mikael Lundmark, 'The European Court of Human Rights and the Protection of Arctic Indigenous Peoples' Rights' (2017) 9 *The Yearbook of Polar Law* 275–303.

It may be important to note here that the protection of rights includes both tangible and intangible objects that have been considered important for Arctic indigenous peoples since their land rights are commonly not understood as giving rise to legal ownership.[90]

Insights may also be gained jurisprudentially, from the field of economic, social and cultural rights, as quite commonly these concern agricultural matters, especially in the context of subsistence-related rights. Interestingly, market rules are given less weight, prioritising animal protection instead as a legitimate objective of collective interest, while tribute is paid to indigenous subsistence rights, more precisely traditional food gathering practices which are granted exceptional status here.[91] This may concern traditional food gathering of a recreational purpose that carries 'significant cultural importance' where competent bodies of the Member States decide so, as argued by Advocate General Kokott.[92] By doing so, due respect must however be paid to other conditions to be fulfilled under EU secondary legislation, allowing, for instance, to derogate from the legal framework.[93] The special treatment that was termed 'the Inuit exception' was later further spelt out in EU Regulation No. 2015/1775, which would require traditional subsistence activities to be 'conducted in a manner which has due regards to animal welfare, taking into consideration the way of life of the community and the subsistence purpose'.[94,95] Any specific conditions and definitions in that regard are left for the Member States to decide, in the process of adopting implementing legislation.[96] The Court also refers to the regulation at issue which in its recital 14 of the Preamble not only refers to indigenous means to ensure their subsistence, but also takes consideration of the 'fundamental economic and social interests of Inui communities' that are being adversely affected in that regard.[97] An economic rationale permeates the judgement, focusing almost entirely on the (economic) effects a prohibition of products may have, and as it may concern indigenous or non-indigenous traders alike: it may be argued that little attention is spent on the particularities and surrounding circumstances that may be concerned by the regulation, more specifically, alluding to the direct or individual concern the act carries. As is established elsewhere, for a violation to be found, evidence is needed as to the direct and adversely effect of a (legislative) measure.[98]

[90] ibid.

[91] Inuit Tapiriit Kanatami and Others v Commission (T-18/10, General Court, 6 September 2011, ECLI:EU:T:2011:419).

[92] Opinion of Advocate General Kokott in Case C-900/19 Stichting Landelijk Informatiecentrum Gezelschapsdieren v Minister van Landbouw, Natuur en Voedselkwaliteit EU:C:2021:1013, para 40.

[93] ibid, para 47.

[94] Regulation (EU) 2015/1775 of the European Parliament and of the Council of 6 October 2015 [2015] OJ L262/1, art 1(2).

[95] Simone Vezzani, 'The Inuit Tapiriit Kanatami II Case and the Protection of Indigenous Peoples' Rights: A Missed Opportunity?' (2016) 1(1) *European Papers* 265–275.

[96] Case C-583/11 P Inuit Tapiriit Kanatami and Others v European Parliament and Council of the European Union EU:C:2013:625, para 19.

[97] ibid, para 65.

[98] *Johtti Sapmelaccat Ry and Others v Finland* (n 29).

Worth mentioning are also civil and political rights, with self-determination constituting a particularly powerful right that has been used, notably, on the basis of the free and genuine will of a territory's population,[99] also gaining special significance against the colonial background of the territory according to Advocate General Wathelet in *Western Sahara Campaign v UK*. Here, the Court addresses the modalities of a referendum that concerned the question of independence, the conditions for complete decolonisation and respective international monitoring of the referendum. Accordingly, the Court declared the respective trade liberalisation in the sector of agriculture and fisheries null and void in the concerned territory.

Another noteworthy development concerns procedural rights, especially standing rights exercised by individuals and groups. In fact, resembling what was observed in the case of the ECtHR, the EU Court has been criticised on grounds of procedural challenges when victims would invoke conventional rights when accessing justice.[100] While the Court generally grants indigenous individuals the right to vindicate rights, it also calls upon domestic courts to soften those criteria (to vindicate rights) as far as indigenous associations are concerned.[101] Notably, the Court of First Instance elaborates on the particularities pertaining to indigenous contexts in that regard. While generally confined to 'direct and individual concerns', the Court establishes a special procedural regime for actions for annulment as far as associations are concerned, in this case, affecting the indigenous organisation Sáminuorra, granting three exceptions that turned complaints by associations admissible. Accordingly, actions of annulment filed by association were considered admissible provided that 'firstly, where a legal provision expressly grants a series of procedural powers to trade associations; secondly, where the association represents the interests of its members, who would themselves be entitled to bring proceedings; and, thirdly, where the association is distinguished individually because its own interests as an association are affected, in particular because its negotiating position has been affected by the act in respect of which annulment is sought'.[102] In other words, the association is considered to be affected owing to the collective good of its members that it strives to protect, that is, the collective traditional right of reindeer herders to make use of grazing land – to be distinguished from the sheer sum of individual interests.[103] Very generic standing rights may also be derived from the court's case-law, holding that 'natural or legal persons satisfy the condition of individual concern only if the contested act affects them by reason of certain attributes which are peculiar to them or by reason

[99] Case T-512/12 Front Polisario v Council of the European Union EU:T:2015:953.

[100] Gerd Winter, 'Armando Carvalho and Others vs. EU: Invoking Human Rights and the Paris Agreement for Better Climate Protection Legislation' (2020) 9(1) *Transnational Environmental Law* 137–147.

[101] Case C-583/11 P Armando Carvalho and Others v European Parliament and Council EU:C:2019:761, para 3.

[102] Case C-583/11 P Inuit Tapiriit Kanatami and Others v European Parliament and Council EU:C:2013:625, para 51; see also Case T-173/98 Unión de Pequeños Agricultores v Council EU:T:1999:296.

[103] Winter (n 100); Armando Carvalho and Others v European Parliament and Council (n 101).

of circumstances in which they are differentiated from all other persons, and by virtue of these factors distinguished them individually'.[104] Indigenous peoples indeed find themselves, very commonly, in the situation of being particularly affected by virtue of, for instance, their dependence on their immediate environment. A related pertinent procedural right lies in the fundamental right to effective judicial protection that also provides the context in which other rights and provisions are to be interpreted, including Article 263 of the Treaty on the Functioning of the European Union (TFEU).[105] Yet another procedural dimension may be found in indigenous participation in environmental protection and sustainability programmes, Advocate General Mengozzi argues, and as relating to biologically diverse territories or endangered ecosystems.[106] Somewhat relatedly, Advocate General Jacobs discusses the role indigenous peoples' traditional lifestyles play as it impacts on the protection of biodiversity.[107]

Wherever looked at as an independent regime, indigenous rights in European legal orders assume a form of ad-hoc function, addressed in the specific context of the violation committed, often concerning land questions and cultural practices related to land use or communal property. Collective claims that largely seem addressed in international law including, essentially, self-determination and autonomies, recognition at organisational level or territorial rights, do not enjoy equivalent protection in European legal orders. While group-differentiated rights in the field of cultural and linguistic matters benefit from wide-reaching safeguards, collective political rights find limited expression, illustrative being the Samediggi Parliaments in Nordic Europe, whose powers have however been curtailed by the domestic government in eg, the Swedish case, acting as a purely 'administrative authority under the domestic government'. These operate under the administrative section of the judiciary,[108] not placing its legislative powers on equal footing with the State, especially in terms of public interest matters. Indeed, decision-making powers are limited to internal affairs, and do not extend to responsibilities regarding third party interests such as land or forestry ownership. From the perspective of legal and political pluralism then, little has been achieved at the institutional level, finding expression instead in the form of sector-specific, arguably temporary rights, commonly being rethought 'minority terms'. The neighbouring regime of 'national' minority rights as articulated in EU law may provide some

[104] Armando Carvalho and Others v European Parliament and Council (n 101), para 46; see also: Inuit Tapiriit Kanatami and Others v Parliament and Council (n 102), paras 71–72; Case C-298/00 Plaumann v Commission EU:C:2003:36; Case C-53/96 Italy v Commission [1998] ECR I-4087; Joined Cases C-71/09 P, C-73/09 P and C-76/09 P Comitato 'Venezia vuole vivere' v Commission EU:C:2010:495.

[105] Consult Art. 263 TFEU permitting 'the institution of proceedings against individual acts, against acts of general application which are of direct and individual concern to a natural or legal person and against a regulatory act which is of direct concern to them and does not entail implementing measures'; see also Plaumann v Commission and Unión de Pequeños Agricultores v Council (n 104).

[106] Opinion of Advocate General Mengozzi in Case C-377/12, *Macedonian Case* EU:C:2013:820.

[107] Opinion of Advocate General Jacobs in Case C-377/98, Netherlands v European Parliament and Council EU:C:2000:388.

[108] Lawrence and Mörkenstamm (n 3).

alternative points of departure. The Court notably establishes a wide understanding of cultural identity including the positive obligation to promote minorities' ways of life.[109]

4. Common Points of Departure, Trends and Derivative Rights Approaches: The ECJ and the ECtHR under Focus

Academic accounts seem to coincide on the observation that the European Courts and their founding documents have given paid only peripherical attention to indigenous peoples' rights and their very collective dimension.[110] Let us shed some light on a rather fragmented legal scenery. Our focus shall remain on relevant contexts giving rise to very context-specific rights as a consequence, which may however be interpreted widely and transposed to other situations. Much emphasis has been placed on external circumstances and measures taken by the State and third parties that produce certain detrimental effects on the communities, often being massive in scale and intensity, interfering with indigenous communities' ways of life, proper customs, procedures and practices. This may concern, classically, extractive operations or infrastructure projects carried out on indigenous lands, affecting their livelihoods and sources of subsistence. What has been given similar attention though concerns climate change[111] affecting the arctic marine and terrestrial environment in Europe's north, which is of relevance to the Inuit in Greenland, the Sámi in Norway, Finland, Sweden and Russia and other groups inhabiting territories in Russia.[112] Commonly, indigenous rights are granted being grounded on their very cultural rights, as an underlying rationale, as well as their traditional subsistence rights. Given the scarcity of rights being specific to indigenous peoples, the ECtHR relies on basic human rights, more specifically, invoking rights relating to the length of proceedings, the right to peaceful enjoyment of possession, and respect for private and family life.[113] Emblematic may be the *G & E v Norway* decision, which extends the classical human right to private life to include the right to cultural identity, hence, turning the right applicable to indigenous peoples and collectivity.[114] Such a derivative approach may be attributable

[109] see, essentially, Buckley v United Kingdom; Chapman v the United Kingdom.

[110] Beqiraj (n 87); Koivurova (n 6).

[111] For an in-depth overview of indigenous environmental rights in Northern Europe, see Lena Gross' work or Leena Heinämäki's dissertation Leena Heinämäki, 'The Right to Be a Part of Nature: Indigenous Peoples and the Environment' (Doctoral dissertation, University of Lapland, 2010).

[112] Beqiraj (n 87).

[113] ibid; see the following cases in particular: Handölsdalen v Sweden (n 55); Johtti Sapmelaccat Ry v Finland (n 29); Könkämä and 38 Other Sami Villages v Sweden (n 22); OB and Others v Norway App no 27824/95 (ECHR, 23 September 2003); Östergren and Others v Sweden App no 42395/98 (ECHR, 12 February 2008); Hingitaq 53 and Others v Denmark App no 18584/91 (ECHR, 25 May 1995).

[114] Beqiraj (n 87).

to the scarce legal framework that largely builds on civil and political rather than cultural rights. Similar conclusions were drawn by the Court in *Chapman v United Kingdom* as relating to the rights of the Roma minority, referring, particularly, to their traditional lifestyle, which was based on their private and family life as a minority. A further important implication of this lies in the Court's benevolent attitude towards reducing the States' margin of appreciation in these cases, and somewhat relatedly, the Court's approach to adopt respective positive obligations as relating to a minority's way of life.[115] Other derivative rights were established in relation to subsistence rights, understanding these as a possession, hence as an extension of the right to property, as decided in *Handölsdalen Sami Village v Sweden*, including the dedicated duty to provide for effective enjoyment of a property right.[116]

Yet another common point of departure is established with a State's extraterritorial obligations, which finds recognition in both EU law[117] and under the ECHR framework,[118] constituting in fact a very welcome avenue for indigenous peoples residing elsewhere. This may, for instance, apply to French Guiana being part of the European Union, that hence falls within the safeguarding umbrella of the ECHR, as well as territories that are affiliated with European States but concern areas outside the EU, such as Greenland or the French Overseas Collectivity of French Polynesia.[119] Much potential hence lies with interpreting the European founding instruments as living documents in consideration of progressive standards developed in international law.[120] A somewhat hesitant attitude is shown by the ECtHR on the matter which, in a decision in the *Chagos Islanders v United Kingdom* judgment, refrains from ultimately pronouncing itself on the continuing validity of Article 56 (territorial application of the Convention) according to which States 'may' declare that the Convention is to be applied to 'all or any of the territories for whose international relations it is responsible'. It merely refers to extraterritorial jurisdiction as remaining exceptional.

What indeed remains disputed, and carrying with it postcolonial implications, concerns the exercise of control as being decisive or not in establishing extraterritorial responsibility. The Court notably refers to the *Al-Skeini and Others v United Kingdom* decision that establishes a clearly outlined set of criteria: jurisdictional competence is to be understood as primarily territorial and for its extraterritorial application to be exceptional only with two principal exceptions to territoriality having found recognition. This includes that of, firstly, circumstances of 'State agent authority and control' applicable where acts are committed by diplomatic or consular agents on that territory or public powers carrying out judicial or executive functions or home State control is exercised over an individual. Secondly, it

[115] ibid.
[116] ibid.
[117] Front Polisario v Council of EU (n 99).
[118] See, for instance, *Chagos Islanders v United Kingdom* App No 35622/04 (ECHR, 11 December 2012).
[119] Kirchner (n 9).
[120] Gismondi (n 5).

extends to 'effective control over an area' in cases of military action. Based on these jurisprudential developments, the Court legitimately reflects on the significance of the *Al-Skeini* decision as far as the extended application of the Convention to overseas territory is concerned, which the Court ultimately does not enter. We may understand such undecidedness as disclosing a (neo)colonial undertone, which becomes yet more visible where the ECtHR merely refers to the Higher Court's acceptance of the applicants (islanders) being subject to oppression or not having realised the settlement was final. It had been maintained by the applicants that 'not all of them had signed the waiver forms in the settlement or that those that did had not understood or properly consented to what was involved',[121] certainly also being indicative of the difficulties indigenous communities had been facing when dealing with the predominant legal system, its technicalities and procedures but also its focus on individual human rights, proving ignorant of the idea of collective land or territory, hence limiting the claims made to 'interferences with respect for their homes'.

Some hope may be placed in Article 56's third paragraph holding that the Convention is to be applied in territories 'with due regard, however, to local requirements' which, it was argued, could carry certain colonial implications, notably 'leaving the suspicion that European colonial powers intended that even when human rights protections were extended to their dependent territories, adjustments would be made in deference to the colonial relationship'.[122] The provision could, however, also be interpreted as for local requirements to 'prove a prescient insight by its drafters in favour of a place for minorities and indigenous peoples inhabiting the last 'colonies' of European Powers'.[123] Indeed, the provision seems to introduce a form of legal pluralism into the context of its extraterritorial application, with a clear decolonising potential, as it explicitly condemns a strict application without considering the local context which, in turn, often concerns indigenous peoples inhabiting those territories. While not explicitly stated as such, we may want to infer from the exception granted that indigenous justice or political systems could gain recognition throughout the process also vis-à-vis local government structures that may not live up to the collective need for autonomies.

[121] Chagos Islanders v the UK (n 118), para 79.

[122] William A Schabas, *The European Convention on Human Rights: A Commentary* (Oxford: Oxford University Press, 2015) art 56, 926.

[123] ibid, 926; see also: Syméon Karagiannis, 'Territorial Scope of Treaties' in Olivier Corten and Pierre Klein (eds), *The Vienna Convention on the Law of Treaties: A Commentary* (Oxford: Oxford University Press, 2011).

11

Anthropological Theory, Stakeholder Inclusion and Minority Rights

*Reflections on the Research and Safeguarding of Serbian Intangible Cultural Heritage in the Western Balkans**

MILOŠ MILENKOVIĆ

1. Introduction

Even seventy-five years after the adoption of the Universal Declaration of Human Rights, the relationship between anthropological theory and real-world social challenges remains uncertain. This is particularly important given that most of the people we study perceive culture, identity, and tradition as real entities – almost as if they were physical facts. These cultural elements are more often linked to groups than to individuals, and they are especially important for communities that do not see themselves reflected in the dominant traditions shaped by those who control representation, memory, and the process of heritagisation. Although anthropology has, for much of its history, stood with minority communities – whether they are Indigenous, marginalised, or countercultural – contemporary anthropology, faced with the tension between individual and collective rights, almost instinctively rejects the collectivisation of human rights and the essentialisation of identity on which that collectivisation relies. This is the source of the discipline's ambivalence toward the Declaration, as it has often taken on the role of devil's advocate in attempts to defend the right to collective distinctiveness without threatening the rights of individuals within the collective.[1] As we will see, anthropology plays a similar role when it comes

* This work was supported by the Science Fund of the Republic of Serbia [Identities 1534].

[1] Kathryn Engle, 'From Skepticism to Embrace: Human Rights and the American Anthropological Association from 1947–1999' (2001) 23 *Human Rights Quarterly* 536; Robert Winthrop, 'Defining a Right to Culture, and Some Alternatives' (2002) 14(2) *Cultural Dynamics* 161; Eva Kalny, 'Against Superciliousness: Revisiting the Debate 60 Years after the Adoption of the Universal Declaration of

to intangible cultural heritage (ICH), shaping a constructivist, anti-realist orientation in contemporary heritage studies.[2]

Twenty-five years after the adoption of the Framework Convention for the Protection of National Minorities, this chapter also reflects on changes in the field of heritage and identity protection in Serbia and the Western Balkans. It especially emphasises how minorities either tend to or are forced to preserve their identities as isolated islands, often operating outside the heritage safeguarding system based on UNESCO, which by definition is tied to nation-states, not minority groups or Indigenous populations.[3] As with global declarations like the Universal Declaration, the European framework poses a challenge to anthropological norms: there are increasing calls for law and policy to adopt a 'more anthropological' perspective on minority cultures, while anthropologists and heritage scholars themselves remain divided over whether something like culture or heritage that can serve as a foundation for collective identity even exists.[4]

These dilemmas are part of a much broader relationship between anthropology and law itself viewed as a cultural practice – a topic we do not have the space to explore in detail here.[5] Yet, this is not only a problem for anthropological theory.

Human Rights' (2009) 29(4) *Critique of Anthropology* 371; Mark Goodale, 'Becoming Irrelevant: The Curious History of Anthropology and Human Rights' in Thomas Cushman (ed), *Handbook of Human Rights* (Routledge, 2012) 180.

[2] Christoph Brumann and David Berliner, 'UNESCO World Heritage – Grounded' in Christoph Brumann and David Berliner (eds), *World Heritage on the Ground: Ethnographic Perspectives* (Berghahn Books, 2016) 1; Lucas Lixinski, 'The Convention for the Safeguarding of the Intangible Cultural Heritage and Human Rights: Relativism and Collectivism 2.0?' in Janet Blake and Lucas Lixinski (eds), *The UNESCO 2003 Intangible Heritage Convention: A Commentary* (Oxford University Press, 2020) 463.

[3] Janet Blake, 'ICH and Safeguarding: Legal Dimensions of Safeguarding the ICH of Nondominant and Counter-Culture Social Groups' in A Jakubowski (ed), *Research Handbook on Contemporary Intangible Cultural Heritage* (Edward Elgar Publishing, 2018) 252; Miloš Milenković, 'Inclusive Intangible Cultural Heritage Protection as an Instrument for the Prevention of Identity-Based Conflicts: The Case of Serbia' in Valery Perry (ed), *Extremism and Violent Extremism in Serbia: 21st Century Manifestations of an Historical Challenge* (Ibidem Press/Columbia University Press, 2019) 319; Jessika Eichler, *Intangible Cultural Heritage under Pressure? Examining Vulnerabilities in ICH Regimes – Minorities, Indigenous Peoples and Refugees* (Institut für Auslandsbeziehungen, 2020).

[4] Ana P Vrdoljak, 'Minorities, Cultural Rights and the Protection of Intangible Cultural Heritage' in Vittorio Mainetti (ed), *ESIL Research Forum on International Law Contemporary Issues* (HEI, 2005) 1; Laurajane Smith, *Uses of Heritage* (Routledge, 2006); Elisabeth Gable and Richard Handler, 'Anthropology and Culture' in Tony Bennett and John Frow (eds), *The SAGE Handbook of Cultural Analysis* (SAGE, 2008) 25; Susanne Oeter, 'Intangible Cultural Heritage in Need of Protection: The Case of Regional and Minority Languages' in Evelyne Lagrange and others (eds), *Cultural Heritage and International Law: Objects, Means and Ends of International Protection* (Springer 2018) 59; Kynan Gentry and Laurajane Smith, 'Critical Heritage Studies and the Legacies of the Late-Twentieth Century Heritage Canon' (2019) 25(11) *International Journal of Heritage Studies* 1148; Stefan Berger, Bella Dicks and Marilyn Fontaine, '"Community": A Useful Concept in Heritage Studies?' (2020) 26(4) *International Journal of Heritage Studies* 325.

[5] Annelise Riles, 'Anthropology, Human Rights, and Legal Knowledge: Culture in the Iron Cage' (2006) 108(1) *American Anthropologist* 52; Stijn Deklerck, Ellen Desmet, Marie-Claire Foblets, Joke Kusters, and Jogchum Vrielink, 'Limits of Human Rights Protection from the Perspective of Legal Anthropology' in Eric Claes, Wouter Devroe, and Bert Keirsbilck (eds), *Facing the Limits of the Law* (Springer Berlin Heidelberg, 2009) 375–414; John L Comaroff and Jean Comaroff, 'Reflections on the Anthropology of Law, Governance and Sovereignty' in Franz von Benda-Beckmann and Keebet von

Other disciplines in the humanities and interpretative social sciences also grapple with the essentialism built into the very notion of collective identity and the collective rights that rely on it.[6] A particular challenge lies in explaining academic business as usual – identity deconstruction – in practical, non-academic contexts, where identity holds such deep meaning that any analysis of what is perceived as 'natural' or 'sacred' is felt as a betrayal. The rigorous academic analysis typical of anthropology often proves insufficient when faced with the complex dynamics of identity preservation in real-world settings. This is why, for over a decade, we have devoted our work to a central question: how can anthropology meaningfully reengage societies and cultures we once proclaimed ourselves the advocates or even guardians of?

This chapter stresses the importance of respecting collective identities in accordance with international conventions – especially in post-conflict societies – even when, from a strictly anthropological theoretical standpoint, those identities promote essentialism. As academically inappropriate as it may sound, this approach is deliberate: it is precisely the dominant essentialist perspectives that must be reconciled and upon which a stable post-conflict framework must be built – and not the scattered networks of individuals whose identity choices align with anthropological or critical social science norms. At the same time, the chapter presents a research program through which this theoretical question is examined in the field itself: how to preserve academic integrity while meaningfully involving the people we study in processes of reconciliation and development in post-conflict societies – bearing in mind that anthropologists and the communities they study often do not share the same views on the reality of identity, culture, tradition, and heritage.[7]

Reflecting on the integration of the Declaration and the Framework with the Convention,[8] we conclude that their coordinated application could represent a powerful model for the protection of minority rights, while simultaneously nurturing and preserving diversity within communities. However,

Benda-Beckmann (eds), *Rules of Law and Laws of Ruling* (Routledge, 2016) 31; Jonatan Kurzwelly, Nigel Rapport and Andrew D Spiegel, 'Encountering, Explaining and Refuting Essentialism' (2020) 43(2) *Anthropology Southern Africa* 65.

[6] Stanley Aronowitz, 'Reflections on Identity' in John Rajchman (ed), *The Identity in Question* (Routledge, 2014) 111; Erich H Matthes, 'Cultural Appropriation Without Cultural Essentialism?' (2016) 42(2) *Social Theory and Practice* 343; Michael Rowlands, 'The Politics of Identity in Archaeology' in GC Bond and A Gilliam (eds), *Social Construction of the Past: Representation as Power* (Routledge, 2020) 129; Benjamin Gregg, 'Against Essentialism in Conceptions of Human Rights and Human Nature' (2021) 43(2) *Human Rights Quarterly* 313.

[7] Michael Sökefeld, 'Debating Self, Identity, and Culture in Anthropology' (1999) 40(4) *Current Anthropology* 417; Jane K Cowan, Marie-Bénédicte Dembour and Richard A Wilson (eds), *Culture and Rights: Anthropological Perspectives* (Cambridge University Press, 2001); Haidy Geismar, 'Anthropology and Heritage Regimes' (2015) 44 *Annual Review of Anthropology* 71; Richard Pfeilstetter, 'Culture in Heritage: On the Socio-Anthropological Notion of Culture in Current Heritage Discourses' (2017) 112(2) *Anthropos* 609; Miloš Milenković, *Intangible Cultural Heritage and Reconciliation in the Western Balkans: An Anthropological Perspective* (Routledge, 2024).

[8] UNESCO Convention for the Safeguarding of the Intangible Cultural Heritage (adopted 17 October 2003, entered into force 20 April 2006) www.ich.unesco.org/en/convention.

especially in many sensitive post-conflict regions around the world, this would require legal, political, and anthropological theory alike to come to terms with the banality of essentialising collective identity if they are to have any influence at all on the communities for whom these rights frameworks were originally intended. In this sense, this chapter should be read as the beginning of an alignment that is still far from complete as it is clear that some will come to terms with essentialism more easily than others as anthropology repositions itself once again.[9] Ethnology is proven to be of assistance in that regard, with its traditional inclination to understand truth and justice as something that the communities being studied themselves truly 'live' as heritage – believing in it even as they are aware of its construed nature.[10]

2. Anthropological Default – Both Academic and a Societal Challenge

Post-conflict societies frequently have a stronger collective identity. People there typically identify primarily through ethnic, religious, or other cultural categories. In the Balkans, this is especially true among young people who were born after the conflicts but whose identities were still shaped by those events.[11] This makes the analysis of these topics particularly challenging. Older generations, who directly experienced identity-based conflicts, often see the deconstruction of those identities as a form of 'betrayal'. The problem is not just that many might see us as traitors when we try to understand how today's identities were formed, but also that younger generations share that same view. The challenge is even greater because it is hard to achieve non-academic goals related to human and minority rights if we do not have legitimacy among the communities we study. In the end, we are often seen as 'antisocial', which complicates our work.[12]

Our analyses, though academically valuable, are usually difficult to apply in practice, especially in politics and administration. The issues arise not just because academic analysis fails to reach the broader public, but also because it often doesn't align with the needs of politics, education, bureaucracy and the media. Moreover, such analyses can unintentionally offend the communities we study, requiring careful methodological attention. It was once believed that compromising with

[9] Thomas H Eriksen, 'The Sustainability of an Anthropology of the Anthropocene' (2022) 14(6) *Sustainability* 3674.

[10] Miloš Milenković, 'The Promises of the Bureaucratisation of Intangible Cultural Heritage Safeguarding in Post-Conflict Regions: Lessons from Anthropological Fieldwork in Four Western Balkan States' (2024) 30(1) *International Journal of Heritage Studies* 1.

[11] Felicia Pratto, Iris Žeželj, Edona Maloku, Vladimir Turjačanin and Marija Branković (eds), *Shaping Social Identities after Violent Conflict: Youth in the Western Balkans* (Palgrave Macmillan, 2017).

[12] David Mosse, 'Anti-Social Anthropology? Objectivity, Objection, and the Ethnography of Public Policy and Professional Communities' (2006) 12(4) *Journal of the Royal Anthropological Institute* 935.

those we study would undermine academic standards. Many actors, for various reasons and interests, may feel threatened when academic truth is pursued in politically sensitive topics. As we often say before heading into the field: 'Truth hurts – that's why science can offend'. This leads us to consider how, in an era when both academic research funders and policymakers expect actor inclusion, and these same actors often turn to populist views on tradition, culture, and identity, we can still maintain academic integrity while striving to change the world.

The default anthropological view of identity as a social construct shaped by power relations is in contrast to the prevailing societal view that identity is innate, almost part of the natural order – something with which we are born, without which we do not exist (and from this, it follows that the people with whom we share an identity – say, ethnoreligious – are practically our relatives). In academic discourse, communities are typically presented as being controlled by official narratives, which can turn entire nations into folkloric societies incapable of modernisation, innovation, and progress. The fate of Serbs is not much different from that of other peoples in post-conflict regions. Today, our young people are experiencing a return to traditionalism and are often more conservative than their parents and grandparents. But who wants to hear that? Who is really ready to accept that they are more conservative, backward, or closed off than their ancestors?

In such an interpretation, heritage is not seen as naturally shaped and collectively constructed, but as something imposed. This bitter truth about imposed identity does not heal the wounds but rather worsens them. Our current research shows that people do not have a reflective distance from the content they receive about tradition, culture, identity, and heritage – they accept it automatically because 'that's how it should be.' As an additional complication, we must also consider the researcher's relationship with the legal and political framework within which processes of heritagisation take place. Many academics view the State and politics as enemies of academia, almost as open adversaries. Although this chapter does not specifically address these attitudes toward the State and bureaucracy, this aspect cannot be overlooked. In related disciplines, there is also a large number of those who see the State as a repressive force rather than as the last bastion of civilisation against the onslaught of populism.

The role of academy in society, especially of the humanities, remains a contentious issue that points to the need to clarify how academic knowledge actually achieves social impact. This opens up numerous challenges for humanities like ethnology and for interpretive social sciences like anthropology, since regulators and donors demand that we not disturb or hurt the feelings of those we study. But what to do when those, whose feelings we are supposed to spare, are in the wrong, or even participate in criminal acts that violate international or domestic laws that protect humanity, individual human rights or collective rights of the minorities? What should we do when we discover that the implementation plans of the Convention are actually being used to consolidate one's power over heritagisation? We are aware, of course, that we ourselves contributed to this phenomenon, unsuccessfully trying to explain to the rest of the world outside of anthropology that cultural relativism is a method of anthropological analysis of ethnographic reality, and not an empirical finding that supposedly confirms – and thereby justifies – the oppression of other people who do not have the power to impose their culture on others. In this sense, a particularly significant problem is the fact that contemporary populist movements use the concept of identity in a perverted way – as if they selectively take only what suits them from anthropological textbooks, ignoring the theoretical introductions and political lessons that always accompany relativistic empiricism in anthropology.

When it comes to the legal and political framework of using anthropological knowledge, the reawakening of cultural relativism in the era of populism imposes challenges in finding a balance between respecting different perspectives and advocating for universal human rights and values. These questions are particularly relevant today, in the era of pseudoscience and populist attacks on the academy, an all-encompassing science denialism. The denial of scientific facts is well known when it comes to human contribution to climate change, or the connection between smoking and cancer, or – in recent years – especially in connection with the anti-vaccine movement. What is less known are populisms' dreadful consequences when directed against the humanities, through attempts to negate centuries of academic study of history, culture, and identity. Populists seek to ban academic research on cultural heritage, as if it were a sacred object immune to scientific analysis. Are these the actors we want to 'include' in research and to 'harmonise' academic knowledge with? Is the engagement of their followers – in traditional and new media, as well as in churches, schools and partly in academic institutions and universities – worth the 'impact' that foundations seek? Balancing the pressure to achieve social impact and benefit, on the one hand, and the critical questioning of culture, on the other, requires a delicate balance between responding to society's needs and preserving the possibility of cultural criticism. That balance is particularly difficult in circumstances in which entrenched positions oppose any attempt to reconcile academic and popular knowledge, as it is seen as a betrayal on both sides.

3. Post-Conflict Heritage Stakeholder Participation – A Challenge for Theory

Stabilisation programs in post-conflict contexts, whose main goal is to foster peace, reconciliation and sustainable development, should in principle be key to the reconstruction of societies devastated by conflicts. These initiatives recognise the interdependence of peace, development and human rights, emphasise the importance of addressing structural inequalities and strive to promote social cohesion through the use of culture as a tool, a function to a goal.[13] However, the implementation of

[13] William Logan, 'Heritage, Sustainable Development and the Achievement of Peace and Security in Our World' in Peter Bille Larsen and William Logan (eds), *World Heritage and Sustainable Development:*

international conventions on human rights within such programs encounters significant obstacles, especially when dealing with issues of collective identity. Although the conventions are designed to protect the rights of individuals, regardless of their belonging to certain groups, the reality on the ground is rooted in political dynamics that direct the implementation of conventions towards goals that are more appropriate for the collectives that need to be reconciled, pacified or controlled, than for the individuals themselves. Of course, there is also a debate about whether communities can even be talked about in this context, and who even has the power to define what a community would even be?[14]

The key challenge in this context is the tension between individual rights and collective identities. International human rights standards put the protection of individual freedoms and rights at the fore, but many conflicts have deep roots in collective frustrations and identities linked to ethnicity or religion. In such contexts, the rights of individuals are suppressed or threatened by the collective interests and demands of their communities for some kind of collective revenge or reconciliation, leading to marginalisation and exclusion, especially of those individuals who do not fit into the dominant norms. Moreover, the implementation of human rights conventions is met with resistance within communities, especially by those who wish to maintain traditional hierarchies and norms. Leaders and elites often instrumentalise collective identities for political purposes, using them to legitimise their own power, resulting in the suppression of minority rights, discrimination against marginalised groups, and the perpetuation of social inequalities. In this sense, the implementation of UNESCO's agenda of intangible cultural heritage shows itself to be susceptible to manipulation through the mythologising of the past, which leads to the cultural supremacy of a dominant community or socio-political elite, the suppression of counter-memories and the exclusion of interpretations that are undesirable for those who have the power to heritagise.

There is abundant evidence from the field that confirms this phenomenon,[15] although this does not necessarily lead to pessimism or the abandonment of the idea that heritage can be used for peaceful purposes. One notable example is the neglect of individuality, especially in the case of those who refuse to conform to practices considered typical of collective traditions: power relations within communities often lead to the oppression of non-conformists by those in

New Directions in World Heritage Management (Routledge, 2018) 134; Robert Wrobel, *Culture in Post-Crisis Situations: Opportunities for Peacebuilding and Sustainable Recovery* (The World Bank, 2019); Sultan Barakat and Sarah Milton, 'Localisation across the Humanitarian-Development-Peace Nexus' (2020) 15(2) *Journal of Peacebuilding & Development* 147.

[14] Miodrag A Jovanović, *Collective Rights: A Legal Theory* (Cambridge University Press, 2012); Philipp Lottholz, 'Critiquing Anthropological Imagination in Peace and Conflict Studies: From Empiricist Positivism to a Dialogical Approach in Ethnographic Peace Research' (2018) 25(5) *International Peacekeeping* 695; Nora Baumgart, 'The European Court of Human Rights and the Protection of National Minorities: Are We There Yet?' (2021) 20(1) *European Yearbook of Minority Issues Online* 93.

[15] Amanda Kearney, 'Intangible Cultural Heritage: Global Awareness and Local Interest' in Natsuko Akagawa and Laurajane Smith (eds), *Intangible Heritage* (Routledge, 2009) 209; Antoinnete Jackson, 'Changing Ideas about Heritage and Heritage Management in Historically Segregated Communities' (2010) 18(1) *Transforming Anthropology* 80.

positions of authority, who strive to preserve traditional norms and values. Another important challenge is the disrespect of different forms of knowledge, whereby scientific knowledge is often privileged over religious, magical or knowledge based on corporate interests – or vice versa, depending on political dynamics (which is especially important at the intersection of environmental issues and intangible cultural heritage).[16] Furthermore, the very idea of truly ethical research-based policy and its implementation is undermined by political pressures on academics to align their findings with the interests of power holders in traditional ethnic and religious communities.

The challenges that stakeholder inclusion poses to the theory are just beginning. Among those who work at the intersection of anthropological theory and legal-political discourse, populist re-traditionalisation represents the most complex problem when it comes to academic approaches to cultural heritage, since the global return to 'traditional' values and practices in post-conflict societies goes directly against the goals of the conventions. Primordialist invocations of ancestors and 'authentic' elements of culture and identity gain particular importance in post-conflict contexts. Since collective identities are by nature relational, reactive and defensive, the identity of young people in post-conflict societies is actually 'reinforced' (when we compare it with the relatively secular and relatively non-national, and certainly non-racist identities of their grandparents). Paradoxically, nationalism and religious fundamentalism tend to become stronger and more deeply rooted in post-conflict societies, such as in the former Yugoslavia. That environment is key to understanding the fate of cultural heritage in the Balkans.

The struggle for collective rights includes efforts by communities to realise their right to cultural heritage and identity, often as a response to historical marginalisation. Zero-sum thinking was regularly recorded in our research. For example, many believe that if one State safeguards a particular element of cultural heritage that is ethnically attributed, it automatically means that this element is 'lost' to everyone else – to other communities within the same State, to other States, and even to heritage experts who see ethnic appropriation as deeply unprofessional and contrary to the essence of UNESCO. This view has led to numerous disputes and accusations of appropriation, laying a firm foundation for the further development of ethnically and religiously based intolerance – precisely the opposite of what the convention was intended to prevent. That is why we are developing a new approach that aims to bring anthropology closer to the communities it studies, while preserving academic integrity, even though the traditional academic position excludes the studied actors themselves from the analysis. This approach could be seen as a response to excessive populism, although the question arises: can there even be such a thing as excessive anti-populism, or should priority always be given to uncovering scientific truths, even when this might lead to new identity-based conflicts?

[16] Miloš Milenković, 'Integrating Debates on Intangible Cultural Heritage, Environment, Identity, and Populism' (2025) 34(1) *Anthropological Journal of European Cultures* 80.

Our research deals with the unique circumstances of the Serbian community – a minority living in the States of the Western Balkans – and explores the specific obstacles and opportunities they face in preserving their cultural heritage. At the centre of this analysis is a fundamental question: can the intangible elements of Serbian culture – customs, beliefs, and folk knowledge, which were of great significance during the turbulent 1990s – be effectively integrated into a regional framework of reconciliation and development? To approach this question, we adopt UNESCO's model of inclusive safeguarding of intangible cultural heritage, which emphasises the active participation of communities in the protection processes. UNESCO has applied this approach in numerous post-conflict regions around the world, often in cooperation with researchers from the social sciences and humanities. However, the differing perspectives that academics and community members hold regarding culture, identity, tradition, and ICH itself is known to lead to tensions. Academics typically approach the topic analytically, aiming to reveal underlying power relations, illusions, and manipulations within the collective. On the other hand, community members prioritise the preservation of collective identity, even at the expense of individual human rights (or are forced to do so by external pressures). What is more, they are willing to compromise the European integration of neighbouring States in the name of identity, within the framework of differentiating EU conditionality on identity basis.[17]

Serbian cultural heritage in the Western Balkan States outside of Serbia is perceived as continuous with the heritage of Serbs in Serbia, just as many Serbs outside of Serbia view Serbia as their primary homeland more than the country in which they reside (even though their ancestors are not from Serbia). Within such a perception, it seems almost impossible to implement the UNESCO's State-based principle of safeguarding, because Serbs in Serbia, Montenegro, and Bosnia and Herzegovina hold different views of the State structures responsible for heritage protection. The model previously developed for the inclusive safeguarding of Bosniak heritage in Serbia – which has proven successful for other minorities as well – requires adaptation, as it appears both promising and risky. It could lead to successful joint safeguarding of Serbian intangible heritage outside Serbia, but it could also contribute to the radicalisation of identity bearers who might perceive attempts at joint safeguarding of heritage elements with Montenegrins and Bosniaks as an attempt at assimilation. Accordingly, we have arrived at a series of recommendations, which are available to the public.[18]

In cases we encountered during fieldwork, there was a clear conflict between ethnic attribution of heritage and the State's power to implement heritage

[17] Marko Milenković, 'The Western Balkans and European Union Enlargement – Exploring Possibilities of Differentiated Integration' in Diane Fromage (ed), *Re-defining Membership? Current and Future Perspectives* (Oxford University Press, 2024) 273.

[18] Miloš Milenković et. al, *Contested Heritage, Negotiated Futures: Policy Insights from the Western Balkans* (Zenodo, 2025) www.doi.org/10.5281/zenodo.15544333.

policies – to map and thereby determine what exists and what does not; to research and thereby select what heritage will be studied and what will not; to nominate and promote, and thereby set aside the heritage that is deemed undesirable. This situation may appear hopeless and could discourage anthropologists, as well as legal and political experts, from even initiating a search for a reconciliation model through the integration of the Convention with the Declaration and the Framework. Still, existing research points to a high level of public trust in Serbian ethnologists – a sentiment shared by colleagues in Montenegro, Bosnia and Herzegovina, and Croatia, based on the perception that they adhere less to official cultural policy and more to professional standards. Ethnology is a discipline oriented toward the preservation of collective identity, and it is precisely on this basis that we argue it can serve as a bridge for the inclusion of various social actors – a bridge for legal and political sciences, and even critical humanities to work from within instead of alienating the general population. Joint work among ethnologists from different Balkan nations has been crucial in establishing inter-ethnic trust – and this is something that should be comparatively tested on a global level. Ethnologists act as metonymic representatives of their communities, and those communities trust them when they work together on preserving cultural heritage that is simultaneously controversial, endangered, and perceived as disappearing under the pressures of modernisation, globalisation, Europeanisation, and similar processes. It is precisely the fear of these processes that emerges as a strong motivator for paradoxically accepting the agenda of the most universal of all actors – that of UNESCO.

When it comes to legal analysis, cooperation with local actors brings a set of familiar challenges as well. While anthropologists have produced extensive research on how to deal with ethical issues in post-conflict settings,[19] with sensitivity to local context becoming a key reflexive component of standard anthropological practice, the role of legal analysis in these processes remains marginal. It is still reserved for sophisticated discourses in legal philosophy, critical legal studies, and 'law and society' approaches, while mainstream legal science stays within normative frameworks for several reasons.[20] The dilemma troubling anthropologists – whether to deconstruct heritage elements because they serve as a basis for conflict-driven discourse, or to accept the lived reality of the communities we study and try to support them by using those same elements as tools of reconciliation – is similar to the dilemma ethnologists face in the field when implementing the UNESCO agenda on intangible cultural heritage. They must decide whether to insist on professional UNESCO standards, which tie heritage to territory and obligate signatory States to protect the heritage of all communities, or to accept the

[19] Jana Krause, 'The Ethics of Ethnographic Methods in Conflict Zones' (2021) 58(3) *Journal of Peace Research* 329; Gearóid Millar, 'The Ethics of Ethnographic Peace and Conflict Research' in Roger MacGinty and others (eds), *The Companion to Peace and Conflict Fieldwork* (Springer, 2021) 147.

[20] Ernst Hirsch Ballin, *Advanced Introduction to Legal Research Methods* (Edward Elgar Publishing, 2020); Roger Cotterrell, 'Social Theory and Legal Theory: Contemporary Interactions' (2021) 17 *Annual Review of Law and Social Science* 15.

reality in which most people ethnically attribute heritage elements – whether we are talking about modern nations or Indigenous populations.[21]

This dilemma demands of anthropologists a balance between ethically sound research and the production of useful knowledge, and lies at the heart of applied anthropology, to which Balkan ethnology is closely related.[22] Like archaeology,[23] anthropology in post-conflict contexts faces the challenge of balancing critical research with building bridges toward reconciliation. The question of how to deal with the past – especially regarding war crimes and systemic injustices based on identity – is not the only challenge anthropologists face in trying to reconcile truth and justice with the need to avoid misinterpretations that might reopen old divisions. What turns out to be most difficult is the responsible preservation and strategic revitalisation of cultural heritage as a key to reconstruction – enabling communities to express their identity and reconnect with the past, while at the same time avoiding conflicts over the ethnic attribution of particular heritage elements. This function of anthropology theoretically contributes to the preservation of unique cultural expressions, and in turn – again in theory – to diversity and coexistence in societies that have gone through traumatic experiences.

However, the negative side of this, as shown by critiques of the paradoxical role of collectivism embedded in the discourse on heritage,[24] is that academic legitimisation often ends up additionally empowering already powerful individuals within traditional communities, who then continue to homogenise their own societies at the expense of the rights and freedoms of 'deviant' individuals (those who do not wish to submit to those authorised to carry out the heritagisation process). While development policies tend to seek external legitimacy, internal disagreements at the community level pose an obstacle to the implementation of the global protection framework.[25] This recalls the general conclusion reached by Kymlicka and Wayland[26] some time ago in the context of multiculturalism: external protection of minority collectives by the State or other authority leads to internal restrictions within those communities, as local power-holders prohibit members of their own collectives from deviating ideologically, ethically, religiously, or in terms of identity from the norm they control. Ideally, the inclusion of local perspectives

[21] Jelena Ćuković and Miloš Milenković, 'Intangible Cultural Heritage as a Resource for "Self-sta keholderisation": Fieldwork Among Politically Active Civil Society Stakeholders in the Province of Vojvodina, Serbia' (2023) 18 *International Journal of Intangible Heritage* 49.

[22] Christina F Kreps, Museums and Anthropology in the Age of Engagement (Routledge, 2020).

[23] John D Giblin, 'Post-conflict Heritage: Symbolic Healing and Cultural Renewal' (2014) 20(5) *International Journal of Heritage Studies* 500.

[24] Rosemary Coombe and Lindsay M Weiss, 'Neoliberalism, Heritage Regimes and Cultural Rights' in Lynn Meskell (ed), *Global Heritage: A Reader* (Wiley-Blackwell, 2015) 43; Lucas Lixinski, *Legalized Identities: Cultural Heritage Law and the Shaping of Transitional Justice* (Cambridge University Press, 2021).

[25] Nicolas Adell, Regina F Bendix, Chiara Bortolotto and Markus Tauschek (eds), *Between Imagined Communities and Communities of Practice: Participation, Territory, and the Making of Heritage* (Universitätsverlag Göttingen, 2015); Jessika Eichler, 'Intangible Cultural Heritage, Inequalities and Participation: Who Decides on Heritage?' (2021) 25(5) *The International Journal of Human Rights* 793.

[26] Will Kymlicka and Stephen V Wayland, 'Multicultural Citizenship: A Liberal Theory of Minority Rights' (1996) 28(2) *Canadian Ethnic Studies* 174.

in reconstruction and stabilisation processes should not only contribute to more appropriate interventions, it should also strengthen the capacity of communities to take control over their own destiny. The problem, however, lies in who defines what 'destiny' is – and the research program of heritage studies confirms that control over the past is the most effective tool for projecting the future.[27]

Anthropologists strive to play a role in reconciliation and development processes by promoting sustainable practices that simultaneously respect local culture, resources, and needs, and protect – at least academically – the right of individuals to differ from their own collectives, regardless of how threatened those collectives may be or how deserving of protection under international conventions. By taking on this role, they try not to deviate from the core principles of a discipline whose purpose is to protect cultural differences within communities, not only between them. And this is a dilemma we faced constantly during our research project. What we discovered while trying to meet the expectations that research must have is that social impact is also theoretically relevant and may be of interest to colleagues in legal and political theory, as well as in related fields. Donors insist on research having social impact, with the goal of bringing tangible benefits to society. However, that focus limits critical thinking (mostly constructivist), especially among researchers who question established norms (mostly historical, identity-based, inherited). A paradox arises when donors imagine social impact exclusively as positive and constructive, which often clashes with the findings of critical researchers. As a result, critical researchers struggle to demonstrate the required 'impact' in the form donors expect, especially when their results provoke discomfort or resistance among actors in the community.

This tension between the expected social impact and the pursuit of critical independence complicates the research process, because in post-conflict and post-communist societies, development strategies prioritise stability over deeper social change. Although international development strategies promote stakeholder inclusion, actual power structures favour traditional elites who oppose democratisation and social transformation. Critical researchers advocating for substantive transformation therefore face resistance from both international actors and local elites who benefit from the status quo. This creates a 'double bind': aligning with expectations of impact on one side and pursuing truth and justice on the other. The dominant concept of the entrepreneurial university in some regions further emphasises applied projects, while neglecting the deeper implications of research findings. Researchers disappointed with academia tend to transition into political or public intellectual careers, or try to keep academic positions while no longer engaging in research, but rather in politics and teaching, which undermines the quality of the university itself, turning it at best into an NGO-like platform for social activism. Despite all of this, the need to include actors – even those who break the law or violate human rights – remains. The fact that the heritagisation

[27] Brian Graham and Greg J Ashworth (eds), *Senses of Place: Senses of Time* (Routledge, 2005).

of intangible culture as the core of identity patterns is still largely in the hands of experts offers some hope in this regard.

4. Conclusion

Anthropology, as an academic discipline concerned with the deconstruction of tradition, culture, heritage, and therefore all collective identities, often comes into direct conflict with identity politics (which, by contrast, strives for stability, homogeneity, and legitimacy as prerequisites for political representation and the realisation of collective rights). This opposition becomes especially pronounced when anthropology criticises the preservation of cultural heritage, particularly ICH, without recognising that such academic critiques can unintentionally alienate precisely those people it aims to understand and support. While our goal is to challenge essentialist narratives and illuminate the complexity of cultural dynamics, we sometimes neglect the need to act with sensitivity and to acknowledge the actual experiences and perspectives of the communities we study. This is especially important when collective identities are appropriated by nationalists, racists, and other powerholders who use them to harm members of their own culture who disagree with them – or members of other cultures, 'in the name' of identity. Negotiating this balance requires a careful approach that maintains academic rigour but also respects the cultural contexts of those involved – their interpretations, interests, and 'voices'.

However, the post-conflict context generally makes it impossible to discuss identity outside of an essentialist framework, because the reconciliation of essentialists – especially those who resort to violence – is prioritised by the international community above all other goals (including respect for intra-cultural differences or the right of individuals to fully diverge from the way power-holders within their communities define collective identities, carry out heritagisation, and claim collective rights on that basis). This has posed a serious challenge for anthropological theory for decades – from its confident (and unreflective) contribution to drafting the Universal Declaration of Human Rights, to its later marginalisation. In post-conflict settings, the imperative of peace and stability often becomes the main goal of international actors, who then give preference to essentialist approaches to identity. Allegedly fixed, immutable traits or elements of tradition are prioritised in reconciliation efforts, in order to address the causes of conflict and prevent future violence – legitimising the authority of those who control memory and heritagisation in a given context: community leaders, elders, clergy, etc. Such a focus, of course, sidelines more complex academic discussions on identity that recognise its constructed nature, fluidity, and internal diversity – both within and between communities.

Focusing exclusively on essentialist narratives in post-conflict reconciliation risks neglecting the diverse range of identities in society and perpetuating a homogenising understanding of culture and heritage – precisely of the kind that often led to conflict in the first place. Moreover, elevating essentialist identities in post-conflict contexts strengthens power imbalances and marginalises voices that do not belong to dominant narratives of folklore, tradition, identity – heritage that is fundamentally important for marginalised groups whose identities have been historically ignored or suppressed. Although the reconciliation of essentialist identities is seen as a pragmatic step toward short-term peace, it can simultaneously reinforce rigid boundaries of identity and obstruct long-term efforts toward inclusivity, diversity, and genuine reconciliation. It is therefore necessary for post-conflict societies, as well as the international community, to include in the dialogue approaches that go beyond essentialism and embrace the complexity and diversity of identity as a path toward lasting peace and social cohesion. Empirically, however, this has proven to be almost impossible. The furthest we have come in our research is to bring essentialists together and reach temporary agreement on the joint safeguarding of contested heritage elements under the auspices of the UN – bearing in mind that those shared elements are also the most conflict-ridden. Despite numerous attempts in several countries, we have not succeeded in moving to the next level, where our model would also work with intra-cultural differences. That, of course, does not mean we will stop trying, nor that colleagues around the world should not keep trying – whether they are anthropologists, legal scholars, or experts from other disciplines who face the paradoxes of essentialising identity in the practical application of conventions that are, in fact, meant to enhance human well-being.

In this sense, we believe not only that the Convention for the Safeguarding of Intangible Cultural Heritage (ICH) can 'ground' the Declaration and the Framework, but also that it can turn them towards respecting individual differences in cases where collectives are deeply essentialised and their heritage is predominantly ethnically attributed. We are developing this model in the sensitive context of the Western Balkans, on the remnants of former Yugoslavia, where a significant number of Serbs still live in other former republics (now independent States), with which they share a large portion of cultural heritage – and with which they are in conflict over – raising issues of appropriation, assimilation, ethnocide, and the like. None of these issues offer any guarantee that they will help prevent future identity-based conflicts. However, we have succeeded – precisely by involving those most invested in identity and by making their cooperation conditional on joint heritage safeguarding (especially ICH, which they see as the very core of identity) – in calming disputes that at times seemed like preludes to new wars. We could not have achieved this without accepting the banality of essentialism, without realising that anthropological theory cannot work outside the State and its bureaucratic structures, just as we cannot fulfil the non-academic aims of anthropology – intercultural understanding and lasting peace – unless we focus precisely on those who see themselves as bearers of identity, who essentialise it, arm it, and are ready to die for it (again).

The inclusion of the humanities and interpretive social sciences in post-conflict stabilisation agendas in the Western Balkans faces serious obstacles, primarily due to the internal tension between excessive nationalism and rigid anti-nationalism. Scholars inclined toward nationalism unintentionally alienate more moderate members of their own nations, members of other nations, and international actors, by promoting exclusionary narratives. On the other hand, those with anti-nationalist views alienate their own communities by challenging entrenched beliefs about history, tradition, identity, and heritage. Nationalist perspectives prioritise the preservation of unique national identities, potentially exacerbating inter-ethnic tensions and hindering reconciliation and cooperation. In contrast, anti-nationalist approaches aim to deconstruct essentialist narratives and promote more inclusive understandings of identity, but they struggle to find support in communities that fear the loss of cultural heritage and collective memory.

This dichotomy poses a serious challenge for integrating our disciplines into sustainable identity management strategies – producing a continuous cycle of obstacles. The goals of anti-realist deconstruction and the pursuit of tangible political outcomes often seem incompatible. While deconstructivist academic approaches aim to challenge existing power structures and dominant narratives, decision-makers and on-the-ground actors prioritise pragmatic solutions and immediate results. In response to this mismatch, academia must explore new paths that reconcile academic integrity with engagement with reality. One promising approach is the adoption of participatory research methods that actively include community members and actors in the research process. By working with local communities in real time, researchers can better respond to sensitive issues, reduce the risk of alienating those they seek to understand and support, and still remain true to academic principles. If anthropology were to close in on itself, it would surely fall into the gap between theory and application – due to excessive self-referential insistence on its own domains and the narcissistic echo chamber effect. Interdisciplinary collaboration with fields such as conflict resolution, peacebuilding, and development studies enriches research efforts and supports stabilisation approaches that do not depend on theoretical specificities. It is precisely through such decentralisation that anthropological theory can – paradoxically – thrive, confronted by reality and perhaps liberated by the solutions offered by already applied disciplines. One could argue that law, in this respect, can turn to anthropology as a bridge to engage with complex social realities.

Over the past decade, we have accepted the concept of knowledge transfer into public policy – not without reservations and not always gladly – trying to collaborate with bureaucratic structures that academia tends to dislike. In the effort to make academic work impactful and to promote interdisciplinary cooperation, we navigated the complexities of identity politics in the Western Balkans. Still, it is important to acknowledge that peacebuilding efforts based on academia in the region remain fragile, and the idea of sustainability often seems more like an aspiration than a reality. This model of integrating actors into the resolution of identity conflicts could, in principle, assist the implementation of the Universal Declaration of Human Rights and the Framework Convention for the Protection of National Minorities, supported by the ethnological infrastructure that implements the UNESCO Convention for the Safeguarding of ICH. However, this requires comparative testing, deeper multidisciplinary collaboration, knowledge exchange, and experience sharing – and above all, the acceptance of the UNESCO Convention on Intangible Cultural Heritage as a tool for achieving human and minority rights – the most important platform for cooperation between the humanities and social sciences in this century.

INDEX

academic integrity 10, 207, 209, 212, 219
accommodation 24, 104, 112, 134, 182, 184
accountability 54, 73–74
actors 21, 35, 79, 158, 209–10, 214, 216, 219–20
non-State 96, 158, 163
adequate representation 129, 132–40, 142–45, 147–49
administrative authorities 76, 80, 200
administrative units 77–78
admissibility 38, 46, 49, 51
Advisory Committee (AC) on the FCNM 8, 30, 114–15, 123, 126–28, 130, 132–46, 148–49
monitoring 131, 135–39, 146–47, 149
Albania 131, 135–36, 138–39, 142
Allott, Philip 5, 16, 19–21, 27
anthropological default 208–10
anthropological theory 10, 205–20
anthropologists 206–7, 214–16, 218
anthropology 10–11, 205–7, 209–10, 212, 215, 217–19
anti-discrimination 7, 9, 87
frameworks 5, 47, 55, 88
practice 38, 46–47
applicability 165, 172, 195
direct 52, 54–55
potential 158
applicants 50–51, 110, 192, 194–95, 203
aspirations 65, 86, 91, 176–77, 220
assimilation 2, 26–27, 173, 213, 218
forced 63, 102, 107, 111–12, 114
Austria 93, 176–77
authorities 79, 81, 116, 118–19, 140–41, 162–63, 215, 217
autonomy 10, 46, 52–53, 86, 159, 192, 200, 203
non-territorial 9, 151–65

barriers 9, 50, 134, 138, 141, 143
'battling' nations 7, 101–24
Belgium 116
beliefs 4, 87, 92–93, 95, 110, 213, 219
Bentham, Jeremy 21
Bill of Rights 66–68
broad margin of appreciation 7, 108–9, 115, 119–20, 124, 147
burden of proof 48, 51, 192
bureaucracy 208–9
bureaucratic structures 218–19

CAJ, *see* **Committee on the Administration of Justice**
case law 48, 83, 104, 110, 124, 189, 199; *see also* ***individual cases***
CAT (Convention Again Torture) 188
Catan 104–5, 118–19, 122–24
Chapman 50, 108–9, 122, 202
Charter for Regional or Minority Languages, *see* **European Charter for Regional or Minority Languages**
Charter of Fundamental Rights 51, 87, 91, 93, 170, 173, 178–79
children 92, 103, 111, 116–18, 122
China 95, 159
citizens 17, 43, 52, 159, 170, 177, 179
citizenship 62, 170–74
civil servants 135, 137, 141
CJEU, *see* **Court of Justice of the European Union**
classifications 39, 47, 154, 178
CoE, *see* **Council of Europe**
coherence 86, 146–47, 149
cohesion, social 52, 175, 181, 183–84, 210, 218
collective identities 10–11, 156, 159, 206–8, 211–14, 217
collective rights 5, 9, 41, 43, 52, 54–55, 62–63, 162–63, 185, 187–90, 205, 207, 209, 212, 217
collective victimhood 50, 54
collectives 11, 43, 61, 203, 205, 211, 213, 215–16, 218
collectivisation 205
Commission on FICT (Flags, Identity, Culture and Tradition) 67–68
commissioners 68, 71–72

commitments 5, 19, 67–68, 73, 87, 95, 97, 112, 127
Committee of Experts 74, 77–81
Committee on the Administration of Justice (CAJ) 70–71
common knowledge 15, 17
communities 64, 69–70, 162, 178–79, 192, 207–9, 211–17, 219
indigenous 9, 188–89, 201, 203
competence 85–86, 88, 161, 202
complaints 103, 116, 118–19, 199
complexities 6, 23, 48, 61, 73, 121, 154, 156, 169, 217–19
compliance 52, 69, 93, 163
conceptions 24–26, 46, 52
political 5, 38, 46, 55
conceptions of equality 24, 26
conceptualisation 151–53, 155–56, 158, 169–70
conditionality 27, 103, 130–31
conflict prevention 8, 94, 126, 129, 143, 145–47, 149
objectives 127–28, 139, 144, 148–49
techniques 8, 125–49
conflict resolution 8, 126, 129, 146, 149, 219
conflicts 8, 43, 59, 64, 70, 139, 144, 187–88, 208, 210–11, 213, 215, 217–18
identity-based 208, 212, 218
violent 125, 129, 144, 146
consciousness 16, 19, 21
consensus 66–67, 122, 154, 156, 170, 183, 190
consistency 136, 147, 149
absence of 146, 157
constitutionalism, domestic 185
constitutions 19–20, 40, 145, 157
constructivism 30, 206, 216
contestations 60, 69–71, 73–74, 106
Convention Again Torture (CAT) 188
conventionalists 19
cooperation 63, 68, 93, 96, 132, 184, 213–14, 218–20
interdisciplinary 11, 219
core tenets/principles 87, 103, 107, 109, 216
core values 124, 184
correlation 128, 137–39, 148
Council Directives 174, 178, 180
Council of Europe (CoE) 1, 5, 37, 81–82, 93, 119–20, 155–56, 188
counterpart rights 5, 17, 30, 36
country-specific opinions 49, 128, 130–31, 135, 137, 140, 143, 148
Court of Justice of the European Union (CJEU) 51–52, 120
crimes 42, 160, 191, 215
Croatia 77–78, 82, 130, 135, 137, 139, 141, 143, 145, 214
cultural heritage 3, 6, 76, 195, 205–20
cultural identities 6, 61, 68–69, 158, 183, 192–93, 201
cultural practices 9, 154, 200, 206
cultural rights 10, 28, 110, 192–93, 198, 201–2
cultural values 34, 76, 186
culture 6, 9–10, 59–60, 62–63, 73, 205–7, 209–10, 217
curricula 111–13, 115–16, 176
customs 177, 201, 213
Cyrillic script 117, 119

data 135, 138, 140–41, 145
disaggregated 134, 160
official 140–41, 145
de Varennes, Fernand 90, 160–61, 164, 172
declarations 3, 89, 103, 155–56, 205–7, 214, 218
draft 42
deconstruction 151, 158, 164, 207–8, 217, 219
deference 187, 203
democracy 85–88, 91–92, 96–97, 107, 170, 195
democratic process 173, 177
Democratic Unionist Party (DUP) 72–73
demographics 6, 74, 134, 154, 173, 175, 181
Denmark 192
Derrida, Jacques 164
development 6–8, 64–66, 87–88, 102, 108–9, 126–27, 135–36, 212–13
differential treatment 47, 108–9, 119, 123
differentiation 15, 26, 35
digital era/age 8–9, 152, 158–61, 163–65
digital minorities 8–9, 151, 158–61
protection 161–64
digital spaces 161, 164
dignity 47, 164
Dinstein, Y. 44
direct applicability 52, 54–55
direct discrimination 179
directives 178–81
disabilities 8, 47, 55, 92, 154, 156, 158, 160
disciplines 10–11, 205, 207, 209, 214, 216–19

discretion 53–54, 101, 106–7, 121–22, 170, 181, 186
broad 5, 7, 123, 189
State 49, 122, 170
discrimination 8–9, 47, 49, 87–89, 153–54, 156, 179–80, 190–92
complaint 119, 121–22
direct 179
employment 134, 138
indirect 23, 88, 179
invidious 106, 108
prohibition 87–89, 91, 108–10, 121, 124, 155–57
structural 48, 144
systemic 48, 51–52, 144
distinct identities 6, 101–2, 106, 108–9, 112, 121–22, 124
distinctiveness 102, 154, 205
distributive justice 23, 129
diversity 9, 162, 164, 173, 175, 215, 217–18
governance 171, 182–84
linguistic 6–7, 51, 75, 88, 91, 196
and unity 181–83
domestic constitutionalism 185
drafters 30, 32, 34, 61–62, 76, 126, 203
DUP (Democratic Unionist Party) 72–73
Durkhan, Mark 65
duties 19–21, 29, 72–73, 79, 133, 140, 169, 191
moral 19
duty-bearers 15, 21, 28, 36
Dworkin, Ronald 26
dynamics 63
complex 207
political 211–12

early adulthood phase 8, 125, 149
ECHR (European Convention on Human Rights) 8–10, 86–87, 107, 109–10, 115–17, 122–24, 156–57, 186
framework 156, 194, 202
economic interests 10, 187
economic systems 29, 33–35
ECtHR (European Court of Human Rights) 7–8, 47–54, 103–5, 107–10, 119–24, 186–89, 201–3; *see also* ***Valiullina* case**
case law 104, 108–10
jurisprudence 104, 108
minorities and language in education 115–18
education 6–7, 50, 52, 76, 78–81, 88, 103–4, 110–24
language in 104, 110, 113–16, 119, 124
mother-tongue 8, 113
private 34, 118
provision 116–17, 123
secondary 80, 118, 120
systems 53, 80, 119
university 79, 81
effective participation 8, 61–62, 93, 102, 128, 133, 135, 148, 155, 175, 188
effectiveness 75, 94, 96, 116, 138, 160–61
egalitarianism 24–25
elections 173, 177
electoral processes 97, 175
elites 211, 216
local 216
emotional development 113
employment 95, 111, 134–35, 144, 179
private-sector 174
Employment Framework Directive 178–79
EMRIP (Expert Mechanism on the Rights of Indigenous Peoples) 90
endangered languages 6, 76
energy 19–20
enforceability 5, 49, 54
enforcement 5, 28, 35, 38, 49, 54, 170
engagement 95, 122, 161, 164, 175, 210, 219
political 170, 177
enjoyment 31, 54, 94, 105, 128, 155, 157, 187
effective 106, 202
peaceful 189, 201
enlargement 128, 130–31, 137
entitlements 28, 54, 169, 176
equal access 16, 112–13, 134
equal opportunities 25, 111, 113–14, 173
equal treatment 109, 112, 115, 174
equality 16, 45, 47–49, 87–88, 91, 110, 112–13
arguments 113, 121
as differentiated difference 22–30
effective 31, 63
index 23–27
of outcome 24, 26
principle 16, 22–23, 157, 175
simple 24
of status 26–27

substantive 8, 104, 107, 109–10, 113, 121, 124
of welfare 25

equity 16, 22, 164
essentialism 26, 207–8, 217–18
Estonia 130–31, 138, 142
ethical behaviour 16, 29
ethical considerations/dimensions/ issues 16, 27–29, 214
ethnic composition 128, 135, 140–42, 145
ethnic conflicts 8, 103, 126, 139–43, 146, 148–49
ethnic data 141, 145
ethnic groups 71, 88, 91, 101, 126, 129, 171, 190
ethnic minorities 24, 55, 88, 144, 195
ethnic origin 48, 87–88, 179, 191
ethnic particularism 2, 42
ethnic profiling 49, 51
ethnicity 46, 62, 92, 148, 155, 172, 211
ethnology 208–9, 214
EU, *see* **European Union**
European Charter for Regional or Minority Languages 6–7, 53–54, 65–69, 72, 75–83
Committee of Experts 74, 77–81
evaluation of success 82–83
monitoring 81–82
novel approach 75–78
Part II 78–79
Part III 79–81

European Charter of Fundamental Rights 51, 87, 91, 93, 170, 173, 178–79
European Commission 86, 88, 180, 194
European consensus 103, 109, 119–20, 122
European Convention on Human Rights, *see* **ECHR**
European Court of Human Rights 4–5, 47, 103, 183, 186
European legal orders 196, 200
European minority rights regime 16, 30, 143, 147–48
European Parliament 89, 97, 177
European Union 5, 51–52, 86–87, 89, 91, 126–28, 130, 148, 170, 202; *see also* ***Introductory Note***
accessions 136–37, 139
citizens 174, 177, 180
citizenship 171, 173–74, 179, 183
conditionality 130–31, 213
enlargement 127–28, 131, 136–37, 148
human rights action 95–96
human rights in external action 85–97
instruments 92, 97, 173
as basis for protection of new minorities 178–81
integration trajectories 8, 148
new (non-EU) minorities 171–74
non-EU citizens, *see* non-EU citizens
Special Representative (EUSR) 96–97
standards 148, 178, 180

evaluations 82–83, 120, 135–41, 143, 145, 148
Committee 134, 148–49

exclusion 8, 27, 156, 211
Expert Mechanism on the Rights of Indigenous Peoples (EMRIP) 90
experts 74, 77–83, 214, 217–18
explanatory reports 30, 43, 62, 188

family life 109, 189, 201–2
family reunification 178, 180–81
FCNM (Framework Convention for the Protection of National Minorities) 5–6, 30–34, 59–74, 103, 111–12, 119–28, 130–33, 186; *see also* **Advisory Committee on the FFCNM**
and the Good Friday/Belfast Agreement 64–66
as human rights treaty 61–64
and Identity and Language (Northern Ireland) Act 2022 71–73
provisions 5, 17, 31–34, 36

feasibility 164–65, 174, 177
feminists 26
Finland 76, 190, 201
First World War 2, 37
Flags, Identity, Culture and Tradition (FICT) Commission 67–68
flash mobs 159
FPIC (free, prior and informed consent) 193
Framework Convention for the Protection of National Minorities, *see* **FCNM**
France 52
free, prior and informed consent (FPIC) 193
free market 24–26
freedoms 24–26, 28, 43, 50, 54, 87, 91, 94
freedom of expression 61–62, 93, 103
religious 51

fundamental freedoms 1, 87, 155, 189
fundamental rights 95, 101–3, 105–8, 169–71, 178–79, 182–84, 196, 200
scope 105, 107

gender 8, 24, 92, 152–54, 156, 160
general human rights 85, 102–5, 122
general rights 10, 15, 18, 103, 107
General System of Preferences (GSP) 96
genocide 42, 44, 160, 175, 183
geopolitical contexts 60, 66, 71, 74
Germany 76, 130, 137, 141, 174
GFA, *see* **Good Friday/Belfast Agreement**
Global Positioning System (GPS) 159
globalisation 152, 158–59, 173, 214
Goikoetxea, Jule 154
Good Friday/Belfast Agreement (GFA) 6, 59, 64–66, 70, 73–74, 139
goods 23–24, 26, 28, 35, 102
governance 65, 133, 162–63, 187
GPS (Global Positioning System) 159
grandparents 209, 212
Greece 40
Greenland 197, 201–2
GSP (General System of Preferences) 96
guidance 62, 72, 108, 122–23, 155

***Handölsdalen* case** 193, 195–96, 202
hate speech 93–94, 160–61, 164
heritage 10–11, 70, 205–9, 211, 213–15, 217–19
linguistic 7, 154
studies 206, 216
heritagisation 205, 209, 211, 215–17
High Commissioner on National Minorities 93, 157, 169
Hohfeld, Wesley 21
Homo Digitalis 159
Homo Videns 159
HRC (Human Rights Council) 91, 93–94
human beings 16–17, 19, 25, 63
human dignity 23, 87, 91, 170, 191
human rights, *see* ***Introductory Note*** **and** ***detailed entries***
Human Rights Committee 132, 155, 172, 188, 196
human rights concepts, doctrine and practice 37–55
Human Rights Council (HRC) 91, 93–94
human rights law 4, 17, 37, 93
international 4–5, 64, 87, 125, 185
human rights standards 9, 35, 83, 149, 182, 184
human rights treaties 6, 55, 59–64, 71
Hunter-Henin, Myriam 52

IACtHR, *see* **Inter-American Court of Human Rights**
ICCPR, *see* **International Covenant on Civil and Political Rights**
ICESCR, *see* **International Covenant on Economic, Social and Cultural Rights**
ICH, *see* **intangible cultural heritage**
identities
collective 10–11, 156, 159, 206–8, 211–14, 217
distinct 6, 101–2, 106, 108–9, 112, 121–22, 124
indigenous 193
intersectional 154, 158
linguistic 42, 106, 155
national 62, 68, 159, 219
religious 63, 156
identity-based conflicts 208, 212, 218
identity bearers 213, 218
identity politics 217, 219
identity preservation 45, 207
imperfect obligations 5, 16, 29, 31–32
implementation, levels of 130, 132, 149
inclusion 7–9, 88, 103, 111–12, 124–25, 172, 177–78, 214–15
stakeholder 212, 216
inclusivity 164, 218
indigenous identity 193
indigenous issues 90–91
indigenous land 192, 196, 201
indigenous peoples 9–10, 86, 88–92, 185–203
indigenous representatives 190, 197
indigenous rights 10, 186–87, 189, 193, 197, 200–201
ECJ and the ECtHR 201–3
and EU human rights order 196–201
and European court cultures 185–88
under Council of Europe framework 188–96
indirect discrimination 23, 88, 179
individual rights 7, 9–10, 41–43, 50, 53–54, 85, 186, 211

inequalities 23–24, 26, 94, 120, 134, 144, 190, 210–11
institutional frameworks/structures 4, 15–36, 46, 94
institutions 17, 24, 29–30, 32–35, 40, 74, 160, 162–63; *see also* ***individual institutions***
intangible cultural heritage (ICH) 10–11, 206, 211–14, 217–18, 220
integral part 1, 4, 37–38, 59, 61, 85, 156
integrated society 102, 107, 111, 169, 179, 182
integration 7, 31, 102, 104, 107, 110–14, 121, 127, 207, 214
  cultural 112, 177
  dimensions 112–13
  measures 181, 183
intentions 5, 15, 17, 22, 24, 36, 61, 67, 114, 192
Inter-American Court of Human Rights (IACtHR) 193, 196
interculturalism 76, 81
interferences 117–18, 189, 203
international courts 105–8, 123; *see also* ***individual courts***
International Covenant on Civil and Political Rights (ICCPR) 2–5, 37, 40, 42, 44, 89, 125, 155, 188, 196
International Covenant on Economic, Social and Cultural Rights 35, 188, 196
international law 38, 42, 44, 53–55, 87–88, 90, 200, 202
internet 159–60
interpretive social sciences 207, 209, 219
intersectional identities 154, 158
intolerance 160, 212
intra-cultural differences 217–18
Inuit 197–98, 201
Ireland 65–66, 68–70
Irish language 65, 69–70, 73–74
Irish Language Commissioner 68–69, 73

Jones, Peter 63
judgements 27, 103–4, 108, 110, 122, 188, 198, 202
judiciary 133, 136, 174, 200
jurisdictions 18, 161, 186, 189, 202
jurisprudence 10, 17, 47, 49, 53, 103, 105, 115, 119, 121–22, 182, 196
justice 5, 22–23, 25–28, 49, 123, 147, 208, 215–16
justiciability 38, 46, 49
justifications 2, 5, 47, 54
justificatory grounds 38–41, 45
justificatory routes 5, 38, 45

kin-States 76, 171
knowledge 11, 21, 28, 51, 111, 114, 120, 210, 212, 215
Könkämä 189
Kosovo 139
Kymlicka, Will 1, 62, 215

land 9–10, 186, 189, 192–93, 197, 200, 203
  rights 187, 193–94, 198
language rights 7, 31, 62, 108, 121, 123
languages 6–7, 53–55, 67–83, 87–88, 103–4, 115–16, 119–21, 154–55
  in education 104, 110, 113–16, 119, 124
  endangered 6, 76
  minority 6, 31, 61–63, 75–76, 78–83, 113–15, 120–21, 137
  national 52, 111, 113, 119–20, 122
  non-territorial 76–77
  official 76, 78, 80–81, 114, 116–18, 121–22
  protection 75, 77, 79
  weaponisation 73
Languages Charter, *see* **European Charter for Regional or Minority Languages**
Latvia 7, 104, 118, 120–21, 123–24
Latvian language 120–21
League of Nations 37, 41, 102
legal analysis 90, 214
legal frameworks 7–8, 10, 54, 62, 91, 144–45, 198, 209–10
  common 86, 97
legal instruments 3, 5, 60, 178, 180; *see also* ***individual instruments***
  international 1, 41–42
legal landscape 10, 48, 186
legal power 16, 21–22
legal regulation 127, 142, 146, 149
legal relations 16, 19–21
legal status 40, 172–73
legal systems 29, 33–35, 55, 91, 203
legislation 35, 68–69, 72–73, 198; *see also* ***individual instruments***
legitimacy 108, 121, 123–24, 208, 215, 217
legitimate aims 105, 118, 120, 123, 179
legitimate interests 43–44, 52
Lenin, Vladimir 2
Levinas, E. 152, 161

libertarians 24
liberty rights 5, 28–29, 34–36
lifestyle 50, 90, 103, 109, 191, 200, 202
limitations 30, 49–50, 52–54, 72, 105–7, 147, 180
linguistic diversity 6–7, 51, 75, 88, 91, 196
linguistic identities 42, 106, 155
linguistic minorities 1, 3, 7–8, 42, 44, 85–86, 89, 91–93, 95, 152, 155, 160, 172, 187–88
linguistic preferences 116–17, 119
local requirements 10, 203
Locke, John 17–18
logos 151, 158, 164
Long-Term Residents Directive (LTRD) 173–74, 178, 180–81
lowest common denominators 41, 87
LTRD, *see* **Long-Term Residents Directive**

Macedonia 148, 157
majority groups 63, 159, 182, 184
Malloy, Tove H. 5, 134, 152, 160, 163, 176
Manx 82
margin of appreciation 7, 47, 50, 106, 108–9, 115, 119–20, 124
marginalisation 94–95, 154, 211–12, 217
marginalised groups 10, 51, 164, 211, 218
Marxism 23–24, 159
material outcomes 5, 15, 17, 36
media 6, 61–63, 76, 80, 83, 115, 117–18, 123–24, 132, 136, 208, 210
  social, *see* social media
memory 89, 177, 205, 211, 217, 219
menu-system 6, 76, 79–81
Meyers, Barton 154, 156
migrant languages 76, 176
migrant workers 180–81
migrants 9, 51, 92, 171–73, 177–78, 180
migration 69, 171, 173–74, 180
migratory background 176–78
minorities, *see* ***Introductory Note*** **and *detailed entries***
minority concept 47–49
minority languages 6, 31, 61–63, 75–76, 78–83, 113–15, 120–21, 137
minority protection 1, 5, 31, 37–38, 46–48, 51–53, 62–64, 103
minority rights, *see* ***Introductory Note***
minority rights instruments/provisions 3, 30–32, 34, 53–54
minority status 8–9, 40, 45, 47–48, 65, 154, 164, 172
missed opportunities 7, 101, 105, 118, 121
Moldova 117
monitoring 127–28, 135–37, 139–40, 142, 144, 147–48
  cycles 131, 135–36, 138, 140, 142, 147
  European Charter 81–82
  process 82, 131, 136–37, 145
Montenegro 131, 136, 138–39, 141, 143, 145, 213–14
Montevideo Convention 157–58
mores 104, 111
mother tongue 104, 113–14, 116, 119, 121–23, 141
  education 8, 113
multiculturalism 25–27, 45, 215
multilingualism 75–76, 81
Muñoz Diaz 110
Musk, Elon 163–64
mutual respect 31, 63, 66, 68
Myanmar 94

nation building 7, 63, 101, 114, 119, 121, 123–24
nation-states 7, 10, 101, 173, 176, 206
national identity 62, 68, 159, 219
national languages 52, 111, 113, 119–20, 122
national minorities 62–63, 68, 70–72, 74–75, 86–87, 128–29, 132–34, 143–44, 188
  participation 128, 132–33, 141, 145
  representation 143, 149
  representatives 96, 142
  Ulster Scots as 69–71
national unity 7, 55
national values 111
nationalism 114, 116, 174, 212, 219
nationalists 65, 68, 217
nationality 62, 155, 179–80
nature of rights 15, 17–19
NDICI (Neighbourhood, Development and International Cooperation Instrument) 96
negotiations 64–65
Neighbourhood, Development and International Cooperation Instrument (NDICI) 96
New Decade, New Approach (NDNA) deal 66–69, 71

new minorities 6, 9, 60, 167, 170, 172–73, 175–78, 183
and protection measures 174–78
relevance of concept 171–74
NGOs, *see* **non-governmental organisations**
NIHRC, *see* **Northern Ireland Human Rights Commission**
non-citizens 173, 180–81
non-discrimination 16, 22, 37, 62, 87–88, 174–75, 178, 180
provisions 51, 187–88, 190
non-EU citizens 9, 169–84
non-EU minorities 9, 169–72, 178–81, 183
non-governmental organisations (NGOs) 81, 188, 194
non-territorial autonomy (NTA) 9, 151–65
non-territorial languages 76–77
normative definition of minorities 155–58
normative frameworks 147, 149, 214
normative power 18, 40
international 156–57
normativisation 156–57
normativity 3
norms 26, 97, 133, 175, 186, 206–7, 211–12, 215–16
North Macedonia 131, 138–39, 141, 143, 145, 148
Northern Ireland 6, 8, 59–74, 139, 148
Assembly 66–67, 69, 74
Good Friday/Belfast Agreement (GFA) 6, 59, 64–66, 70, 73–74, 139
Human Rights Commission (NIHRC) 66, 71–72
Identity and Language (Northern Ireland) Act 2022 71–73
New Decade, New Approach (NDNA) deal 66–69, 71
Protestant/Unionist community 70
SDLP (Social Democratic and Labour Party) 65, 73
Sinn Féin 66–67
Ulster Scots 65, 68–74
UUP (Ulster Unionist Party) 64
Norway 82, 179, 201
NTA, *see* **non-territorial autonomy**

obligation-bearers 17, 27, 29–30
obligations 3, 5–6, 16–19, 53–54, 61, 155–56, 191
extraterritorial 187, 202
imperfect 5, 16, 29, 31–32
and institutional frameworks 32–35
perfect 29, 33–36
positive, *see* positive obligations
special, *see* special rights
State 32, 105–6, 109, 115, 120–21
occupations 104, 117, 123–24
official languages 76, 78, 80–81, 114, 116–18, 121–22
old minorities 48, 170, 173, 175–77, 184
O'Neill, Onora 5, 27–30, 32–36
oppression 2, 203, 210–11
Organization for Security and Co-operation in Europe (OSCE) 111, 169
origin, racial 87–88, 179
otherness 151–52
over-simplification 61, 71, 74

parents 104, 115–16, 118–19, 122–23, 209
linguistic preferences 118, 122
participation
effective 8, 61–62, 93, 102, 128, 133, 135, 148, 155, 175, 188
in public affairs 125–49
particularisation 60, 66, 69, 74
particularism, ethnic 2, 42
peace 59, 70, 103, 126, 210, 217–18
accords 146–47, 149
process 6, 59, 64–65, 139
sustainable 94, 129
peacebuilding 8, 126, 219
perceptions 60, 64–65, 68, 73, 172, 213–14
perfect obligations 29, 33–36
philosophical convictions 117–19, 122–23
platforms 159, 161, 163, 216, 220
pluralism 50, 173, 191, 195, 200
Poland 50, 76–77
police 132–33, 139, 148
policy documents 7, 85–87, 90–92, 94–95, 97
policymakers 177, 181, 209
political dynamics 211–12
political engagement 170, 177
political framework 209–10
political participation 9, 114, 177
political representation 24, 133, 217
political rights 42, 106, 199
politicisation 59–60, 70, 73–74, 148
politics 208–9, 216
of recognition 38, 45
of social exchange 16, 19–22

population groups 112–13, 124, 193
populism 11, 209–10, 212
populist nationalism 160
positive measures 34, 136
positive obligations 48, 106, 186, 201–2
State 106, 108–9, 115, 118, 121–22
possessions 187, 189, 192, 201–2
post-conflict heritage stakeholder participation 210–17
post-conflict regions 208–9, 213
post-conflict settings/situations 114, 131, 144, 214, 217
post-conflict societies 10, 83, 207–8, 212, 218
power relations 193, 209, 211, 213
power(s) 16, 18, 21–22, 154, 199–200, 202, 209–11, 213
natural 19–20
shared 16, 22
social 19–21
powerholders 7, 217
pre-political substratum 40, 45
preferences 26, 113, 123, 217
prejudice 134, 153
preservation 55, 78, 83, 113, 174, 213–15, 217, 219
pressures 7, 10, 210, 213–14
prioritisation 8, 38, 54–55, 156, 160, 186, 195, 219
private education 34, 118
private life 109, 186, 189, 196, 201
professional standards 214
profiling, ethnic 49, 51
proof, burden of 48, 51, 192
property 10, 18, 25, 185, 189, 192, 196, 202
rights 186, 196, 202
proportional representation 129, 175
proportionality 105–6, 118, 120–22, 124, 189, 195
protection 9–10, 37–38, 47–55, 76–83, 101–2, 106–9, 160–61, 178–80
effective 106, 112, 163
levels of 77, 80, 181, 187
protection measures/mechanisms 6, 170, 174–76, 178, 183
Protestant/Unionist community 70
public administration 132–33, 135, 137
public affairs 8, 188
minority participation in 125–49
participation in 131–32, 134–35
public authorities 72–74, 95, 122
public bodies 79, 143
adequate representation of national minorities 132–35
public interests 105, 187, 189–90
public life 6, 76, 78, 83, 85, 93, 118, 175
public sector 131–38, 144–45, 148
employment 134, 138, 143–44
representation 138
workforce 132, 135–36, 141, 145, 149

qualifications 63, 73, 104, 111
qualifiers 114, 123

race 24, 48, 92, 154–55, 190–91, 196
racial discrimination 48, 183, 192, 196
Racial Equality Directive 178–79
racism 51, 160–61, 191, 217
Rawls, John 26, 46
Raz, Joseph 39, 44, 46
reasoning 27, 30, 38, 108, 117–24, 143
recognition 5–6, 9–10, 27–28, 50–51, 61–65, 78, 151–53, 202–3
explicit 37, 122
legal 40, 64, 188
official 69, 172
recommendations 49, 74, 77, 82–83, 96, 213
reconciliation 68, 131, 207, 210–11, 213–19
reconstruction 210, 215–16
reforms 49, 81–82, 116, 131, 174
refugees 92, 131, 171
regional organisations 85, 92, 96
regulation 115, 117, 198
reindeer 192, 194, 199
relationships 4, 7, 18–20, 28–30, 32–35, 102, 112, 127, 132, 143–44, 148, 205–6, 209
religion 46–48, 50, 93, 95, 111, 154–55, 179, 181
freedom of 92–93, 95, 103
religious identities 63, 156
religious minorities 1, 7, 42, 44, 85, 89, 91, 93, 95, 109, 155
religious neutrality 52
representation 131, 133–34, 136, 144–45, 148, 162, 194, 205
adequate 129, 132–40, 142–45, 147–49
levels of 128, 140–41
political 24, 133, 217
proportional 129, 175

representativeness 135, 137
representatives 51, 92–93, 97, 130, 177
indigenous 190, 197
research
findings 6, 38, 129, 135–44, 148–49, 216
process 216, 219
programs 207, 216
reservations 77–78, 219
residence 51, 161, 171–72, 179, 181
residents 70, 173, 177, 179–80
long-term 171–73, 180
resistance 11, 181, 211, 216
resources 25–26, 181, 187, 197, 216
respondents 176–78
responsibilities 24, 30, 55, 69, 74, 170, 176, 194, 200
restrictions 52, 54, 161, 215
land use 50
rhetoric 1, 27–28, 38
rights, *see* ***Introductory Note*** **and** ***detailed entries***
rights framework 52, 188, 208
rights-holders 15, 18, 21, 27–29, 35–36, 39, 86, 89
rights language 6, 61–62
risks 6, 27, 47, 71, 124, 164, 195, 219
Rohingya 94, 97
Roma 7, 88, 95, 109, 136, 144, 183, 191
children 52
communities 25, 50, 110, 187
marriages 110
stateless 177
Romani Chib 77–78
Romania 130–31, 138, 141
Romansh 76
Ross, Alf 18
Roter, Petra 38
rule of law 68, 87, 91, 95, 148, 170
Russia 117–18, 197, 201
Russian-speaking minorities 104, 120–21, 138, 180

safeguards 44, 53, 164, 180–81, 186, 190, 194–96, 200
Şahin **case** 48
Sami 77, 185, 190, 192, 194–95, 201
villages 189–90, 194
schools 117–18, 120, 176, 210
scrutiny 8, 47, 106, 108, 115–16, 128, 154
levels of 106–8
SDLP (Social Democratic and Labour Party) 65, 73
Second World War 2, 8, 37, 124–25
secondary education 80, 118, 120
security 54, 59, 93, 103, 126, 132, 147, 180, 191
self-determination 65, 160, 199–200
self-identification 6, 34, 60, 72
sensitivities 68, 73, 214, 217
sentences 115–16, 122
Serbia 10, 131, 138–39, 141, 143, 145, 148, 164, 179, 206, 213
Serbian intangible cultural heritage 205–20
Serbs 209, 213, 218
sex 47, 155
sexual orientation 47, 55, 92
simple equality 24
Sinn Féin 66–67
Slovakia 77, 130–31, 137, 140
Slovenia 93
social cohesion 52, 175, 181, 183–84, 210, 218
Social Democratic and Labour Party (SDLP) 65, 73
social exchange 5, 16, 19–22
social impact 209–10, 216
social interests 21, 147, 198
social life 76, 80, 143
social media 160–61, 163
platforms 159–60, 163
social power 19–21
social sciences 11, 112, 213, 220
interpretive 207, 209, 219
socialisation 104, 111, 124
socioeconomic status/situation 8, 144, 154, 156, 158
soft law 3, 132
South Tyrol 176
sovereignty 5, 7, 46, 101, 156, 171, 185, 197
State 53, 55, 114
sovereignty-limiting capacity of minority rights 53–54
Spain 78, 82, 110, 130, 136–37, 152
special measures 48, 106, 109, 175
special rights 4–5, 15, 17–19, 21, 23, 27–30, 33–36, 193

stability 8, 126, 134, 147, 149, 156, 163, 216–17
stakeholder inclusion 10, 205–20
State discretion 49, 122, 170
State obligations 32, 105–6, 109, 115, 120–21
State sovereignty 53, 55, 114
statehood 157–58, 171
status 3–5, 23, 39–40, 44, 54–55, 120–21, 169, 171–72
  equality of 26–27
  legal 40, 172–73
  minority 8–9, 40, 45, 47–48, 65, 154, 164, 172
  socioeconomic 8, 144, 154, 156, 158
structural discrimination 48, 144
structure-system 19, 21–22
subsistence 198, 201
  activities 189, 196, 198
  rights 198, 201–2
substantive equality 8, 104, 107, 109–10, 113, 121, 124
supervisory practice 112, 114–15, 120–23
suppression 120, 154, 211
survey respondents 176–78
sustainability 200, 216, 220
Sweden 82–83, 130, 137, 193, 201–2
Switzerland 50–51, 76, 179
synergies 65, 146–47, 149
systemic discrimination 48, 51–52, 144

TCNs, *see* **third-country nationals**
terminology 3, 61–62, 158
territorial integrity 65, 101, 124
territoriality 156, 185, 202
territories 8–10, 31, 76–77, 101–2, 152–53, 156–58, 199–200, 202–3
TEU, *see* **Treaty on European Union**
TFEU, *see* **Treaty on the Functioning of the European Union**
Thematic Commentaries 16–17, 30–32, 34–35, 49, 114, 133, 188
theorists 18
third countries 92–93, 95–97
third-country nationals (TCNs) 9, 171–74, 179–81, 183
third party interests 185, 200
Thlimmenos 108–9
Thornberry, Patrick 41, 50
Thrace 40
threats 7, 55, 70, 94, 124, 174, 191
thresholds 77, 81, 114, 188
Tibetans 95
Ticino 76
tolerance 54, 61, 63, 68, 195
traditionalism 10, 209
traditions 177, 182, 205, 207, 209, 211, 213, 217–19
treaties 7, 37, 54–55, 61, 75–76, 81–82, 86–87, 170; *see also* ***individual instruments***
Treaty on European Union (TEU) 51, 86–87
Treaty on the Functioning of the European Union (TFEU) 87, 200
'Tree Model' for diversity governance 9, 182–84
'trump-over-sovereignty' rights 38, 46, 49, 53–55
trust 175, 181, 214
Turkey 48, 95, 117
tweets 163–64

UDHR, *see* **Universal Declaration of Human Rights**
Ulster Scots 65, 68–74
Ulster Unionist Party (UUP) 64
undertakings 65, 76, 79–81, 195
UNDRIP, *see* **United Nation, Declaration on the Rights of Indigenous Peoples**
UNESCO (United Nations Educational, Scientific and Cultural Organization) 10, 206, 211–14
United Kingdom 6, 59–60, 65–67, 71, 135, 137, 139, 141, 143, 145, 199, 202
  government 67–68
United Nations 1–2, 37, 89–90, 126, 155–56, 172
  Charter 17, 87–88
  Conventions 72, 196
  Declaration on Human Rights 2
  Declaration on Minorities 1, 42, 125, 155
  Declaration on the Rights of Indigenous Peoples (UNDRIP) 90–93, 196
  General Assembly 91, 94
  Special Rapporteur 94, 153, 157, 172
unity 162–63
  and diversity 181–83
Universal Declaration of Human Rights (UDHR) 11, 37, 47, 87, 89, 156, 205–6, 217, 220
universal rights 15, 17, 28, 33, 35, 43–45
universality 5, 21, 35, 43–45, 87

universities 48, 79, 210, 216
UUP (Ulster Unionist Party) 64
Uyghurs 95, 97

***Valiullina* case** 7, 101, 104–5, 118–24
  shifts in interpretation before 115–18
van der Stoel, Max 169
VDPA (Vienna Declaration and Programme of Action) 86
Verstichel, Annelies 134, 144
Vienna Declaration and Programme of Action (VDPA) 86
violence 1, 146, 160, 191, 217
visibility 82–83, 94, 96, 177
voting rights 9, 177, 184
vulnerabilities 30, 97, 154, 161, 164
vulnerable groups 7, 95

***Wa Baile* case** 51
Waldron, Jeremy 18, 27
Walzer, Michael 23
Wayland, SV 215
welfare
  equality of 25
  rights 29, 35
Weller, Mark 134
Western Balkans 10, 95, 205–20; *see also* ***individual countries***
Westphalian era 37, 157
Wilson, Woodrow 2
Wirth, Louis 153
Woehrling, J-M 76
women 24, 94, 97, 103, 152–54, 156–58
workforce 128, 132–33, 146, 148, 173
World War I, *see* **First World War**
World War II, *see* **Second World War**

Xanthaki, Alexandra 50

young people 10, 177, 208–9, 212
Yugoslavia 8, 42, 212, 218

Ziemele, Judge 193–94

www.ingramcontent.com/pod-product-compliance
Ingram Content Group UK Ltd.
Pitfield, Milton Keynes, MK11 3LW, UK
UKHW020806290926
15470UKWH00003B/985

9 781509 984541